Cult Controversies

Cult
Controversies

*The societal response
to new religious movements*

JAMES A. BECKFORD

 105146

TAVISTOCK PUBLICATIONS

LONDON AND NEW YORK

First published in 1985 by
Tavistock Publications Ltd
11 New Fetter Lane, London EC4P 4EE

Published in the USA by
Tavistock Publications
in association with Methuen, Inc.
733 Third Avenue, New York, NY 10017

© 1985 James A. Beckford

Photoset by Rowland Phototypesetting Ltd
Bury St Edmunds, Suffolk
Printed in Great Britain by
Richard Clay (The Chaucer Press) Ltd,
Bungay, Suffolk

British Library Cataloguing in Publication Data

Beckford, James A.
  Cult controversies: the societal response
  to new religious movements.
  1. Cults—Social aspects
  I. Title
  306'.6   BP603

  ISBN 0-422-79630-1
  ISBN 0-422-79640-9 Pbk

Library of Congress Cataloging in Publication Data

Beckford, James A.
  Cult controversies.
  Bibliography; P.
  Includes indexes.
  1. Cults—Controversial literature—History and
  criticism. 2. Religions—Controversial literature—
  History and criticism. 3. Religion and sociology.
  I. Title.
  BL98.B4 1985   291   84–26833

  ISBN 0-422-79630-1
  ISBN 0-422-79640-9 (pbk.)

CONTENTS

*For Martin Sheldon John, this time
In memory of John Henry Beckford*

PREFACE

The list of people and institutions who have helped me to complete my research on the controversies surrounding new religious movements is very long. Pride of place must go to the people who agreed to be interviewed by me. They all gave their time generously; many provided kind hospitality; some found it distressing to talk about their experiences of 'cults'. None of them is likely to agree totally with my interpretations of what they said, but I sincerely hope that they will at least find our differences of opinion challenging and constructive.

Intellectual criticism, stimulation, and support have come from many colleagues and friends. Special thanks are owed to Eileen Barker, David Bromley, Diane Choquette, Bert Hardin, John Lofland, Meredith McGuire, Jacob Needleman, Jim Richardson, Tom Robbins, Paul Schwartz, Jean Séguy, Andy Shupe, and Bryan Wilson. Joan McArthur, Margaret Bell, and Lynda Nurse worked wonders with all manner of secretarial skills, and Julie Beckford's contributions went well beyond the call of duty.

Many members of Family Action Information and Rescue were supportive, none more so than Paul Rose. Assistance also came from Caryl Williams, Thierry Baffoy, Alexandra Schmidt, Klaus Karbe, Henrietta and Curt Crampton, John Clark, and Mr Yamada of Nagoya. I am grateful to them all. Gratitude is also owed to numerous members and erstwhile members of new religious movements who answered my irreverent questions instead of suing me for libel or trying to buy my favour.

Research expenses were met at various times by the generous support of the Social Science Research Council, the Nuffield Foundation, the Japan Society for the Promotion of Science, the US/UK

Educational Commission, Durham University's Research Fund Committee, and the Center for the Study of New Religious Movements at the Graduate Theological Union, Berkeley, California. Financial assistance from the Council of Durham University and the Association of University Teachers enabled me to maintain equanimity in the face of harassment from leading members of a new religious movement in Britain. It is a pleasure to record my thanks to all these institutions.

Parts of Chapters 6, 7, and 8 have already appeared in, respectively, D. G. Bromley and J. T. Richardson (eds) The *Brainwashing/ Deprogramming Controversy*, New York and Toronto, Edwin Mellen Press, 1984; *Social Compass* 30 (1), 1983; and *Sociological Analysis* 42 (3), 1981. The editors and publishers are thanked for their kind permission to reprint parts of these materials.

INTRODUCTION

The study

This book is about controversy. It tries to explain how and why a particular kind of controversy has developed in various countries in the past two decades. The controversy in question concerns what are popularly called 'cults'. They are relatively small, new, and unconventional religious groups which grew rapidly in the 1960s and 1970s. They have attracted a great deal of interest among people in all walks of life, and a sizeable literature about them now exists in many languages.

My purpose in writing about the cult controversy is mainly to chart its development as a social phenomenon. The sociological approach is therefore the most appropriate angle, although my interpretation of events also draws extensively on the insights of psychology, history, and religious studies. The reason for giving priority to sociology is that it enables me to explore the social processes whereby the interactions between individual human beings and between human groups can generate controversy. After all, controversy is not something that exists independently from human beings: they construct it. At the same time, their actions are guided by culture or shared meanings. It is essential therefore to examine not only the social construction of controversy but also its cultural setting and the meaning that it has for the people involved.

The material on which the book is based is drawn mainly from two kinds of sources. First, I interviewed a large number of people who had been associated in different ways with probably the most controversial of the cults – the Unification Church (UC). They included twenty-six ex-members of the UC, thirteen of their close relatives, thirty-five parents of practising members, twenty-six activists in organized campaigns against cults, and journalists and official policy makers.[1] They can all be considered as participants in the controversy, although their viewpoints are diverse and in some cases contradictory. Second, I analysed the publications of anti-cult campaigns, the (auto-)biographies of ex-members of cults, journalists' accounts of cult-related matters, official reports of inquiry into cults, transcripts of legal cases bearing on cults, and social scientific works on minority religions.

Most of the interviews were conducted in Britain between 1977 and 1979, but the other material was collected in Britain, France, the Federal Republic of Germany, the USA, and Japan from 1975 to 1984.

A discussion of the issues raised by my use of these varied methods of inquiry can be found in Chapter 4. But it is important to anticipate the discussion in one respect at this point. The whole project was designed not so much to test a specific hypothesis as to try to chart and to interpret the meanings of the cult controversy that my informants had already formulated for themselves. In other words, my task was to search for patterns in the actions, feelings, and ideas that were reported to me. I was definitely not seeking a single cause of the controversy. Much less was my intention to take sides in it or to apportion blame for it. Nor was my intention to arbitrate between competing versions of the truth. I merely tried to understand how it came about that the various participants accounted for the controversy and how they reacted accordingly. The linkage between accounts and actions took on special significance in my analysis of interview transcripts.

But it would be untrue to deny that there was any theoretical context for my work. As Chapter 2 makes clear, some of the most fundamental aspects of my research were designed to remedy perceived inadequacies in more conventional social scientific study of new religious movements (NRMs). I was particularly concerned to make some existing concepts more flexible, to explore ways of avoiding theoretical blind alleys, to make the sociology of religion more responsive to insights arising from other sociological specialisms, and to test the limits of comparative study. And running through the whole project was a note of scepticism about the uses to which sociologists have often put their informants' accounts of religious experience.[2] In other words, there is a constant dialogue in this book with alternative possibilities of conducting the research that it reports.

This book is certainly and centrally about the cult controversy that began to develop in the mid 1960s, but it is also about the extent to which sociology can explain such a phenomenon. At no point is it taken for granted that sociology is the only valid approach to the topic. I am convinced, however, that it *can* explain things cogently and distinctively.

One of the reasons for being cautious about the capacity of sociology to make sense of religious controversy is that, by virtue of its predilection for 'snapshot' survey methods and one-off interviews, it may appear to be ill-equipped to explain any phenomenon which lasts for a long time or which undergoes change. In many cases the sociologist is simply too close in time to events to appreciate their long-term significance. In other cases, the sociologist is so personally immersed in the process of trying to see the world through the eyes of his or her informants that it becomes difficult to take an objective or distanced view of things. These difficulties are aggravated, of course, in sociological studies of religion because notions of change, growth, and maturity are widely considered to be integral to the very definition of the religious life. There is all the more reason, then, to be cautious about a sociological interpretation of a controversy that, on the one hand, has been developing for no less than twenty years and, on the other, is still ramifying and assuming new forms.

It was very much with these difficulties in mind that I decided some years ago to delay completion of this work until I was confident that the cult controversy was not likely to take any further dramatic turns in the foreseeable future. It would be foolish to try to make accurate predictions about this, but it seems to me that the principal parties have now come forward and that the pattern of the controversy's future is, within limits, determinable.

Another reason for not rushing into print was that I wanted to distance myself to some extent from the emotional impact that the experience of interviewing frequently distressed and angry people had produced on me. As I argue in Chapter 4, I believed in the value of 'combative rapport' with informants, and this often led to emotionally demanding, but rewarding, encounters. It was important to conduct interviews with ex-members of the UC, for example, while they were still experiencing strong emotions about their membership. The same consideration applied to interviews with the close relatives of ex-members and of practising members alike: the freshness of their experiences was reflected in the vividness of their accounts. It was essential for me to capture their thoughts and feelings while they were still fresh and vivid.

Yet, the interpretation of the interview transcripts, the search for common patterns, and the pondering of their meaning were best done over a long period of time and after considerable reflection. The collection and interpretation of research material can never be entirely separate exercises, of course, and there is much to be said for the researcher's immersion in the informants' life-world. But, on balance, I believe that some distance must be preserved between the observer and the observed. Clifford Geertz, borrowing terms from Heinz Kohut, neatly captured the essence of my argument as follows:

> 'Confinement to experience-near concepts leaves an ethnographer awash in immediacies as well as entangled in vernacular. Confinement to experience-distant ones leaves him stranded in abstraction and smothered in jargon. . . . The real question is . . . how, in each case, should they be deployed so as to produce an interpretation of the way a people live which is neither imprisoned within their mental horizons, an ethnography of witchcraft as written by a witch, nor systematically deaf to the distinctive tonalities of witchcraft as written by a geometer?'
>
> (Geertz 1979: 227)

One way of overcoming this problem was to allow the interpretation to mature slowly and to take on the colour of experiences, perspectives, and information acquired subsequently to the interviews. This was an attempt to get the best of both worlds: to feel immersed in the informants' life-world but also to achieve some distance from it for the purposes of interpretation.

While this book is not an in-depth study of particular NRMs it does, of course, offer a lot of information about them and it may even reveal some new aspects of them. But the important task of empirically analysing the movements themselves is left primarily to others;[3] in any case, some NRMs are only tenuously implicated in the cult controversy. My principal aim has been to account for the controversy's development.

A full sociological understanding of controversial NRMs would ideally take special cognizance of the cult controversy. It constitutes, from one point of view, a set of conditions limiting the scope of their activities and, from another point of view, a situation to which many of them have contributed significantly. From both points of view,

NRMs can be fully understood only in the context of the controversy surrounding them.

It follows that the 'interface' between NRMs and the cult controversy deserves special attention. An analytic framework for this purpose is presented in Chapter 2. Drawing on the findings of empirical research into the structure and dynamics of many NRMs it sets out the major factors which affect each movement's 'mode of insertion in society'. This refers to the characteristic profile of social relationships linking individual members to their movements, and movements, as collectivities, to the societies in which they operate.

This approach to the study of NRMs is deliberately contrasted with other approaches that tend for the most part to explain them in terms of either ideological or organizational factors. The main advantage of the focus on modes of insertion in society is that it makes comparisons across time and space much easier. Indeed, it *requires* that ideological or organizational typologies or classifications of NRMs should be closely inspected for what they reveal or conceal about the diverse and changing ways in which religious groups may be inserted in different societies.

The controversy

Many books and articles about religious cults begin with stories about the painful or embarrassing incidents that first brought to their authors' attention the fact that young people had begun to experiment with novel and often frightening forms of religion in the 1960s and 1970s. The impression is sometimes given that the struggles, anguish, anger, and suspiciousness directed against cults are the most important things about them. Readers could be forgiven for thinking that the very fabric of society was being rent asunder by invading hordes of insidious cult recruiters. Reliable estimates of the actual number of recruits were never available, of course, but the idea was quickly created in the early 1970s that recruitment of youth on a massive scale had already taken place.

From the beginning, therefore, cults were pictured in the mass media and in book-length descriptions of them as controversial and threatening. There was virtually no 'honeymoon period' and, as I explain in Chapter 8, a wide variety of techniques was employed to keep the controversy surrounding cults in the public eye. No matter what the different groups did, they were indelibly marked as basically all the same and all problematic.

If the general public learned anything about NRMs, it was wrapped up in stories of destructive mind-control techniques, the tragic ruination of promising careers, and the anguished despair of relatives who were to all intents and purposes mourning the 'loss' of their beloved to cultic abductors. Information about the movements was simply not available to the public in any other form. In any case, most people were ignorant about the history of minority religious groups of any kind in the west, so they had no way of putting all the fuss and suspicion about the new cults into a historical perspective. And, in an age of widespread indifference to organized religion, there was little likelihood that they could have made any independent assessment of the movements' religious merits or demerits. The cults were inescapably inseparable from controversy in most people's minds.

In time, the cult controversy took on more aspects. The alleged greed and unscrupulousness of the founders and leaders of cults were highlighted by those who wanted to expose their alleged manipulativeness. Then there were scares and scandals about allegations that some cults were buying influence in political circles. Soon they were being accused of creating economic empires and tax havens. Further allegations concerned the supposedly authoritarian character of their organization structures, sexual promiscuity among leaders and/or rank-and-file members, and hazards to the health of participants.

On the other side, some NRMs tried to fight back against what they saw as intimidation, oppression, and denial of various rights. The rate of litigation increased sharply in the mid 1970s; attempts were made to counter the effects of adverse publicity on members; and steps were taken in some NRMs to organize a concerted defence against a phenomenon that was only vaguely becoming conceptualized as 'anti-cultism'.

The late 1970s, and especially the period following the destruction of the People's Temple community in Jonestown, Guyana,[4] saw the firm establishment of associations dedicated to suppressing 'destructive cultism' or, at least, to ensuring that the cults conformed with existing laws. At the same time, some official and quasi-official bodies began to commission reports and to organize public hearings on the dangers of cults. In some places, attempts were also made to introduce legislation designed specifically to control cults and to punish those which refused to comply with the law. In response, various organizations and caucuses were mobilized to block any such proposed legislation and to combat attempts to single out cults for special penalties under the terms of existing laws. This mainly involved appealing against legal verdicts in favour of granting conservatorships over cult members to their parents, and persuading law-enforcement agencies to prosecute people who captured members for the purpose of 'deprogramming' them.

In the early 1980s the cult controversy was sustained by long-running legal battles involving a small number of NRMs. In conjunction with contemporary concerns about the legality of the practices of some other religious groups, the controversy began to feed into debates about church–state relations in the USA. It retained a degree of distinctiveness, however, because of continuing agitation about the allegedly deceptive and exploitative recruitment methods employed by some movements, but it had to some extent been subsumed under a broader heading concerning the powers of the state to oversee *any* religious group. This was partly because the proliferation of NRMs had slowed down and partly because the rate of membership growth had also declined in the most controversial movements.

This brief sketch of the trajectory of the cult controversy is qualified and amplified in Chapters 7, 8, and 9, but it has already served to illustrate the need for a comprehensive and direct approach to the phenomenon. Enough has already been said to show that studies of NRMs in isolation or of anti-cult associations cannot do justice to it. This is because it emerges from the interaction of numerous individual and collective actors drawn from circles extending far beyond cults and anti-cults. It is a social product which is simply ignored in studies which artificially separate NRMs from anti-cults.[5] My belief is that they cannot be properly understood in isolation from each other. Rather, the relationship between them and the wider social context of their inter-relatedness are the best focus for a sociological study.

Lack of attention to the controversy is puzzling, especially when it is borne in mind that cults are controversial in spite of the relatively small number of people who have joined them, the high drop-out rates, and the very limited public knowledge about their practices. We need to ask why public sentiment has been so hostile towards NRMs and why such an apparently marginal phenomenon has given rise to such energetic attempts at control. It is also important to discover how and why the impressive diversity of NRMs has been consistently denied or ignored in anti-cult sentiment. An essential task of historical reconstruction is therefore to be accomplished in the search for factors to explain the translation of basically personal and familial grievances into an orchestrated public campaign against cultic phenomena. In order to approach these questions, the cult controversy must be identified as a topic in its own right.

Existing studies of anti-cult groups and campaigns have suggested that an all-out *conflict* has been raging between cults and their detractors. Attention has been focused narrowly on their mutual hostility and their head-on collisions. A certain amount of attention has also been given to the violence occasionally employed by one side against the other, and ample evidence exists to support the view that nothing short of the total capitulation of one side would be accepted as success by the other.

The conflict has been punctuated by numerous episodes in the nature of scandals, panics, atrocity-accusations, and outrages. For example, France was the location of a scandal about a little-known group called Les Trois Saints Coeurs (Lecerf 1975); the small town of East Grinstead in England was the scene of a panic over the activities of Scientologists in the mid 1960s; atrocity tales about the Children of God or Family of Love movement have been widely circulated in the USA; and moral outrage has been a common response to the arranged marriages and mass-weddings of UC members. Although it may be unwise to lump all these disparate groups together as 'cults', the fact remains that reports of their activities all stress the conflicts between apparently cult-like groups and a critical public for whom the mass-media act as moral gatekeepers.

If evidence were needed of the public's critical attitude towards groups labelled 'cults', the findings of an opinion poll in the USA concerning the leader of the UC are instructive:

> 'In 1977 the Gallup Poll invited a cross section of Americans to express their attitudes towards Billy Graham, Pope Paul VI, and Reverend Sun Myung Moon. The most famous practitioner of alternative religion in the United States, the Reverend Sun Myung Moon, elicited one of the most overwhelmingly negative responses ever reported by a major national poll.'
>
> (Gallup and Poling 1980: 27–8)

In short, the term 'conflict' is entirely appropriate in connection with the public response to 'cults', but it fails to capture adequately the character of all the numerous ramifications and reverberations of the head-on collision between cultists and anti-cultists, cult-defenders and cult-detractors, the person in the cult and the person in the street.

'Controversy' is better suited to the latter task because it conveys the ambivalent, uncertain, and perplexed character of much of the argument and activity accompanying the major conflict. It conveys the idea that contrary opinions are in dispute over a matter that is considered problematic. It is not a matter of taste but, frequently, of principles and values. There is also the notion of a debate between the contending parties and, therefore, the possibility that some common ground exists between them. This is the general sense in which 'controversy' is used in this book. But more needs to be said about the distinctive character of the cult controversy and about its connections with the conflict between cults and anti-cults.

It is a *public* controversy in so far as the merits and demerits of cults have been discussed in the media of mass communication. Of course, such discussions have not been even-handed or unbiased, and the audience has had little opportunity to respond. On some of the occasions that members of NRMs have agreed to participate in radio or television programmes, they have complained either that subsequent editing of the recorded material distorted their opinions or that on live shows the presenters did not give them a fair opportunity to represent their viewpoint. Similarly, journalists writing for newspapers and magazines have often been accused of misrepresenting the cults. So, there has to be some doubt about the degree to which the mass media accounts of cults really allow, or provide, for a public debate. But there is no denying that the public is encouraged to believe that such a debate actually takes place in the mass media. All that can be reasonably stated, then, is that cults have been turned into a public 'issue'. The dispute is not confined to the very small number of people personally concerned about them; it spills over into many unrelated spheres of life.

The cult controversy originally arose from conflicts between members and their close relatives whose objections to cults included allegations about, for example, the way in which members are recruited, their alienation from relatives and former friends, the disruption of their careers and courses of education, their harsh living conditions, the deterioration of their intellect, and the induction of inappropriate or strange affect. The character and tone of these persisting allegations are examined in Chapters 3, 5, and 6. But, as was indicated above, this original conflict was taken up selectively by other parties, each of whom had different reasons for entering the dispute. The cults also fought back with publicity and litigation. The matter was then taken up by academics, jurists, civil rights activists, educators, and churchmen. It even inspired novelists, playwrights, film makers, and cartoonists.

This continuing *extension* of the debate is a powerful reason for choosing the term 'controversy'. The initial issue has become overlain with so many different issues that the sense of a simple conflict of interests has been lost. More importantly, it has become clear that some of the issues have serious implications for major institutions such as the law, law enforcement, medicine, and the family.

One implication of the extension of the dispute into a full-scale controversy is that a lot of the sensationalism and anger has been diluted by more impersonal issues of *principle*. The dispute may still be active and occasionally heated, and some individuals continue to wage a private war against the cults, but in other circles it is conducted in terms of evidence and reason, proof, and justification. The public probably catches only rare glimpses of this part of the controversy when an 'expert' makes a statement in public or is quoted by a journalist. But in the long term, the outcome of the controversy involving academics, churchmen, jurists, psychiatrists, and clinical psychologists is likely to have a lasting influence on public policy. This is not to say that the elements of scandal, panic, atrocity, and outrage are ignored. It simply means that they cease to be the main focus of attention and, instead, become rather suspect and questionable 'exhibits' in reasoned argument.

In one important respect the controversy has been partly *formalized* in some countries. It has become the subject of legal cases and of official inquiries. This marks a crucial turning-point in the evolution of a controversy, as I argue in Chapter 7. It signals the end of the private phase of a conflict and the beginning of a much more public scrutiny of the issues. For not only do court hearings and official inquiries generate evidence which may supersede earlier journalistic accounts but they also provide the contending parties with opportunities to publicize their cases. They rarely settle disputes but they can certainly raise them to a higher level on which different issues may come into play. In this way, the cult controversy has been partly transformed as a result of a process of formalization in some countries.

Chapters 7, 8, and 9 examine in detail the distinctive trajectory of the cult controversy in various countries and make comparisons with other and earlier kinds of religious conflicts. But it may be helpful simply to indicate here that I believe that there are some major differences between the present-day phenomena and those of the past. They have to do with the role played by theological issues; the geographical extent of the dispute; the number of groups targeted; the degree of organization among all contending parties; and the nature of the physical violence employed. In combination, these factors turn the modern cult controversy into a very distinctive phenomenon.

I believe that today's cult controversy is proving to be not only distinctive but also important. In fact, the issues raised by the controversy are probably more significant for the future of western societies than are the NRMs themselves. Even if the movements were suddenly to disappear, the consequences of some of their practices would still be felt for years to come. In particular, they have inadvertently and indirectly helped to reinforce (a) major cultural and social boundaries between images of the normal and abnormal person, (b) legal definitions of the limits of defensible action to be taken against an individual's wishes but allegedly in his or her own best interests as determined by agents of the state or close relatives, and (c) new ideas about the extent to which the economic base of religious groups can benefit from protection by the law on charities. In these, and other, respects the cult controversy is a barometer of changes taking place in a number of different societies. NRMs represent an 'extreme situation' which, precisely because it is extreme, throws into sharp relief many of the assumptions hidden behind legal, cultural, and social structures. The operation of many NRMs has, as it were, forced society to show its hand and to declare itself.

One of the main aims of this book is therefore to go beyond the conventional thinking about NRMs. Their sociological significance, it will be argued, exceeds the limits of problems about brainwashing, deprogramming, family disputes, and economic exploitation. They are undoubtedly serious social and psychological problems; but they are far from exhausting the *sociological* implications of NRMs. At a deeper level of analysis, the presence, methods of operation, and problems of NRMs can help to trace changes and tensions in whole societies. To adapt the argument of Léger and Hervieu (1983), NRMs can be seen as a microcosm of their host societies. I shall be content if those who have experienced NRMs as a private predicament or affliction are persuaded that social and societal problems are also at work. The former cannot be entirely reduced to the latter, of course, but their inter-relatedness has so far escaped the scientific attention that it deserves. Similarly, I shall be content if members of NRMs are persuaded that both the opportunities and the problems facing their movements were conditioned by various states of society.

Finally, I shall be content if social scientists are persuaded that the study of NRMs goes beyond the categorization of their ideologies and the search for factors pushing and pulling people towards membership. These aspects of the topic have greatly outweighed others, but it is time to appreciate the fact that NRMs have wider theoretical significance. Steps in the right direction have already been taken by Wilson's (1976) assessment of their potential for integrating societies; Bird's (1979) and Tipton's (1982) analyses of the movements' moral logics; Wuthnow's (1978) analysis of their experimentalism; Robbins and Anthony's (1980) insights into the social mechanisms for controlling them; and Robertson's (1979) understanding of the problematic relationship that they symbolize between identity, authority, and self-formation in modern societies. It remains now to examine what cult controversies can also reveal about the processes whereby social and personal problems are generated, defined, and managed.

Definitions

Even the terms that are used in a study of the cult controversy are controversial. We must therefore discuss the problem of definition at this juncture. One complication lies in the fact that not only are sociologists in disagreement over the most appropriate designation for religious groups such as the UC, Scientology, the Children of God, and the International Society for Krishna Consciousness (ISKCON) or Hare Krishna, but in a book dealing with the public response to them it is also necessary to use a popular term, namely 'cult'. To add further complication, 'cult' has a respectable, if contentious, pedigree among sociological terms (see, for example, Richardson 1979; Wallis 1974; Campbell 1977).

In order to preserve the character and feel of popular sentiment I shall use 'cult' whenever I report or paraphrase popular usage. This would normally be signposted by the use of inverted commas – 'sneer marks', as they have been called – but in a book-length treatment of the topic, this practice would become tedious. The important point to establish, then, is that 'cult' is used here in its popular sense to refer

to groups considered small, insignificant, inward-looking, unortho-
dox, weird, and possibly threatening. I believe that this is a fair
representation of widespread public views of cults. I do not endorse
these pejorative connotations; but it would be intellectually dishonest for me to ignore them. Whenever I refer to the groups in question
for analytic purposes, my preference is for 'new religious movements' (NRMs). Since this term is not without its own problems,
however, a further discussion of definitions is necessary.

No universally acceptable, hard-and-fast distinction can be made
between NRMs and other religious collectivities. For, just as the
term 'religion' and its cognates can be conceptualized and defined in
vastly differing ways (see McGuire 1981), so there are disagreements
about the kind of boundaries that could or should be drawn around
NRMs. It is a term which has become popular in both academic and
popular discourse, and this may be one reason for the ambiguities
that attach to it. Moreover, the question of boundaries is not simply a
matter of pedantry or logic-chopping: it has serious implications for
the public response to all religious groups.

Some characterizations of NRMs are based on quasi-doctrinal or
theological considerations. They amount to assessments of orthodoxy and are therefore useful for distinguishing primarily between
something akin to 'real' religion on the one hand and NRMs on the
other. In this usage, the term comes very close to the sense in which
'religious cult' is used in popular language. The underlying assumption is that a cult is not an authentic expression of what every
right-minded person knows to be religion. Its inauthenticity may
stem from fraudulent intentions on the part of founders or leaders;
from doctrinal aberrations from 'normal' standards; or from excesses in its religious practices. The variety of reasons for attributing
these cultic characteristics to NRMs is immaterial for present purposes but it illustrates part of the difficulty facing anyone who tries to
bring some order and clarity to this topic. Terms are chosen for
broadly political reasons.

Among academic students of NRMs, and especially social scientists, the tendency has been to regard religious movements which
either emerged or came into prominence in the west after about 1960
as 'new'. This is a convenient procedure because it accommodates
more or less all the well-known groups which have qualified as
NRMs by most people's definitions. Strictly speaking, of course, the
UC and Scientology were founded before this date. And it is a point
of some importance in many movements to claim that they operate in

direct line of succession from much older traditions. In fact, it seems to be almost *de rigueur* for some of them to deny that they could justifiably be called 'new'. For social scientific purposes, however, it matters little that such movements may have ancient forbears. Nor does the question of whether NRMs date from the 1960s or from, say, 1940 have much significance for purely definitional purposes.

Given the constant turmoil and change in all the world's great religious traditions at virtually any time in their history, it may even appear unwise to use the term 'new' for social scientific purposes. For it implies that there had previously been a time when 'new' movements did not exist; and this is patently untrue. There have always been NRMs.[6]

On the other hand, it is undeniable that in popular, as well as informed, opinion there occasionally comes a time when it is agreed that a significant change has taken place and that the beginning of something distinctly new can be identified even in the midst of constant flux.

This was the opinion of those social scientists and others who observed the more or less simultaneous emergence of a number of ostensibly similar religious movements in North America and Western Europe in the 1960s and 1970s. An indistinct, but qualitatively distinctive, phenomenon was initially registered at that time. Since then, of course, disagreements about the identity and meaning of the supposedly new phenomenon have been rife, but the claim that, whatever it was, it was new has scarcely been challenged.

It is important to emphasize, therefore, that the term 'NRM' was originally applied to a *plurality* of freshly observed groups. It did not refer to any particular group in isolation from the wider phenomenon. This means that, in its application to separate movements in isolation, the term is problematic: it applies more appropriately to them collectively. It refers to the perception of a pattern. There is not much to be gained from referring to movements in isolation as 'new'. It is only because a number of separate religious groups became popular among some young people at roughly the same time that use of the term 'NRM' can be defended. For it refers to them collectively – not separately.

The situation would be clearer if a term such as '*the* new religious movement' in the generic singular had been adopted. This would at least have emphasized the point that, while the separate groups may not be entirely new and may fall short of being movements, their collective impact is novel and is perceived as amounting to a movement. The statistical evidence about the rate at which religious groups were formed in the USA in the 1960s justifies such a view (see Melton 1978; Stark, Bainbridge, and Doyle 1979; Wuthnow 1978).

From this perspective, questions about the extent to which any single, so-called NRM displays the requisite novelty are beside the point. What is more important is that, once the perception of a general movement towards new kinds of religion or religiosity had been made, the dynamics of the general phenomenon came to override considerations of its constituent parts. For example, explanations were commonly sought for the tendency of young people to join religious movements in general rather than any particular religious movement. The cultural impact of NRMs in general was of greater interest to most observers than was the precise contribution of any particular movement in isolation.

One of the implications of this is that the available terminology referring individually to minority religious groups as 'church', 'sect', 'cult', etc. was bypassed, presumably because it was felt that it could not accommodate the new collective phenomenon. A large number of religious groups had been observed which were so qualitatively different from other religious innovations that they collectively warranted the special designation of 'new'. Some commentators implied even greater degrees of innovation by referring to these groups as 'new religions', thereby suggesting complete departures from prevailing norms in theology, metaphysics, rituals, etc. This designation has not proved popular, however, in spite of the popularity of Jacob Needleman's (1972) book of that title. Incidentally, Ahlstrom (1978) even designated three nineteenth-century innovations 'new religions', namely the Mormons, Jehovah's Witnesses, and Christian Scientists.

The term 'NRM' had not been at all widely used in the study of religion prior to its application to some post-Second World War innovations in the USA and Europe. More specific and purposive terms such as 'cult', 'sect', 'heresy', 'deviation', 'separatist church', 'independent church', etc. had previously held sway, and some of them are still applied to groups which are nowadays more commonly called 'NRMs'. But the currency of the older terms is now declining in the face of the increasing acceptability of the new term. There are two main reasons for its acceptance.

In the first place, 'NRM' is an entirely appropriate, value-free term to be used at a time when there is a strong tendency to regard virtually all expressions of religion as equally valid. When religious beliefs, convictions, experiences, and commitments are treated as expressions of personal preference or taste, there is much to commend the adoption of terms which reflect the prevailing ethos of pluralism and emotivism (see MacIntyre 1981). The older vocabulary was shot through with the theological and social resonances of an age when the boundary between entrenched truth and marginal aberrations was much clearer. But cultural pressure to adopt a less judgemental and divisive vocabulary has increased in recent years. An allied consideration may have been the recognition that the sharp distinctions that had formerly prevailed in some countries between established churches and all other minority religious groups was no longer a fair representation of the balance of material and cultural relations between them. In the course of secularization, the declining power and influence of the major churches seemed to induce the idea that virtually all religious groups were to be treated alike. The persistence of English-language terms like 'church', 'sect', and 'cult' therefore became unacceptable.

Comparisons with the vocabularies used in some other western European countries suggest that older terms have tended to be applied to the phenomena designated as NRMs in the USA. Thus, in the French language, terms meaning 'new sects' or 'new deviations' tend to prevail, thereby confirming that the Roman Catholic church is still a major socio-cultural force representing the norm from which all departures are, at best, suspect. But in the German and Dutch languages there is little implication that NRMs constitute an affront to a religious hegemony. Rather, terms meaning 'youth religions' or 'youth sects' clearly indicate that the most salient feature of NRMs in Austria, West Germany, and the Netherlands is felt to be their youthful following. In Britain, the term 'cult' has long been applied to small, exotic groups operating outside the mainstream of Christian churches, denominations, and sects. It has therefore been applied without any change of meaning to the new groups which first began appearing in the 1960s. This usage does not imply the existence of a religious hegemony in the country; but it does reflect the widespread feeling that a variety of churches and denominations share a common core of values, teachings, and practices. 'Cults' are definitely felt to lie outside this broad mainstream.

The case of the Italian language is particularly interesting because the groups which are called 'NRMs' in the USA were slow to make an impact in Italy. Before they became an object of popular interest, a term meaning 'NRMs' had already been applied primarily to transformations taking place *within* the dominant Roman Catholic church. It referred to such things as the movement for liturgical reform, the popularization of charismatic experiences, and changes in authority relations between clergy and laity. Groups such as the UC, ISKCON, and the Children of God have therefore been categorized as 'popular religions' along with the neo-pagan secret societies, witchcraft groups, associations for the veneration of popular saints, and major complexes of superstition. In social scientific studies of religion, however, it seems likely that the American usage will eventually prevail even among Europeans.

The second reason for adopting the term 'NRM' has to do with the perception that many of the innovations in belief and ritual which attracted public attention in the west in the 1960s for the first time had been imported from, or influenced by, non-Christian and non-western sources. The movements conveying them were not, therefore, modifications or permutations of the kind of ideas and sentiments which had inspired earlier deviations from mainstream churches and denominations. They were perceived to be radically new in that they drew on completely alien cultural and social traditions.

'The range of the new in contemporary American religious life and thought has moved beyond the experience of earlier generations. The movement is away from the boundaries of the Judaeo-Christian heritage of Western civilization. Whereas the religious diversity within that heritage continues to flourish in peculiarly American innovative forms, Eastern spirituality and third world religiosity are profoundly and innovatively expressed in America.'

(Ernst 1979: 44)

Moreover, unlike some earlier attempts to interest western audiences in oriental philosophies and religions, many of the movements which developed in the 1960s were clearly aiming to attract a mass-following by determined, if not very sophisticated, methods. They bore little resemblance to the decorous and elitist groups of *aficionados* who had dabbled in Indian, Chinese, and Japanese spirituality in the nineteenth century.

Sense of movement

There are sound reasons for choosing a term which emphasizes the radically new character of NRMs in preference to the more dated and culture-bound notions of 'sect', 'cult', etc. In addition, there are good reasons for drawing attention to the sense of *movement* implied by the new groups. Some of them very quickly achieved notoriety and acquired an enthusiastic following among young people who were apparently prepared to devote themselves without much reservation to the new-found cause. The combination of a speedy rise to prominence with an unusual capacity to sweep young people into selfless action on behalf of the groups was thought to be almost without precedent in modern religious history, although some perspicacious observers have commented on parallels with the early years of Methodism and Mormonism. In consequence, it seemed as if an extensive and unprecedented movement of minds, hearts, and bodies was taking place among youth.

Furthermore, it quickly became apparent that the most visible NRMs were energetically planning to expand their outreach by all manner of means. Enthusiasm for their teachings and practices was allegedly not developing 'naturally' but was being artificially cultivated by leaders who possessed ambitious schemes for their movements' growth. Journalists began to sense the pace and the direction of some movements in the late 1960s. Their sensationalist reports only reinforced the public feeling that a large-scale abduction of western youth was being orchestrated by ruthless gurus and meretricious messiahs. Some accounts of NRMs even suggested that the phenomenon bore a resemblance to such patterns of collective behaviour as 'crazes' and 'panics'. In the circumstances, then, the idea of a new *movement* in religion found a ready response in public opinion, if not among academic students of religion.

The reasons for the adoption of the term 'NRM' are connected with both the character of the phenomena and with the circumstances in which they came to public notice. These reasons should not be allowed to obscure the fact, however, that other less visible or newsworthy changes had also been taking place at the same time. The growing popularity of communes and of various self-help therapies on the fringes of the 1960s Counterculture gave rise to spiritual and explicitly religious innovations which were eventually incorporated under the increasingly inclusive rubric of NRMs. Some, like Scientology, were quite independent of the Counterculture in their intellectual roots and social composition, but the timing of their emergence was such that they were incongruously bracketed together with very different kinds of group. Others, like Zen Buddhism and Nichiren Buddhism, were simultaneously undergoing transformations of their traditional methods of public outreach and of their recruitment base which seemed to indicate a closer affinity with the genuinely new movements than was actually warranted. Still others were up-dated evangelical Christian groups embodying some aspects of the countercultural life-style whilst rejecting all vestiges of hedonism and promiscuity. Their doctrines usually remained close to the Protestant mainstream, although a few exceptions also achieved notoriety. Moreover, the major Christian denominations in the USA were facing increasing pressure to recognize as authentic a number of lobbies and pressure-groups representing the advocates of charismatic experiences, ethnic minorities, and feminist and homosexual constituencies.

None of these innovations, however, took place in a vacuum. The late 1950s and the 1960s witnessed serious upheavals in the doctrinal, organizational, and ethical aspects of many conventional churches. The growing popularity of liberal and radical theologies was eliciting the first backlash from conservative quarters. Mergers between churches were becoming frequent, but at the same time resistance to them was taking the form of separatist groupings of independent congregations and rival federations of protesting churches. But it was the increasing salience of liberal church programmes for the protection of various minorities and disprivileged groups, coupled with rising resistance to American military involvement in South-East Asia which caused the greatest amount of disruption in American churches. Taken together, these upheavals heralded the declining power and popularity of both liberal and radical causes in mainstream Christianity in the USA. They reflected deep-seated unease about basic social institutions and they were to provide the justification for the conservative evangelical revival that gathered momentum during the 1970s.

In the 1960s, however, these upheavals were largely unrecognized as such outside the inner elites of various churches. The attention of many observers was more easily attracted by phenomena which appeared to be genuinely new and even exotic. Their apparent irrelevance to questions of theology, ecumenism, and social justice perhaps enhanced their attractiveness. Coming as they did at a time of confusion and turbulence in other sectors of the religious world, the most visible and exotic NRMs offered a welcome departure from the norm.

In short, the movements of Asian provenance were only the most visible and perhaps the most novel of all the groups which were eventually to fall under the heading of 'cults' and NRMs' in popular and academic discourse. But the fact that they caught public attention in the first place and that they clearly warranted the designation of 'new movements' had created the unjustifiable impression that they are somehow representative of *all* the other groups which came to share their label. In reality, there is great diversity among NRMs – so great, in fact, that there are grounds for doubting the term's usefulness in social scientific analysis of religious innovations. As I argue in Chapter 2, one helpful response to this situation has been to divide NRMs into various sub-types. There is no sign of this kind of discrimination in popular discourse about cults.

For the moment, however, the significance of this terminological discussion is that, while the term 'NRM' is conveniently neutral and compatible with public perceptions, it is also misleading and insufficiently discriminating for scientific purposes. One possible solution would be to avoid using the term altogether and to employ a better alternative. It is doubtful, however, whether the available alternatives are any less problematic. 'Marginal religious movement' (Harper 1982), for example, avoids the misleading impression that religious innovation only began in the 1960s but it also creates problems with the implication that there are agreed standards by which to assess marginality in religion. There is also some ambiguity about the precise reference of marginality – doctrinal? social? or cultural? The same kind of difficulties attend such other terms as 'alternative religious movement' (Tipton 1982) or 'unconventional religious movement'. If anything, these two terms present even thornier problems than does 'NRM'. And a term such as 'post-movement movement' (Foss and Larkin 1976) is too closely tied into specific theories of modern culture and of the dynamics of particular groups to be acceptable as an all-purpose designation for the phenomena commonly called 'cults'.

On balance, then, it seems reasonable to retain 'NRM', but it is also essential to emphasize the need for an awareness of the potential difficulties that the term presents. My usage of the term in this book therefore makes heavily qualified assumptions about the movements' degree of novelty and it is certainly not meant to conceal the enormous diversity among them. For this reason, Chapter 1 emphasizes the doctrinal and social differences between the four most controversial NRMs in North America and Western Europe.

Notes

1   The identity of all informants has been deliberately disguised. See Beckford 1978a and 1985a for the reasons behind my choice of methods.

2   See Beckford 1978b for expanded views on how to make sociological sense of reports of religious experiences.

3   Recent publications on this topic are simply too numerous to be listed here. The reader is referred to the bibliography prepared by Beckford and Richardson 1983.

4   Deliberate attempts to counteract the sensationalism that pervaded many accounts of the tragedy were made by Richardson 1980 and Naipaul 1980.

5   It is to be regretted that major studies of the UC in the USA and of the anti-cult movement have been kept virtually separate in, for example, Bromley and Shupe 1979 and Shupe and Bromley 1980.

6   Ahlstrom's sardonic comment is worth quoting in this connection:

> 'Both humorists and outraged establishmentarians of all hues have been ridiculing the American's penchant for religious novelty ever since a Puritan minister in Boston referred to Roger Williams' sect-filled commonwealth of Rhode Island as "the Sewer of New England".... Given the extraordinary pluralism and, more importantly, the unremitting fecundity of the American religious tradition, the general observation is warranted that the appearance of many new religious impulses during the 1960s and 1970s can best be seen as a continuation of a venerable tradition − not only because they continue to be formed but because they also maintain an explicit or implicit social critique.'
>
> (1978: 4, 19)

See also John F. Wilson 1974. But for a dissenting opinion see Chinnici 1979.

ONE

The distinctiveness of
new religious movements

Introduction

The phrase 'new religious movement' (NRM) has achieved wide-spread popularity among social scientists and other commentators as an all-purpose way of designating distinctive groups which began to come into prominence in the 1960s and early 1970s. 'NRM' refers principally to the groups which have attracted the most publicity and/or notoriety. They include the Unification Church (UC), the Children of God (COG) or Family of Love, the International Society for Krishna Consciousness (ISKCON), Scientology, The Divine Light Mission (DLM), Transcendental Meditation (TM), and the Rajneesh Foundation. Yet, anyone with only a passing knowledge of even this small sample of controversial groups will know that there are many more broadly comparable groups and that there are major differences between them all. When some of the many less well-known groups are considered, it really becomes a problem to decide what they all have in common – if anything.

To some extent, I have made matters easier for myself by choosing to concentrate on the *controversy* surrounding NRMs or so-called cults. This allows me to focus very largely on those groups which have been labelled controversial by the public and therefore to duck some of the awkward questions about the wisdom of using a term which implies an unwarranted degree of homogeneity among all possible candidates for the designation of 'NRM'. It is a relatively simple matter for me, then, to turn aside from nagging problems of definition by stipulating that, for my purposes, the term 'NRM' refers at least to the following: the UC, Scientology, COG, and ISKCON. Amongst other things, they are all widely regarded as controversial.

Before examining this sample of NRMs in detail, I shall reflect on three characteristics of the socio-cultural context in which the controversy about cults has developed.

First, NRMs, in the most general sense of the term, are by no means restricted to the present historical juncture. Indeed, the religious history of the west in modern times could be written as a continuous dynamic activating, at one moment, massive structures of religious stability and, at another, forces for change and restructuring. One does not have to subscribe to structuralist theories of culture-change to realize the essentially contested character of religious expressions and sentiments. Whether it concerns teachings, beliefs, values, feelings, experiences, symbols, forms of social organization, or patterns of social relationships, the very fact of a religious expression seems to invite elaboration, challenge, or refutation. Undercurrents of enthusiasms and energies running tangentially or counter to orthodoxies have been an important feature of all religious traditions (see Knox 1950; Cohn 1957; Ellwood 1979a). In the nature of things, their importance has usually been played down by the upholders of tradition and continuity, but this only makes it all the more essential for sociological analysis to try to gain a more inclusive view of the diversity of religion at every historical juncture.

NRMs have been a recurrent feature of the major religious traditions, but their salience has not been constant. Historical comparisons are hazardous, but it seems likely that present-day NRMs are significantly different at least from their predecessors in the post-Reformation era in the western world in respect of their visibility, the form of opposition to them, the religious 'career' of their members and their political economy. All these points will be examined below.

Second, studies of religious phenomena have shown that the NRMs of the west are not alone in the world at present. Of course, local conditions affect the form of religious movements and produce highly variegated effects, but all the same it is possible to discern at least a minimal pattern in phenomena occurring in many parts of the world. On the one hand are movements aiming at the revitalization of religious traditions without introducing fundamentally new elements of belief, value, or practice. Such movements are distinctive mainly for their capacity to mobilize resources in novel ways for the achievement of ends which may not be at odds with those of traditionally valued spirituality. On the other hand are movements which seem to be seeking genuinely novel spiritual ends and/or means to their attainment.

This is an admittedly crude distinction which is fraught with problems, but it serves a simple purpose here in underlining the fact that 'new' religion is not necessarily destructive of 'old' forms in their entirety. There is a complex dynamic between them, and the outcomes are always provisional in the sense that new orthodoxies themselves elicit their own critical responses from even newer movements.

More to the point is the observation that spiritual change appears to be taking place on a large scale in many non-western countries and that the change is in part orchestrated by identifiable 'movement organizations'. In some cases, the organizations are sufficiently powerful and effective to cross national, regional, and tribal boundaries. There may also be links with political, educational, and economic institutions which serve to heighten the NRMs' capacity to bring about far-reaching transformations in the social life of members *and* non-members. At the same time, there may be tensions and conflicts with such other institutions as the state, the military, the family, and medicine (traditional no less than modern/western). These are all dimensions of what I call the 'insertion' of NRMs in their host societies. This notion will be developed more thoroughly in the next chapter.

Third, not all western countries have given rise to the level of NRM activity that has been detected in the USA. Most western NRMs originated there or assumed their present form in that country, but not all movements have been equally successfully transposed to other countries. Canada, Britain, West Germany, France, and the Netherlands have been relatively fruitful sites for many movements; but Italy, Greece, Spain, Ireland, Switzerland, and Austria have seen little in the way of their activities. Belgium and the Scandinavian countries fall somewhere in the middle of a scale extending between the countries of high and low degrees of NRM activity.

The NRMs of the western world are not unique in the perspective of either history or geopolitics (see Wilson, J. 1974). They have had counterparts in earlier times and they continue to have them in other regions of the world (see Wilson, B. 1976). This does not mean, however, that no marks of distinctiveness can be detected. Rather, it means that the characteristics of today's western NRMs have to be carefully specified if we are to understand their distinctiveness as

separate groups and as a category of religious collectivity giving rise
to public controversy. I shall begin to examine their distinctiveness
by describing each of the four major controversial movements.

A vignette of each movement will be sketched. Descriptive exhaus-
tiveness is not among my objectives, but I shall cite references to
authoritative literature whenever possible. Priority will be given here
to doctrinal distinctiveness since the movements' teachings serve as
the basic template for conditioning their other features. It would be
fruitless to open a discussion about the relative importance of
doctrine, beliefs, values, organization, material resources, etc. They
are obviously interrelated in complex and changing ways. But for the
purpose of accentuating each movement's distinctiveness, it makes
sense to begin with their doctrines. An attempt will be made in
Chapter 2 to construct a composite profile of selected movements
based on their characteristic mode of insertion in society. The full
complexity of the web of doctrinal, organizational, ethical, and
economic factors will then become apparent.

The International Society for Krishna Consciousness

Until the arrival of the Rajneesh movement in the west in the late
1970s the most colourful and instantly recognizable of the controversial NRMs was the ISKCON. It is better known as the Hare
Krishna movement – a title based on a phrase from the movement's
public chant. It was founded in the USA in 1965 by an enterprising
Indian businessman, A. C. Bhaktivedanta Swami Prabhupada
(1896–1977), who devoted the latter part of his life to export-
ing to the west a form of Vaishnavite Hinduism that had been
practised for hundreds of years in Bengal. The movement's communal style of living and public chanting, singing, and dancing, as well
as men's shaven heads, topknots, and saffron robes, quickly became
a symbol for many other exotic movements which were sinking
roots in America during the heyday of the youth Counterculture.
Good accounts of ISKCON's early development can be found in
Judah 1974; Daner 1976; Johnson 1976; Goswami 1980; Rochford
1982a.

Beginning in the mid 1970s, ISKCON lost much of its symbolic
resonance with the Counterculture in the process of cultivating a
more businesslike approach to the task of popularizing its teachings.
This was done through the sale of literature, public solicitation of
donations, and the development of numerous schemes for serving the

religious needs of the Hindu population of some major cities in the west. This brought ISKCON into legal conflict with various public agencies, private individuals, and anti-cult organizations. As a result, the number of young western people volunteering to join the movement's monastic order went into decline, but a category of sympathetic lay supporters expanded at the same time. The number of children born to members is also increasing steadily, and special educational facilities have been provided for them. Total membership is probably less than 20,000 worldwide.

The sophistication of ISKCON's public relations initiatives increased sharply in the early 1980s as it moved into the production of video cassettes and the marketing of tourist visits to its newly-completed Temple complex in West Virginia. Despite the massive changes that have taken place in the movement's outreach and social composition, however, no significant modifications have been detected in its metaphysics or teachings.

Some religious movements propel their members' focus of attention into an imminent future of apocalyptic destructiveness. Others instil and encourage an intense preoccupation with the self's progressive actualization in the present moment. Still more situate their followers individually and collectively at the culminating point of a progression of global dispensations or ages. But the distinctive characteristic of the Hare Krishna movement is that it dissolves the dominant western categories of time in a potent fusion of myth, ancient history, and actuality. As a result, selfhood and subjectivity are experienced in a way which has parallels in other Indian modes of religious consciousness but which is very different from the 'ways of being' characteristic of other new religious movements in the west. To understand this, one must begin with the movement's basic conceptualization of history.

According to the teachings of the Hare Krishna movement, time has no beginning and no end. Eternity is ever present. But unique events do occur in time, and they may lend meaning to the experience of the never-ending present. In particular, the reported actions of the forms assumed by the supreme deity, Krishna, on earth about 5,000 years ago hold great significance for the Hare Krishna followers. He is believed to be the Supreme Personality of Godhead and, as such, worthy of devotion, sacrifice, and worship. It follows, then, that the historical writings which relate his deeds are regarded as no less sacred and authoritative than the older scriptures revered in brahmanical Hinduism.

While Brahman is generally considered in most Indian philosophies to be the ultimate reality, the devotees of Krishna regard Krishna as its supreme personalization. He is therefore believed to have (or to be) supreme powers, including the power to take on many different forms.[1] Some of these forms are visible to humans; and some are recognized as being deities. Krishna therefore comprises within himself the whole of (his) creation but is also separable from, and greater than, it. He is considered to be at once universal and personal, for he responds warmly to the love of his devotees. Thus the philosophical categories of dualism and monism are unable to contain Krishna in all his forms.

True awareness of the knowledge of Krishna's nature is believed to be the source of unsurpassable bliss, for it is in this consciousness that all divisive categories of subject/object, matter/spirit, time/eternity, and difference/identity are transcended. Just as Krishna's nature fuses the eternal and the present, so consciousness of his nature is thought to intensify the devotees' sense of their location in time through identification with the timeless. This is the experience of Krishna's personal love for his devotees, and the expression of their love for him is believed to fill him with joy. In this way, the spiritual unity between Krishna and his 'parts' transcends, but also affirms, their different forms.

Time is therefore important since it is the medium within which Krishna 'expanded himself' into all living people and within which human beings have the possibility of regaining the full consciousness of their divine or spiritual origins. Accordingly, the *Bhagavadgita*, composed between the fifth and second centuries BC, is regarded as a literally true record of Krishna's historical acts, but it is also supplemented with the anonymous ninth or tenth century *Bhagavatam* which elaborates on the personal qualities of Krishna and explains the need for personal devotion to him. This latter work is central to the Hare Krishna movement's teachings and worship practices – as, indeed, it has been for centuries to the Bengali Vaishnavite current of Hinduism with which A. C. Bhaktivedanta Swami Prabhupada was deeply involved prior to the separate establishment of ISKCON in 1965.

Alongside the belief in the infinitude of time, there is also a belief that the physical world and all other creations are limited to an existence of four billion three hundred million years. At the conclusion of this period all living things are expected to be drawn back into the original godhead in the form of Vishnu for many millions of years. Only Krishna Conscious beings are believed then to transfer to a realm of eternal bliss (Goloka-Vrindavan), while others resume the round of rebirths in accordance with the law of karma. In comparison with western millennial philosophies of history, however, the outlook induced in Hare Krishna devotees is less apocalyptic and fatalistic. Perhaps the vastness of the time-scale discourages preoccupation with these cosmic transformations. It should not be overlooked, however, that the present age is regarded as the end of a materialistic phase of cosmic history in which increasing turmoil and distress are envisaged unless consciousness of Krishna's love for his creation can be instilled in enough people to usher in a new age of peace. Transformation of consciousness on a massive scale is believed to be the key to liberation from the world's travails, but it is conditional upon individuals' readiness to devote themselves to Krishna. Fatalism and apocalypticism thus play little part in the outlook of ISKCON's devotees.

Another reason for the relative lack of interest in grand historical designs is the fact that devotees are encouraged to concentrate on their personal progression through five determinate stages of spiritual growth. Each stage reflects a closer loving relationship to the deity, and each one is governed by strict rules. This is possible because man's original nature is held to be spiritual. He was created as part of Krishna, containing a tiny speck of 'Supersoul' in the form of Vishnu and a personalized soul as the seat of consciousness. But man's material body distorts his consciousness into thinking that he is identical with his body. It is taught that release from the distortion is attainable through devotion to Krishna, in the course of which the 'correct' relationship between creator and creatures is restored. Krishna Consciousness teaches that man's imperfections and problems derive from ignorance of dependence on the Godhead and from the mistaken belief that human lust was a faithful representation of Krishna's love for his creation. Man is therefore consigned to live in the material world unless or until he achieves a rebirth in a higher, spiritual world as a result of continuous, sincere worship of Krishna.

The moral economy of Krishna Consciousness is quite straightforward. Man's adversity is attributed to forgetfulness of his originally and potentially loving relationship with Krishna. The continual reproduction of adversity is assured by the principle that the condition of each soul's rebirth in human, animal, or vegetable form is determined by the degree of faithfulness to Krishna displayed in previous existences. The more a person invests in the material world,

the more remote he or she becomes from Krishna. Only by progressive distancing from the basically illusory attractions of the material
world can a person cultivate true Krishna Consciousness and, in
consequence, rebirth in higher and higher spiritual forms. The Hare
Krishna movement does not acknowledge any connection between
the discipline required to achieve progressive liberation from illusion
and the duties traditionally associated with the Hindu caste system.
The objective is, rather, to transcend human categories of good and
evil by ceaseless devotion to ensuring Krishna's happiness through
selfless love for him.

The monks devote many hours of each day to contemplating and
reciting the names, forms, and pastimes of Krishna in a continuous
round of joyful worship. At the same time, however, their life is
strictly moulded by a regime demanding vegetarianism, avoidance of
stimulants and of sexual relations even among married couples
except for the purpose of procreation, and early rising. This combination of ecstasy and discipline is one of the movement's intriguing
hallmarks. Critics have interpreted it as a sign of infantilism.

Nevertheless, complete withdrawal from conventional social and
intellectual life is not considered a prerequisite for spiritual advance
towards Krishna Consciousness.[2] What is required is the peaceful
observance of prevailing laws, the pursuit of compassion, and
avoidance of self-indulgence. Above all, Krishna Consciousness is
believed to imply love and concern for the whole creation since it is
all part of Krishna's being. But this does not mean attachment to
things or people. It means having the sincere desire to bring others to
Krishna Consciousness, for only in this way can their real happiness,
as distinct from the illusory and temporary benefits of physical
pleasure, be assured.

The elevated status of ISKCON's founder, A. C. Bhaktivedanta
Swami Prabhupada, in the movement's teachings and practices is
closely connected to its teachings on history and on Krishna's love
for his creation. He is regarded as the latest in an unbroken line of
Krishna's disciples whose task has been to bring people to consciousness of the illusory distortion of reality in everyday life and to
consciousness of the loving reciprocity between Krishna and mankind that has been forgotten. In the case of Prabhupada, this has
entailed translation and wide dissemination of the allegedly divine
wisdom contained in a large number of Hindu scriptures. His
credentials were therefore impeccable for the role of Guru or spiritual master, for his life is believed to have been faithfully modelled on

scriptural precepts. It was devoted to loving service of Krishna; and he had conquered the temptations of the material world. Prabhupada could claim to be a pure devotee and a representative of Krishna, and this is what made (and still makes) him an object of veneration by other devotees. Yet, he is treated as distinct from Krishna. He is the perfect guide to Krishna because of his spiritual gifts and his command of the sacred wisdom of the *Bhagavadgita*; but he is not to be confused with the Godhead.

Similarly, the ISKCON organization is accorded respect for its contribution towards the dissemination of what is considered absolute truth. Aside from the scriptural precepts relating to the discipline of personal worship of Krishna, however, no special rules apply to the collective instrument of sacred truth. It has therefore developed in a flexible and rather pragmatic fashion[3] very largely in accordance with the personal decisions of Prabhupada. Towards the end of his life he established a governing body commission (GBC) composed of twelve mature male appointees who would exercise responsibility for the management of ISKCON in all parts of the world. Their authority was derived from the Swami's personal spiritual status, although it was also envisaged that after his death they would be elected by one vote of all temple presidents for fixed terms of office. The status of the GBC was subsequently modified to that of an international administrative board of twenty-four members among whom eleven of the original appointees function as spiritual masters and initiators of new disciples.[4] Alongside its original pragmatism, however, the ISKCON insists on its unbroken continuity with the Bengali Vaishnavite tradition. Indeed, this was cited as the first reason why it should not be confused with 'cults' in the west. The latter are considered to be 'generally recent creations, without definite roots in traditional religion or cultural systems', whereas ISKCON describes itself as 'an ancient and principal denomination of Hinduism (the world's oldest religion), with a long-standing spiritual, philosophical, and cultural heritage' (ISKCON *A Report to the Media: Please Don't Lump Us In*, p. 2).

For all their public displays of ecstasy and bliss, members of the Hare Krishna movement actually participate in a form of 'fundamentalist' Hinduism. Their sacred scriptures are regarded as literally true, and there is no sympathy with the 'all-paths-lead-to-one-God' philosophy characteristic of many brands of westernized Hinduism. Authority relationships are clear-cut, although sometimes hotly challenged. The daily regime of early rising, chanting, study, vegetarianism, ritual purification, worship, and work is strictly enforced on all members of the monastic order who live in temples. And all their social relationships are closely monitored for signs of unfaithfulness to Krishna.

The monks are the most visible members, but several categories of lay members are also associated with Hare Krishna temples.[5] They may be relatives of monks, aspiring members, curious outsiders, or would-be members whose material circumstances prevent them from abandoning ties to the secular world. An increasingly important category of lay members nowadays includes expatriate Indians who wish to support a Hindu temple and make use of its ritual services. In their different ways all these lay members contribute towards the Hare Krishna movement's material prosperity (see Carey 1983).[6]

The movement is also active in sustaining itself through various profit-making and publicity ventures such as vegetarian restaurants; the manufacture and/or distribution of incense, posters, soaps, herbal toothpaste, fragrances, Yoga clothing, musical instruments, and meditation supplies; radio broadcasting in Italy; newspaper publication in India; book production and sale; the management of private schools; sale of sound and video cassettes; tourism at New Vrindaban Palace in West Virginia ('Krishnaland'); and the door-to-door sale of various types of membership to raise money for temple construction in northern California. It has acquired extensive property in many countries and is now generating enough funds in the west to support missionary work in India.

In sum, the ISKCON movement has skilfully adapted an ancient form of Hindu spiritual practice to the conditions prevailing in modern, western, urbanized societies. Its 'launch' coincided with the rise of a youth Counterculture among well-educated people, but it has nowadays achieved considerable independence from the countercultural milieu. It is still in the process of finding a more complex, albeit no less controversial, mode of social insertion.

I believe that Wallis (1984: 87–8) creates a misleading impression of the Hare Krishna movement's dynamics by describing the changes that have taken place in ISKCON as adaptations to the loss of its countercultural constituency and as ways of exploiting a less marginal constituency by means of 'progressive accommodation' to the world. In fact, the countercultural 'phase' of the movement had lasted only a few years in the late 1960s and had never really disturbed the tight control that Prabhupada had always exercised over its path of development. The Counterculture has merely helped to generate interest in Asian worldviews but in many respects it was incompatible with Krishna Consciousness.

The declining number of recruits from countercultural mileux did not therefore call for major adaptations in the movement. Rather, it was the death of Prabhupada in 1977 and the subsequent struggle for power among his appointed successors which led to laxity in some sections of ISKCON and to ambitious commercial ventures in others. It was at this time that about 25 per cent of members were reported to have withdrawn from the movement. The stronger links that were then forged with some Indian communities in western cities, far from being a closer accommodation to the world or an adaptation to the loss of the countercultural 'market' for recruits, were actually illustrations of the movement's roots in India. They do not represent compromise or enforced accommodation. They represent continuity with an ancient tradition that was temporarily overshadowed by the brief and hectic interlude of the late 1960s. To speak of 'world accommodation' in this context is to miss an important point about long-term continuity.

The Children of God

The origins of the Children of God (COG)[7] are to be found in the luxuriant growth of Hippie-style evangelical missions to young people that developed in the mid 1960s on the fringes of some Christian denominations in the southern USA. Beads and beards, sandals and smiles were the outward symbols of the so-called Jesus People movement which attracted numerous followers among college-age students, drop-outs, beach bums, and other denizens of the countercultural world.

Some evangelical campaigns among youth are still in operation, but many groups of enthusiastic converts were short-lived. Others achieved stability and independence; still more fused with established denominations. But the group which came to be called the COG took a completely different path and has survived for more than fifteen years as a network of itinerant bands preaching radical condemnation of conventional styles of life and of ruling powers (see Davis and Richardson 1976; Richardson and Davis 1983; Wallis 1979: 74–90, 1981; Pritchett 1979).

Some of the COG's practices are highly controversial and have given the group a degree of visibility, at least among anti-cultists, which is out of all proportion to its numerical strength of no more than a few thousand. One reason for this is that COG's teachings are recognizably Christian in very many respects but radically different in other respects. The combination of orthodoxy with what its critics consider blasphemy has elicited severe condemnation, vilification, and rejection.

Whereas the doctrines and practices of some NRMs have evolved slowly over decades under the guidance of increasingly prosperous and sophisticated organizations, backed in some cases by considerable wealth, the Children of God movement has evolved in a more halting but none the less dramatic fashion in the past fifteen years or so. In another sharp contrast with what has happened in some other NRMs, COG has developed less in response to increasing exposure to dialogue with outside commentators and more in response to the leader's quasi-experimental practice of 'trying out' successive schemes for expressing his millennial Christian ideas in practice. Within five years of the beginning of David Berg's independent evangelism in 1967, for example, he had experimented with a coffee-shop-cum-crash-pad for Hippies in southern California, a gypsy-like nomadic trek with his followers to Canada and back, ranch-style communes in Texas and California, and finally, smaller colonies dispersed over vast tracts of North America, South America, Europe, and Asia.[8] Eventually they extended to the Caribbean, Asia, Africa, the Middle East, Australasia, the Pacific, and India, but it is unlikely that the total of members has ever exceeded about six thousand.

Berg's earliest teachings were in the mould of many fire-and-brimstone Christian evangelists of the southern and south-western USA. A Bible-based understanding of the need to repent for sins in the saving grace of Jesus Christ animated his warnings of an impending apocalyptic destruction of the sinful world. Salvation was offered in return for heart-felt repentance and an ascetic life devoted to warning others of the harsh punishments about to be administered by a righteous Old Testament God, although Berg was admitting by 1978 that '"Faith without works is dead" (James 2: 17), and love without some material manifestations is doubly dead!' (MO Letter 682, 1978).[9]

Berg's vision was originally pre-millennial and fundamentalist.[10] As such, special prominence was accorded to biblical inerrancy, prophetic chronology, and the interpretation of apocalyptic symbolism. To this repertoire of conventional, if not popular, teachings Berg came to add more idiosyncratic elements concerned with glossolalia, astrology, the interpretation of dreams, the degeneration of the Jews, the nobility of the Arabs, and the historic significance of the Gypsies as a model for Christian communities. And running through it all was the theme that conventional religious groups were worthless corruptions of authentic Christianity. In fact, the whole western system was condemned, including the institutions of politics, law, government, the economy, the family, and medicine. Revolutionary rhetoric became common in Berg's writings in the early 1970s.

In keeping with the pre-millennial tradition, Berg originally taught that, beginning in 1968, the world[11] would be devastated by a series of natural and man-made disasters leading to the advent of Anti-Christ. Only people who were alienated from the 'system' and who were prepared to abandon everything for the sake of learning how to survive the Great Confusion and the Great Tribulation were welcome to COG groups. They alone were believed to have the mandate to warn the rest of mankind about the impending Apocalypse; and they alone were expected to rule over the millennial paradise on earth following the Great Tribulation.

The idea of the Great Confusion is based on a Third World War scenario set in the early 1980s. It turns on an Arab–Israeli conflict, Soviet assistance to the Arabs, and the crippling of the USA. Thus, 'The White powers of the Western World are about to collapse under the rising Red tide of color. . . . The White Man's Doomsday impends!' (MO Letter 105, 1971). The succeeding decennium was expected to witness the installation of a communistic regime under the presidency of Anti-Christ,[12] followed by the persecution of the few remaining faithful Christians in the Great Tribulation, and their 'translation' as Saints into a heavenly condition as the Bride of Christ. Christ is expected to destroy Anti-Christ in a Battle of Armageddon in 1993, thereby marking the beginning of the millennial kingdom culminating in the final destruction of Satan and the judgement of all mankind. The Righteous are believed then to enter a Heavenly City for eternity, and apparently there is a prospect of universal redemption even at this late stage of the historical drama. For example, members of the People's Temple who died at Jonestown in 1978 were said by Berg to have taken the coward's way out of life but that, since they had been 'saved' through faith in Christ, they would be admitted to Heaven although with lower spiritual status than COG members.

Berg's particular brand of millennialism is distinguishable from that of the majority of Adventist preachers in a number of respects.[13] First, it is pervaded by a righteous indignation against the rich nations of the northern hemisphere and their ruling classes. No attempt is made to disguise a class-based animus against what Berg considers to be unjust distributions of material and symbolic resources. This gives his preaching in MO Letters a degree of social 'relevance' which was persuasive to many young people alienated from western societies in the late 1960s and 1970s.

More recently Berg has combined anti-system feelings with a virulent strain of anti-semitism. Following an unhappy visit to Israel in 1970, during which he attempted to take out Israeli citizenship, he steadily increased the anti-semitic tone of his writings to the point where he could vent his anger as follows:

> 'May God damn those God-damned Jews! . . . How can God tolerate those God-damned Jews! . . . O God, if I had a gun I would shoot them myself! . . . God damn those rich US Jews, those anti-Christ, God-hating Jews who hate us, Thy children, and are trying to destroy us . . . May God damn every Israeli! They are all robbers! – all terrorists! And all thieves! All oppressors!'
>
> (MO Letter 681, 1978)

Berg's anti-Semitism sets him clearly apart from many Christian Adventists who show great sympathy for Israel and interest in her fortunes.

Second, Berg's understanding of his personal role in the millennial vision became progressively stronger and more intrusive in the COG's set of teachings. By the early 1970s it was accepted that he had been 'filled with the Gift of Faith' in his mother's womb (MO Letter 77, 1971) and was acting as God's mouthpiece for the dissemination of 'the Truth'. A common claim was that doctrinal pronouncements were not Berg's own ideas: they were the word of God – conveyed by means of his servant on Earth.[14] In fact, Berg claimed that originally God had virtually forced him into the prophetic role (MO Letter 329, 1974).

By the end of the 1970s this idea had developed into the claim that the COG's success, unlike that of other 'youth sects', was due to God's leadership:

> '*We have had worldwide fame! . . . All I do is just give the word!* It's not been my "hypnotic personality", it has not been my "magnetic charisma", it has been just the *Truth – the Word of God*

– that has done it. This is totally different from any of these other sects.'

(MO Letter 748, 1978. Emphasis original)

This is a further indication of Berg's highly reflexive style of preaching and 'situating' his movement.

Third, the COG organization quickly acquired more than merely instrumental importance in Berg's writings. In addition to being considered as an effective and necessary instrument of God's purpose in the 'end-time' heralding the advent of Anti-Christ, the organization also assumed a collective sacredness in itself as the only true church. Its committed members were considered an exclusive elite with the unique responsibility to rescue God's faithful from the impending destruction. Unwillingness to obey its proper authorities therefore amounted to sacrilege and symbolized the forfeit of God's grace. Salvation was by faith alone and was available to all who would show it; but failure to conform with Berg's account of God's will was deemed to deny all access to saving grace. And countries which abused the COG were expected to suffer from divine retribution.[15]

Fourth, the underlying sense of COG as a heroic pariah community had been present from the beginning (see, for example, MO Letter 'Nehemiah' of 1 March 1970) but was boosted in the late 1970s by perceived persecution at the hands of various anti-cult forces. In particular, the tragic (self-) destruction of the People's Temple at Jonestown, Guyana was identified by Berg as a major source of the growing repression of all religious minorities in the 'end-time': '*It's all a part of the Devil's own conspiracy* against *the Lord* and his *people*! They *hounded* those poor people literally to death! ... *They've beaten, kidnapped, imprisoned, tortured and even killed us*' (MO Letter 742, 1978. Emphasis original). The practical response was to advise the COG to '*Dive underground* totally out of the picture into some *unknown* place and destroy or carry with you any high-security materials such as *mailing lists, files, financial records* etc.' (MO Letter 750, 1978). In fact, this period witnessed the instigation of a major programme entitled 'Nationalize-Re-organize Security-wise' (NRS) which changed many aspects of COG organization and coincided with a massive defection of members.

Fifth, COG's exclusivity is closely connected with two precepts: to keep the organization pure from the corrupting influence of less-than-fully committed people; and to feel unconstrained by any 'worldly' standards, provided that the injunction to Love Thy Neighbour (the 'Law of Love') is not compromised. The seeds of a doctrinal and moral perfectionism were thus implanted in the COG from its earliest stage as a separate growth of the burgeoning Jesus People movement in southern California.

In combination, all these distinguishing features of Berg's teachings paved the way for COG's collective image as a heroic, persecuted minority whose misfortunes merely confirmed the 'end-time' teachings. Through all the group's trials and tribulations the overriding sense of the urgency and deadly seriousness of its divine mission has never been clouded by other considerations. This can be illustrated by analysing the COG's most controversial teaching, namely, the sacred obligation to use sex as an aid to conversion.

Berg has claimed that, since being seduced by his baby-sitter at the age of three, he has never fully understood the taboos and oppressive restrictions against free expression of human love and sexuality. Not surprisingly, he has repeatedly emphasized the benefits to be gained from a robust attitude towards heterosexual relations. But it was only in the mid 1970s that he openly articulated ideas about the sacred duty of women to have sexual intercourse with men for the deliberate purpose of bringing them to faith in Christ. More recently, the doctrinal justification for so-called Flirty Fishing (FFing) has been further refined with references to the status within the community of resulting 'Jesus babies', 'mateless mothers', and 'promiscuous profligates'.

At the centre of this teaching lies a very important principle: the Mosaic law, which would have condemned FFing as fornication or adultery, is no longer considered applicable to COG because this spiritual elite benefits from the newer dispensation of Christ's 'Law of Love'. The new law makes it an obligation of faith to reflect and embody God's love in *all* things. Offering sexual relations to potential converts therefore amounts to an act of divine love which is beyond reproach. More than that, it is highly commendable as a test of faith in the 'end-time', or, as Berg put it: '*That revelation about Flirty Fishing was the ultimate test* that really divided the sheep from the goats, both wives and husbands' (MO Letter No. 1012, June 1981). At the same time, however, a distinction was introduced between sex and love:

> 'Let's have no more of this careless, unloving, purely lustful, wicked, sinful, irresponsible, flagrant, profligate, promiscuous sex

that is unwilling to lovingly take care of the results! *Such sex is not love, but pure, wicked, sinful, iniquitous, selfish lust* with no regard for the consequences and no feeling of responsibility for the results and broken hearts, bodies and fatherless children left behind!'

(MO Letter No. 1012, June 1981)

Expulsion and excommunication are therefore threatened to all male members of COG who do not accept responsibility for caring for their sexual partners and children who require assistance. '*So trespassers beware!* Don't trespass against [a female member] unless you're willing to become her mate and the father of your child that she bears you, if she so desires' (MO Letter No. 1012, June 1981). The necessity for a lengthy and repeated treatment of these matters between 1974 and 1975 (see MO Letters No. 302C; 314B; 332C; 359) indicates that FFing took place within the group as well as with outsiders.

The new dispensation of the Law of Love in the peculiarly threatening 'end-time' therefore serves to justify FFing in COG groups. It is also used as a justification for the practice of condoning extra-marital sexual relations. Husbands in particular are warned to be magnanimous and forgiving of their wives' liaisons:

'"Judge not that ye be not judged, for with what measure ye mete it out it shall be meted unto you again" (Matthew 7: 1, 2). Even if your wife is guilty, you'd better forgive her if you want to be forgiven for your sins. For if you self-righteously and hypocritically judge her harshly God will judge you the same, but justly. "For whatsoever a man soweth, that shall he also reap." (Galatians 6:7).'

(MO Letter No. 1012, June 1981)

To this justification in personal terms is added a type of *collective* responsibility which hints at the idea of a perfectionist community of love.[16] Thus, Berg reasoned that true love and genuine concern for the welfare of *all* COG members should dispose the men to accept responsibility even for children whose paternity was in doubt, for,

'If they are in your family they *are* yours and every child is ours and *some* father should take care of it. And every mother is our sister and our widow and someone should mate her in love and consideration for the mateless and fatherless. . . . God's Law of Love requires that, and He will reward you accordingly.'

(MO Letter No. 1012, June 1981)

It is widely recognized that tight-knit communities find it difficult to overcome the problems arising from tensions between the tendency of married couples to form a relatively closed unit and the communal need to maintain common ownership of, and access to, major resources (see Abrams and McCulloch 1976). In the case of groups like COG, in which contraception and abortion are taboo and in which the production of large numbers of children is regarded as a sign of divine blessing, the tensions are to some extent aggravated. For over against the primacy placed on sexuality and child-rearing there is the equally salient obligation to keep the whole community permanently united and mobilized in the pursuit of pressing evangelistic goals.[17] Berg's way of controlling these tensions is apparently to stress the over-riding importance of the Law of Love and to extend its applicability to virtually all social relationships generated in evangelism.

Other considerations, as Wallis (1979) has argued, include Berg's growing awareness in the mid 1970s of the need to find ways of making converts and recruiting well-qualified members among social strata more sophisticated and less other-worldly than the college drop-outs who had predominated in the early COG groups. Recruiting in discotheques, bars, and night-clubs in tourist centres supposedly called for the novel strategy of FFing. Now, strategic considerations were no doubt important in the decision to extend the privileges of sexual freedom to non-elite members of the movement, but they should not be separated from more strictly doctrinal developments in the evolution of Berg's thought.

This potted description of COG's evolution may give a misleading impression of stability. The fact is that, in addition to the tensions found in any system of millennial-cum-evangelical beliefs, Berg appears to have given differential salience to particular teachings at particular times (see Wallis 1979: 70–3). There is certainly continuity of insistence on the millennial vision of history and of the imminent future, but this has at times been coupled with an evangelical outreach and, at others, with a more withdrawn perfectionism. One can only speculate on the social and psychological factors which may have disposed Berg to swing from one set of priorities to another. What is not in question, however, is Berg's own awareness of the predicaments and dilemmas facing the COG's determined efforts to be 'in the world, but not of it'; evangelical but exclusive; successful but ascetic in life-style; organized but not organization-minded. His MO letters display a high degree of reflexivity and of sensitivity to changes in COG's collective fortunes. Berg's critics prefer to interpret this as false naivety or manipulativeness (State of New York 1974).

Speculation about Berg's motivations and intentions is beguiling but frustrating because so little reliable information about him is available to outside observers. We do know something, however, about the evolution of the social bonds which tie members to COG. It is clear, for example, that the movement has at times been centred on communes in both rural and urban settings. At other times, smaller 'colonies' and house groups have served as the principal organizational unit. Most recently, the trend has been towards a much more loosely federated structure of 'homes' and isolated missionary families.

Since the late 1970s, MO Letters have consistently encouraged members to disperse to various Third World countries[18] and to engage in whatever evangelical ventures seem most appropriate in the circumstances. The outcome has been a proliferation of diverse initiatives with mixed results. But the common thread running through these experiments is a heightened notion of individual responsibility for the collective fortunes of COG. Members are encouraged to arrange their lives in such a way that they can afford to meet the costs of travel to the new mission fields; they must ensure that they have sufficient resources to carry on effective evangelism virtually independently from the rest of the COG organization; yet, they must somehow maintain contact with other members; and they are under pressure to send cash donations to COG leaders on a regular basis.

Today's practices are a far cry from those of the early 1970s when COG communities survived largely on the strength of their begging ('provisioning'). Nor is the sale of MO Letters ('litnessing') a main-stay of local groups. But whereas 'going solo' was an unusual initiative[19] in the mid 1970s when most members lived in colonies under the direct supervision of appointed leaders, it began to become a normal procedure in the 1980s. This was closely associated with the exodus from western Europe, the migration to the Third World, the increasing modal age of members, and the growing number of members' children.[20]

While the model of a federated organization is appropriate to COG's present mode of operation, it should not be overlooked that the doctrinal and administrative centre of affairs is still controlled by Berg and his immediate entourage. Their public visibility may have declined since the late 1970s but their control over COG's fortunes is no weaker for that. They still control the movement's literature output; they still organize the movement's finances; and they still run the World Wide Mail Ministry in which members are expected to participate by writing to outsiders who have reportedly shown interest in COG's activities.

One implication of the transfer of the main evangelistic effort to Third World countries is that there seems to be a greater readiness to co-operate with public officials. In fact, the *Family News International* of 1 March 1982 urged members 'Please let's try to make ourselves as popular with governments as possible'. Advice was therefore given on how to receive visitations from inspectors and from the police. 'Be respectful and honest' seemed to be the rule. Despite some problems with immigration officials and the police in a few Third World countries, Berg's letters have largely avoided criticism of the COG's new 'hosts'. At the same time, of course, excoriation of the western world's evil and corruption has not waned. In fact, the contrast between the west's allegedly imminent destruction and the Third World's possibly bright future forms a common theme in his writings after 1979.

The evolution of the COG movement illustrates the overwhelming power that its leader has been consistently able to exercise over its members. Many have left the movement, of course, but a continually renewed body of followers has been prepared to conform with each of Berg's bewildering changes of strategy for the movement's development (Wallis 1982). The persistent refusal to sanction compromise has ensured that the public controversies surrounding COG have remained out of all proportion to its numerical and material strength. There is no sign that its marginal status is being revised, despite energetic moves to adopt fresh modes of social insertion. This may be why the eclipse of most Jesus People groups has not yet brought the COG to a halt, although it must be recognized that the movement has been on the wane since the mid 1970s.

The Unification Church

The origins of the Unification Church (UC) are shrouded in mystery but they seem to involve a charismatic and spiritualistic innovation among Korean Presbyterians.[21] It was led by a spiritually sensitive young man from the North of the country who had been partly educated in Japan during the period of annexation. His name was

Sun Myung Moon (1920–   ). After fleeing from the Communist forces he eventually registered his schismatic group in South Korea under the title The Holy Spirit Association for the Unification of World Christianity in 1954. It appears that Moon's spiritual curiosity and energies outraged the Presbyterians and lay behind charges of minor criminal activity that were never proven.

If the circumstances of the UC's origins were not very auspicious, it rapidly attracted a dedicated following in the Republic of Korea and subsequently in Japan. Eventually, the Japanese branch prospered to such an extent that enough funds were generated to sustain extensive missionary work in the USA. But it is not clear whether financial assistance also came from Moon's increasingly successful businesses in Korea or indeed from other sources as well.[22]

The American mission field did not immediately yield good results in the 1960s (see Lofland 1966; 1977; Mickler 1980), but when Moon began to make speaking tours of the country in the early 1970s, recruitment of new members (soon to be nicknamed 'Moonies') expanded rapidly. A series of well publicized and orchestrated rallies in major cities, culminating in spectacular gatherings in New York City gave the UC a massive boost in the mid 1970s. Large numbers of mainly college-age, middle-class people joined the movement (at least briefly), and its activities quickly proliferated in diverse ways. A similar pattern of events took place in West Germany, France, and Britain.

The rate of membership growth in the western democracies slowed down in the late 1970s, although expansion was only just beginning in other parts of the world. The combined effect of organized campaigns of opposition and of several well publicized scandals limited the UC's growth in the west, but the 1980s saw the introduction of new strategies which may have taken it in the direction of a more flexible and less unitary kind of organization. Parallel transformations have been observed in the movement's teachings.

Discussion of the doctrine taught by the Unification Church is made easier by the fact that Christian theologians and philosophers have commented at some length on its development and structure (see, for example, Bryant and Hodges 1978; Bryant and Richardson 1978; Quebedeaux and Sawatsky 1979; Bryant and Foster 1980; H. Richardson 1981; Flasche 1981; Bryant 1980). It has also elicited more critical commentary in general terms than has any other NRM (see, for example, Bjornstad 1976; Levitt 1976; Sparks 1977; Sontag

1977; Yamamoto 1977; MacCollam 1979; Allan 1980). And Christian groups of various persuasions have commented on Unificationist theology (see, for example, British Council of Churches n.d.; National Council of Churches in Christ 1977; Evangelische Zentralstelle n.d.). Among today's NRMs the UC is distinctive in positively seeking opportunities to discuss its doctrine with nonmembers and with the members of competing groups.

The UC acknowledges a single authoritative source of doctrine,[23] although references to the Bible and to other religious traditions are occasionally made in the course of expositions of Unificationist thought. The central source is entitled *Divine Principle* and consists of the wisdom channelled through[24] Sun Myung Moon and assembled over many years by his disciples, translators, and editors.[25] Controversy rages in some circles over the relative contribution of Christian and non-Christian components to Unificationist thought, but there is no doubt about the general influence of Korean shamanism, Taoist philosophy, Confucianism, and Buddhism over Moon's unique blend of traditions. Equally, there can be no doubt about the UC's aspiration to act as the solvent of religious differences and as the catalyst of universal religious harmony.

Divine Principle is a systematic exposition of thought intended to complete, by unifying, the wisdoms of Judaeo-Christianity through a fresh denouement of the history of mankind's fall from divine grace and restoration to original perfection. The guiding theme is therefore a very intrusive philosophy of history – but not conceived solely as an external patterning of events. Rather, the levels of personal development and universal history are fused into a single perspective, namely, the progressive restoration of original perfection. In so far as this is historicism, then, it is conditional upon the readiness of individual people to 'glimpse a panorama of the good that could be' (Kim 1976: 284) and to associate themselves with God's revealed plan to 'transform the world according to his dispensation of restoration' (Kim 1976: 284). Man's role is to fulfil what are called the Three Blessings, namely; to achieve perfection of individual minds and bodies; to perfect human relationships from the level of the family upwards to that of world unity; and to perfect man's relationship with the physical environment. Only the Fall of Adam and Eve is believed to have prevented the fulfilment of these Blessings in an earlier age.

Eschatology therefore looms large in Unificationist theology but it eschews violent apocalypticism in favour of a vision of progressively maturing intuition, intelligence, and spiritual power. The culmination of this process is believed to usher in a rage for higher truths which will complete the Old and New Testaments and herald the beginning of a new epoch in God's creation. Unificationist theology has a dramatic, sweeping character. History is represented as a drama of conflicting forces, a steadily unfolding plot, and a 'cliff hanging' finale.

The major actors in Unificationist theology are God, mankind, two Messiahs, and Satan. The conception of God is of a living, compassionate Creator caring in anguish about the fate of fallen man and caring in love for his restoration. Originally, He formed intimate relations with His creatures who, in turn, reflected His love and had the capacity to reflect His perfection. He was hurt by the Fall of Man, which was attributed by Moon to the sexual seduction of Eve by Lucifer and He has been continually grieving and seeking since then to restore the basis for the broken father–child relationship.

God's scheme for restoration calls for men to display humility, sincere contrition, and a readiness to obey His chosen intermediaries. Indemnity has to be paid voluntarily for the Fall, since it was an expression of free will. Much of *Divine Principle* is therefore devoted to a scriptural and numerological analysis of the past six thousand years designed to reveal the progress of restoration and the special significance of the present era. The main idea is that the conditions are presently ripe for the Lord of the Second Advent to achieve the physical salvation of mankind.

According to the Unificationist doctrine of man, he was created potentially perfect by God in order to enjoy nature, to fulfil himself, and to glorify God. As a result of the Fall, however, this three-fold purpose has been frustrated and will only be achieved when man progressively re-establishes the conditions for a restoration of the original father–child relationship. This entails awareness of God's plans as well as procreation in a God-centred marriage so that the experience of mutual love in the family can reactivate God–man relationships on an increasing scale. This process is termed 'resurrection'. Eventually, harmonious relations would be formed with the whole of God's creation, thereby fulfilling its purpose. Man, as a physical and a spiritual being, mediates between God and nature and can therefore establish a dominion over it for the purpose of bringing it, like himself, to perfection. But, like everything else in creation, development must pass through the three stages of formation, growth, and completion. This applies to men individually and collectively; it also applies to phases of history. Moreover, the development does not cease with physical death but continues in a spirit realm.

In conformity with the Unificationist disposition to find homologies and parallels between things on different symbolic or material, divine or human, levels, the doctrine of the two Messiahs parallels the plan for the progressive restoration of perfection to man and nature. It holds that, since everything has a male and a female aspect or polarity, true harmony is conditional on the establishment of a proper relationship of mutual love or 'give and take' between them. Jesus, the first Messiah, failed to marry (amongst other things) and consequently failed to produce children who would, by virtue of their conception in a marriage based on a faithful reflection of divine love, have instigated the re-peopling of the world with spiritually perfect beings. Christian doctrines of the atonement are therefore rejected in favour of the supposedly less mysterious idea that a non-divine Jesus partially failed in His mission and succeeded only in providing the opportunity for men to attain the growth stage on the route to perfection, i.e. a spiritual, not a physical, salvation.

Progress towards the stage of completion or perfection in everything is said to have been occurring for the past six thousand years, and the recent outpourings of charismatic enthusiasm and interest in the supernatural are taken as signs that a critical juncture is at hand. But progress has to be earned through indemnity or suffering. This means that man must make an effort to be restored, and the effort must aim to restore the supposedly correct relationship between man and God.

The role of the Lord of the Second Advent, the second Messiah, or the Third Adam, is to act as God's interpreter of the meaning of present-day events. It is believed that under his guidance identification with God will inspire bonds of love which will then be progressively reflected in all social relationships, thereby completing the restoration of perfection and man's dominion over nature. This is the doctrinal basis for the supreme importance attached to the ceremonial Blessing conferred by Moon on couples who have been matched by him for marriage. This is considered to be the fundamental contribution to the progressive transformation of the human race on to a plane of higher spirituality.

Nothing short of the establishment of the Kingdom of Heaven on earth is the second Messiah's task. He is expected, on the basis of scriptural evidence, to be born in the East and, on the basis of an argument by elimination, to be Korean. The religious history of the USA allegedly qualifies it for a special providential role in supporting the new Messiah's mission, particularly in the struggle to destroy Satanic communism.

The arrival of the Third Adam coincides with the descent of good and bad spirits to earth. For they will share with the living the opportunity to achieve the completion stage of restoration. The resurrection of the dead (i.e. spirits without bodies) and the Judgement are therefore interpreted symbolically: not literally.

The fourth actor in this historical drama, Satan, is conceived of as a fallen Angel who tempted Adam and Eve to have sexual intercourse before being married by God and who has constantly opposed man to God. This is the source of sin, and it is an hereditary condition from which recovery can only be achieved by reasserting a loving relationship with God and by being willing to 'buy back' the accumulated debt of sin through indemnity. This involves taking on the responsibility for denying Satan through sacrifices appropriate to the historical moment of God's plan. Indemnity has to be orchestrated by a central figure (for example, Noah, Abraham, Moses, Jesus) who is responsible for ensuring that all the God-ordained conditions are fulfilled for redressing the historical balance of sin and obedience.

A number of general observations can be made about the overall character of Unificationist doctrine. The most striking thing is that it is presented in such a systematic fashion that it seems to be intended for use in teaching situations.[26] This is true of *Divine Principle* as well as of the more esoteric documents. As we shall see later, this is a crucial feature of the UC's primary mode of operation in the west.

It is also a strikingly positive system. In addition to carrying the full weight of a dispensationalist and messianic philosophy of history, it provides for an unusually significant input of voluntarism. The plan for the restoration of perfection is never in question, but the timing of its denouement allegedly depends on the success of God's prophets in creating the right conditions for its successful completion.

The starker and darker Christian doctrines touching on Hell, the Apocalypse, and predestination are rejected by the UC in favour of a more optimistic vision of universal salvation, the harmonious resolution of all ideological differences in a world of unified truth, and the establishment of a physically perfect Kingdom of Heaven on earth. Happiness, for example, is described as the goal of existence.

Yet, for all its systematic character,[27] Unificationist theology also makes great play with strong emotions. God seems to be motivated by a highly anthropomorphic love for His creation, and His feelings about the Fall of man include lamentation, grieving, and compassion. Similarly, His prophets are believed to have experienced intense emotions of guilt and pain in their efforts to turn people back to a God-centred existence. The private devotions of individual members have also been described as highly emotional.[28]

The visitor to a UC centre is certainly struck by the members' outward signs of joy and intense concern for others. Closer acquaintance with their spiritual practices also reveals great emotional intensity in their praying, singing, teaching, testifying, and interpreting dreams, visions, and omens. Premium is placed on 'spiritual openness' or capacity to communicate with the spirit world.

The person of the Revd Moon plays an important role in relation to Unificationist doctrine not only because he is usually credited with its revelation, nor simply because he is widely thought to be the Lord of the Second Advent depicted in it, but also because he is regarded as the movement's mediator with God and other eminent spirits. The written or formal doctrine therefore matters less than his capacity to reveal absolute truth. Moreover, the success of his mission is still conditional upon his being able to generate the right circumstances for physical and spiritual salvation.[29] This may explain why many members acquire a deeply personal attachment to Moon and why one of the few regular rituals involves taking a Pledge which venerates him and his wife (see Carlson 1981).

There is an open-endedness to Unificationist theology which deserves examination. On one level this means that the formalized doctrine undergoes change in time. But on a more subtle level it means that, over time, members of the UC come to experience doctrine differently. Its meaning and significance also change in accordance with changing outlooks and circumstances. Thus, differences in interpretation of doctrine can be attributed to different backgrounds, etc. In fact, this is carefully built into the indoctrination procedures in such a way that the central teachings are revealed to neophytes only in a fixed sequence and only at a pace considered suitable for each individual. Notions such as perfection and salvation are given a processual, rather than a fixed, meaning. This has contributed to the suspicion that the inner elite has access to esoteric doctrines concealed from other members and from the public. It has also disturbed some of the UC's critics who interpret doctrinal open-endedness and variability as signs of nothing more elevated than deceptiveness and manipulativeness. They seem to demand of the movement's members a degree of intellectual uniformity and rigour that would confirm theories of brainwashing and mind-control. As it happens, the range of doctrinal understanding found among members is probably no wider or narrower than that found in other religious groups of similar size and maturity.

Since the UC has gone to exceptional lengths in the past five years to finance and organize a number of conferences and symposia at which Christian and Jewish theologians have commented on Unificationist theology, the question of the movement's relationship to standards of orthodoxy has been openly discussed.[30] Needless to say, opinion is divided with, for example, Carney (1981) asserting that the UC is clearly not Christian, and Richardson (1978) affirming that it is an authentic Christian group. Somewhere in the middle comes Sontag (1977; 1981). No other NRM has received (or solicited) so much commentary from outsiders, although it must be added that some commentators have cultivated such close and lasting ties with the UC that they can scarcely be called outsiders any longer. Herbert Richardson, for example, describes himself as a 'Moon supporter'. It will be interesting to assess the long-term impact of exposure to external theological criticism on the development of the UC's theology.

The long-term impact of external criticism may actually be less significant than the current practice of putting the movement's most promising, committed members through intensive Masters-level courses at the Unification Theological Seminary (UTS) in Barrytown, New York. The syllabus ranges over most of the core and optional subjects offered in mainstream seminaries, so that exposure to non-UC scholarship is extensive. A closely allied strategy is to encourage the best UTS graduates to study for doctorates in a number of universities and schools of theology in the USA. What is more, the prestigious schools and departments of religious studies or theology are clearly preferred. One can therefore expect that the results of this two-pronged engagement in higher education will eventually feed back into the presentation of Unificationist doctrine in myriad ways. At present, the signs are that the graduate students are primarily intent on situating the distinctiveness of their religion in the context of contemporary schools of philosophy and theology. It remains to be seen whether their interaction with fellow-students and teachers in non-UC schools will produce any modifications of their own or of other people's beliefs.

An earlier modification of the emphasis placed on certain aspects of Unificationist theology seems to have occurred in the mid 1970s when a so-called 'heartistic revolution' took place. This term refers to a relative shift away from the doctrines of indemnity towards the notion that the UC, as a human community trying to inspire a transformation of the world's values, was based on bonds of love. The significance of this shift lay mainly in the suggestion that the heroic stage of grim struggle to establish the UC on a firm footing in the west was passing and that a new, more expansive stage was beginning. In symbolic terms, the 'suffering minority' self-image gave way partially to a new self-image as a confident, welcoming, and loving community. This symbolic change no doubt reflects the UC's growing prosperity and organizational stability.

Other changes paralleling the 'heartistic revolution' included the cultivation of the Home Church movement and the development of various services for the benefit of communities in the neighbourhood of UC centres. The Home Church is an attempt to meet the religious needs of people who are unable to abandon their secular responsibilities in order to join the UC. It therefore consists mainly of sympathizers who are either too young or too old to participate on a full-time basis in the full round of fund-raising, study, worship, and work in Unificationist enterprises. Its activities are largely confined to meetings for instruction and worship. It may also come to serve as an organizational convenience for providing such communal services as street-cleaning and musical entertainment in public places. At present, however, neighbourhoods are served by groups of full-time members who are drafted for this express purpose.

In these various ways, the centre of gravity of the UC's public activities is gradually shifting away from the preoccupation with fund-raising and with the recruitment of young, full-time members. The movement's social base is slowly widening and diversifying, although the young mobile 'zealots' are still very much the modal members. Yet, even *their* public visibility has declined in recent years as they have become progressively more deeply involved in UC businesses. They are no less active: but their activity is less public.

The UC's present strategy for transforming western societies seems to involve infiltrating higher educational, religious, and scientific institutions in order to create a public image of itself as a credible source of new values. This is paralleled by expensive forays into newspaper publishing in New York, Washington DC, and Tokyo. The Unificationist philosophy is marketed in increasingly diverse ways as the dissolution of ideological antinomies and as the basis for harmonious existence among all parties, interests, and nations. The precise character of the envisioned world order is left vague, just as the UC's highly energetic campaigns for ecumenism studiously avoid judgements between contending theological positions. The preferred tactic is to imply that all differences can be overcome if and when all parties agree to acknowledge the oneness of God and, presumably, the unique competence of Sun Myung Moon to reveal His will. It is as if the UC were offering to organize a debate on all the major issues of the day – but only on condition that the speakers agree in advance to accept the Unificationist way of resolving their differences.

It is not entirely unlikely that the UC is evolving towards the kind of utopianism that was eclipsed by the massive fund-raising campaigns of the early and mid 1970s. Now that the movement has achieved public visibility and material prosperity, there may be a return to building the kind of 'ideal' society envisaged during Sang Ik Choi's leadership of the first major Unificationist centre in San Francisco. This pattern of evolution would certainly be compatible with the observed decline in the rate at which young, unattached people are prepared to devote themselves wholeheartedly to the UC. A closer integration between the movement and dominant social institutions is also more feasible at a time when the turn-over rate among members is slowing down. These changes in the UC's social composition in many western countries may allow it to be more influential in circles where social values are shaped.

Another implication of these changes is that the character of the controversies surrounding the UC in the west may be modified. As we shall see below, controversy has been mainly attached to the methods whereby the movement recruited, indoctrinated, and removed young people from conventional roles and routines. With the declining rate of recruitment and the rising average age of members, however, critical attention is now being switched to the UC's business operations and political programmes. It remains a highly controversial movement – but for rather different reasons.

Scientology

The founder, chief ideologue, and present-day figurehead of Scientology proclaimed that it was a *religious* movement only some years after his major book on Dianetics had begun to sell in large numbers in the early 1950s. Lafayette Ron Hubbard's (1911–   ) background had been in physics and engineering, but when he retired from the United States Navy after the Second World War he returned to a pre-war interest in writing science fiction stories. Indeed, the early sketches for Dianetics, a form of self-help mental training and therapy, were developed in the science fiction genre. The hugely positive response from the reading public seemed to convince Hubbard that there was a real need for a more elaborated version of his ideas about the relationship between mind, body, and spirit. Accordingly, *Dianetics, the Modern Science of Mental Health* was published in 1950 with the claim to be 'the common people's science of life and betterment' (for histories of Scientology see Wallis 1976; Kaufman 1972; Malko 1970; Whitehead 1974).

The early years of Hubbard's transformation of Dianetics, and then Scientology, into a religious movement were punctuated by unsatisfactory alliances with collaborators, disputes over the ownership of ideas, and organizational failures. The Hubbard Association of Scientologists finally emerged in 1952, however, as the stable basis for the promotion of Hubbard's ideas. It was superseded two years later by the Founding Church of Scientology which has continued with the addition of numerous organizational adjuncts to serve as the movement's intellectual, material and moral centre. From 1959 until 1964 Hubbard's base of operations was at Saint Hill Manor, England, and he subsequently controlled the movement from aboard a small flotilla of yachts based in the Mediterranean. His whereabouts have been secret since the mid 1970s, so secret in fact that there have been repeated rumours of his death.[31] But there is no reason to believe that Scientology's current teachings have departed significantly from Hubbard's own ideas. The continuous introduction of new programmes, routines, and spiritual objectives certainly indicates that Scientology has not ossified and is able to supply its practitioners with fresh goals and activities.

The fundamental assumptions of Scientology are really very different from those of the other NRMs under consideration in this chapter. Not only does it lack an explicit grounding in the scriptures of any major world religion but it also possesses a historical perspective which differs radically from that of the other movements. Scientology has no conception of the kind of grand historical design common to, for example, the Children of God or the Unification Church. Nor does it share with ISKCON the view that myth, history, and personal growth can be fused in a single moment. By contrast, Scientology's teachings refer to history as the scene of the conditional evolution of life-forms, and little emphasis is placed on the benefits that might be derived from a broad historical perspective. I doubt whether this was the reason why one of its critics dubbed Scientology 'the Now Religion', but the title is apt in so far as it draws attention to the historical 'flatness' of its teachings.

The starting point for the highly complex and programmatic set of Scientology teachings is a series of claims about the nature of the human spirit and brain as they operate in the human body. These claims were first systematically arranged in the late 1940s by Lafayette Ron Hubbard, the movement's founder, into a scheme called Dianetics. Its aim was to deal with both ontological and existential problems, but it was quickly adapted to suit the needs of people seeking practical solutions to psychological and social problems in their own lives.

Long before the days of popularized micro-electronics, Hubbard was speculating in various writings about the computer-like nature of the brain and about its capacity to promote the organism's survival by suppressing some of the body's painful experiences. But survival was supposedly obtained at a cost. The repressed memories acted as blocks to, or distortions of, the efficient operation of some normal brain functions. The normally rational and analytic mind is overridden by a different, reactive mind in situations which resemble, however tenuously, the conditions in which the originally painful experience had been registered and repressed. These experiences are called 'engrams'[32] in Scientology, and it is believed that chains of them can be built up in body cells on the basis of similar experiences. Each of them can subsequently be 'keyed in' by sense perceptions similar to those registered by the reactive mind during the period of shock-like response that followed the originally painful experience. Prenatal engrams have been estimated to constitute between two-thirds and three-quarters of all the engrams acquired by the average forty-year old person. 'Anaten' is the term used in Dianetics to refer to this shock response which closes off the analytic mind in a way which may misleadingly suggest unconsciousness. Irrationality is supposed to be the hallmark of behaviour conditioned by engrams.

In an effort to overcome engram-conditioned irrationality and to restore computer-like efficiency to human minds, Dianeticists were taught to practise a wide variety of methods for emptying the 'bank' of engrams from the reactive mind. The underlying belief is that by bringing to consciousness the conditions of the originally painful experience, engrams can be transformed into memories which are then made subject to the normal control of the analytic mind. The formal parallels between Dianetics and varieties of psychiatry and psychotherapy have been commented on by many students of Hubbard's writings. Following the immense success of his book, *Dianetics: The Modern Science of Mental Health* (1950), Hubbard embarked on writing and research projects which attracted the interest of large numbers of people. In order to satisfy the public demand for Dianetics, he published more and more practical works designed to enable readers to put Dianetics into practice for themselves and for the benefit of others. Eventually, the Church of Scientology was founded in 1954 as an organizational instrument for supervising Dianetics and introducing Scientology. It progressively controlled and standardized all of Scientology's burgeoning operations in several parts of the world so that by the early 1960s it constituted a powerful, centralized movement-organization with effective procedures for disseminating the teachings of Dianetics and Scientology, marketing their products, supervising their practice, and defending their interests against mounting criticism from public agencies and private individuals.

The relationship between Dianetics and Scientology is complementary. The latter did not repudiate or replace the former. Scientology basically placed the 'technologies' of Dianetics in a more spiritual framework. Dianetics is primarily concerned with the problems of the reactive mind, whereas Scientology deals with learning about mankind's spiritual nature. But little attention seems to be given by Scientologists to the differences between them.

It was in the mid 1950s that Hubbard clearly situated the psychological assumptions of Dianetics in a framework of spiritual or religious evolution. It was claimed that Dianetics was descended from ancient Asian hymns, theories of evolution in Vedic scriptures, Taoism, etc. But the most explicit claim to descent from ancient spiritual sources relates to the Buddha, who was

> 'called actually *Bohdi*, and a Bohdi is one *who has* attained intellectual and ethical perfection by human means. This probably would be a Dianetic Release ... or something of this level. Another level has been mentioned to me – *Arhat*, with which I am not particularly familiar, said to be more comparable to our idea of Theta Clear. ...

Any work that I am doing or have done, and that any Scientologist is doing, has a tremendously long and interesting background. We are delving with [sic] and working with the oldest civilised factors known to Man. . . . Scientology is a religion in the very oldest and fullest sense.'

(Hubbard 1968: 18, 34–5. Emphasis original)

At the same time, Hubbard clarified his thinking about the ramifications of the human urge to survive by specifying its eight 'dynamics' or manifestations at levels ranging from the individual person to mankind as a spiritual ward of a Supreme Being. Similarly, the notion of 'theta', spirit or soul, emerged as the undying human life-form which is subject to disturbance in the physical world of Matter-Energy-Space-Time (MEST) and which survives the death of the body. It was subsequently reconceptualized in the plural as 'Thetans', spiritually perfect beings considered to be all-knowing and all-powerful, creators of the universe, and such playful designers of life's 'games' that they eventually forgot their transcendental origins and identified themselves with the physical bodies that they inhabited, between intervals, in endless succession.[33]

The process of systematically uncovering engrams by means of question-and-answer sessions ('auditing') is the major practical application of both Dianetics and Scientology. Auditing is designed to eradicate engrams progressively to the point where the Thetan is liberated to regain its self-identity as the spirit which animates the body. A person who 'goes clear' is believed to have realized his or her identity apart from the physical body and to have gained dominion over the physical world. Beyond the status of 'clear' there is a complex hierarchy of progressively elevated spiritual states, all of which are allegedly attainable as a result of training and counselling. Progress is achieved by studying Scientology material, following courses of instruction, practising newly acquired skills and drills, and being audited by a qualified Auditor. The Auditor asks questions designed to expose the traces of engrams, and the client's response is measured (in Scientology auditing) on a skin galvanometer called an E-meter. The objective is to reach a point where the questions reveal no further traces of engrams or other disturbances of communication which would be shown in deflections of the meter's needle.

Liberation from the effects of engrams is believed to free the Thetan to the point where it can put itself 'at cause' in any course of action, i.e. it can knowingly take responsibility for, and control over, its actions. The contrasting position is to be 'an effect' of external forces and causes. The person who is 'at cause' tends to live life more fully than other people by virtue of being thoroughly involved in the 'ARC triangle'. This refers to the web of reciprocal relationships between (A) feeling emotional *affinity* for others, (R) agreeing with others on the *reality* of situations, and (C) being able to *communicate* without hindrance. The degree of involvement is measured on various scales. The 'Tone Scale', for example, measures emotions on the dimension of affinity, extending from Cheerfulness to Apathy. Extensive quotation from Scientology's own literature is indispensable at this point as a way of conveying the most highly valued characteristics of the successful Scientologist:

> 'The characteristics and potentiality at the top of the scale or near the top are unbounded creation, outflow, certainty, certainty of awareness, going-awayness, explosion, holding apart, spreading apart, letting go, reaching, goals of a causative nature, widening space, freedom from time, separateness, differentiation, givingness of sensation, vaporizingness, glowingness, lightness, whiteness, desolidifyingness, total awareness, total understanding, total ARC.'

(Hubbard 1969: 99–100)

As a Scientologist goes up the scale of Auditing, so his or her ratings on all the various scales are also expected to rise. This is believed to find reflection in an enhanced sense of self-actualization and satisfaction as well as in higher rates of success in whatever the Scientologist sets out to achieve.

Does this liberating technology find expression in a social ethic? Or is it limited to purely personal gratification? Hubbard's earliest writings on this point are quite consistent with present-day teachings. The whole point of Scientological wisdom is supposedly to facilitate improvements in all the conditions of living.[34] Thus, there have been constant references to the civilizing mission of Scientology, to its attempts to deliver mankind from a state of barbarism, and to restore the limitless creative powers to Thetans. In reality, this mission has primarily taken the form of several specific projects for changing the institutionalized practice of mental health care, implementing a new programme for breaking drug-addiction and for rehabilitating former addicts, and supporting various campaigns against perceived violations of human rights. The justification is that 'A church cannot advocate spiritual freedom for man, and turn a blind eye to injustice, suffering or dishonesty' (*Freedom* (39) May 1979: 17). Claims that Scientology campaigns have been successful are given extensive publicity in its publications (see, for example, *Freedom* (42) August 1979: 11 ff.).

The range of Scientology's reform campaigns is indicative of its underlying theory of pathology, i.e. failure of communication. Dissatisfactions, failures, and evil in general are all traced back to distortions of, or breaks in, communication at the personal and collective levels. It follows, then, that accusations of conspiracy to mislead, defraud, hoodwink, or otherwise cheat honest citizens form a *Leitmotiv* in Scientology publications. Topics that are given special prominence have included: federal taxation in the USA; the abuses of institutionalized psychiatry; corruption in the American CIA; dishonest implementation of the Freedom of Information Act in America and of its counterparts in some other countries; complacency about the dangers of nuclear radiation; official cover-ups of prison-service malfunctions; discrimination in the US Justice Department; abuses of Interpol; violation of the constitutional separation of Church and State in the USA; connivance at the criminal activities of deprogrammers; conspiracy in the health care professions; collusion between journalists and security services; unauthorized experimentation with drugs in the armed forces; and illicit compilation of data banks on private citizens.

Communication failures are not considered accidental. They are explained by reference to anti-social personalities which oppose all plans for improvement in any sphere of life (Hubbard 1974). Twenty per cent of the population is estimated to be 'anti-social' and, consequently, unable to communicate successfully with others or to understand the inter-relatedness of affinity–reality–communication. The remainder constitute 'social personalities'. 'Basically the social personality wants others to be happy and do well, whereas the anti-social personality is very clever in making others do very badly indeed' (Hubbard 1974: 20). The difference between the two types can allegedly be measured in terms of the empirical results of their respective actions ('statistics') and expressed in terms of a scale of 'conditions' ranging from 'treason' to 'power'.

The connection between this individualized moral psychology and the wider moral economy of the whole society is effected by means of a classically liberal notion.[35] It holds that, if creativity and productivity are encouraged in individuals, there will be a comfortable material surplus to be distributed among the needy. Socialism and communism can therefore be tolerated only as strictly temporary expedients to overcome crises of under- or over-production. Progressive income taxes amount to an unethical suppression of potential and actual talents. Capitalism, in the sense of 'living off interest from loans' (Hubbard 1974: 62) is found to be equally objectionable. Thus, 'All I beat a drum for is that the working worker deserves a break and the working manager deserves his pay and the successful company deserves the fruit of its success' (Hubbard 1974: 62).

The religious philosophy of Scientology, or 'wisdom' as Hubbard has often termed it, combines several distinctive and potent components. It contains, for example, a theory of evolution which is both ontogenetic and phylogenetic, accounting for the conditions under which liberation from ignorance, suffering, and weakness can be overcome by mankind and by the individual Scientologist.[36] This is coupled with a claim to scientificity based on realist principles. That is, Scientology claims to lay bare the fundamental structures and mechanisms of reality. The greater a person's understanding of reality, the more successful will he or she allegedly become. The techniques and skills taught by Scientology are expected to make that understanding accessible and applicable in everyday life. Conformity with the underlying structure of reality is the primary requirement, then, for realizing the full potentials of the liberated Thetan which supposedly inhabits every body. But Scientology contains no suggestion of historical necessity or inevitability. On the contrary, it has a thoroughly voluntarist metaphysics which stresses the conditional character of liberation for the individual whilst also holding out the prospect of collective spiritual and material progress on condition of individual progress. It is fully consistent with this highly positivistic perspective, therefore, that personal and social pathologies are attributed to failures of understanding.[37] They are believed to be at the root of negativity, apathy, hostility, unawareness, and withdrawal.

In accordance with the ethos of 'positive thinking' which pervades Scientology, membership is strictly voluntary and goal-directed. That is, people choose to participate because they believe that they will become more 'aware' and 'better able to handle life' as a result. The absolute value of Scientology in itself is probably of less importance to most participants than is the belief that it can help them to achieve whatever goals they have. It follows, then, that the form of their participation will vary with their changing perception of goals, ideals, and values. The result is that participation may entail not much more than the purchase of courses of training and counselling. But it *could* entail deep involvement in the movement's organization, advanced courses, religious ministry, and campaigns of social reform. In short, the notion of membership is flexible and the forms of participation are diverse.

The social composition of Scientology is equally complicated. Research conducted for the movement's own purposes showed that there is a wide range in the distribution of members' age, social class, and occupation (Church of Scientology of California 1978). But the modal characteristics are those of a married, white person in their late twenties with above-average educational qualifications and white collar occupation. The ratio of men to women is roughly 3:2. This profile is quite different from that of the other NRMs considered in this chapter. It shows that Scientology is definitely not a creation of the youth Counterculture and has never been a 'youth religion', although it may have benefited from the spiritual ferment of the 1960s.

The intensity of a Scientologist's participation can be measured in terms of the number of courses completed. But other indicators include periods spent working as 'staff' in Scientology establishments; promotion to positions of responsibility in the organization; and ordination in the Church of Scientology's ministry. There is no single route to success or power in the movement. Rather, the Scientologist's 'career' can take any number of directions at different times. Fresh training and re-training are constantly available options.

The strategy of marketing and promoting Scientology primarily through the sale of courses of training and counselling has given rise to a set of very distinctive controversies. They partly concern the practice of encouraging participants to purchase more and more expensive courses in pursuit of progressively higher qualifications. Other sources of controversy concern some Scientologists' occasionally over-zealous attempts to unearth evidence of various agencies' alleged campaigns of vilification against, and subversion of, the movement. The treatment of putative 'enemies' has incurred severe criticism and punishment. So has the kind of 'tug-of-love' situations which arise when one parent decides to remain in Scientology while the other decides to seek legal custody of their children and to leave the movement. This problem occurs in many religious groups, of course, but it has sometimes been aggravated in cases

concerning Scientologists by accusations that the movement insidiously defends the interests of its members against those of its
defectors.[38]

Conclusion

Three points emerge clearly from these brief descriptions of today's
four most controversial NRMs.

First, their metaphysical assumptions, doctrines, and ideological
views display great *diversity*. Leaving aside the obvious fact that they
are engaged in cultivating and disseminating metaphysics, doctrines,
and ideology, it is not easy to identify points of substantive similarity
among their respective positions. They each convey a different
notion of man's origins, reasons for existence, historical development, and future prospects. Their respective accounts of the ontological and existential problems besetting mankind are at least
incompatible, if not contradictory in some cases. There is considerable disagreement between them in respect of the programmes
designed to overcome these problems. And, despite some superficial
similarities, they do not share the same reasons for justifying their
respective attempts to mobilize collective resources for the attainment of their remedial programmes.

Second, each movement is based on a self-contained system of
assumptions, teachings, and recipes for action. There are, of course,
wide variations in the degree of systematization and sophistication.
But strenuous efforts have clearly been made to mark the system's
boundaries and to eliminate internal inconsistencies. This has been
achieved in different ways and is still taking place.

In the case of the UC, for example, continual elaboration of
theology and ideology is produced partly by its own experts and
partly by interactions with outside intellectuals. The result is
progressive refinement of the movement's understanding of *Divine
Principle* and a constantly expanding awareness of its relation to
other systems of thought. A question therefore arises about the
system's capacity to retain a separate and distinctive character at a
time when its boundaries are shifting.

By contrast, COG's system of teachings appears to be less systematic but more impervious to outside influences. The movement
lacks a sacred text other than the Bible, although MO Letters do fulfil
many of the functions that *Divine Principle* fulfils for the UC. But the
Letters' wisdom is not summarized or categorized for teaching

purposes; nor does there appear to be any mechanism or institution within COG for critically reviewing, or elaborating on, them. There is certainly no provision for intellectual dialogue with outsiders, although Berg's writings suggest that he at least keeps abreast of some currents of thought outside the movement.

Part of ISKCON's distinctiveness resides in the fact that its most revered sacred texts, the *Bhagavadgita* and the *Srimad Bhagavatam*, are shared with millions of Hindus outside the movement. On the one hand, this means that it does not have to work very hard to gain some degree of respect for its system of thought but, on the other, competing interpretations of the same texts constitute a threat to the movement's credibility. In the circumstances, emphasis has been placed on the distinctive features of Swami Prabhupada's interpretations of the sacred texts and, in particular, on their translation into precepts for practical action. In this way ISKCON participates in the historical and philosophical richness of ancient Hinduism without forfeiting claims to represent a unique and exclusivist embodiment of the tradition's practical wisdom.

The wisdom of Scientology may appear to have much in common with many other systems of positive thinking, New Thought, religious science, psychotherapy, etc., although Scientologists usually protest the absolute uniqueness of Hubbard's thought. But it is distinctive in at least two ways. On the one hand, the organization's publications are highly programmatic and mutually reinforcing. The formalization of a common yet abstruse technical vocabulary is very important in this respect. On the other hand, the full benefits of the wisdom are said to be available only through the official courses of training and counselling. The design of such courses is in the hands of the movement's highest ideologues and is not open to discussion or criticism by rank-and-file participants. In combination, then, these two features of Scientology help to counteract the tendency for its ideological boundaries to be blurred by similarities with other systems of comparable thought.

Third, the overall diversity of NRMs' systems of thought and their different modes of systemicity go a long way towards characterizing their appeal to members. The accounts that many members have given of their 'conversion' to a NRM frequently lay great stress on the attractiveness of a distinctive, internally consistent system of thought. Similarly, the accounts typically given by ex-members of their reason for leaving a NRM also allude to problems that were eventually perceived in the thought system. In short, the people most

directly involved in, or affected by, NRMs attribute great importance to their distinctive teachings. Yet, it is questionable whether
doctrinal distinctiveness has contributed much to the public *controversy* about NRMs.

The diversification of Christian churches, sects, and cults in the
modern era has been accompanied by a rich culture of theological
criticism. Heresy-hunting has thrived alongside growing pluralism
and religious tolerance. Numerous individuals, groups, and institutes have published tracts, brochures, and books against the perceived errors of their antagonists. Insider-stories by apostates frequently add spice to the charges of heresy, blasphemy, and infamy.
It is not surprising, therefore, that today's NRMs have attracted the
wrath of countless theological critics. A sample of the better-known
works includes W. J. Martin 1980; Enroth 1977; Haack 1976 and
1979; Sparks 1977; Vernette 1979. It is a mistake, however, to
believe that today's anti-cultism is merely an extension of the Christian evangelical's time-honoured practice of criticizing doctrines
perceived as heretical or cultic (cf. Melton and Moore 1982). There
may be superficial similarities, but the underlying social and organizational base is quite different, as will become apparent in
Chapter 2.

Anti-cultists are aware of this tide of critical commentary emanating mainly from the evangelical wing of Christian churches in the
USA and they have sometimes put it to good effect in support of their
campaigns. But there has been a tendency to play down the specifically theological criticism because they fear that it might make them
vulnerable to the charge of interfering with the *beliefs* of NRM
members (Shapiro 1983). This is especially noticeable in the USA
where any suspicion of a threat to the freedom of belief is treated very
seriously. In any case, many anti-cultists are aware of the danger of
being accused of the very charges that they level at NRMs, namely,
interference with, or manipulation of, belief. This distinction is
crucial to the strategy of jurists seeking legal remedies for the alleged
crimes of NRMs against their members (see Delgado 1977).

Moreover, other contributors to the public controversy about
cults usually refrain from direct criticism of teachings and beliefs.
Representatives of mainstream religious groups outside France and
West Germany have been increasingly reluctant to issue condemnations of NRMs' teachings. State officials have no brief for theological
criticism. Mental health professionals tend to discount the importance
of religious beliefs. And professional deprogrammers/rehabilitators

seem to regard professed belief as a mere cover for deeper considerations of self-identity, self-worth, etc. All of this is very apparent in the expert testimony typically offered in courts of law hearing cases concerning NRMs. It is as if discussion of beliefs and teachings were taboo. Religiously inspired action is thereby reduced to a variety of socially and psychologically determined behaviours.

The roots of the cult controversy cannot be entirely separated from criticism of NRMs' teachings, but the controversy is more importantly fuelled by other considerations. In order to understand them, we must carefully examine the ways in which controversial NRMs structure the relationships between their members, individually and collectively, and the 'outside' society. For my argument is that these relationships generate the strongest anti-cult feelings and thereby feed directly into the public controversy. This is the topic of the next chapter.

Notes

1   'Lord Krsna shines with unlimited energies. Everything, from planets whirling around the sun to the electrons whirling around the nucleus, from the huge banyan tree to the delicate rose, comes from Krsna through His energies. But because His energies act in automatic accordance with His will, He doesn't have to do anything Himself. He simply enjoys His pastimes in the spiritual world.'

     (*Back to Godhead* 17 [10] 1982: 3)

2   Recent years have seen the growth of Hare Krishna interest in ecological matters.

     'We do not advocate that man should live as a primitive. There can be Krishna conscious cities and farm communities, along with the development of culture and science at the highest level. But we should create nothing for exaggerated sense pleasure or for the exploitation of the many by the few. When we center all our activities on Krishna and work for His satisfaction, there will naturally be economic, political and social harmony.'

     (*Back to Godhead* 17 [10] 1982: 32)

3   Rochford (1982b: 400) describes ISKCON's development as 'opportunistic' in the sense that its 'recruitment strategies have been tailored to local conditions rather than tied to the movement's ideology or structure'. My preference is for an interpretation which does not separate strategy from ideology or structure. See Beckford 1975a

for this kind of interpretation of the Watchtower movement's development.

4   Divisions of opinion, expulsions, and schisms began to destabilize ISKCON in the late 1970s. The main problem, centred on the Berkeley Temple in California, seemed to be a conflict of ideas about styles of management. One effect was increased differentiation between temples and, consequently, declining rates of mobility between them.

5   Rochford (1982a) argues that sympathizers with ISKCON have come to play an important role in the recruitment of new members.

6   A small indicator of the increasingly harmonious relations between ISKCON and expatriate Indian communities was the annual Gandhi Community Award that the movement received in 1982 from the *India Tribune*, a newspaper with a circulation of 15,000 in Chicago.

7   The name was changed to Family of Love (FOL) about 1978, but for the sake of simplicity I shall refer to the movement by its better known name of COG.

8   According to Sparks 1977:159 and Streiker 1978:54 COG also grew by deliberately taking over a number of other Jesus People groups and communes.

9   MO Letters (MOLs) are illustrated newsletters-cum-tracts which serve as Berg's longest running and most authoritative link with COG's members. I shall identify them by their serial number and year of publication.

10 For accounts of the early years of Berg's ministry to young people in California, see Enroth, Ericson, and Peters 1972; Ellwood 1973; McBeth 1977.

11 Berg's most vituperative criticism of the System has always been aimed specifically at the USA. The caption to a drawing of America as a brazen whore, for example, ran:

> 'This is how God sees America! She sits with a crushing weight on *you*!! Rich world rulers fornicate with her by partaking of her delicacies to satisfy their selfish lusts! And they sell *you* into a drunken stupor of her job-slavery, idol-making, bloodshed (war) and dollar worship!! Get out of her *today*! Before she gets *you*!'
>
> (MOL 216, 1973)

12 Beginning in the mid 1970s Berg dropped many hints that COG might initially co-operate with the Antichrist before being persecuted. This may have been a reflection of his increasing readiness to co-operate

with a bewildering variety of Arab, socialist, and Third World governments. See, for example, MOL 709 'Islam' of May 1975. On the other hand, some countries were definitely beyond the pale: 'Much of Africa is a *hell hole!*' (MOL 'Black holes!' 706, June 1978)

13 See Martin 1980 for a discussion of Berg's doctrinal departures from one standard of evangelical Christian orthodoxy.

14 'To ignore the Word of the Lord through his Prophet is to ignore the Voice of God Himself. . . . *God made me your shepherd – and you* had better follow, or you're going to miss God and His will! It was not my idea! – it was God's. If you think you can be a part of God's mighty Movement without following its leadership – His chosen leadership – you are mistaken.'
('Dad's wee word of Introduction' to Children of God, 1976: 10)

15 '*The US ran us out,* and now their dollar is declining . . . Iran threw us out, and now the Shah's losing his country' (MOL 749, 1978). Comparable disasters were also perceived in England, Malta, Sicily, Tenerife, Nicaragua, Australia, Italy, and Greece.

16 MOL 'The Law of Love' of March 1974 had foreshadowed many of the subsequent developments of communal sexuality and of MO's attempts to regulate it by reference to Scripture and reason. In this particular letter he adumbrated the theme of a perfectionist community in the end-time: 'We are the last church! We are God's last church, the last step in God's progress towards total freedom for His Church and the last chance to prove that the ultimate Church can be trusted with total freedom in this last generation.' (quoted in Wallis 1979: 77).

17 But, as Wallis 1979 points out, there are structural and motivational factors which also tend to reduce these tensions in the particular circumstances of COG colonies. The logic of Wallis' argument even makes it difficult to understand why *any* marital partnerships are tolerated in this movement. But the fact that Berg reverts so frequently and outspokenly to discussion of the *problems* surrounding sexual bonding in the COG suggests that Wallis' account may be exaggerated.

18 It was announced in 1982, for example, that, as an inducement to move away from 'rich' northern countries, 'baby bonuses' would be paid only to mothers in the world's poorer countries.

19 This could also be a form of punishment for disobedience.

20 '*We have come to the point where we now have families with lots of children who need homes and therefore jobs* and the kids need

an education we can't give them. So they are going to have to settle down sometime, somehow and somewhere!'

(MOL 770 1979)

21   The parents of the UC's founder were members of the Presbyterian Church, but he is said to have been more influenced by the spiritual ideas of Baik Moon Kim, creator of the 'Israel Monastery' movement and author of *Sungsin-sinhak* (The Theology of the Holy Spirit) (see Kim 1981: 58–64).

22   The difficulty of distinguishing between Moon's personal wealth and the assets of the UC, along with its many associated businesses, institutes, and trusts, was recognized by both sides in Moon's protracted trial for tax fraud in the State of New York. It culminated in a verdict of guilty and an eighteen-month jail sentence beginning in July 1984. See Tribe 1982 for expert views on some of the constitutional problems arising from this case.

23   Critics often accuse the UC of concealing esoteric doctrines in such publications as *The Master Speaks* and *The 120-Day Training Manual*. These documents contain explicit claims about Moon's messiahship, his relations with the world of spirits, and his frank views on the UC's opponents.

24   Moon said in an interview that

'The *DP* is not a philosophy, not a theory; it is a principle. It is an unchanging truth of God. . . . Truth must become incarnate. It must be lived or fulfilled within a living person. . . . This is why I do not reveal truth until the conditions are all met and the truth is embodied to a certain point. In a way then, the *DP*, this new revelation, is the documentary of my life. . . . The *DP* is in me, and I am the *DP*. . . . There is a much greater area of truth yet to be revealed. I have already received this revelation, yet I am purposely reserving certain truths to be revealed in future days'

(quoted in Sontag 1977: 147).

25   It is important to recognize that Moon did not personally write *DP*. In fact there are numerous versions of the text, each one representing a different interpretation and translation of ideas attributed to Moon. See Mickler 1980 and Lofland 1966 for difficulties with the establishment of an authorized version in the English language.

26   Mickler's (1980) account of the numerous attempts made in the 1960s to establish a workable version of the *DP* in English emphasizes the fact that it was considered critical for the UC's evangelism. Far from being a once-and-for-all-time-fixed kind of scripture, *DP* has under-

gone continual modification, with each succeeding version being considered better suited for teaching purposes.

27 Systematization is taken to extremes of abstraction and formalization in, for example, Unification Thought Institute 1973; 1974.

28 See, for example, the characterization of 'the Unification attitude' by a Barrytown seminarian as 'sowing sweat for earth, tears for man, and blood for heaven, as a servant, but with a Father's heart', in Bryant and Hodges 1978: 156.

29 See, for example, the half-jocular discussion of whether Moon's mission could be accomplished if he was to leave the UC, in Bryant and Hodges 1978: 17–18.

30 The relationship with the Koran has been explored in one of the UC's own publications, *Introduction to the Principle. An Islamic Perspective.* The author admits that many of the concepts presented in the book may not coincide with traditional views of Islam but he adds 'neither do they contradict them. The reader is asked to try to keep an open mind in studying these pages, remembering how Islam itself was born in the midst of great misunderstanding and blind opposition' (p. 3).

31 Hubbard's son applied to a California court in 1982 to have his father declared either dead or mentally incompetent and to have his estate distributed among the next-of-kin. The court received letters purporting to be from Hubbard himself and denying that his affairs were being mishandled. The son's petition was rejected. A further twist to stories about Hubbard's disappearance occurred when the transcript of a lengthy interview with him was published in Denver's *Rocky Mountain News* on 20 February 1983 and subsequently reprinted by the Church of Scientology, presumably in order to scotch the rumours of Hubbard's death or incompetence.

32 For a history of Hubbard's terminology, see Wallis 1976: 31–8.

33 In 1954 Hubbard estimated that the average weight of a Thetan was 1.5 ounces but that some 'heavy Thetans' weighed as much as two ounces (Hubbard 1968). The estimates were based on the differences in weight between live and dead bodies.

34 'A civilization without insanity, without criminals and without war, where the able can prosper and honest beings can have rights, and where Man is free to rise to greater heights, are the aims of Scientology' (Hubbard 1982: 8).

35 'When religion is not influential in a society or has ceased to be,

the State inherits the entire burden of public morality, crime and tolerance. It must use punishment and police. Yet this is unsuccessful as morality, integrity and self-respect not already inherent in the individual, cannot be enforced with any great success. Only by a spiritual awareness and inculcation of the spiritual value of these attributes can they come about. There must be more reason and more emotional motivation to be moral etc., than threat of human discipline.'

(Hubbard in *Freedom* 41, July 1979: 16)

36   'We seek only evolution to higher states of being for the individual and for Society.'

(Hubbard 1982: 8)

37   'There is no national problem in the world today which cannot be resolved by reason alone. . . . My purpose is to form, here on Earth, a civilization based on human understanding, not violence.'

(Hubbard in *Freedom* 51, 1980:16)

38   A classic statement of all the major grievances against Scientology was made by Mr Justice Latey, a British High Court Judge, who ruled in July 1984 that an ex-Scientologist mother should be given custody of two children who were being raised by their Scientologist father:

'Scientology is both immoral and socially obnoxious. In my judgement it is corrupt, sinister and dangerous. It is corrupt because it is based on lies and deceit and has as its real objective money and power for Mr Hubbard, his wife, and those close to him at the top.

It is sinister because it indulges in infamous practices both to its adherents, who do not toe the line unquestionably, and to those outside who criticize or oppose it.

It is dangerous because it is out to capture people, especially children and impressionable young people, and indoctrinate and brainwash them so that they become the unquestioning captives and tools of the cult, withdrawn from ordinary thought, living and relationships with others.'

(reported in *The Times*, 24 July 1984)

TWO

A new conceptual framework

Introduction

A sociological investigation of religious phenomena involves the study of broad patterns of social relationships between individuals, between groups, and between institutions of society. The object is to see how these different types of relationship can act as the 'vehicles' of religion. But sociological perspectives can only be partial and one-sided attempts to make sense of religion. Moreover, there are no grounds for claiming the superiority of sociological over all other perspectives. Nor is there less variety among sociological perspectives than among 'lay' or non-sociological interpretations of religion. Finally, many problematic or puzzling features of the social reality of religion simply overflow sociological categories and remain stubbornly resistant to them.

What, then, is the competence of sociology when applied to religion? It can do two things which are not usually part of any other intellectual enterprise. On the one hand it can investigate the complex mutual influence between social arrangements and religious institutions; and, on the other, it can study the ways in which social 'forms' (in the sense of basic configurations of social relationships) can convey religious thought, feeling, and practice. On balance, the tendency has been for sociologists of religion to concentrate on the former. My intention here, however, is to develop the latter possibility by focusing attention on what Geertz (1968) termed the social 'vehicles' of religion. In particular, I shall try to identify some basic social relationships expressing (or carrying) *controversial* kinds of religion.

The chapter begins with a discussion of typological approaches to the sociological understanding of new religious movements (NRMs). A framework for interpreting the social forms produced and reproduced by NRMs is then proposed as a device for improving our understanding of them as distinctive sociological objects. Finally, some generalizations about the typical forms of contemporary NRMs are offered as a background for the ensuing discussion of cult-related controversies.

Typologies

A number of sociologists have designed typologies and classifications for the purpose of highlighting what they consider to be the typical forms of NRMs and their typical responses to societal conditions. Their work has informed my own interpretation of NRMs and must therefore claim our first consideration.

Orientations to the world

Among the most general schemes for understanding NRMs in the West is Roy Wallis' (1984) tripartite typology of their 'orientations to the world'. Movements are said to accommodate to, reject, or affirm the world. These three orientations are considered to be 'logically exhaustive', but they are also thought to permit a variety of mixed empirical cases. The *world-accommodating* type is characterized by the primacy that it places on providing 'solace or stimulation to personal, interior life. Although it may invigorate the individual for life in the world, it has relatively few implications for how that life should be lived' (Wallis 1984: 35–6). The *world-rejecting* type demands a life of service to a guru or prophet in consequence of condemning society and its values and of anticipating an imminent upheaval in social arrangements. A better world order is expected to follow this upheaval. The *world-affirming* type emphasizes the potential that human beings have for improving the world. It therefore offers techniques for releasing or enhancing the human potential to achieve whatever goals are set.

Underlying Wallis' typology is the belief that 'new religious movements have – in substantial measure – developed in response to, and as attempts to grapple with the consequences of, rationalization' (Wallis 1984: 41). But this general condition is further broken down into specific factors allegedly disposing people in particular social circumstances to favour one or other of the three types of NRM.

Moreover, it is recognized that an extensive 'middle ground' between the types is occupied by NRMs which combine facets of at least two of them. The tension and conflicts arising from combinations of distinct orientations are believed to help explain changes that have been observed in all movements.

Wallis' scheme is helpful in two ways. First, it emphasizes the fact that no NRM actually conforms with the depiction of any logical type and that empirical cases may represent complex mixtures of orientations. Second, it draws attention to affinities between the message of certain NRMs and the social circumstances in which potential recruits find themselves. It therefore recognizes that different types of movement tend to have different constituencies which, in turn, are differentially affected by the general process of rationalization.

On the other hand, Wallis' scheme cannot, and perhaps was not intended to, serve as a detailed guide to the empirical complexities of specific movements. Rather, its usefulness lies in the sweeping economy with which it promises to handle empirical detail. And, in particular, it offers clarification of the affinities between members' experience of life in rationalized societies and the message of typical NRMs. There are problems, of course, about the operationalization of a scheme based on such a broad interpretative criterion as 'orientation to the world', for it is not entirely clear how any particular movement's teachings and practices are related to the beliefs and outlooks of individual members. Moreover, Wallis' scheme takes little or no cognizance of the differences that have been shown to exist between the outlooks of members of any given movement. For these reasons the scheme may need to be refined in order to improve its usefulness in empirical research. The next scheme for typifying NRMs goes some way towards meeting the requirements for a more refined and precise research instrument.

Moral accountability

Bird's (1979) tripartite typology of NRMs is designed to demonstate typical variations in the extent and manner of 'moral accountability' among movement members. This refers to 'individual awareness that a person is expected to act in keeping with moral expectations'. The theoretical backdrop to Bird's scheme is the belief that, following the advent of 'multiple, relativistic and comparatively permissive moral expectations' (Bird 1979: 344), feelings of moral accountability have been aggravated. This is because the prevalence of utilitarian, situational, and emotivist ethics in a rationalized, bureaucratized, and largely secularized world creates tension with older, more objective sources of moral obligation. External and internal expectations are out of balance, and the resulting moral dilemmas are thought to be one of the factors disposing people to participate in NRMs for the sake of reducing painful feelings of moral accountability.

Each type of NRM is believed to offer a distinctive way of reducing moral accountability in the face of societal conditions which only exacerbate it. Bird's argument is that the relationship between followers, masters and/or the source of sacred power revered in NRMs falls into three types: (a) *Devotees* surrender themselves to a 'holy master or ultimate reality to whom they attribute superhuman powers and consciousness' (Bird 1979: 336); (b) *Disciples* 'progressively seek to master spiritual and/or physical disciplines in order to achieve a state of enlightenment and self-harmony, often following the example of a revered teacher' (1979: 336); (c) *Apprentices* 'seek to master particular psychic, shamanic and therapeutic skills in order to tap and realize sacred powers within themselves' (1979: 336). These roles, in turn, are said to be the vehicles of each movement's typical relationship to sacred power, form of authority, and moral model.

In combination, these features of NRMs are believed to reduce moral accountability in distinctive ways. Devotee groups induce 'innocence' by relativizing moral expectations arising from other sources and by encouraging members to identify their real selves with their sacred alter egos. In this way, occasions for feeling moral guilt or dissatisfaction are reduced in frequency and significance. In discipleship groups the overriding goal of achieving compassionate detachment from distracting commitments and desires tends to find expression in an image of life as a harmonious, holistic focus of all energies and interests. Consequently, standards defined as extraneous or imposed lose their authority and are ideally replaced by a sense of self-discipline which is non-judgemental because it is based on an important distinction between intention and action. Apprenticeship groups reduce moral accountability by inducing members to think that they alone are the best judges of their own accomplishments and that other people's standards are irrelevant.

One of the main strengths of Bird's approach is that it pays specific attention to the doctrinal, metaphysical, and moral teachings of NRMs in such a way that their practical ethics can be thrown into sharp relief. This focus on teachings facilitates fine distinctions between movements whilst also offering the advantage of protecting their doctrinal integrity from reductionism. The usefulness of typologies based on such sweeping criteria as Oriental/western origins or monistic/dualistic philosophies is thereby called in question.

Bird's approach is also valuable for its capacity to lay bare the lineaments connecting together the metaphysical, doctrinal, experiential, moral, and organizational features of NRMs. It therefore encourages an image of each movement as a distinctive whole based on inner metaphysical strengths and inducing definite patterns of belief, conviction, and action. At the same time, however, this scheme serves the very useful purpose of linking the discussion of types of NRMs to discussions of moral change and conflict in modern societies. NRMs are thereby shown to exist in an important relationship with major societal trends and forces.

Responses to moral ambiguity

The typology of NRMs devised by Robbins and Anthony (1979a) also addresses the question of their relationship to the moral problems of modern societies. Instead of being focussed on the means whereby individual members seek to reduce moral accountability, however, it is pitched at a much higher level of analysis and abstraction. In fact, the typology deals with NRMs at the level of the metaphysics inherent in their teachings and underlying philosophies.

NRMs are classified according to their respective responses to what Robbins and Anthony term the present climate of moral ambiguity. This climate is attributed to the failure of utilitarian individualism to legitimize the present social order in western societies. The rise of an urbanized mass-society dominated by massive bureaucracies is said to be at odds with the formerly prevalent moral values extolling the virtues of hard work, competitiveness, personal autonomy, and deferment of gratification (see also Bellah 1975; and Sullivan 1982). The success of NRMs is therefore explained in terms of their attempts either to bolster a declining value system or to replace it with an alternative.

The first major axis of this typology distinguishes between *dualistic* movements which affirm traditional moral absolutism and theocentric ethical dualism whilst protesting against permissiveness in all spheres of life and *monistic* movements which assert the 'oneness' of the universe and the consequent invalidity of any concepts separating 'self' from 'the whole' or implying the existence

of absolutist moral standards. Monistic movements are then sub-
typified first into (a) *technical* movements which teach procedures
for attaining the desired states of mind and dispositions and (b)
charismatic movements which make such attainments dependent on
the emulation of spiritual leaders/masters/exemplars. Monistic
movements are further broken down in terms of two different
conceptualizations of procedures for achieving spiritual goals and
benefits: (c) *One-level* monistic systems offer the once-and-for-all
achievement of a state of enlightenment, whereas (d) *two-level*
systems offer the prospect of long-term evolution towards higher
states of consciousness.

The analysis therefore allows four distinct subtypes of monism in
NRMs but only one type of dualism. There has admittedly been
speculation about the possibility that there may be one-level and
two-level, technical and charismatic subtypes of dualistic movements as well (Robbins, Anthony, and Richardson 1978: 108), but
the problems with such a development probably outweigh the
advantages.

The overall conceptual scheme may therefore be considered unbalanced on strictly logical grounds. A more serious problem, however,
concerns the possibility that a wrong impression may be created of
the relative numerical importance of dualistic and monistic movements. For the fact is that, if due account is taken of all the
ramifications of the Jesus People and Charismatic Christian movements that emerged in the 1960s, dualism has attracted more people
than has monism. The latter has certainly proved to be attractive to
sections of the young and affluent liberal middle classes – 'the secret
religion of the educated classes' (Campbell 1978 after Troeltsch
1931) – but varieties of philosophical and religious dualism are still
the dominant component of the meaning-systems of western
societies.

Robbins and Anthony's typology has the great merit of being
directed at a number of high-level theoretical problems about the
evolution of modern western societies. It is intended to show the
reciprocal relationship between NRMs and problems of societal
order, meaning, identity, legitimation, and integration. But the
precise articulation between the various subtypes of movement and
the diverse facets of these high-level problems has not been clarified.
The scheme is both plausible and suggestive; but it remains to be seen
whether it can be fruitfully applied in empirical investigations of
NRMs.

Corporateness

Lofland and Richardson (in press) have designed a typology which promises to facilitate detailed comparisons between NRMs as well as provocative comparisons with non-religious social movements. They isolate a distinctive phenomenon called the 'religious movement organization' (RMO) which serves as the major focus of their interest. It is therefore a more narrowly defined topic than that of Wallis, Bird, or Robbins and Anthony. For it refers to only one facet of NRMs, namely, their 'corporateness' or 'the degree to which a set of persons actively promotes and participates in a shared, positively valued and collective life' (Lofland and Richardson, in press). The degrees of RMOs' corporateness or 'elemental forms' are labelled 'clinics', 'congregations', 'collectives', 'corps', and 'colonies'.

The five types of RMO are presented as ideal-types: not empirical descriptions. Moreover, they are said to represent only the most important and most distinct elemental forms of RMO. Nevertheless, it is clear that the typology can serve as the basis for stimulating and refining various postulates about the organizational dynamics of RMOs without losing sight of the differences between primary attributes and secondary correlates. The case is made, then, for regarding the movements' organizational forms as at least as important as their meaning-systems and values. This typology therefore represents a reaction against what Lofland and Richardson seem to consider the excessive 'insensitivity to corporate and collective life' that characterizes some other approaches to the typification of NRMs. One of their main reasons for emphasizing the need for closer attention to RMOs as a specific form of religious collectivity is that they believe that it will facilitate fruitful comparison with such other phenomena as social movement organizations, ego movement organizations, and political movement organizations.

An interesting implication of this approach is that the terms 'sect' and 'cult' should be 'de-emphasized or at least defined in a more specific, lean, and organizational manner' (Lofland and Richardson, in press). Their argument is that these terms have become 'too general and imprecise' and that they obstruct comparative analysis of social movement organizations. This is precisely the burden of my criticism of the whole church-sect-cult conceptual tradition (Beckford 1975b; 1976; 1984; 1985b). Robertson (1979) misunderstood my argument as a plea to confine the application of 'sect' and 'cult' exclusively to organizational matters. What I was actually advocating, and what Lofland and Richardson have come to recognize, is that the multifunctionality of these time-honoured terms allows culture-specific and time-specific complications to cloud considerations of the purely organizational aspects of NRMs. Clearly, these considerations do not exhaust the wide range of problematics associated with church—sect theorizing.

Other typologies of NRMs are mentioned in later chapters, but it should already be evident that the movements are sufficiently numerous, varied, and complex to warrant close examination. They have been shown to vary with regard to their 'orientation to the world'; their capacity to reduce feelings of 'moral accountability'; their proposals for coping with 'moral ambiguity'; and their degree of 'corporateness'. The need for typologies and classifications is beyond doubt if we are to understand more about the social dynamics of these distinctive movements.

A new framework

One sociological aspect of NRMs which has not yet been methodically examined is their typical relationships with other groups, organizations, institutions, and currents of ideas in society. The existing concepts tend to isolate NRMs from their surroundings by focusing attention narrowly on their 'internal' arrangements. I have therefore designed a conceptual framework for the purpose of emphasizing the variety of ways in which NRMs are related to their social environments. The framework will be introduced in two parts – the first dealing with social relationships internal to NRMs, and the second with external relationships. A fairly lengthy preamble is necessary to explain the framework's structure and purpose.

The framework is formed by the intersection of a number of factors which all have a bearing on the complex life-process of NRMs. No single factor is all-important, and there is no mechanical necessity in the framework. Rather, it serves the purpose of drawing attention to ways in which the empirically observed relationships between NRMs and other sections of society can be sociologically interpreted. It also serves the purpose of facilitating comparisons between NRMs in respect of their different historical careers or trajectories.

The reasons for choosing the constituent factors of the framework are different from those informing the construction and use of existing classifications and ideal-types. Briefly, the difference lies in the fact that I am not trying to place NRMs in mutually exclusive classes on the basis of one or more critical criteria. And, unlike ideal-types, the framework is not based on a sense of the logic which impels NRMs 'rationally' towards determinate positions. Rather, my framework helps to locate them empirically and flexibly.

The fundamental question is 'How are NRMs inserted into their societies?' A more formal way of putting this is to ask 'What is distinctive about the way in which members of NRMs are individually and collectively related to other people, groups, institutions, and social processes?'. This approach enables us to consider NRMs as distinctive sets of social relationships.

A basic distinction is made between those relationships which link members of NRMs to one another and those which exist between the collectivity of members and non-members. For the sake of convenience I shall call this the 'internal–external axis'. Already, however, it is clear that this kind of distinction is elusive in practice – if not inoperative in some cases. But this is precisely the point of constructing a framework: it summarizes and guides one's thinking about comparisons which are inherently challenging or problematic.

It is well known that members of, for example, the UC tend to be immersed in a demanding and carefully regulated set of relationships which largely preclude close bonds with people outside the movement. On the other hand, it is much more difficult to make such a distinction in the case of most members of Scientology who retain jobs, homes, and social relationships in the 'outside' world. Other movements present variations on, and combinations of, these typical relationships. *Figure 2.1* shows the range of possible modes of insertion in society.

Within the basic framework established by the internal–external axis, special attention can be given to the processes whereby NRMs are produced, reproduced, and transformed. The material conditions of their continuing existence are of great importance in this connection. But it is not easy to separate them from the production of ideas, sentiments, aspirations, controls, and dispositions, for these things are part of the life-blood of all religious collectivities. Their successful production contributes just as directly to the survival and adaptability of religious groups as do their more visible fund-raising and resource-mobilizing practices.

The main object of the proposed framework is to emphasize the association between NRMs' profiles of internal relationships and their differential susceptibility to controversy. In short, the ways in which people join, participate in, and eventually leave NRMs all

Figure 2.1   NRMs' modes of insertion in society

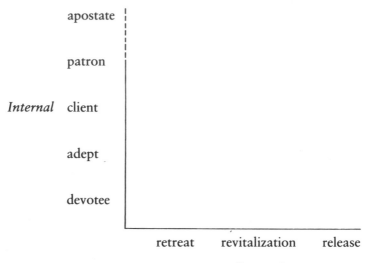

help to explain why certain movements become embroiled in particular controversies. In turn, the character of the controversies feeds back into the ways in which NRMs recruit, mobilize, and lose their members. The framework is designed to highlight this dynamic association.

Any given movement may display more than one combination of internal and external relationships at any time, and changes in their configuration can often be observed. Thus, the Church of Scientology has progressively accommodated more and more members as staff workers whose position in the movement closely resembles that of devotees in other movements with quite different ideologies and organizational structures. At the same time, however, the great majority of Scientologists are still clients who pay determinate fees for the consumption of specific services. The movement's 'internal' relationships are therefore of these two main types, and their coexistence entails both costs and benefits. Tensions are certainly created between the interests of devotees and clients. But their coexistence also gives the movement a degree of flexibility which protects it from the worst vagaries of 'enrolment economies'. The pattern of a movement's internal relationships is a central part of its 'political and moral economy'. This term has been chosen to convey the complexity of the active processes whereby NRMs produce and reproduce themselves in society.

The political and moral economy of NRMs is concerned with the production of both ideas and material resources. It emphasizes the fact that ideas and values do not evolve in a vacuum but, rather, play an important part in reflecting and affecting the material circumstances in which religious movements have to operate. Accordingly, the framework is sensitive to the strong inter-relatedness between these two aspects which have sometimes been separated in other typologies (see, for example, Woodrum 1982).

The framework is also focused on the political and moral economy of NRMs in recognition of the fact that they display relatively high degrees of organizational purpose, control, and direction. Far from being currents of diffuse sentiments or dispositions, they actually have at their core quite carefully circumscribed collectivities of actors and resources orientated towards specific goals or end-states. I must stress that the NRMs which have been at the centre of controversy are guided by powerful 'movement-organizations': they are not amorphous currents or tendencies. This is not to say that the changing fortunes of particular NRMs are not somehow bound up with general shifts in public sentiment, taste, or interest; but the point must be made that, as movement-organizations, NRMs follow specific managerial strategies. Two striking examples are provided by the COG and Synanon. Both of these very different movements have been led, if not dominated, by charismatic individuals who effectively dictated virtually all aspects of their sometimes bewildering developments. But they did so by means of complex organizations which assured that strategic decisions were put into practice at grass-roots level. They did not always achieve their goals, but neither the COG nor Synanon can be said to have drifted along in accordance with vague public sentiments.

The evolution of NRMs reflects complex and changing equations of ideas, values, people, and material resources. Of course, the path is neither smooth nor straight for any of them. All manner of deflections, diversions, and disruptions complicate (or frustrate) their intended developments. And it is most unwise to assume homogeneity among members in respect of background, beliefs, or commitments. On the other hand, however, as was shown in Chapter 1, NRMs are at least guided by identifiable values, teachings, priorities, and principles. What is needed is a framework which is sensitive to all these elements and their inter-relations. The notion of a 'political and moral economy' is believed to satisfy this need and to be particularly useful in helping to explain the controversies which have grown up around some NRMs.

The inclusion of 'economy' is essential to the aim of explaining the *processes of change* which take place in NRMs' mode of insertion in society. It tries to account for the establishment of priorities and for the calculations of relative advantage which help to determine changes in the way in which the members of NRMs relate separately and collectively to outside people, groups, and institutions. Not all of these changes are intended or foreseen, of course, but they certainly occur partly as a result of deliberate strategies, policies, or decisions. The relatively brief history of the UC's mission to the west, for example, has been strewn with changes of strategy. The formation of 'new ideal communities' in California was the original aim but it was eclipsed by a programme for the massive mobilization of small teams of evangelist-fundraisers. This, in turn, gave way to more selective and discriminating schemes for influencing spheres of public life and for creating successful businesses. The mid 1980s was a period of retrenchment and of reorientation towards a more denominational form of organization on the local level.

It is important to point out the differences between my framework based on the political and moral economy of NRMs and the more narrowly economic approach of some other commentators. Richardson (1982), for example, has reflected in a timely manner on the sheer diversity of NRMs' financial, fiscal and productive arrangements. The range is considerably wider than most of the movements' critics have usually acknowledged; their reliance on methods of soliciting donations in public is much weaker than one might expect; and their willingness to experiment with novel fund-raising methods sets them apart from most other types of social movement. It is also suggested that interesting insights into the economic management of NRMs could be derived from Kanter's (1973) study of the 'primary economic stance' of communes. Richardson's article certainly sets an important agenda for future research, but I am advocating a more inclusive approach which would relate economic management to movements' conceptions of their changing place in society.

Bird and Westley (1983) have also attempted to delineate the political economy of new religious and para-religious movements, but they differ from Richardson in emphasizing continuities and discontinuities with more conventional religious groups. The most salient differences are said to stem from the fact that, whereas religious groups tend to have traditionally depended on their adherents' willingness to make regular donations of cash, new religious and para-religious movements may sell services; accept their members' donated labour; beg for donations in public; encourage members to be indifferent towards secular occupations and therefore available for movement-related activities; and they tend to have much smaller overheads than do other religious groups. These differences are related to patterns of belonging to the new groups, with 'members' being outnumbered by 'adepts', 'clients', and 'affiliates'. Bird and Westley conclude that new religious and para-religious movements have 'intrinsically unstable' political economies in so far as the centripetal and centrifugal forces experienced by different types of member prevent the movements from developing stable sources of revenue.

I think it is important to avoid construing 'economy' so narrowly as to exclude non-material considerations. For it is clear that in the interplay of intellectual argument, moral suasion, and emotional excitement that takes place in NRMs, beliefs, feelings, values, ideas, and doubts make a major contribution. They help to identify and assess the relative advantages of the different material circumstances within which religious movements operate, but it is rare for the balance of advantage to be unambiguously identified – let alone agreed upon. Consequently, the process of intellectual and practical experimentation with, and testing of, competing schemes is never-ending. And there is no point in trying to identify the relative strengths of the material and cultural components of the process because they are inextricably intertwined in each movement. All that is required is a framework which permits a 'simultaneous equation' of their contributions to each movement's distinctive life-process, i.e. the changing modes of insertion in society for the purpose of producing and reproducing the conditions of their collective mission. The main components of the framework can now be introduced.

Internal relationships

The typification of internal relationships is based primarily on the character, strength, and valency of the bonds between people in NRMs. The configuration of bonds reflects a movement's distinctive profile.

The devotee

The position of devotees[1] in NRMs is characterized by high intensity, inclusiveness, and polyvalency. Devotees devote themselves fully to the promotion of their movements' values, teachings, and material security. At the same time they reduce the significance in their lives of bonds to people who are not fellow-members. This is frequently expressed in decisions to live exclusively in the company of fellow-devotees and to minimize contact with others. It certainly entails restrictions on the choice of marriage partners and strict limitations on the circle of social relationships permitted to devotees' young children. Residential members of the COG, ISKCON, and the UC can usually be described as devotees.

One of the major concomitants of the devotee-type of relationship to a religious movement is submission to a source of authority having dominion over virtually all aspects of life. This authority may be invested in an individual person or a collectivity. Another major concomitant is that a devotee's material conditions of life are more dependent on the movement's collective prosperity and internal arrangements for distributing resources than on his or her personal efforts or possessions. Indeed, abandonment of personal possessions is often a pre-requisite of becoming a devotee and it has the effect of increasing the degree of dependence on the movement's leadership.

The adept

The position of the adept is characterized by the fact that many of his or her relationships are confined to fellow-religionists and that the NRM articulates most of these relationships. But it is possible for adepts to combine a high degree of commitment to an NRM with at least periods of involvement in kinship, affectual, economic, and occupational relations extending beyond its boundaries. The difference is not just a matter of the strength of commitment: it reflects different modes of commitment which are, in turn, geared to variations in NRMs' structures and strategies.

There is no logical reason to suppose that adepts in such movements as TM, the Divine Light Mission (DLM), or Rajneesh do not submit themselves to the authority of individual or collective leaders with the same degree of compliance as do devotees. If there is a difference it lies in the *range* of areas over which authority is likely to be exercised without competition from other sources. Countervailing pressures may be felt from the different networks of social relationships in which adepts are engaged.

Similarly, adepts experience greater variety of social relationships at work and in the home. But this is not to say that, by definition, they cannot also choose their occupations and intimate associations with a view to preserving the primacy of their religious convictions. Thus, Scientologists and Rajneeshees, for example, may occupy the adept position without necessarily confining all their social relationships to members only.

The client

The position of the client[2] in relation to certain NRMs is characterized by the largely instrumental purposes which draw him or her into association with other members. In most cases, clients accept whatever the movements are offering – wisdom, skills, therapy, friendship – on a contractual basis with very limited assumptions about the movements' impact on the conduct of their life. This is not, of course, to say that clients do not take their attachment to NRMs seriously. It merely underscores the point that seriousness in this context does not necessarily take the form of abandoning all associations outside the movement. Conversely, it is possible for clients to take their religion seriously without confining all their social life to fellow-religionists.

Recent studies of NRMs in which the position of client seems to be modal have shown that the exercise of authority is both complicated and subtle (see, for example, Ofshe 1980; Wallis 1976; Tipton 1982). They have made it clear that such movements do not lack the resources to impose sanctions on members whose degree of dependence on them may seem to be considerably weaker than that of devotees or adepts.

Similarly, the degree of clients' economic dependence on their NRMs has been found to be just as great in some cases as in that of, for example, communal movements. The methods of marketing courses or services, the methods of paying for them, and the opportunities for accepting employment in NRMs in return for services can all help to create and sustain a relationship of dependence.[3] These findings go some way towards questioning the widespread view that clients are by definition only loosely associated with NRMs.

The patron

The position of the patron is probably the least well documented type of involvement in NRMs – not because it is especially rare but because, in the nature of things, it tends to be overlooked in most kinds of research. This is because patrons are not usually present at many meetings or services and because they are not eligible for positions of responsibility. Nevertheless, they may contribute by offering moral support, material assistance, and occasional advice or services. They usually appear on NRMs' mailing lists for publications but have few personal relationships with other categories of member. This may be a consequence of infirmity, physical isolation, or lack of time/opportunity to attend gatherings. Indeed, their support may be invisible to all except a few privileged members who may from time to time ask them to show support for the movement by, for example, writing letters to the press or to influential people in defence of the movement's interests. Another possible mode of patronal relationship to NRMs is through support for their campaigns of reform in areas of secular life such as drug rehabilitation, civil rights, education, and social welfare.

Patrons are not directly subject to the authority of NRM leaders and they enjoy the freedom to maintain other commitments. The relationship is therefore based mainly on mutual respect and convenience and, as such, is neither intense nor demanding. It is particularly evident among, for example, Indian families in western cities where lay support for ISKCON and some other 'bhakti' movements is growing stronger (Carey 1981; 1983). Similarly, the UC is steadily building up a body of patrons who are unlikely ever to join the movement formally but who are willing on occasion to lend it moral and/or material support. They include academics, parents of members, and ministers of religion. Perhaps most interesting is the way in which non-committed supporters of the Rajneesh movement are increasing in the ranks of the liberal and caring professions in several western countries.

The apostate

The position of the apostate should never be overlooked in any attempt to understand the full complexity and variability of NRMs' insertion in society. Much more research is needed on this topic, but the indications from available sources (Beckford 1985a; Solomon 1981; Wright 1983) are that the possible modes of apostasy are no less variable than those of membership. Since the range of possibilities in the apostate's relationship with a NRM are examined at length in Chapters 5 and 6, nothing more will be added at this point.

Collective insertion in society

The typification of *external* relationships is based on NRMs' modes of association with various institutional spheres and organizations. It marks the variety of ways in which they produce and reproduce themselves through links with the 'outside' world such as direct evangelism, sale of therapeutic services, or provision of utopian refuges. It is not simply an indication of their formal links with other organizations, although this is definitely an important dimension of their societal location. The typification actually extends into the wider range of relationships generated, sustained and occasionally broken, with people who are not NRM members. The character of these external relationships is not entirely within the control of the movements, but they certainly contribute to them in their own distinctive and creative ways. Compare, for example, the different responses of the COG and the Church of Scientology to the threats posed by anti-cult groups and hostile public authorities in various parts of the world.[4]

It should be stressed that my aim is not to typify movements as such but, rather, to set out the patterns of relationships that have been observed between NRMs and the wider society. Every actual movement displays more than one type of relationship. The framework is therefore helpful in identifying a *profile* of each movement's insertion in society. Some tend to give priority to one particular mode, but we should not lose sight of the variety of modes observed in many movements.

Refuge

NRMs which seek to produce and preserve the social and material conditions in which a model or blueprint for avoiding the world's evil or illusions can be realized on earth are termed 'refuges'. They can be characterized by weak and severely limited ties with non-members. Nevertheless, there are variations in the ways of offering this service and of putting it into practice in the form of refuges. Some involve isolated and largely self-sufficient communes where physical contact with potential sources of impurity can be minimized. But others define the purity/impurity boundary in different ways which permit social contact with the outside world under specified conditions. A good empirical indicator of the precise mode of translating NRMs' blueprints into social practice is therefore the method of recruiting, socializing, and inducting their new members. Some, like ISKCON, permit rapid entry to monkhood; others, like the Johannine Daist Communion, restrict the monastic way of life to a chosen, experienced elite. In the case of movements like the San Francisco Zen Center, the refuge is only one of several simultaneous modes of insertion in society. Through complex sequences of initiations and by means of organizational secrecy it is possible for utopian ideals to be maintained even in movements like the COG or the Healthy-Happy-Holy organization (Tobey 1976) which choose to secure their material means of subsistence through daily contact with the 'outside' world.

The contacts are confined to the minimum necessary to ensure the movements' survival. This means that few attempts are made to improve the outside world by instruction or example; and few attempts are made to use outside facilities for generating interest or support. The primary mode of production is self-initiated and self-controlled. Success is therefore assessed solely in terms of approximation to internal ideals which may have no counterparts or equivalents outside the movement. Numerical growth or material prosperity are not necessarily considered useful indicators of success unless they occur in conjunction with spiritual achievements corresponding to utopian ideals.[5] It goes without saying that the purity of the refuge must be constantly monitored. This is more important than an increase in numbers.

NRMs whose mission includes the provision of a refuge from evil or illusion are not constrained to withdraw from contact with them. The admonition to shun the world or at least to turn one's back on it is compatible with activities having the effect of thrusting members into daily contact with the perceived sphere of evil influence. Preaching the good news of the refuge is clearly one such activity. And using the very media of communication through which evil has allegedly been broadcast is considered to be an acceptable practice in some cases. Similarly, the economic and financial practices of the corrupt world are not always believed to be disqualified as instruments for furthering the cause of salvation.

It follows that movements offering a refuge may be inserted into the conventional world in various ways. Some such NRMs, like ISKCON, practise a form of enrolment economy which depends for its success on a through-put of fresh recruits and on the continuing services of those already sheltering in the refuge. Any interruption or failure in this process threatens to drive refuge movements towards a different relationship with the outside world. Clear examples of this are provided by the successive transformations of the COG (Wallis 1981) and by the changing priorities of ISKCON (Rochford 1982a). In both cases, the primacy of the refuge mode has alternated with that of a mode that I shall call 'revitalization'.

Revitalization

The position of NRMs which seek to revitalize and transform the secular world in accordance with their particular values and teachings is perhaps the most complex. 'Revitalization' in this context means a deliberate attempt to transform important social processes and institutions through the application of distinctive values rooted in comprehensive meaning-systems.[6] The strategy of acting as the leaven of a potentially regenerated world necessarily brings NRMs into extensive contact with the realities of a less-than-ideal world. A fine balance must be sought between confrontation and compromise, and this entails the difficult task of working with the existing arrangements without allowing them to determine the limits of possible reform. Yet, the political and moral economy of NRMs adopting revitalization as the principal mode of insertion in society is very sensitive to changes in public issues and sensibilities. Unless the appropriate balance is struck between confrontation and compromise, NRMs are in danger of becoming either too isolated to produce the leavening effect or too compromised to exert any leverage on the status quo.[7] The COG and the UC illustrate, respectively, the extreme alternatives.

For the same reason it is difficult to assess the success of revitalization. The recruitment of members and the mobilization of their energies, sympathies, and material resources are essential to the reforming and transforming task. Yet, it is no less important that members should also retain positions in the social world outside their movements if they are to exert influence. The position of NRMs committed to revitalization is therefore similar to that of many non-religious voluntary associations in advanced democratic polities.

A variation on the way in which revitalization can be approached is to provide a largely separate and *hallowed universe* in which a number of major institutional tasks are fulfilled in a distinctively religious way. The result is the formation of parallel universes or 'pillars' designed to supplant the available secular provisions in as many respects as possible (see Wuthnow 1981). In the course of the construction of such universes, the conventional boundary lines between 'sacred' and 'secular' are re-drawn, and relationships with the world beyond the movement are consequently variable. This is clearly illustrated by the UC's creation of numerous businesses, institutes, and academies through which a revitalization of secular spheres of life is planned. Incidentally, this strategy has been followed with considerable success by a number of New Religions of Japan since the 1950s.

The political economy of movements in this mode involves the continual recruitment and transformation of people; but it also requires that, as far as possible, members' lives are lived in and through the movements' own hallowed institutions. They therefore provide a life-world parallel to that of non-members. In time, the result is that the movements become partly self-regenerating through the retention of people born into, or reared in, them. This is obviously true of the schools established by, for example, ISKCON, the UC, and the Rajneesh movement. But it also applies to NRMs' colleges, clinics, farms, factories, publishing houses, and cultural or recreational facilities.

The economic basis of many movements which operate as a revitalized and revitalizing section of society rests heavily on the availability of members (usually in the position of devotees) as full-time workers in their own enterprises and agencies. Moreover, members normally renounce personal possessions on committing themselves to such movements and thereby accentuate their dependence on them. Nevertheless, as Jean Séguy has argued with reference to the UC (Séguy 1977: 304–05), its collective economic practices remain unquestionably capitalistic. It cannot therefore be considered primarily as a utopian refuge. This is also true of ISKCON and the DLM, for they both operate on capitalistic lines. By contrast, the COG has at times tried to combine capitalism with principles that were indifferent to accumulation in a market.

Comprehensive, self-regenerating movements may eventually exert considerable influence on their host societies and may therefore be thought capable of creating serious problems of a politico-legal nature. This is mainly because they are perceived as a challenge to mainstream values and conventional social arrangements (see Robbins 1981). Their radicalism, unlike that of the movements offering refuge, is translated into practical projects which often reproduce 'secular' practices in a recognizable, yet significantly different, form. Family and commercial relationships, for example, may retain sufficient similarities to the conventional pattern to be perceived as a threat. The similarity is often claimed to be insidious.

Release

From the point of view of practicalities, the least difficult mode of insertion in society is maintained by those NRMs which specialize in offering to release people from conditions allegedly obstructing the full realization of their potential.

NRMs like Scientology, TM, the Rajneesh Foundation, and Synanon instruct people in the effective use of knowledge, skills, or techniques which are said to increase their capacity to lead fulfilling lives. The production and dissemination of this knowledge necessarily entail contact with the market of would-be and actual clients. Problems may arise, however, from the vulnerability of such movements to co-option or modification by clients who claim to be able eventually to improve on the original teachings (see Wallis 1979: 25–43).

It is inappropriate to think of these movements as 'enrolment economies' because the sale and delivery of 'release' services often mark the conclusion of the relationship between the movement and the client. Of course, if follow-up services are also supplied, then the relationship is extended – but it does not necessarily become more intense or inclusive as a result. The political and moral economy of NRMs in this mode is therefore much more akin to that of commercial businesses. Success is directly assessed in terms of sales performance. And concern is shown for 'after sales' only to the extent that they have implications for 'customer satisfaction' and 'product design'.

This particular form of relationship with the world outside the movement tends to be associated with a flexible distinction between staff-members and clients. Staff-members are also clients in so far as they consume the movements' services, but their form of association can be quite different from that of clients who do not join the staff. This fact is all the more significant in movements which make little or no use of 'amateur' or 'volunteer' officers, i.e. adepts who may have careers outside the movement but who are retained on an unpaid, non-contractual basis to service the needs of new clients.

Discussion

The main aim of my framework of modes of insertion in society is to help explain cult controversies. It is helpful because it is sensitive to the diverse and changing relationships among NRMs' members and between the movements and their host societies. It can thus indicate the social sources of tension, misunderstanding, suspicion, and outright conflict which fuel the controversies. The framework is also useful in stimulating generalizations about NRMs which set the background for the chapters that follow.

In the first place, the dominant modes of economic activity in the host society are reproduced to varying degrees in all but the most rigorously utopian refuges. To the extent that NRMs choose not to reject, for example, the logic of the market, economies of scale, the profits of investment, the value of diversification, etc., their very survival as collectivities depends upon participation in the prevailing economic system. And, to judge by the fate of such earlier utopian enterprises as medieval Christian monastic orders and Moravian communities in the modern era, the prospects for the success of utopian modes of production based on non-standard economic principles are not good. To put this point in terms of the concepts used by Wallis (1984) and others, rejection of the capitalistic world's economic logic is only possible if the rejection is practically total. In consequence, would-be 'world-rejecting' movements find it very difficult to faithfully translate their ideological impetus into appropriate practice. This is not to say that they cannot be successful as NRMs: it is, rather, that their success depends precisely on their *not* rejecting dominant economic principles. Incidentally, this calls in question the very usefulness of the notion of 'world-rejecting' NRMs even as a rational ideal-type.

Second, the association between the modal types of internal and external relationships in NRMs is both loose and variable. The empirical diversity of movements calls for a conceptual framework which is refined and flexible. Moreover, it should be especially attentive to the complexity of each NRM's modes of production and reproduction. Tipton's study of the San Francisco Zen Center makes this point very clearly:

> 'Backed by a constituency of sixties youth and led by a handful of older students contemporary with the Beat generation, Zen Center developed its informal, nonresidential householder's practice of the early 1960s into its more rigorous, routinized, and residential monastic practice of today. Between periods of monastic retreat, students live communally in and around Zen Center's urban headquarters, working at unskilled service jobs, living on several hundred dollars per month, and saving money to return to the

monastery or farm community. Students employed outside and in Zen Center's own enterprises ... make Zen Center financially self-sufficient in its operation, with donations going for mortgage and interest payments on its plant. Zen Center's income and frugality have enabled some fifty students, most of them ordained as priests, to "go on scholarship", living and working within the Center.'

(Tipton 1982: 96)

Another example of the complexity of a movement's insertion in society and the corresponding flexibility of membership status can be found in the Scientologists' and Rajneeshees' practice of switching between periods of employment as (perhaps) residential staff members and secular employment whilst still continuing to take courses as clients. This is why my framework deals with the range of possibilities open to NRMs rather than with 'types' of movement. The profile of each movement's modes of insertion can then help to explain how and why it is involved in controversies.

Third, there seems to be a positive relationship between the strength of a movement's links with the outside world and its readiness to defend its interests by recourse to judicial process and to secular notions of constitutional rights. This is, in fact, just another aspect of some NRMs' modes of social insertion, namely, furthering or protecting their collective interests by using the resources of the wider society. They are thereby inserted in society in a way which differs markedly from that of, for example, movements offering a utopian refuge whose ideologies might place no value on supposedly universalizing ideals of justice. It is instructive in this respect to compare the strategies of the COG and the UC. Both movements appear in some typologies of NRMs as world-rejecting, dualistic, or world-transforming; but their respective profiles of modes of insertion in society give them quite different stances towards the law as a resource. Incidentally, the People's Temple can be seen as a movement which changed its dominant mode of production from that of an enrolment economy geared towards influencing the shape of its urban environment to that of a would-be refuge with its own internal, and increasingly peculiar, ideals and practices. In the course of this transformation, the recourse to judicial process was largely abandoned along with many other links to the outside world.[8]

Fourth, and this observation owes much to the work of Jean Séguy (1977; 1980), it is not sufficient simply to divide NRMs into those which socialize people into dominant values and those which do not.

This distinction may be helpful as a preliminary step in analysis. But there are also major differences between movements in respect of the particular selection that they may make from values which could be considered 'dominant'. From my point of view, therefore, it is important to regard this selection and its subsequent modifications as one aspect of each NRM's mode of production. It is intimately connected with their collective mode of insertion in society and is no less changeable than the more material features of their use of resources.

Conclusion

One important difference between the approach proposed in this chapter and the typologies produced by other sociologists in recent years concerns the fundamental thing to be typified. Whereas other typologies have tended to focus on such ideological criteria as 'response to the world' (Wilson, B. 1967), 'orientation to the world' (Wallis 1984), and 'response to moral ambiguity' (Anthony and Robbins 1982), all of which rest crucially on movements' values and teachings, the primary focus of my framework is the range of social relationships through which NRMs try to achieve their aims and to reproduce themselves. The shift of focus is important because it means that my framework attributes greater creativity and agency to the movements. I do not consider them to be just reflections of, or responses to, socio-cultural conditions.

My work is also different in so far as it tries to explain not *why* people in NRMs hold certain beliefs (which may, in any case, be shared by people outside the movements) but, rather *how* those beliefs are cultivated by NRMs; how the state of believing is collectively managed;[9] and how NRMs thereby become embroiled in controversies. My project is therefore substantially different from those which have given rise to typologies based mainly in ideological criteria. It insists on the need to take seriously the patterns of social relationships through which NRMs are active in society. Public controversies are an important instance of such activity.

Notes

1   The term 'devotee' is being used here in a sense broadly similar to that used in Bird (1979). But I have tried to situate the different types of

member within a wider framework of NRMs' relationship to their host societies.

2   The term 'client' has been used by others to depict the partial nature of the relationships between members of instrumental types of NRM. See, for example, Bird 1979; Ofshe 1980; Wallis 1976. My usage is distinctive for acknowledging that the client-type relationship is found in a wider variety of movements and in conjunction with more diverse modes of insertion in society.

3   See Ofshe's (1980) instructive comments on the 'absorption' of Synanon graduates into low-paid positions in the movement's staff during its therapeutic community phase between 1958 and 1968.

4   See Chapters 7 and 8 below.

5   For fascinating accounts of the political and moral economy of movements whose religious character was actually generated in the very processes of defending otherwise secular ideals, see Hervieu and Léger 1980; Léger and Hervieu 1983.

6   Other uses of 'revitalization' stress the attempt to 'reconstruct patterns of life that have been radically disrupted or threatened' (Wuthnow 1982: 51). But this fails to give adequate weight to the future-orientation of most such outlooks. They are far from being entirely backward-looking.

7   The similarities to Yinger's (1946) 'dilemma of power' should not be exaggerated. I reject the commonly held view that ideological purity is necessarily short-lived. Rather, I regard purity as a contestable quality which is not necessarily sacrificed for the sake of power. More to the point is the struggle that takes place in most social movements for the control of strategy.

8   By contrast, Synanon's development from an 'alternative society' to a religion in the mid 1970s is said by Ofshe (1980: 114–15) to have coincided with the onset of litigiousness. The more deeply involved it became in profit-making business, the more active it became in using the law to defend its interests.

9   Ofshe's (1980) study of Synanon also makes use of the notion of 'managerial strategies' in terms of which the successive transformations of this movement from a voluntary association to a religious movement can be understood.

THREE
Recruitment and controversy

The modern cult controversy is actually a result of numerous over-lapping fears and grievances about NRMs. Distinctions between them can be made for analytical purposes but in practice they tend to be combined into an all-embracing anti-cult animus. The major issues form a litany of allegations about brainwashing; deception and fraud in the recruitment processes; systematic undermining of personal autonomy and freedom of will; exploitation, bordering on extortion, in the remuneration of paid workers; profiteering and dishonesty in setting the level of fees for services; excessively harsh living conditions; physical and mental impairment resulting from inadequate diet and health care; deliberate alienation of members from their families; manipulative arranging of marriages; psycho-logical terrorism and blackmail against would-be defectors; separation of members from their young children; authoritarian styles of leadership; collusion with undemocratic political forces and regimes; and unjustifiably harsh treatment of perceived 'enemies'.

This chapter will begin with an analysis of the main themes found in public sentiment against NRMs. The rest of the chapter and Chapters 5 and 6 will give special attention to the factors which explain how and why these particular grievances have come to dominate anti-cultism. A recurrent question is why particular NRMs give rise to specific grievances. I believe that only a sociologi-cal perspective can provide an answer.

This chapter therefore begins the broad task of relating anti-cultism to features of NRMs' modes of insertion in society.

Although anti-cultism is normally expressed in psychological and/or physiological terms, I shall show that the cult controversy also makes sociological sense when proper account is taken of its socio-cultural background. This does not mean that the accusations of the anti-cultists are thereby rendered any more or any less tenable: it simply means that the surface appearance can be questioned in the light of sociological observations about underlying social factors. In particular, the largely psychological evidence about conversion and disengagement will be reinterpreted in sociological terms, and sociological factors will be used to explain the dynamics of anti-cult movements in various countries. The general aim is not to 'correct' the prevailing views so much as to cast them in a new light which makes them more understandable.

The lineaments of anti-cultism

The most persistent and salient issue in the cult controversy in many countries concerns recruitment. Anti-cultists charge NRMs with using immoral and/or illegal means of persuading people to become members. Terms like 'brainwashing', 'deception', 'coercive persuasion', and 'mind control' abound in the rhetoric, and some psychiatrists and psychologists have attempted to lend them scientific status (see Clark 1979; Singer 1979; West 1982; Clark et al. 1981). It should not be assumed, however, that 'lay' and 'professional' usages are identical. They undoubtedly share many features, as we shall see below, but they stem from different reasons for being interested in NRMs. And they vary considerably in degrees of subtlety and precision.

Anti-cultist arguments usually begin with the claim that recruits are deliberately prevented from knowing all that they supposedly need to know about NRMs in order to make a reasoned decision about joining. Strenuous efforts are therefore made to distinguish between 'authentic' conversion to a religious group and the kind of distorted judgement allegedly displayed by 'cult' recruits. Indeed, this perspective has been formalized in terms of a syndrome called 'information disease' (Conway and Siegelman 1982) which, in turn, has been effectively criticized by Kilbourne (1983).

The tactics by which NRMs are said to conduct deceptive recruitment are varied. They include social and sensory deprivation, emotional blackmail, spiritual and physical threats, unbalanced diets, repetitive chanting, childish games, straightforward concealment of the movement's real teachings or practices, flattery, impoverishment of linguistic capacity, relations of dependency on existing members, and deliberate attempts to alienate recruits from all 'outside' ịnfluences. These allegations are woven into the fabric of anti-cult sentiment at various levels of society. They are focused on (a) the induced abnormality of the recruit as a person and (b) the abnormality of the cult as a social group.[1]

The person

One of the many ironies in the current agitation surrounding religious cults in the west is that both the cultists and their opponents agree on the efficacy of cultic operations. Neither side denies that cults actually 'do something' to their recruits. What is more, the formal structure of their respective accounts of what cults do is similar: both sides make ample use of strong contrasts between the before-and-after states of recruits. In fact, the opposing accounts only differ importantly in the meaning attributed to the perceived contrasts. On the one hand some people see enlightenment, salvation, and higher spirituality; on the other hand there is a dark tale of brainwashing, deception, and victimization. There is clearly a political, i.e. strategic, benefit to be derived from sharp contrast-structures on both sides.

What is at issue in everyday talk about the effect of NRMs on the person is a fundamental image of normality and abnormality. Discussion of the topic usually centres on the location of an acceptable boundary between these two states of the person. The political focus of such discussions is often sharpened in disputes between NRM members and their close relatives, for in this context there is a struggle to impose a particular, one-sided definition of the situation. The qualities, rights, and obligations of the 'normal' person are all at issue.

Perhaps the commonest opposition made by the person-in-the-street is that between a person who 'thinks for himself' and a 'brainwashed' person. It is in the nature of everyday speech that key terms are rarely specified in detail, but it is clear from the way in which these two states of being are discussed that an opposition is intended between, on the one hand, images of the person as a responsible and rational agent and, on the other, as an unthinking, uncritical puppet. The former state is assumed to be the norm, while the latter is believed to require explanation. Only a person in the former state is thought to be sensitive to moral arguments, while a person in the latter state is treated as being incapable of responsible social interaction. In the manifold differences between these two states of the person lies the usually unexposed stuff of mutual faith and trust which underwrites relationships between people who think and feel alike. The gulf is felt to be wider than that between friend and stranger because the relationship between NRM member and close relative often changes rapidly from one of intimacy to one of incomprehension. Explanation of the rapid change is given in terms of either brainwashing by an external agent or organically induced abnormal psychology. But the result is the same in one important respect: the NRM member is perceived as being a less than fully competent person.

The essentially *political* nature of the dispute at the level of the person-in-the-street is reproduced with obvious modifications in the arguments which have been heard in law-courts and in deliberations among jurists about cases involving NRMs. The arguments are more elaborate and sophisticated, but one of the central issues is no less frequently a matter of the criteria for distinguishing between the normal person and the unacceptably abnormal person (see Shapiro 1983).

Legal discussion of NRMs is based on the assumption that the person is not normally harmful to himself, and that such conventional institutions as the family are not normally harmful to the fabric of society. Intervention by the state in the affairs of a NRM or of individual members can only be legally justified, therefore, if it can be shown that these basic assumptions are threatened by NRM activities. This is why psychological, psychiatric, and sociological evidence is given prominence in cases involving NRM members. And this is why the arguments revolve around identifying the boundary between normal and abnormal (i.e. harmless and harmful) states of the person and of the NRM.

The same contrast-structures are found again in the discourse of social scientists. In this case there are fewer references to such emotive and value-laden terms as 'normal' and 'harmful', but the basic assumptions about the nature of the person and society remain the same as those of the person-in-the-street and the jurist. This is reflected in the underlying conventional problematic of the sociology and psychology of religion, namely, the need to explain participation in minority religious groups but not in mainstream religious organizations.

The most salient boundary for psychological and sociological studies of NRM members is that which divides the autonomous, free agent from the victim of a controlling milieu. At issue again is an image of the normal person as someone who maintains a balance between self-impulsion and social regulation. The balance may be struck in various ways, and the existence of an ill-defined grey area between the two extremes is widely recognized. But it is still thought useful to discuss NRM members in terms of such contrasting characteristics as autonomous/controlled; open/closed mind; moderate/fanatical; and centred/non-centred life.

The NRM

NRMs are predominantly characterized in the indigenous sociologies of the person-in-the-street by their allegedly harmful or destructive effects on members, whereas non-cultic groups are assumed to be relatively harmless. There may be a grudging recognition of the difficulty of distinguishing harmful from harmless groups, but this is not a sign that the distinction is regarded as invalid. If anything, such a recognition signifies commitment to the boundary regardless of the difficulties that it presents in practice. This has been observed, for example, among evangelical Christian groups during discussion of NRMs: the willing recognition of their similarities with some movements only serves to reinforce their sense of difference in respects which are claimed to be more important.[2] This may be a sociological instance of 'like poles repel'. The closer the parties are to each other, the more they insist on their differences.[3]

Another feature of indigenous sociologies of NRMs is the overlap between the harmful and harmless categories and the categories of 'really' religious and 'not really' religious. The former distinction is often used to justify the latter. This is an important strategic move because it signifies a transition from a basically analytical mode of discourse to an overtly practical mode. Evidence of the harm that some NRMs allegedly do is taken to show that they are not really religious and must therefore fail to qualify for the protection and privileges usually enjoyed by 'really' religious groups. To oppose NRMs is not, according to this argument, to oppose religion: it is, rather, to separate the bogus from the authentic. This particular strategy of boundary-enforcement is vital to the longer-term objectives of those whose concern is to get a relative out of a particular NRM.

On the level of advocacy in courts of law, the struggle to impose and to break down various boundaries follows very similar lines. The definition of terms and situations is fraught with political significance. In American courts of law, for example, the term 'religion' enjoys great strategic importance by virtue of its role in the First

Amendment to the US Constitution which holds in part that 'Congress shall make no law respecting an establishment of religion, or prohibiting the free exercise thereof.' Consequently, cases both for and against some NRMs hang on the decision whether or not they fall within the class of 'religion' for purposes of the law.[4] Even in countries lacking the same constitutional protection of the freedom of religion, the definitional boundary can still be critical. Scientologists in the Australian State of Victoria, for example, have been struggling for years to have their movement legally defined as religious. The deliberations of the justices in the High Court of Australia are extremely revealing about the kind of criteria by which something could be judged to be religious or not.[5]

A second dispute in legal circles rages over the question of whether the professed teachings of a NRM and the professed beliefs of its members are really *central* in their lives. This is a question about sincerity.

A third legal dispute turns on the question of whether NRMs are harmful to their members and, if so, to what extent the state has an obligation to protect them from harm (see Robbins 1979).

'Boundary politics' are no less central to social scientific discussion of NRMs than they are to everyday speech and to legal arguments. Psychological and psychiatric research is, for example, crucially concerned with distinguishing between normal and abnormal milieux. Even some sociological research has been focused on the boundary between 'marginal' and 'adaptive' NRMs in an attempt to understand whether or not they help members to achieve re-integration into mainstream culture and society (see Robbins, Anthony, and Curtis 1975). A closely allied concern is with the distinction between authoritarian and non-authoritarian styles of leadership in NRMs.

The general controversy about NRMs throws into sharp relief some of the deep assumptions shared by people in western societies about the nature of the individual person and his or her relationship with society. The controversy is a reminder that these assumptions are contested. It may be an exaggeration to claim that the disputes concerning NRMs are causing serious revisions of these usually taken-for-granted assumptions, but they do at least indicate the broad limits within which current thinking about the individual/society relationship takes place. NRMs can therefore be compared with trace elements which mark out the flow and blockages of present opinion.

There are two broad assumptions underlying these boundary disputes. They concern the nature of the individual person and the nature of human societies. We shall examine each in turn.

In reaction against what are considered to be the intensely communal ideologies and regimes of many NRMs, there is an implied view that a normally socialized person is resistant to pressures towards collective thought, sentiment, and action. At the root of many fears and panics about 'cultism' lies an image of the normal person as a balanced compromise between egoism and communalism. Not only has such an idea been a lynch-pin in western philosophy for many centuries but it has also been a cornerstone of post-Enlightenment jurisprudence. There are numerous literary, dramatic, and artistic symbolizations of this fundamental conception as well as of the comic and tragic outcomes of tension, conflict, and confusion between the individual and society. The operation of NRMs in the west has precipitated an unusually elaborate and assertive statement of the typically western model of the person in contradistinction to the kind of person allegedly found in NRMs.[6]

Central to this model is the idea that individuals should enjoy a *dignity* in their own right regardless of the social groups or categories to which they may belong. The 'real' self is felt to inhere in this abstracted individual and is considered an end in itself. It follows that an ideal state for the individual is *autonomy* or self-direction, but this is said to be precluded by the intensely collective-cum-organic nature of life in some NRMs. They are also said to deprive members of a further essential characteristic of an autonomous person, namely, *privacy*. The boundary between the sphere of what properly belongs to the individual and what is considered legitimately 'public' displays wide cultural variation. But a common complaint against some NRMs is that they exceed the accepted limits of public intrusion into private affairs. In doing so, they allegedly prevent the individual from realizing his or her full potential as a person. There is more than an echo in this allegation of the Romantic attachment to the ideal of *self-development* as a guarantee of full personhood. According to this outlook, it would be a sign of weakness to align the path of personal development too closely with the programme of a collectivity such as a NRM.

A good illustration of the kind of opposition shown by some parents to what NRMs are believed to do to their recruits' personhood was given in an interview that I conducted with the mother of a

Moonie who, at the time of interview had been serving as a missionary in Japan for several years:

> 'No, I want my son back in a job. . . . I wouldn't mind at all if he was, say, living with Moonies. . . . What I don't like is this business of Moon chooses their wives and then they are separated for so long; and then they're told more or less when to have a baby and when not to have a baby; and then they're brought up as so-called perfect children. Well, I've met a couple of these so-called perfect children, and if they were mine they'd get a spanked bottom very quickly. No, I don't like this sort of dictatorship which is, you know, to me it smacks too much of the Hitler Youth Movement. I mean, it really is that sort of organization because, if you read back in history, . . . I mean, they were so dedicated to Hitler that they betrayed their own mothers and fathers, didn't they? And this, to me, smacks very much of the same sort of thing. . . . I think everyone should, you know, do their own thing and not be at the command of somebody like Mr Moon or [the leader of the UC in Britain] for that matter.'

Variations on this kind of tirade against the UC were collected from many of my informants.

The second assumption underlying much of the critical comment on NRMs derives from a model of the kind of society that is considered normal. The centrepiece is a liberal conception of society as a stable system of relationships in which the interests of competing or complementary groups are kept in balance either by an Unseen Hand or by the law.

The controversial NRMs have a special significance in the context of a liberal model of society by virtue of their capacity (real or imaginary) to dominate and control nearly all aspects of a member's life. It is this kind of 'totalism' which angers and alarms the anti-cultist; which raises thorny legal problems for the jurist; and which gives rise to theoretical speculation among social scientists about the very grounds of sociability. Their respective questions are 'Why should we tolerate anti-social cults in our society?', 'What are the acceptable limits of state intervention in regulating NRMs?', and 'What does the attraction of NRMs to young people imply about the state of social integration now and in the future?'

Controversies about NRMs are not confined solely to aggrieved relatives and to ex-members. Rather, they raise fundamental questions about the possibility of 'deviant' religious thought and action in societies dominated by liberal ideologies. Anti-cult agitation is a symptom of the deep-seated resistance that is widely felt towards non-liberal ways of thinking and acting. 'Cult controversies' are more than just storms in a teacup. And, although sensationalism in mass-media accounts of NRMs is rampant, the controversies are not simply inspired by the media. Finally, it has to be said that anti-cultism is much more than an irrational response to novel phenomena. It certainly feeds on a wealth of reactionary prejudice in some quarters, but at the same time is also articulates serious, considered misgivings about the threat that some NRMs allegedly represent to the dominant models of the normal person and the healthy society.

Conversion and coercion

Having sketched the main lineaments of anti-cult sentiment I now want to examine the ways in which people directly involved in controversies concerning the UC in Britain were found to construct their own interpretation of cultism. As we shall see in Chapter 5, it is common for the close relatives of recruits to the UC to claim that the latter had undergone such drastic changes in personality, attitudes, and values that they had become different people. A thoroughgoing identity change had supposedly been engineered for them without their knowledge, let alone consent. This is not the place to discuss them in detail, but these arguments loom large in the testimony given against NRMs in courts of law hearing cases centring on the capacity of recruits to act freely and rationally (see Shapiro 1983).

Since none of the psychological categories associated with brainwashing amounts to a category of legally actionable behaviour, attempts to invoke the law either for or against NRMs tend to turn on the question of whether their recruitment practices can be justifiably translated into terms for which the criminal or civil law offers remedies. This usually means that cases revolve around the question of whether *coercion* was employed (see Delgado 1977). The argument quickly moves to consider whether coercion is necessarily confined to physical restraint; and whether the recruit's acquiescence at any stage of the recruiting process negates the charge of coercion (see Robbins 1983; Shepherd 1982).

The cult controversy extends well beyond the confines of law courts, and the definitional precision of legal discourse is quite alien to the frame of reference within which NRMs are popularly discussed. Nevertheless, what happens in the law courts is an inseparable part of the public controversy, although the rules of legal discourse impose constraints which have no counterpart in popular discussions of NRMs.

It is also important to bear firmly in mind that although the UC is highly controversial it has contributed to only a limited number of themes in the wider cult controversy. The problem of distinguishing between the extent to which the Moonies are, and are not, implicated in controversy cannot be ignored. No simple solutions exist, but the following chapters will at least document exactly the kind of complaints made about the Unificationist movement. It might be helpful, therefore, to begin by drawing up a list of cult-related controversies in which the Moonies are *not* implicated. We shall then have a clearer idea of the controversies which will be considered here.

A small number of possibly exceptional cases might be suggested, but I believe that *grosso modo* the UC has not been seriously or widely suspected of the following:

Physical violence against members or non-members
Drug consumption
Promiscuous sexual practices
Questionable forms of mental or physical therapy
Stockpiling of weapons
Lack of control over 'marginal elements' in the membership
Criminal activity
Psychopathological leadership
Encouraging members to commit suicide

Yet, other NRMs have given rise to suspicions of implication in each of these controversial activities. They are therefore part of the folk-image of 'cultism' and may occasionally influence people's thinking about the UC.

The following chapters investigate the ways in which this particular movement's modes of operation have helped to generate distinctive grounds for the cult controversy. I shall begin with some observations on the social sources of controversy about the UC's mode of recruitment. My aim is not so much to counteract what has been called 'the demonology of cults' (Anthony and Robbins 1980) as to explain the social processes whereby the demonology has been constructed.

Social perception of recruitment

This section will present a series of generalizations about the process of recruitment to the UC. They are partly based on statements made to me by ex-members and aggrieved relatives of members and ex-members of the movement in Britain. They also draw on the published findings of research conducted by other social scientists.

The first point to make about recruitment to the UC is that it mainly concerns people between the ages of eighteen and thirty, many of whom had not chosen a life-long career[7] or established their own household before joining the Moonies. The findings of Galanter's (1980, 1985) research into a sample of more than 100 American participants in Unificationist workshops depict 77 per cent of them as male; 95 per cent as unmarried; and 77 per cent as white. Their median age at the time of starting the workshop in the late 1970s was 21.6 years.

There are no grounds for thinking that the social composition of recruit groups in Europe is significantly different. Barker's (1981) survey of British Moonies in 1980 showed, for example, that about half of them were from the middle and upper-middle classes and were aged between twenty-one and twenty-six. Males amounted to 68 per cent of the membership. In comparison with a carefully matched control group, Moonies were less likely to have left the parental home and/or to have been married at the time of first contact with the UC. Although the majority of recruits are far from being drifters or drop-outs, they can be characterized as relatively less 'independent' than many of their peers. This means that parents and other close relatives tended to feel continuing responsibility for them, as we shall see below.

The fact that recruitment to the UC normally proceeds by way of individual attendance at meetings, meals, workshops, and celebrations creates tension in some families, especially if it represents the first instance of the recruit's independent activities outside the family circle. In itself, of course, this hardly amounts to a cause for public controversy. What comes as a shock to many families, however, is the realization that something claiming to be a religion can engage the interests of a member of the family to the exclusion of other interests and in isolation from other kin. It is the contrast between this atomism and the deeply entrenched cultural model of religion as a communal and/or familial activity which alarms so many close kin of UC recruits. This is only the first source of alarm, however.

Since some NRMs teach their members that it is difficult to practise their religion without incurring the scorn or anger of close kin, it is rare for new recruits to offer to share their religious convictions with their relatives. More often they remain defensive and secretive about the precise details of their new faith. More to the point is the fact that few recruits to the UC, for example, understood their newly adopted religion well enough to be able to present it credibly to sceptical outsiders. Numerous studies have shown that active involvement in religious groups tends to precede full awareness of their teachings, let alone intellectual assent to them (see, for example, Hardin and Kehrer 1978; Buckle 1971; Downton 1979; Balch 1980; and in particular, Bromley and Shupe 1979). The long-term implications of this for the 'cultic career' and particularly for defection from the UC are discussed in Chapter 6.

The result is that many close kin become very suspicious when they realize that a young member of the family is beginning to participate actively in a religious movement without showing much inclination to discuss its teachings or practices with them. The case of Susan, a drop-out from medical school, was typical in this respect. She had been contacted on campus and persuaded to attend a UC workshop, but in her father's words,

> 'She said she was going to a meeting place, you know, a conference, and she'd been told to starve. And she didn't eat for a week, but she wouldn't tell us where or what it was or anything about it. She was extraordinarily busy doing things, and we didn't really discover until afterwards what she'd been doing. She had in fact been sorting out all her things, putting everything up in the attic, making little piles of things for [her brother] and piles of records and so on which are still there. She was getting ready for going [into the UC] but she didn't tell us.'

Susan's secrecy was one of the most difficult things for her father to accept because the relationship had reportedly always been close and confidential. Similarly, the mother of a Welsh Moonie had been horrified to discover a copy of *Divine Principle* hidden in his bedroom before he had announced his connection with the UC. Incidentally, she took her Roman Catholic priest's advice and burned the book.

An unusual, but equally secretive, set of circumstances surrounded the sudden recruitment of Terry, a technical draughtsman in his late twenties who was married and had an infant daughter. He was contacted by the Moonies while he was temporarily living alone after taking a new job in another city. Instead of visiting his wife and child as usual he simply announced that he was going to spend the weekend on a farm with a religious group. Some weeks later he renounced sexual relations with his wife on the grounds that the Reverend Moon had said that they were unnecessary. Finally, he packed a suitcase and left home, redeemed an insurance policy, and closed his bank account. But he returned home after six months with no warning just a few days following the publication of an article in a Sunday newspaper which had sensationalized the case. He eventually slipped back into the routine of visiting the UC centre, and in his former wife's words 'We had prayers at breakfast and songs every night. It was just becoming intolerable.' Ten months after returning home he declined the offer of a job as a schoolteacher in a local school and told his wife that he could no longer live with her because she was keeping him away from God. A divorce ensued, and at the time of interview with his former wife he had been a Moonie for four years.

The case of Simon, an unemployed labourer from a working-class family, is interesting because he spent three or four months visiting a UC centre almost daily before he actually became a member. He told his parents nothing about his activities, however. In fact, Simon had been helping to paint and decorate the local UC centre, but his parents knew nothing about the connection with the Moonies until their Anglican vicar enlightened them. The vicar had discovered Simon's connection with the UC in the course of a casual conversation with him in the street.

Matters are aggravated when the recruiting movement does not share the basic components of Judaeo-Christian theology. Recruits to movements based on, for example, Asian philosophies take a long time to assimilate all the new assumptions underlying the movements' teachings. Yet, close kin are reluctant to allow the new recruit the benefit of any doubts that they may have about the wisdom of adopting a radically different philosophy of life. They usually demand an immediate explanation of this apparent perversity, but it is precisely at the very beginning of involvement with an Asian-based NRM that a recruit finds it most difficult to explain its attraction. In some cases it may be felt that the shift in perspective is so demanding that it is better to avoid even trying to convey its meaning to others who are likely to be sceptical.

It is also precisely at the beginning stages of induction into movements like the UC that close relatives feel fully justified in adopting virtually any tactics to combat the recruit's new commitments. All too often, however, the outcome resembles the account given by the mother of Anthony, an undergraduate who had joined the Moonies in his final year at Oxford:

'[Anthony] was clearly obsessed and he wanted to talk about it. Unfortunately, try as hard as we could, this always led to arguments, and then he was distressed. You know, he would come home, and we would say "Yes, we'll listen", but we, we just couldn't keep quiet. It was so patently absurd.'

But, as his mother pointed out,

'There was a certain emotional blackmail because his finals were about four or five months away, and we realized it would be just as well not to upset him too much because, if he walked out of his university, what then?'

A 'silent bargain' was therefore struck among family members that Anthony was not to be attacked for his new beliefs. His own response to the heated arguments at home is interesting. He regretted the mutual lack of understanding but added that his parents would have to realize that he was going to change a great deal and that the 'old him wouldn't exist any more'. This was paralleled by Susan's reply to her father's statement that, shortly after joining the UC, she no longer seemed to be the same person. She was quite happy to accept this; she was *not* the same person.

In many cases, close relatives were disturbed by the recruit's willingness to give property or money to the UC. The disturbing thing was not so much the loss of material possessions as the abandonment of, for example, musical instruments, record collections, and hi-fi equipment. In parents' eyes, they symbolized the recruits' unique identity and independence. Thus, Anthony's mother described the sale of his prized recordings and hi-fi equipment and the donation of the proceeds to the UC as 'one of the things which made us feel that this was something terribly significant because music then was his most overwhelming interest, and he sold it all.'

The mother of Annabel, another highly intelligent Moonie, struck a slightly different note in regretting that her daughter had apparently given up her love of good literature and drama when she became a Moonie. Similarly, the relatives of Susan were alarmed by her sudden loss of interest in animals and ecology. But more distressing to her father and younger brother was the loss of the kind of 'close involvement in Susan's own enthusiasms' which had previously been a feature of their relationships. Her father claimed,

'I would read the *Guardian* . . . with as much involvement about Susan as about myself. And if I saw things which I thought would interest Susan I would cut them out and send them. And when she was here, we always had these sort of conservations about that sort of thing. And I think the absence of that is the sort of partition, really. We don't feel we can get involved in this movement in the same way as we could in her previous enthusiasms.'

Silence on the part of the recruit is interpreted in various ways. In some families it is taken to reflect an impairment of normal mental capacity. The movement is then accused of insidiously interfering with mental processes. The ostensible impoverishment of vocabulary is widely cited by laypeople and some psychologists alike as evidence of serious functional problems with the mind. Speculation is rife about the techniques that are allegedly employed to induce such an apparently sudden and unexpected collapse of the capacity to reason and to communicate normally.

The worst suspicions of close kin are aggravated when a young person appears to commit himself or herself wholeheartedly to a NRM after only a brief exposure to it.[8] The suddenness of the decision to join is deeply disturbing to many observers because it smacks of irrationality or deception. 'What else could account for such bizarre behaviour?' is often their question.

This was clearly illustrated in the case of Philip, a student of physics in his home town university, who simply left a note for his parents that he was going to spend a few days at the UC's centre in the south of England to learn about the Reverend Moon. They had never heard of this man or his movement. But on his return home Philip burst into their bedroom in the early morning and, as his father described the scene,

'He was quite beside himself, wasn't natural at all, demented and . . . in a hectic state . . . completely confused and convinced that he had just had a message from Mr Moon. It was just to confirm that everything [the Centre] had told him was to be accepted. . . . And he just talked in this excited, hectic state that he was convinced that he must consider full commitment.'

Philip continued to visit the Centre despite a promise to his father that he would complete the final year of his degree course before going back there. He moved into the local UC residence six weeks after his first visit, and at the time of interview with his father it was expected that he would take his final examinations on schedule. His father interpreted Philip's actions as the effect of deliberate deception and psychological manipulation.

This view was echoed by the mother of Brian, a former teacher of music in his late twenties, who joined the UC without warning whilst on a camping holiday. His mother knew nothing at that time about the movement but,

> 'He left everything, library books which I had to take back, he just joined overnight. . . . It made me suspicious because it all happened so quickly. I felt, when he'd gone actually, I was empty and I felt that he'd been brainwashed. . . . And then I had letters full of the preaching and so on, and I just felt he was completely taken over. And, of course, since then I feel that he's become retarded.'

The mother and step-father of Mike, a university drop-out, were less hostile to the UC but they did feel that he had deliberately hidden the true identity of the movement from them for several months after being recruited. He simply referred to it as a big group of friends sharing a house and trying to promote religious unity.

Interestingly, his father's suspicions were aroused by Mike's sudden cultivation of more polished manners and by his preference for short hair and tidy clothes

> 'I said, "Well, I've seen it happen before with different organizations." I said, "With Jehovah's Witnesses, only not to the same extent obviously and with people like the Mormons." I said, "I've seen it happen dozens of times. . . . They come along with their natty suits and their short haircuts and their Bible under one arm." I said, "He's been taken for a ride."'

The name and purpose of the UC were revealed only when the parents visited its London headquarters.

A closely allied misgiving about the way in which some people have been recruited by NRMs arises from the lack of any obvious period of probation or apprenticeship. Some movements do, of course, operate with informal notions of probation, and the spiritual traditions in which other movements are grounded make apprenticeship to a spiritual master a definite requirement of membership. But these qualifications miss the point of the relatives' objection to the apparently irrevocable manner in which fresh recruits are 'swallowed up' by the UC movement. It is mainly the lack of a 'breathing space' or of time for re-consideration which worried many relatives.

There was also anxiety about the lack of holidays for Moonies.

Some even went as far as the father of John in regarding this as proof that the UC was not a Christian organization:

'We had no idea whatever that this Christian movement, or so-called Christian movement, was going to turn out to be a cult, a brainwashed cult. . . . The reason I say this is that any other movement, I don't care what it is, any other Christian movement or religious movement in any part of the world, they're all allowed home to see their people or to get back for a rest – normal, healthy rest and to think things over. But in this movement . . . it's a case of you just have to go on to the bitter end. There's no holiday.'

The alleged uniqueness of the UC in this man's opinion was emphasized by the fact that his elder son had joined a Roman Catholic order but had been allowed to take a one-year break before taking final vows. Other parents echoed the same opinion, and some agreed with the mother of Kingsley, a British Moonie who had spent several years in Japan, 'This is what they do, you see. Anybody they think is wavering they whip them as far away from their parents as they can get them, and I haven't seen him since [the first few weeks of his membership].' He had been moved in quick succession from Germany to France and finally to Japan.

Comparisons between recruitment to religious orders and NRMs are often made in this context but they miss an essential point. The crucial difference between the respective recruiting organizations is the degree of urgency and spiritual effervescence affecting the would-be member. Many NRMs are animated by a driving sense of the urgency and importance of their mission – especially those which set out to transform the world. Recruits find this exciting and compelling. Unless they act on it immediately, there is a strong likelihood that enthusiasm would wane. Some movements also cultivate the thought that hesitation is a sign of spiritual weakness or danger. These considerations would be rejected by would-be religious because they smack of immaturity and lack of serious intent or commitment.[9] The notions of probation and novitiate make good sense in the context of long-established institutions dedicated to a long-term mission requiring discipline and steady devotion to largely intangible, spiritual goals. But they are quite out of place in new movements seeking to mobilize recruits in the energetic pursuit of often ill-defined but practical goals.

The apparent suddenness of conversion (although, as we shall see below, this may be an inappropriate term to employ in this context) is usually coupled with the suspicion among close kin that recruitment was accomplished by a conspiracy. Just as they find it difficult to conceive of authentic religion as something practised outside the bounds of the family and conventional religious groups, so they also object to the notion that important commitments can be made without the knowledge of, or consultation with, members of the immediate family. From their point of view, the suddenness and secretiveness of recruitment suggest that the recruit has been surreptitiously manipulated. The implication is that the NRM would have been unable to do this if close kin had been allowed to reason with the recruit. This is a particularly prominent theme in the accounts given by close relatives of people recruited overseas or in places a long way from home.

A good case in point concerns Robert who was recruited by the UC in San Francisco at the end of a ten-week vacation in 1977. The first news that his parents received simply informed them that he had failed to return on the designated charter flight. Only when his travelling companion gave them details of the communal group that Robert had joined, did his parents begin to grow anxious. Robert had actually instructed his friend not to reveal the identity of the UC. Eventually he telephoned home and, according to his mother

'His voice was flat and he just spouted this religious thing: he wanted to serve the world and what he was going to do. He was going to stay there for a year, have a year out. And it was all in a tone like this [i.e. monotone], it was just – well, no feeling in it, no expression or anything, you know. And it sounded . . . well, if we hadn't, odd little things we asked him, if he hadn't given us the right answer we would have said "That wasn't Robert." He was as strange as that.'

The chance discovery of an article about the UC in *Reader's Digest* alerted the parents to the true identity of the group that Robert had joined. It also gave them contact with FAIR, the main anti-cult organization in Britain. Believing that their son had been brainwashed they protested to the then President Carter, the British Prime Minister, the FBI, the Chief of Police and the British Consulate in San Francisco, the Commissioner of Police for London, the Foreign Secretary, the American Ambassador and their own Member of Parliament. With help from Rotary International, Robert's father and uncle then flew to San Francisco in an attempt to persuade him to leave. The UC's attorney in Oakland, California located Robert, and

the British Consul alerted the Immigration and Naturalization Service to the impending expiry of his visitor's visa. On the day of expiry
Robert was jailed for one night and released on bail. He was allowed
to fly to London using a ticket provided by his father, but his only
greeting to his parents at Heathrow Airport was, 'I'm meeting some
friends; I haven't come to meet you.' Nevertheless, he went home
after spending only one night with the UC in England, took a job six
weeks later and eventually completed his interrupted degree course
successfully.

The fact that recruitment to NRMs like the UC is often sudden
and invisible to close relatives of the recruit has the practical
consequence that communication between them is very difficult.[10] A
large number of parents complained bitterly about the difficulties
that they had had in trying to contact a member of the UC which is
scattered across the country and whose members tend to be highly
mobile between centres. Just as wandering 'Holy Men' and itinerant
bands of *illuminati* were suspect in medieval Europe, so today's
NRMs attract suspicion because of the propensity of some of them
to keep their members circulating around different centres, workshops, headquarters, etc. As a result, members have little time to keep
in touch with their families, and the latter find it hard to make regular
contact with them.[11]

My interviews with close relatives of members and ex-members
generated numerous complaints that telephone calls to UC centres
were not answered properly; that mail was censored or interfered
with; that other members stood beside Moonies phoning their
parents in order to counteract their supposedly evil influences; and
that the whereabouts of members was rarely known for certain. The
mother of a British Moonie in Japan had been told that he would no
longer write to her unless she withdrew from FAIR. She believed that
the UC's leaders in London had sent her son press cuttings about her
anti-cult activities in order to persuade him to bring pressure to bear
on her. The plight of many parents was summed up by the mother of
two children in the UC who had both abandoned higher education to
join the movement:

> 'The UC attacks family structure, because I don't think you can be
> a fully committed member of the UC and live a normal family life;
> it isn't possible. They don't encourage them to pop home for the
> weekend or if mother's ill, come home and nurse her or. . . . You
> cannot have a normal family relationship.'

On the other hand, some parents reported no difficulties at all in maintaining contact with their children at any point of their career in the UC. Such parents were very much in the minority in my sample of informants. Large numbers of Moonies' parents have, however, publicly signified their support for the UC by joining a Parents' Association, attending its occasional gatherings, and by signing statements circulated by the movement in an attempt to influence public opinion (see UC 1978: 10). It has even been claimed that '75 per cent of parents of members are positive towards their children's involvement in the UC, or at least respect their right to their own religious viewpoint' (UC 1977: 3).

Once again, the problem is aggravated when members are recruited, or sent, abroad.[12] For, although some NRMs now have sophisticated management structures and international agencies, there is still insufficient organizational infrastructure to permit efficient transfer of information about individual members. Relatives therefore have to rely on informal and accidental contacts with other members – or on titbits gleaned from the press. All of this creates an atmosphere of intrigue and conspiracy which, in turn, adversely affects the quality of any communication which is established between members and their kin.

Communication with the devotees of NRMs which are inserted in society as refuges or as agents of revitalization is particularly difficult when outsiders cannot obtain reliable information about the movements' activities. The mass media and the publications of anti-cult groups convey sensationalized accounts, as we shall see in Chapter 7, but there are very few ways for outsiders to learn what goes on in movements which are suspicious about the ulterior motives of people seeking information. Matters are made worse by the fact that the only publicly visible activities of some movements are fund-raising and public evangelism. Neither of these activities conveys the richness and variety of the experiences enjoyed by some members. There is certainly no opportunity to observe the acts of worship, the discussion of doctrine and the day-to-day fellowship in such movements. Nor do occasional 'open days' for the benefit of parents make much difference. They are by definition 'rigged' in the eyes of unsympathetic observers. The frustration felt by many parents is well captured in one father's indignant cry of 'Even the Jehovah's Witnesses invite the public to *their* meetings'.

Among the parents whom I interviewed, there seemed to be unanimity that the occasions to which they had been invited had been 'set up' for public relations purposes. Restrictions on space unfortunately prevent me from retelling more than a few of the many tragi-comic anecdotes about parents' visits to UC centres, but some episodes would not have been out of place in a Feydeau farce. They mostly concerned the parents' desperate attempts to talk among themselves in private and the Moonies' equally determined efforts to obstruct such conversations. Clandestine trysts were therefore arranged on staircases at night or in bathrooms. All manner of ploys were also devised to isolate individual Moonies from the community, but vigilant supervisors usually frustrated them. Some half-glimpsed rituals only heightened the general atmosphere of intrigue and secrecy. As one mother put it:

> 'The visitors go to bed, but the Moonies don't. And there was certainly one night, because Annabel was in the same dormitory as I was, and I don't think she went to bed at all, or if she did, for a very short time. And when [Annabel's younger brother] was there, there's a wing at Cleeve House which sticks out and he was in there and he could see through the window a room with a portrait of Moon up on the wall. It must have been a Sunday night when they have their little thing, and they were all bowing to this portrait, which put him off completely. So, what they get up to during the night I don't know.'

Another mother could hardly wait to get away from Cleeve House:

> 'We stayed there one night and, oh dear, if I'd stayed there much longer I would've been running up the wall myself. We got up in the morning, and they were all out on the lawn singing for about half an hour before they had a meal. After dinner I said to Geoffrey, "We're not stopping here, Geoffrey. We're going back". . . . Unfortunately I'd made a mistake and booked my bus ticket to go back on a certain date and I couldn't get it changed. So we went down to the farm, and oh dear, everything was so secretive, you know, an awful atmosphere it was, terrible. Oh, I was glad to get away from there.'

Only one person reported the following type of incident that had occurred while she was strolling through Stanton Fitzwarren, a village where the British Moonies operated a small farming estate. A lady leaning over her garden gate asked,

> '"Is that your son?" I said "Yes". "Well," she said, "for God's sake take him back with you quickly before they get him." So, I

said "Whatever are you talking about?" She said, "I am so tired of having mothers and fathers in tears in my house by what's been done to them. Take him home with you now. Get him and take him while you've still got the chance."'

Her son laughed the incident off with 'Oh, she's an old crank. I've heard about her'. But his mother's fears were far from allayed.

Part of the anxiety of close relatives stems from the fact that they have no opportunity to observe members at work in their day-to-day activities other than fund-raising. They have very little conception of how members regularly spend their time; nor is it likely that members will be very forthcoming about their routines when they face aggressive and unsympathetic interrogators in the family home. In fact, it has been widely reported that members of the UC, for example, appear too exhausted even to want to talk about their experiences when they go home. Ex-Moonies have confirmed that brief visits to the parental home were welcomed largely for the opportunity to take a rest from the tiring routines of fund-raising and proselytizing. Not surprisingly, this was frequently interpreted by anxious relatives as evidence for the claim that members were badly fed and overworked in order to keep them compliant and unquestioning. Many ex-members used these rest periods, however, as valuable occasions for taking stock of their situation in the UC and for comparing it with life outside the movement. The decision to leave the movement was ironically traced back to these occasions when their relatives considered them to be most zombie-like.

Another aspect of the general difficulty about access to reliable information on NRMs concerns the role of well-meaning anti-cult activists. Informally, certain individuals emerge as significant sources of 'insider' information about particular NRMs. Some of them maintain good relations with members and are therefore in a position to pick up items of the kind of gossip which is avidly sought and consumed by outsiders. Others are known to operate 'safe houses' for defecting members and are therefore able to 'debrief' them before their experience is lost to the audience of cult-watchers. Journalists have often played a key role in identifying these informal experts and in keeping them in touch with people seeking advice or information.

Formal groups of anti-cult activists have been formed, as we shall see in Chapters 7 and 8, in many western countries for the general purpose of combating the influence of NRMs and of assisting people adversely affected by them. The details of their operations are less important at this point than is their understandable tendency to inflate the significance of 'worst cases'. That is, they tend to be informed about the most serious cases of abuse attributed to the influence of NRMs. Moreover, their staff is usually motivated to work against cults by exposure to particularly distressing episodes. In all, then, formal organizations of anti-cultists can be expected to present the most damaging and hostile image of NRMs to any enquirer who simply seeks information about them. More than this, these organizations actively exploit opportunities to publicize their case against cults. The information that they disseminate therefore comes to exert the strongest influence over public opinion and, as a result of their lobbying activities, over official agents of social control at various governmental levels.

Since anti-cult organizations have the single purpose of combating what they consider to be destructive cultism, the energies, emotions, and resources of their members are concentrated on a narrow range of activities. Interactions among members are virtually confined to this single purpose for fear of diffusing their efforts and reducing their impact. As a result, and as has been discovered in other single-purpose voluntary associations (see Knoke and Wood 1981), there are fewer obstacles to extremism than are usually found in voluntary associations which bring people together for a diversity of purposes. The normal processes of negotiation, mutual accommodation, and compromise are therefore hampered by the fact that members of anti-cult organizations all tend to be motivated by the same single, overriding concern to combat cults with the utmost urgency. Far from each activist's strong feelings being mollified by the cross-cutting interests of other members' interests, the effect of aggregating their shared feelings is only to sharpen their organization's collective resolve.

The public influence of anti-cult organizations is enhanced by the fact that aggrieved relatives of members of NRMs have very few other options open to them in their often frantic search for information. Many turn to ministers of religion, family doctors, public librarians and, of course, other family members. But very little is gained in this way. Nor does recourse to lawyers and the police prove any more profitable, for remarkably little is known in these circles about NRMs. More to the point, there are neither civil nor criminal remedies for most of the grievances entertained by the relatives of NRM members.

In countries where NRMs have proliferated, no agencies of

government at regional or national levels have any special responsibilities for religious affairs. The response to governments of all political persuasions has been uniform: only if evidence of criminal activity is provided can law enforcement agencies act against NRMs. Relatives may receive sympathetic responses from certain officials, but official agencies have been unble to answer most of the questions addressed to them on the topic of NRMs. The case of West Germany is something of an anomaly in this respect and will be treated accordingly in Chapter 8.

The search for information about NRMs is made all the more imperative for some people because the movements appear to have no continuity or contact with other social groups. This is an important sociological aspect of their mode of insertion in society, to which we shall return later in this chapter. They are different, then, from more conventional religious groups which tend to recruit members from particular families, neighbourhoods, or communities. What is more, NRMs lack the normal conduits for bringing people into association. Sunday School, local study groups, community action groups, artistic circles and choirs are notably lacking in most NRMs. In addition, although devotees can be regarded as full-time professionals, there are no theological colleges or seminaries to prepare them for ordination. Movements which have seminaries actually use them for different purposes. Continuity with schools, colleges, and universities is non-existent. Questions therefore arise about the credentials and credibility of the movements' leaders. This is not a problem concerning only NRMs for it arises in connection with a wide variety of other religious groups outside the mainstream. But it is particularly acute in this context because NRMs have so few links with other organizations through which enquiring outsiders might be able to learn something about them. Just as important is the consideration in the minds of aggrieved relatives that the lack of inter-organizational linkages prevents them from bringing indirect pressure to bear on what are regarded as 'wayward cults'.

Recruitment and modes of social insertion

The preceding section was written in terms of generalizations which allowed for little or no discrimination between NRMs. More importantly, it made no references to the differential contribution of particular NRMs to the public's perception of the 'typical' recruitment process. I shall now remedy the situation by explaining how the controversial aspects of recruitment are conditioned by the movements' modes of insertion in society. This will be done by examining in turn the tendencies towards collective insertion as refuges, agents of revitalization, and of release.

Refuge

Although movements which strive to provide a utopian setting in which to realize their highest ideals in isolation from the presumably corrupting influences of the world might be thought to be highly controversial, this has only rarely been the case in the modern period. In fact, the findings of research on utopian communities generally indicate that religiously inspired ones are more likely to avoid controversy and to survive for longer than their purely secular counterparts (Kanter 1972: 137). Numerous examples of successful and non-controversial religious refuges can be cited. The reasons are not hard to find.

NRMs which are insulated against, and isolated from, the influence of the outside world either by vicinal segregation or by strict rules restricting contact with outside influences to a minimum tend to have stringent entry requirements and relatively liberal procedures for withdrawal. The only people who are recruited are those who have actively sought out the movements and who have shown themselves to be suitable for admission. In the case of the Californian movement formed around Master Da Free John, the Johannine Daist Communion, for example, there is a very elaborate hierarchy of spiritual statuses which entitle the members to sharply differentiated kinds of access to the community. Some live outside and attend only certain ceremonies and functions. Others are permitted to reside inside the community's sanctuary but are denied access to specified places and occasions. Only a very small minority has full residential and ceremonial privileges. It can be safely assumed that this arrangement helps to prevent unsuitable people from getting into a position where they could cause difficulty. It also provides members with varied opportunities for materially supporting the community and thereby enhancing its prospects for success.

Other examples include the San Francisco Zen Center (Tipton 1982), the Ananda Co-operative Village (Nordquist 1978) and the pseudonymous Christ Communal Organization (Richardson, Stewart, and Simmonds 1979). All of these communities have created procedures for making would-be recruits aware of their practices and requirements and for granting proselytes a gradual transition towards the status of full member. But perhaps equally important is their capacity to admit members to different kinds of relationship with the community. Some live in monastic conditions; others live as temporary but full-time residents; while still more spend only brief amounts of time in residence between much longer periods of life and work on the outside. In terms of my framework these communities contain devotees, adepts, patrons, and (with the exception of Christ Communal Organization) clients. People in the last category simply consume specific services such as weekend retreats at the Zen Center or seminars run by the Laughing Man Institute associated with the Johannine Daist Communion.

Interestingly, the category of 'apostate' hardly seems appropriate in this context. Of course, many people pass through the communities, but it seems safe to say that very few devotees have left them in circumstances which could lead to controversy. The primary reason is that the process of becoming a devotee is so lengthy and demanding that (a) mistakes are relatively rare, (b) transfer to the position of adept, patron, or client is usually possible, and (c) there are few grounds for recrimination against the community in terms of deception or fraud.

The objection might be raised that some communally-based movements *have* become controversial in the recent past. The UC, the International Krishna Consciousness Society (ISKCON), and the Rajneesh Foundation are probably the most frequently cited examples. But, as I shall show, there are good reasons for believing that they actually confirm my general argument that the refuge mode of insertion is not in itself a cause of major controversy. This is because the refuge is only one relatively minor mode of these three movements' social insertion. The controversial aspects of these very different movements primarily concern their attempts to find a location in society as agents of transformation or release.

Even the most hostile critics of the UC, ISKCON, and the Rajneesh Foundation usually concede that their communal living practices give relatively little cause for alarm. Some are disturbed by the 'unnatural' segregation or mixing of the sexes, the spartan living conditions, and the allegedly poor diet, but these things pale into insignificance compared with accusations about deception, manipulation, and exploitation. These accusations are not directed at the fact that the movements are communal organizations. Rather, they attack the movements' allegedly unscrupulous exploitation of members as unwitting workers for their material, ideological, and political aggrandizement. The communal form of organization is certainly treated as a contributory factor, but there is little hostility towards either the goal of creating an ideal community or the manner in which these movements attempt to do so.

The case of Scientology is particularly interesting because it concerns a movement which has some communal residences for staff members. It would be an exaggeration to say that they served as refuges from error or illusion, but they undoubtedly provide a unique opportunity for the practical realization of the movement's philosophy. Yet, controversies surrounding Scientology have rarely concerned the communal living arrangements, with the exception of rumours about the way of life on board the flotilla of boats which formerly served as its organizational headquarters. Far more controversial have been the psychological effects attributed to the training or counselling routines practised by all members whether communal residents or not.

In Chapter 9 I shall also bring evidence to show that the agencies of the state which monitor and control the activities of NRMs do not act out of prejudice against communally based movements as such. It is largely their involvement in state-regulated activities which attracts a higher level of supervision than do non-communal movements (Beckford 1983a). On balance, I believe that movements which are inserted in society as nothing more than a refuge very rarely give rise to controversy. And, if they do, there is nothing specific to their being NRMs which contributes to the controversy.

As we shall see in the next sub-section, the really controversial aspects of NRMs which are at least partially inserted in society as refuges arise from attempts to weaken the criteria governing admittance to the community or from attempts to use the community as a basis for transforming the external world.

Agent of revitalization

NRMs which are inserted in society in such a way as to attempt the revitalization and transformation of important features of the external world have given rise to some of the most serious controversies. The UC, the Children of God, and Scientology are the most infamous in this respect, but the differences between them help to produce distinctive profiles of controversy.

In the first place, the socio-logic of revitalization ideally requires high rates of recruitment and mobilization. Emphasis is put on expanding the movements' operations and outreach as quickly as possible. The immediate goal is to mobilize all available people and material resources in pursuit of the goal of expansion. This is achieved differently in each movement, but the common characteristic among them is their drive towards collective growth and influence.

With the possible exception of some recent developments in the UC, these movements conceive of their work as a unique and exclusive task or mission. There is usually strong resistance to the idea of co-operating with other groups or of learning from them. They believe that they hold the truth and that only by their exclusive efforts can crucial features of the world be transformed in accordance with their special blueprint for reality. It follows, then, that the increase of members is of prime importance, for there is no expectation that other groups can be relied upon to achieve their tasks on their behalf. On the contrary, the activities of other groups are usually denigrated and anathematized as not only erroneous but also dangerous. Nor is there any hope that outsiders will simply absorb the transformative ideas of their own accord and thereby gradually bring about the desired revitalization. The only defensible strategy is therefore to build the largest possible force of converts who can put the movements' strategies directly into action.

One tactic is to diversify activities so that a wide coverage of different fields of influence can be achieved. Again, this requires high rates of recruitment, and this can lead, in turn, to some of the difficulties alluded to in the previous section. Outsiders become suspicious of movements which recruit young people suddenly, unexpectedly and, as it were, invisibly. Their suspicions are further aroused when the new recruits are instantly mobilized in fund-raising or proselytizing.

The contrast with movements primarily offering a refuge is sharp, for there is often little evidence of premeditation, reconsideration, or probation in movements aiming at revitalization. Moreover, outsiders rarely glimpse anything that would suggest the existence of gradations of spiritual maturity through which recruits might pass. In the eyes of outsiders, it is as if recruitment marked the end-point of their spiritual development.

Thus, although revitalization has been the aim of countless religious groups in all times and places, it is only in movements such as the UC and the Children of God that aggressive recruiting among specifically young people has produced widespread public alarm in recent times. There are good grounds for believing, however, that the public response to Mormons in Illinois in the 1830s and 1840s may have been similar in some respects (Hampshire and Beckford 1983; Robbins and Anthony 1979b). Certainly, tales of abduction, exploitation, and political conspiracy are common to anti-Mormonism and to today's anti-cultism. By contrast, aggressive recruitment in the twentieth century by, for example, Jehovah's Witnesses, Seventh Day Adventists, and Pentecostal groups has rarely been controversial to the same extent. The difference stems from the fact that the latter movements have not targeted single, middle-class, young people. Nor have they drawn their recruits so swiftly into full-time work for the movements' growth. Finally, their basically local and congregational form of organization lends them a degree of stability, public visibility, and accountability which is noticeably lower in today's NRMs.

We should not close this topic without acknowledging, however, that even the revitalizing NRMs may lose some of their controversial character if they evolve towards a pattern of recruitment based on family groups or neighbourhoods. In other words, there is nothing inherently controversial about revitalization as such: it is merely that the NRMs which pursue this goal by rapid induction and full-time mobilization of young adults leave themselves open to attack from recruits' close relatives. At present, the UC shows signs of moving towards a more diversified social base and a closer integration with existing organizations which could help to promote its particular form of revitalization.

Given the history of controversy surrounding the UC, however, it is unlikely that its putative attempts to diversify and to co-operate with other organizations will be widely interpreted as anything other than self-serving and duplicitous. Anti-cult organizations are usually quick to discredit such moves and to cite them as instances of the very manipulativeness of which they have always complained.

Movements such as the Children of God and the Way International seem content to spread their influence by largely ideological means. They try to 'process' as many recruits as possible by inculcating their special versions of the Christian religion and by providing appropriate frameworks for embodying the ideology in everyday life. Resources are mainly directed towards disseminating the message by means of literature and study groups. Additional outreach in the Children of God has taken the form of running coffee bars, radio programmes, schools, and discotheques. But the aim is always to use these channels as ways of increasing the number of people sharing the group's teachings, providing, of course, that they can pay for themselves.[13] Infiltration of mainstream churches has also been an approved tactic for winning new recruits and/or supporters, but this has occasionally led to counter-productive controversy.[14] A more productive tactic has been begging for supplies, or soliciting donations, regular subscriptions, and bequests from well-wishers.

Most members of the Children of God can be characterized either as devotees if they are full-time residents in the movement's communal centres or as adepts if they hold secular jobs and live in households as part of its network of members in different regions of the world. The latter are integrated into the movement by regular communications with leaders and by a complex system of tithing. The number of patrons is therefore negligible, and the client-type relationship is simply inappropriate in movements based on millennial ideas.

Children of God members tend to be effectively insulated against outside influences despite the fact that many of them earn a living in employments which regularly bring them into contact with outsiders. But this is virtually the limit of their relationships with non-members. As a collectivity, the Children of God does not participate in activities with other groups; nor does it involve itself in community organizations. The tactic of operating through front-organizations has not been common, nor is the movement known to be involved in many profit-making enterprises.

Controversies surrounding the Children of God have therefore tended to centre on recruitment methods, the lifestyle of members, and David Berg's style of leadership. Again, it is worth mentioning that a large number of Jesus Movement groups originating in the late 1960s in the USA shared the Children of God's communal form of organization without attracting adverse publicity.[15] Living in community as such is not controversial. The Children of God became highly controversial because their particular version of community offended public taste in various ways. It was nomadic and lacked any stable basis for generating the resources to meet everyday needs. Begging for food and money have been a regular part of the Children of God's way of life, although the recent move to Third World countries has necessitated a break from this practice. Concern for the well-being of the many children born to the movement's parents has also figured prominently in public agitation for control over some of its practices. Many members were recruited unexpectedly and quickly removed from the influence of former friends and relatives. The style of leadership from Berg downwards was autocratic and unpredictable. And sexual relations among members, as well as between members and potential recruits, were allegedly promiscuous. Significantly, for my purposes, the Children of God have often been categorized as a Christian community which 'went wrong'. The idea of a Christian refuge is perfectly acceptable to many people, but they cannot accept the idea that that community could be ruthlessly manipulated for the purpose of implementing one man's vision of world-transformation.

By comparison, the UC has inserted itself in society in far more diverse ways and has sparked off correspondingly different controversies. But it shares with the Children of God and ISKCON the fact that its recruitment methods give the greatest cause for alarm, at least, in the English-speaking world. That is to say, it is accused of deceiving 'structurally available' young people into believing that they are being invited to participate in an idealistic movement to create a better world with no connection to the Moon movement. The apparent suddenness, invisibility, and irrevocability of recruitment were explained at the beginning of this chapter, as were the psychological devices by which the Moonies are said to break down the resistance of prospective converts.

In order to forestall possible objections, let me make it clear that these widespread beliefs about recruitment are not necessarily confirmed by the evidence collected by social scientists (see, for example, Barker 1978, 1981, 1983; Rochford 1982b; Taylor 1982). But they demand our attention because they nevertheless contribute directly to the public controversy over 'cults'. They are important in another respect: the model of allegedly deceptive and manipulative recruitment practices is often attributed indiscriminately to all NRMs, but it seems to be based very largely on 'evidence' about the UC and COG alone. What is more, it is highly questionable whether the practices attributed to the UC have ever been widespread even among Unificationist groups. It seems likely that only the 'Oakland Family' branch of the UC in California could realistically have given rise to the anecdotes about systematic mind control which are now a virtually standard feature of popular accounts not only of the UC but also of all cults. The influence of just a few early eye-witnesses (for example, Rice 1976; Rasmussen 1976; Edwards 1979) has been overwhelming in this respect, and the highly selective endorsement of available information by anti-cult organizations has also helped to perpetuate the unidimensional image of cult recruitment.

Unlike the Children of God, however, the UC has always striven to increase its chances of revitalization by exploiting a wide variety of 'ways into' target societies. That is, it has never been content simply to mobilize the maximum number of individual members for the purposes of fund-raising or proselytizing. It has, from the very beginnings of its missionary operations in the West (Lofland 1977; Mickler 1980) sought other ways of bringing its message and its practical schemes for transforming the world to bear on diverse spheres of life. Partly, this has served to broaden the movement's economic base and to generate funds for conventional missionary activity; but it has also served to put the UC in a better position for influencing public values and opinions. Some of the schemes for a diversified mode of insertion in society have created highly distinctive controversies.

It is virtually impossible to discover what the connection is between the Reverend Moon's extensive business interests and the fortunes of the UC. The Fraser Committee which investigated, among other things, the possibility that the Reverend Moon had been implicated in attempts by agencies of the South Korean government to buy influence in America was unable to answer this question satisfactorily (US House of Representatives 1978). Nor did the UC's official response shed much additional light (Unification Church 1979). All that is known for certain is that Reverend Moon and a large number of organizations associated with the UC have extensive investments in real estate, banking, manufacturing, newspapers, and service industries. It is not known how the UC's missionaries' activity is related to these investments, and the uncertainty has fuelled controversy. The Reverend Moon's conviction in 1982 for tax-evasion has further affected his public image and, by implication, that of his church. Nothing is more likely to arouse suspicion in the west than the idea that a religious group may be used for the purpose of increasing the leader's personal fortune and corporate power.

Controversy is complicated by the widespread public distaste for some of the UC's fund-raising tactics. Richardson (1982) is probably correct in denying that they have been the major source of the movement's income but they have certainly aroused hostility, cynicism, and organized opposition in some quarters. In fact, the mobile fund-raising teams (MFTs) which were deployed in many countries in the mid 1970s and which came to symbolize the UC's allegedly exploitative procedures have now ceased to operate in many places. Door-to-door sales of plants, clothing, candy, and candles are no longer a prime source of income. The formerly lucrative sale of flowers at street corners has been cut back, and the straightforward soliciting of cash donations for various causes is nowadays rare. But it was these fund-raising activities which earned the Moonies a reputation for being unwitting agents of unscrupulous profiteers, and the reputation has outlived the objectionable practices. I can only speculate that the movement's leaders' calculation was that, at a time when new recruits were arriving in a steady flow, the disadvantages of the reputation were cancelled out by the scale of revenue and by the rate of membership growth.

By the late 1970s, however, the rate of growth had begun to decline in the USA and in other western countries. The adverse effects of bad publicity may have slowed the flow of recruits, although other factors associated with a worsening economic situation must have been at least equally unhelpful. As the 1980s wore on, recruitment slowed to a trickle in the west, and there simply were not enough Moonies available to mount fund-raising campaigns.

In any case, a shift had already begun towards a different strategy for growth. Local Unificationist centres had always raised income from the sale of various services. They ranged from distributing ginseng to house cleaning; from dry cleaning to the production of stationery. The list of known enterprises is now simply too long to reproduce here, but the most important observation on the diversification of these scattered enterprises is that they have prospered so much that the available Moonies are fully occupied in running them. The slowing down of recruitment rates has led to a proportionate shift of emphasis away from street-solicitation towards work in small-scale service industries. One result is that Moonies are considerably less visible to the public in their economic capacity and therefore less controversial.

Another, longer-term consequence is that Moonies acquire more regular opportunities to interact with outsiders in the course of work. They are in a better position to give practical demonstrations of their faith and they are less likely to be ignored or criticized if the interaction takes place during working hours. I am not suggesting that this mode of social insertion is going to increase the number of recruits in the short term. But it may help to change the Moonies' public image as well as providing new opportunities for disseminating their message in social circles from which they had previously felt virtually excluded. The same could be said for the UC's extraordinarily ambitious and expensive launch of two daily newspapers in the USA: *Newsworld*[16] and the *Washington Times*. Of course, the movement has had extensive experience of publishing all manner of magazines and newsletters as part of the routine missionary process, but the resources required to publish daily newspapers are of a quite different order. It remains to be seen whether this publishing venture will have the effect of making new openings for the movement's message and whether the large investment will prove profitable. Meanwhile, all that can be said for certain is that the two newspapers provide employment for many Moonies as well as for non-members.

For some years the UC has also been organizing public entertainments. They included an orchestra, several choirs, dancers, and even a martial arts display team. During the Reverend Moon's evangelistic rallies in major American cities, for example, Moonies staged a variety of dramatic and musical performances on a spectacular scale. It is impossible to know what effect these entertainments have on the movement's recruitment pattern, but in the long-term it is not unlikely that they may improve UC's rather tarnished public image. They at least evince a desire to integrate Unificationist principles into the wider society's cultural patterns. On the other hand, this is precisely the kind of strategy which arouses the anxiety of anti-cultists who fear that the UC is bent on surreptitiously co-opting influential people and important institutions.

A more conventional strategy has been the establishment on many college campuses of branches of the Collegiate Association for the Research of Principles (CARP) as a mechanism for channelling students in higher education towards membership of the UC. Local groups act as organizers of recreational, sporting, and cultural events to which outsiders are often invited. A national office oversees CARP activities in many countries and maintains contact with the international organization. To some extent this cuts across the principal axis of organization based on local centres, but the only noticeable consequence is that the UC is far more in evidence in university centres than in other towns. CARP has the advantage of being more flexible as a mobilizing instrument, especially in connection with international activities. But it is also controversial because of its role in allegedly distracting students from their studies.[17] Many students' organizations and campus authorities have therefore tried to prevent it from gaining recognition as an approved student group and from enjoying the corresponding privileges.

Controversy in the higher education sphere is not, however, confined to CARP. For quite different reasons there has been criticism of the UC's various efforts to attract the attention of academics. Foremost is the annual series of International Conferences on the Unity of the Sciences (ICUS) which began in 1972 as a UC-sponsored forum in which distinguished scholars could discuss broad, humanistic questions in the comfortable surroundings of luxury hotels at the movement's expense. The programme is mainly arranged by scholars, and the Moonies play little part in the proceedings. But they have used the occasions for publicity purposes, and the presence of Nobel Prize winners enhances the prospects for controversy. Anti-cultists have had some success in dissuading scholars from participating. Opinion among academics seems to be divided on the ethics of accepting the UC's hospitality (see the symposium in *Sociological Analysis* 44 (3) 1983), but there can be no doubt that the conferences have won considerable support for the Moonies among academics worried by the thought that freedom of discussion may be jeopardized by opponents of the UC. In this respect, the ICUS conferences have been an interesting way of indirectly introducing the movement's message into circles normally closed to NRMs.

The UC has also sponsored other kinds of meetings and conferences for academics but none of them has contributed significantly to the controversy (Beckford 1983b). This is partly because the movement has not tried to use these occasions for publicity purposes and partly because most of the participants have had legitimate professional interests in the conference themes. Anti-cultists have not therefore tried to exploit these meetings as occasions for publicizing what they claim to be the UC's harmful effects on young people in general and on students in particular.

Although other missionary strategies have also provoked controversy they have not had direct implications for recruitment and therefore do not concern us here. But mention should simply be made of the fact that the UC has invested considerable resources in lobbying legislators, monitoring the progress of legislation which might adversely affect it, and actively pursuing litigation in defence of its own interests. These activities represent another aspect of the movement's mode of social insertion and they indicate a determination to take advantage of every opportunity to further its implantation in all spheres of life. In certain circumstances this has even entailed co-operation with other religious groups, as in attempts to block potentially damaging legislation against 'cults'. An alliance of

NRMs and civil libertarians is currently forming in the USA in reaction against attempts to impose legal curbs on various activities of NRMs.

Release

A number of NRMs which primarily offer neither a refuge nor a mission to revitalize the world fall into the category designated 'release'. This means that people seek services from these movements as a way of being released from an unwanted condition or of having inner potential released from conditions which supposedly obstruct its full realization. The two aspects of release are frequently com·bined in a single service or 'treatment', but movements also vary in the relative emphasis placed on them.

The central feature of the release mode of social insertion is the existence of a client-like relationship between the NRM and the would-be 'members'. That is, the movement makes itself available to clients of its services on a rational, supply-and-demand basis usually mediated by the payment of fees. This is not, of course, to deny that more spiritual, metaphysical considerations are not also at work on both sides. It simply draws attention to the segmental and in-strumental nature of the client–movement relationship. The move-ments' services are not necessarily the guiding spirit of the clients' whole life; nor are they 'consumed' for their own sake. But there is usually the opportunity in most such movements for *some* clients to centre their life on the services provided and to regard their practice as an end in itself. These people stand in the relation of adepts to the movement. Some may even become devotees if the possibility for communal living exists. On balance, however, the clients are the overwhelming majority of participants in NRMs in the release mode of social insertion.

A wide variety of NRMs are at least partially active in offering release to their clients. Some, like Scientology and Synanon, have sought and achieved the legal status of religions in some countries. Others, like *est*, Arica, Silva Mind Control, Psychosynthesis, and the Rajneesh Foundation, occupy a more ambiguous territory on the borderlines of religion, mysticism, the occult, psychotherapy, and positive mind control. For my purposes, the question of definition is not important here. What matters is that these diverse groups have enough in common in terms of the relationships through which people typically participate in them that they illustrate my thesis about the patterns of controversy associated with certain modes of social insertion. They all tend to offer their clients various means of achieving release from feelings of dissatisfaction and release of their untapped inner potential.

As might be expected, the controversies that have grown up around NRMs in this category are rather different from those besetting movements primarily offering refuge or the prospect of revitalization. These differences reflect differences in the movements' social composition; the location of release movements in a cultic milieu of comparable groups; the modes of entry to, and progression through, grades of expertise in the movements' practices; and the typical ways of withdrawing from them. In all, then, the patterns and sources of controversy in the context of movements offering release are highly distinctive.

Accusations of fraud and charlatanry are perennial problems for movements having clients who pay fees in return for the promised benefits of various kinds of release. There is a contractual basis to the relationship. More accurately, a contract is implied but rarely made explicit. This is understandable in view of the necessary vagueness about spiritual phenomena. But it can become a matter of serious controversy when movements offer to improve their clients' physical condition or material well-being. Significantly, many NRMs in this mode of social insertion teach that conventional distinctions between the psychical, the physical, and the material are false or misleading. They try to inculcate a monistic view of reality which asserts the basic oneness of all being, experience, and matter.

One possible consequence of some monistic doctrines is that things on one level of reality or perception are collapsed into those on a different level. The psychical, for example, can be translated into the psychological or even the physical. This allows practitioners to employ psychological criteria to judge their psychical states. It is but a short step to the measurement or assessment of inherently elusive conditions in terms of a supposedly closely related bodily or material state. Unless the overall framework of monism is kept firmly in mind, practitioners may give priority to the purely empirical criteria for judging non-empirical qualities.

This may induce them to become dissatisfied with the empirically measurable aspects of their association with NRMs which had promised a variety of benefits from the consumption of their services. The movements are therefore somewhat vulnerable to charges ranging from ineffectiveness to fraud. The fact that services are purchased for a fee only aggravates the dissatisfied clients' sense of grievance.

Another kind of controversy surrounding NRMs offering release to clients arises from claims that the services supplied are actually harmful. Sometimes the claims are made by aggrieved clients, but it has also been known for officials of state agencies to anticipate problems and to ban the supply of certain services or the use of certain equipment. The American Food and Drug Administration, for example, confiscated the Scientologists' E-Meter in 1963 on the grounds that it could be damaging to health.[18]

These controversies are often fuelled by the opposition of health care professionals to any practice considered potentially damaging to mental or physical health. The medical profession, including associations of psychiatrists, has indeed sought more stringent legislation in many countries to control the use of, for example, hypnosis and hypnotherapy in NRMs and quasi-religious groups. There is an underlying concern with control over entry to the field of therapy, but this is complemented by misgivings about the potentially harmful effects on clients of allegedly religious practices.

The case of Scientology is particularly interesting because this movement has repeatedly fought back against official and professional attempts to control or to discredit those of its practices which appear to have a therapeutic purpose. It has done so by aggressive litigation, by publishing exposés of alleged conspiracies to halt its operations, by monitoring the activities of its 'enemies', and by sponsoring public debate about alleged abuses of human rights. The last strategy represents a clever politicization of the issue. For the movement's counter-accusation is that it is under attack for exposing the psychiatric establishment's connivance at gross abuses of mental patients' rights. Scientology has published a number of eloquent statements about the ramifications of this supposed conspiracy and especially about what is seen as the unwholesome collusion between the American medical establishment, the federal government, and secret service agencies. The Scientologists seem to be trying to elevate the controversy to a much more serious political level, but the conviction of some leading members for burglary of the US Justice Department may have confounded their plans.

Conclusion

I have tried to show in this chapter that it is mistaken to believe that there is a single controversy surrounding NRMs. Their various recruiting practices actually give rise to different sources of controversy. More precisely, NRMs' modes of insertion in society carry the potential for particular kinds of scandal, conflict, and protest. But, since no movement is confined to a single mode, controversy tends to have more than one root. There is also a tendency for public opinion to lump all NRMs together in a catch-all category. This is all the more reason, then, to separate the factors making for certain kinds of controversy.

We shall see in Chapter 6 that the recruitment practices distinctive of certain NRMs are also connected with distinctive patterns of disengagement from them. Again, the 'profile' of disengagement will be seen to condition the kind of controversies associated with particular movements. But in view of the generally unsatisfactory state of sociological thinking about disengagement from NRMs I shall first introduce the concept and its concomitant problems.

Notes

1   An expanded version of the argument that follows can be found in Beckford 1979.

2   The literature published by the Spiritual Counterfeits Project of Berkeley, California, for example, illustrates the difficult, but urgent, task facing an embattled Christian group trying to defend a notion of orthodoxy against what are considered to be the dangerous deviations and heresies of many contemporary cults.

3   The Spring 1982 Newsletter of FAIR, a British anti-cult organization, admitted that, 'While it is comparatively easy to detect and recognize a cult with a strong doctrine of its own, it may be very difficult to decide whether a small Bible-based charismatic group is still acceptable and beneficial for its members, or whether it has gone "off the rails".'

4   In the late 1960s the criterion of religion seems to have shifted away from an insistence on theistic beliefs towards a requirement for intensely held moral convictions.

> 'First amendment protection for one's religious faith does not require a person to articulate an explicit set of beliefs, or to present a solid basis for them. Indeed, the beliefs need not be acceptable, logical, consistent, or comprehensible to others.
>
> The hallmark of religion thus becomes the willingness to stake one's all on the belief system one adopts. The person must have conviction; he must have a faith that binds him to an ultimate concern.'
>
> (Shapiro 1983: 1306)

5   In overturning a judgment of the Supreme Court of Victoria that the
     Church of the New Faith (i.e. Scientology) did not qualify as a religion
     for the purposes of exemption from Pay Roll Tax in Australia, two of
     the five High Court justices stipulated that:

> 'for the purposes of the law, the criteria of religion are twofold:
> first, belief in a supernatural Being, Thing, or Principle; and
> second, the acceptance of canons of conduct in order to give
> effect to that belief, though canons of conduct which offend
> against the ordinary laws are outside the area of any immunity,
> privilege, or right conferred on the grounds of religion.'

But a third judge was less sanguine about the possibility of identifying
definitional criteria: 'There is no single characteristic which can be
laid down as constituting a formularized legal criterion, whether of
inclusion or exclusion, [of religion].' He nevertheless stipulated that,
'One of the more important indicia of "a religion" is that the
particular collection of ideas and/or practices involves belief in the
supernatural, that is to say, belief that reality extends beyond that
which is capable of perception by the senses. If that be absent, it is
unlikely that one has "a religion".' Despite their differences of
approach, however, the High Court judges agreed that the Church of
the New Faith could be fairly described as a religion (High Court of
Australia. *The Church of the New Faith* v. *the Commissioner for
Payroll Tax*. 27 October 1983. Transcript pp. 10, 55–6).

6   I am indebted to Lukes 1973 for many of the ideas in this section.
     Additional help has come from Hollis 1976 and from Benn and Peters,
     1959.

7   The findings of Barker's study of British Moonies showed them to
     have had settled, and in many cases good, jobs before joining the UC.
     What is less clear is whether her respondents were committed to
     life-long careers. This seems unlikely in view of her comment that 'the
     potential Moonie had fairly clear ideas that he wanted to achieve a
     definite goal – but that he might have found that he had either become
     disillusioned about the goal that he had originally chosen, or thwarted
     in his ambitions to achieve it' (Barker 1981: 74). Compare the findings
     from a study of back-to-the-land communes in France (Léger and
     Hervieu 1983).

8   Balch (1980: 6) argues that controversy over the Bo and Peep UFO
     cult centred on the notion of 'sudden disappearances'. Anti-cultists'
     fears about this have been caricatured in terms of such themes as the
     'invasion of the body-snatchers', 'youthnappers' or 'the Pied Piper'
     phenomenon.

9   See Beckford 1978b for a discussion of group influences on accounts of religious conversion.

10   On Moonies' relationships with close kin, see Beckford 1981a.

11   Matters are aggravated when young children are kept circulating around NRM centres. See, for example, Durham 1981; Yanoff 1981.

12   It is significant that the Member of the French Parliament who led a parliamentary inquiry into NRMs in France from 1981 to 1983 had orginally been interested in them because of complaints that he had received about the plight of young people who joined cults on *foreign* travel. See Lanarès 1982.

13   The following comment on Flirty Fishing is instructive: 'Fishing can be fun, but fun doesn't pay the bills! You've got to catch a few to make the fun pay for itself! So don't do it for nothing! We're not in it for the money but we are in it for the men!' (MOL 673 '7 Supporters', February 1978).

14   'By 1972 [the COG] were on the enemies' list of every Jesus-movement group on the West Coast [of the USA]' (Streiker 1978: 54).

15   See Richardson, Stewart, and Simmonds 1979 for an extended case-study of a relatively non-controversial, communal Jesus People movement.

16   Now re-named *The New York Tribune*.

17   A sister organization, the High School Association for the Research of Principles (HARP), is potentially even more controversial but it has so far failed to attract many members.

18   According to Garrison (1980: 27) the seizure of the E-Meters was only a cover for the 'vicious effort of a despotic government to destroy a new religious sect through the misapplication of a consumer statute'.

FOUR

Disengagement

Introduction

Disengagement from NRMs has attracted far less attention in both scholarly and popular contexts than has the topic of recruitment. This is perfectly understandable in view of the animosity widely shown towards some of these movements. Public attention has therefore been fixed on such questions as 'How could anyone in their right mind *join* a religious cult?' or 'How do cults manage to lure new recruits?' It follows that disengagement from NRMs is considered relatively unproblematic: it makes sense that people should eventually leave movements that in the popular view, 'have no right to recruit people in the first place'. Certainly, anti-cultists have generally not found it interesting to ask how and why some people do in fact defect. I find it significant, however, that anti-cultists have given attention to ways of understanding the situation of ex-members so that they can be prevented from relapsing into membership.

If public opinion shows relatively little interest in the topic of disengagement from NRMs, social scientists have fewer excuses for ignoring it. But only recently have theorizing and empirical research on the topic begun to make an impact on social scientific interpretations of religious action. This brief chapter is designed to make contributions to both the theoretical and empirical understanding of religious disengagement. It begins with some reflections on terminology and concepts; this is followed by a critical review of existing models of disengagement from religious groups of various kinds; and it finishes with a discussion of some of the philosophical and methodological issues surrounding the sociological study of this phenomenon. This serves as an introduction to the detailed analysis of disengagement from the UC which begins in Chapter 5.

A brief discussion of terminology is necessary at this point because of the lack of an agreed-upon, all-purpose term designating the act or process of leaving a religious group of any kind – not just NRMs. This problem is the counterpart of the difficulty that has already been experienced of finding a term for conveying all the different nuances of belonging to, or participating in, a NRM. 'Membership', for example, is too weak in connection with devotee status in a movement operating mainly as a refuge and is simply inappropriate to the case of movements having only clients who consume their services.

The most obvious candidates (for example, 'leaving', 'withdrawing', 'switching') all connote a kind of physical separation that is out of place in the context of many NRMs. The same is true of quasi-legal expressions such as 'resignation' or 'disaffiliation'. And terms such as 'disenchantment', which reflect only changes in mood or feelings, cover only one aspect of the whole phenomenon.

Oddly enough, one of the most favoured terms, 'apostasy', has a technical meaning that is largely ignored by those who have used it in connection with leaving NRMs. It implies that the abandonment of a religious group is accompanied by active hostility towards it. Moreover, the Oxford English Dictionary defines the 'apostate' as 'one guilty of apostasy', thereby reminding us that it is a value-laden term. Similar connotations may also attach to 'defector' and 'drop-out'.

In the circumstances, there are good grounds for adopting an ugly-sounding term which never actually appears in the vocabulary of NRM members – 'disengagement'. It has the advantages of being neutral and of not pre-empting any of the diversity found in people's experiences of leaving NRMs. 'Disengagement' can serve, then, as the basic reference term, but stylistic considerations dictate wide use of alternatives. The aim of this discussion has not been to legislate for terms but merely to draw attention to a lexicographic quirk which accurately mirrors the elusive nature of the phenomena in question.

It should be added that, in the sense in which 'disengagement' is used in this book, it refers exclusively to the actions of individual people. In other contexts, of course, it may be appropriate to consider defection from religious groups as a collective phenomenon. For example, Peter *et al.* (1982) have described the processes whereby whole family units are currently withdrawing from Hutterite communities in North America, many as a result of their collective conversion to evangelical Protestantism. Other examples could be cited of so-called mass conversions and defections of people from one type of religious faith to another. But for present purposes, 'disengagement' refers to the actions of individuals who terminate their own membership of a religious movement.

Disengagement from religious groups is elusive in practical and conceptual senses. On the one hand, there are serious methodological difficulties about studying the topic. For example, very few groups compile reliable data on disengagement; and even fewer are willing to make the data available to researchers. So, even the most basic information required for assessing the phenomenon's fre-quency and strength is largely missing. There are also problems about gaining access to people who have disengaged from NRMs. It is usually impossible to know how many they are in total even for a single movement. The identity of any of them is hard to discover. And some of those whose identity is known are understandably reluctant to answer questions about their disengagement. It all adds up to a major methodological problem which often results in the necessity to rely on whatever meagre information happens to be available.[1] This is sometimes dignified with the title of 'snowball sampling' of willing informants (see Beckford 1978a).

On the other hand, in addition to the practical difficulties of gaining access to reliable information and informants, there are also formidable problems of conceptualization. Even if one takes the relatively easy step of borrowing the widely adopted conception of 'religion' as a multi-dimensional phenomenon involving, at least, knowledge, belief, practice, experience, and ethical consequences, there is no guarantee that disengagement from a religious group will necessarily entail a decline on any or all of these dimensions. Similarly, schemes that categorize the motives for disengagement in terms of, for example, intellectual, emotional, and social consider-ations provide only crude check-lists or frameworks which are only incidentally related to the empirically discoverable mainsprings of action. They can only alert us to a certain range of possibilities. Empirical investigation alone can determine the meaning of disen-gagement to the actors concerned, but this kind of research is still in its infancy. All that can be safely stated at present is that disengage-ment from religious groups can take many different forms and may take place on a multiplicity of dimensions and levels. There can be no point in imposing particular limits on the scope of its meaning in advance of empirical research.

Models of disengagement

Although reliable evidence about disengagement from religious groups is sparse, to say the least, there is no shortage of conceptual schemes for organizing our thoughts about the topic. They can be divided into two broad categories. Some are concerned mainly with disengagement as a multi-dimensional phenomenon frozen at a given point in time (*synchronic*), whereas others are mainly concerned with disengagement as a process occurring across time (*diachronic*).

Synchronic models

The typology of religious defection produced by Mauss (1969) is based on the recognition that (a) each of the three dimensions of the phenomenon (intellectual, social, and emotional) can be combined with the others, and (b) the response of any individual defector may be high or low on each dimension. The result is an 8-fold typology over which Mauss was able to distribute the sixty respondents to a mailed questionnaire survey of a sample of defectors from the Mormon Church in California.

By contrast, Seidler's (1979) innovative proposal for explaining differential rates of priest resignations in American dioceses of the Roman Catholic Church in terms of the structural model of a 'lazy monopoly' is concerned more with the sociological factors facilitating defection than with a typology of its forms. In brief, his argument is that the strategy of organizations approximating in crucial respects to the model of a lazy monopoly as conceptualized by Hirschman (1970) 'apparently consists of developing a product that is adequate for most clients, consumers, or members, but not equal to the standards of their most quality-conscious customers or personnel. . . . Such a tactic is that of a lazy person – pleasing mediocre tastes and satisfying those who seek no changes' (Seidler 1979: 774–75). In his view this is a defensible characterization of a key feature of American dioceses, but he also suggests that movements such as the People's Temple and the UC might equally well be understood as would-be monopolies.

Synchronic models of disengagement tend to emphasize the calculation of gains and losses to be made from leaving a religious group. It is assumed that actors always attempt to maximize their advantages and to minimize their costs. Accordingly, the strength of pre-existing ties to people outside the movement is compared with the value of gains from membership. It follows in this line of reasoning that people who join a movement are believed to have previously enjoyed relatively weak relationships with non-members, whereas non-joiners are assumed to have previously enjoyed relatively strong 'outside' relationships (see Snow, Zurcher, and Ekland-Olson 1980). Thus, Galanter found that drop-outs from the UC's induction workshops in 1978 were characterized by 'greater affiliative ties to people outside the sect' (Galanter 1980: 1578).

Wright was also able to show that 'more defectors than members reported family closeness' (Wright 1984: 5) and that parental dis-approval of cult membership seemed to be significantly more effec-tive in encouraging defection among members with strong family ties than among those whose relations with their family were more distant. But we have no way of knowing how the experience of membership and/or defection coloured the kind of accounts that informants gave of their relations with their families.

In their different ways, then, synchronic models of disengagement from religious groups are limited to the background conditions affecting the decision to leave. They are useful in indicating the statistical probabilities that certain conditions will provoke disen-gagement. In this sense, they help to explain in broad terms why NRMs display their distinctive profiles of disengagement. What they cannot illuminate, however, is the process whereby disengage-ment is achieved by individuals. This requires a completely dif-ferent approach which I have labelled 'diachronic' by virtue of its special sensitivity to the *durée* experienced by people who leave NRMs.

Diachronic models

Diachronic models have been used in a few studies of resignations from the professional ministry or from religious orders (see, for example, Hall and Schneider 1973; Hunsberger 1980; Jud, Mills, and Burch 1970; SanGiovanni 1978) but they are more frequently found in studies of new or unconventional religious groups. This reflects a curious fact about the sociology of religion, namely, the relative lack of concern with the process of joining and leaving *conventional* religious groups. It is only with regard to such uncon-ventional groups as NRMs that serious attention has been consist-ently given to questions about the processes of entry and exit. This reflects a basic puzzlement over 'How could anyone join an NRM?' and 'How can anyone ever get out of one?' But as we shall see, there is considerable diversity in the proposed answers.

According to Brinkerhoff and Burke (1980), for example,

'Religious disaffiliation is a gradual, cumulative social process in which negative labelling may act as a "catalyst" accelerating the journey to apostasy while giving it form and direction. Signs of disbelief stemming from doctrinal questions or violation or behavioural codes may serve as the basis for the label.'

(Brinkerhoff and Burke 1980: 52)

This is indeed what may happen when a potential heretic or deviant is identified in some religious groups. But not all cases of apostasy can be reduced to the process of negative labelling.

Skonovd's (1979) multi-dimensional model of defection (based on the six dimensions of: theological belief; spiritual experience; participation in ritual; ethical commitment; compliance with authority; and self-identity as a member) defines apostasy as 'the rejection or loss of religiosity along all six of these dimensions' (1979: 2). The sequence of stages leading to apostasy begins with 'crisis' and moves through 'review and reflection', 'disaffection', 'withdrawal', 'cognitive transition', and 'cognitive reorganization'. The titles reflect accurately Skonovd's underlying commitment to a theory of *cognitive dissonance*. The movement into the sequence and subsequently from each stage to the next is explained in terms of the defecting member's attempts to 'lessen the dissonance' felt between various factors internal and external to the religious group in question. A similar theoretical position had been adopted in an earlier attempt by Prus (1976) to account for both recruitment to, and defection from, religious groups in terms of actors' strategies for minimizing the perceived inconsistency between their cognitions. One of the points of difference from Skonovd's approach is that Prus acknowledges that *many* actors, standing in various relationships to the potential recruit or defector may be engaged in their own separate attempts to control cognitive dissonance. The outcome is said to be negotiated among them, but Prus's theory specifies no factors or conditions that might facilitate prediction of the terms on which the dissonance is actually resolved. Moreover, insufficient attention is given to the possibility that the outcome may be felt as unsatisfactory by some or all actors in the situation. No doubt interpersonal negotiation is an important aspect or dimension of religious defection (Beckford 1978a), but the reduction of cognitive dissonance may not always be its most important feature. Other considerations also enter into such events, and there is a danger that they will be omitted from would-be explanatory accounts that limit the substance of negotiation to the drive to reduce cognitive dissonance.

Balch's (1982) interpretation of defection from the 'Bo and Peep' UFO cult rejected the notion that a 'crisis of belief' had affected his subjects and informants. Members' beliefs seemed to be so vague, flexible, and shifting that they could accommodate virtually all cognitive difficulties. Only disruptions of social support for the beliefs' plausibility were found to precipitate serious reconsideration of intellectual and personal commitment to Bo and Peep. Many echoes of Balch's findings occur in the report of my work among ex-Moonies in Chapter 5.

Shupe and Bromley's (1981) work on apostasy is also interesting but limited in its relevance to withdrawal from NRMs outside the USA by two operational features. First, they limit the discussion of withdrawal from the UC to cases in which either a persuasive or coercive attempt was made by parents to 'deprogramme' their offspring. This is such a drastic intervention that its effects on the process of withdrawal cannot simply be discounted when comparisons are made with cases in which no deliberate deprogramming of any kind has taken place (see Solomon 1981). Second, Shupe and Bromley define 'apostasy' as 'leaving a NRM, and then joining an organized countermovement' (1981: 193). There are defensible etymological grounds for this definition, but it is unfortunately out of line with the practice of other American sociologists who have used the term in a more general sense to designate simply 'withdrawal from a religious group'.

Of all the available models of disengagement, the most sensitively and clearly oriented towards the processual aspects of the phenomenon are those based on the concepts of *role-passage* as used by, for example, SanGiovanni (1978) in her study of 'ex-nuns', and *status-passage* as used by Glaser and Strauss (1971). Going beyond the commonplace observation that in the course of their life people are continuously involved in transitions from one role to another or from one role-set to another, these authors have sought to understand the processes whereby the emergence or creation of *novel* role- and status-passages is managed. That is to say they examined 'new modes of transition' outside the institutionalized structures of roles and statuses. These include such relatively new and still emergent possibilities for 'role-making' as 'Jesus people, feminists, single parents, acupuncturists, bisexuals and mystics' (SanGiovanni 1978: 5).

Emergent role-passages involve major and multiple transformations of identity, status, and behavioural expectations which have
not yet been absorbed into the body of more regular and more
familiar transitions in personal and social identity. Indeed, the nature
of emergent role-passage is 'created, discovered and shaped by the
parties as they go along' (SanGiovanni 1978: 5), although there may
well be social and cultural forces inducing or demanding that certain
people should move outside the range of conventional role-passages
(see Ebaugh 1977).

For my purposes the primary advantage of the concept of 'emergent role-passage' is that it does justice to the evidence supplied by my
informants about the *indeterminacy* and confused character of their
experiences in withdrawing from the UC. From the point of view of
both defectors and their close relatives or friends, defection was not
experienced as an unambiguous transition from one set of roles to
another. They did not feel that they clearly understood what was
happening, although they were certainly under pressure to impose
particular interpretations on events. The outcome in most cases was
a lengthy period of unsettling confusion and tentative moves to
resolve the problem by *ad hoc* adjustments, trials, and errors. As I
shall show in Chapter 5, the passage from being a member of the UC
to being cast in the role of a defector illustrates unambiguously its
complex, subtle, and difficult character in a society lacking an
appropriate blueprint or 'scenario' for such a change.

My conclusion is that most of the available models of religious
defection, synchronic and diachronic, are unsuitable for my purposes on three grounds. First, they tend to depict the process of
leaving a NRM as being considerably smoother and more programmatic than is indicated by the findings of my study of ex-
members of the UC. It is almost as if the models were based on the
assumption that the actors possessed total rationality and total
understanding of their situation. Second, there is a tendency for the
models that *do* have a grounding in research findings to reflect a
rather narrow and extreme range of episodes of defection. Those that
rely upon psychological or psychiatric evidence, for example, tend to
be heavily conditioned by the fact that the evidence is often collected
in clinical and therapeutic encounters between obviously distressed
defectors and professional therapists. Third, many models of religious disengagement (with the signal exception of SanGiovanni
1978) have a tendency to isolate artificially the defector's thoughts,
feelings, and actions from the influence of other people. The findings

from my research in Britain clearly indicate, by contrast, the immense importance of various 'significant others' in affecting the path and the outcome of 'careers' in the UC.

Ever mindful of the maxim that 'a model is never defeated by facts, however damaging, but only by another model' (quoted by Hirschman 1970: 68) I do not expect that the findings that follow in the next chapter will 'defeat' any of the foregoing models. My only hope is that they will bring about a more critical attitude towards what I consider to be premature modelling on the basis of occasionally inadequate information.

Methods and motives

Before reporting in detail my findings on the processes of disengagement from the UC and its bearing on 'cult controversies' however, I have to explain the strategies of my research.[2] They were quite distinctive in two respects. First, I considered it important to move away from the conventional practice of interviewing only isolated, individual defectors. In wanting to understand the processes of joining and leaving the movement in all their ramifications, I realized that it was necessary to abandon the 'members only' approach that had previously been the norm in the sociology of religion. My plan was therefore to question the close relatives and friends of people who were still in the movement and of those who had left it. My reasoning was that these people were likely to have had an influence on members and ex-members alike and thus to have contributed to the controversies surrounding the UC. Their views were consequently considered as important as those of any other informants.

My method of research was primarily based on intensive interviews with close relatives and friends of members and ex-members as well as with some of the ex-members themselves. By a process of 'triangulation' I wanted to compare the several accounts of one person's membership and disengagement – not with the intention of piecing together a single, accurate account but, rather, with a view to understanding their different interpretations of what had happened. I was especially interested in the ways in which the various actors' accounts reflected the influence of significant others and of how they were internally structured to sound plausible. This is examined in Chapter 6.

Second, I recognized that my informants gave me accounts of their disengagement experience that had been constructed in consideration of all kinds of influences and intentions. They were not objective, neutral reports. They were interpretations that made the reported events and states of mind meaningful in particular ways. Consequently, they could not serve simply as factual resources: they were interpretive in nature and they required further interpretation from me.

Thus, when a parent reported that her child had been brainwashed into joining the UC, for example, I was interested to discover how she assembled an account which drew on what she knew about brainwashing without offending the norms of non-scientific discourse. That is, her use of examples of 'telling' behaviour revealed her grasp of what the term 'brainwashing' meant to her. Accounts are skilful constructions that can be put to a variety of uses. By interpreting the way in which they are assembled, one can gain an important insight into the body of intersubjective and taken-for-granted meanings that characterize whole cultures and sub-groups.[3]

Special mention should be made here of the highly distinctive character of the accounts that ex-cultists and their close relatives have published in the form of biographies and autobiographies.[4] These books are a clear indication of how widely shared are many assumptions about the ways of getting into and out of NRMs, but this is not to say that there is total unanimity. The variations are few but significant. Thus, while some accounts present the cult recruit as the innocent victim of unscrupulous exploiters, others depict recruitment as the culmination of a long process of demoralization and alienation. The narrative structure of these two types of account turns on, respectively, violated innocence and foolish complicity. Not surprisingly, the accounts of disengagement also fall into two broad types. On the one hand, defection is presented as a sudden, unthinking response to a disturbing event or circumstance that 'brought the subject to his or her senses'. On the other hand, defection takes the form of a protracted, almost imperceptible slide towards confusion or disillusion. The central image is either the sharp shock or the slow slide.

Leaving aside these structural differences, there are some striking parallels among books in the ex-cultist genre. Concern with the quality of food, clothing, and lodging in cults invariably obscures questions of belief or doctrine. The intricacies of religious rituals and unusual social practices are given more prominence than are the realities of power and authority relationships. Episodes of excitement and danger alternate with periods of drudgery and despair, although the reader usually gains little insight into the everyday life of cult members. The peaks and troughs of emotion are emphasized above all else.

My views on the special importance of adopting an interpretive strategy for studies of cult controversies have been explained at length elsewhere (Beckford 1983c). It merely remains to add that several other researchers have recently adopted similar positions regarding the accounts given by ex-members of religious movements. Jules-Rosette (1985) has, for example, analysed the kinds of 'disavowal account' given by ex-members of NRMs in Africa and the USA in terms of rationalizations for departure. She identifies accounts which attribute disengagement to (a) single, external causes; (b) sudden revelations; (c) moral denunciation of leaders; (d) faults in the movement; and (e) a mature appreciation of the movement's strengths and weaknesses. She also stresses that the character of these accounts reflects the social organization of NRMs and that, through them, members and ex-members come to a clearer understanding of their self-identity in rapidly changing circumstances.

Skonovd (1981) does not typify the accounts of defection that he collected from ex-members of NRMs in California but insists that 'they are not objective, impartial descriptions of events and experiences' (1981: 21). It follows, therefore, that accounts cannot be taken at face value, although paradoxically they are among the best material that we can have on disengagement. Balch (1982) agreed that defectors' retrospective accounts may obscure or ignore crucial aspects of the defection process but felt that he was able to overcome this problem in his study of a UFO cult by observing members as they became progressively disillusioned and disaffected.

Not all sociologists are in agreement, however, on the interpretive status of accounts. Mention should be made of the argument that accounts are adequate evidence of actors' own motives and that, as such, they can serve as relatively unproblematic resources for the sociologist who is trying to explain social action (see, for example, Wallis and Bruce 1983). This allegedly 'commonsensical' position may be appropriate for certain kinds of explanation, but I believe it to be insensitive to the special requirements of research into actors' changing sense of self-identity, meaning, etc. The subtleties and complexities of experience so frequently confound commonsense that sociologists would be well advised to shun any philosophical position that limits their scope for interpretive manoeuvre.

The next chapter demonstrates the usefulness of listening carefully
to what actors say and of interpreting their statements partly in terms
of the conditions constraining what could be said. 'Accounting'
means 'reckoning' or 'making sense'. It is an assumption of my work
that my informants reported on their past experiences in such a way
as to make sense of them in the light of the position in which they
found themselves at the time of talking to me. As we shall see, this
primarily involved accounting for disengagement in terms of their
'disengageability'. The sharp contrast with accounts given by their
close relatives will serve to emphasize the situated character of
accounts of ostensibly the same subject-matter.

Finally, I make no assumptions about the motives for ex-members'
accounts. They may be many, various, and complex, but my research
was not designed to explore this area. I therefore dissociate myself
from those who, on principle, discount the stories that defectors
tell about NRMs (see, for example, Melton and Moore 1982;
Tworuschka 1981). This may be particularly important in the
case of very small movements such as the Bo and Peep UFO cult
studied by Balch, for he believed that all the bad publicity surrounding this movement originated with only one disgruntled defector
whose experiences with it had been allegedly atypical.

My position on the admissibility of ex-members' accounts was
well expressed by Lindner (1981: 219) who, while admitting that one
had to be aware of the deliberately bad impressions created by some
ex-Moonies, nevertheless thought that the testimony of ex-members
should be taken just as seriously as that of practising members.[5]
Similarly, I reject the idea that ex-members' accounts can all be
subsumed under the heading of 'atrocity tales'. It would certainly be
indefensible to rely on them exclusively for information about the
structure or functioning of NRMs; but it is equally indefensible to
deny that their accounts can tell us anything interesting about the
social position of ex-members. One might have thought that professional sociologists did not need to be reminded that having an
academic interest in a certain group of people does not necessarily
imply any degree of personal support for their cause. Unfortunately,
however, some of the 'professional' response to my work indicates
that I am taken to be an anti-cultist because of my interest in
ex-Moonies and in the aggrieved relatives of practising members
of the UC. I am therefore obliged to preface the following chapters with an express denial of the charge that my interest in
apostates' and critics' accounts of the UC evinces any personal

antipathy on my part towards this particular NRM or, indeed, any others.

Notes

1   Hoge (1981) found that about 50 per cent of a sample of former Roman Catholics in the USA between the ages of eighteen and thirty-two declined to be interviewed on the telephone about their disengagement. See also Kaslow and Schwartz (forthcoming) on the difficulty of getting a representative sample of ex-cultists and parents.

2   See Beckford, 1978a and 1985a for further details on research methods and strategies.

3   This argument is expanded in Beckford 1983c.

4   A modest sample of the (auto-)biographies of former cult members includes:

         P. Cooper 1971
         D. Durham 1981
         C. Edwards 1979
         C. Elkins 1980
         J. Freed 1980
         D. Gerstel 1982
         O. Hammerstein 1980
         E. Heftman 1983
         L. Hultquist 1977
         R. Kaufman 1972
         S. Kemperman 1981
         U. McManus and J. Cooper 1980
         B. Magnouloux 1977
         R. Martin 1979
         S. and A. Swatland 1982
         A. Tate Wood 1979
         B. and B. Underwood 1979
         C. Vosper 1971
         M. Yanoff 1981

I have not included any of the numerous (auto-)biographical articles about former cultists that have appeared in newspapers and magazines.

5   I think that there are grave problems with reliance on 'self-selected' samples of practising cultists. Ungerleider and Wellisch, for example, administered psychological tests to members of a Californian NRM who had *offered themselves* for testing in the expectation that the

results would prove useful to them if they ever had to seek legal redress against deprogramming. I find it significant, therefore, that the results showed that cult members 'had an elevation on the Lie scale [of the Minnesota Multiphasic Personality Inventory] such that their group profile must be regarded as exemplifying: (1) an intentional attempt to make a good impression and to deny faults ("fake good") and (2) neurotic characteristics including the prominent use of the defences of repression and denial, coupled with a generalized lack of insight' (Ungerleider and Wellisch 1983: 208).

FIVE

The moral career of the ex-Moonie

Introduction

Resisting the temptation to impose a mechanical model of the stages of religious disengagement on the material that I collected from ex-Moonies in Britain I shall simply interpret it in terms of salient experiences and recurrent themes. In fact, I shall not even try to compare my findings with the available models of disengagement since I find them all of limited value on various grounds. Instead, this chapter will begin with a brief survey of information about the rate of disengagement from the Unification Church and will go on to examine ex-Moonies' accounts of their disillusionment with the movement, their means of separating from it, their attempts to cope with the problems of disengagement, their persistent ambivalence towards Unificationism and, finally, their 'moral career' at home. In the next chapter I shall comment on the contributions made by the UC's distinctive 'profile' of disengagement to cult controversies in general.

One distinctive feature of the material analysed in this chapter is that it is largely restricted to cases of *voluntary* disengagement from the UC. Of the twenty-six ex-members who spoke to me at length about leaving, only one was initially lured away from the movement by a ruse and confined more or less against her will in her parents' home for several days. One other was deported from the USA largely at his father's instigation, and his departure from the UC followed quickly on return to Britain. Attempts were unsuccessfully made to remove some of the other informants from the movement, but only one case of professional deprogramming was reported to me.

At the time of my research there were no programmes of therapy or rehabilitation for ex-members of NRMs in Britain. A few individual members of Family Action Information and Rescue (FAIR), the first anti-cult organization in the country, gave informal counselling and assistance to people who requested it. But no official or formal programmes existed at that time. This is another factor affecting comparisons between my findings and those of American researchers.

In fact, my interpretation of disengagement from the UC differs in many respects from that of American scholars, primarily psychologists and psychiatrists, who have dealt almost exclusively with deprogrammed Moonies. The differences between voluntary and involuntary ex-members are briefly discussed by Solomon (1981) and Wright (1984), and further comments will be added below. It is important to recognize at this point, then, that many divergences between the respective interpretations of disengagement from NRMs stem from differences in the type of cases considered.

Comparisons in this context are not so much odious as methodologically difficult. This is mainly because ex-members vary considerably in terms of the length and intensity of their participation in NRMs. Some were strongly involved for many years; others had no more than a fleeting association. It is unfortunately impossible, given the methodological problems summarized in the previous chapter, to construct an adequate sampling frame which would control for these important variables. But they will certainly be taken into account in my analysis of disengagement from the UC. A second reason for the difficulty of comparisons is that ex-members are not all at a common point of destination in social or psychological terms. Some make a clean and total break from a movement, whereas others hover on a movement's periphery without achieving significant distance from it. This is a dimension of disengagement which calls for explicit treatment. If an analogy were made with studies of social mobility, these difficulties would be said to arise from the fact that ex-members vary widely in their status of origin and destination. Finally, as this book continually emphasizes, there are considerable differences between NRMs on many dimensions. It is therefore clear that disengagement is a difficult topic for comparative research. One of the aims of this book is, through the framework of modes of insertion in society, to facilitate careful comparisons wherever possible. But the difficulties should not be underestimated at the outset.

Rate of disengagement

In accordance with my characterization of its insertion in society as primarily an agent of revitalization, the UC has tended until quite recently to recruit young people quickly, to mobilize them in pursuit of its many goals, and to lose a large proportion of them within a year or so. This has been called the 'revolving door' syndrome. It characterized the situation in several NRMs in the early 1970s. As I suggested in Chapter 2, this is congruent with the 'in-between' status of many recruits. They are willing to make themselves available at short notice, to travel widely, to accept spartan living conditions, to switch frequently from one task to another, and to have no permanent place of residence.

The picture began to change in the early 1980s when the flow of new recruits slowed down and the continuing proliferation of UC enterprises absorbed a growing proportion of mature members.[1] There are indications that by the mid 1980s the movement will have virtually abandoned its notorious mobile fund-raising teams (MFTs) in favour of less visible and less controversial means of generating its material resources. Nevertheless, the focus in this chapter will have to remain on the former mode of operation, since this is what gave rise to so much of the controversy. There is a long delay between the introduction of changes in a social movement and public recognition of the changes. It is important to acknowledge, however, that some aspects of the UC have changed drastically in the last few years.

Until the late 1970s, then, the UC's political economy was based on the mobilization of relatively large numbers of members with brief service. Only a small proportion of them was absorbed into the *cadres*, but again, this has now changed. Moonies who have been members for longer than one or two years now constitute a much larger proportion of the total.

The evidence from my British informants suggests that the high rate of turnover followed from the UC's distinctive processes of recruitment and mobilization. Firm facts about this are notoriously hard to obtain, but there seems to be agreement that during the 1970s roughly 75 per cent of recruits disengaged from the movement in Britain within a year of joining.

This is naturally a sensitive topic from the viewpoint of those people in the movement who might be in a position to know with certainty how many recruits have actually left it. The most authoritative estimate for the UC in Britain (Barker 1981) is that 18 per cent of respondents to a questionnaire who had participated in two-day courses failed to complete them and have presumably taken no further part in UC activities. Of Barker's total questionnaire sample, only 12 per cent eventually became full-time members and 9 per cent Home Church members, but many of these 'joiners' subsequently left the movement. Barker considers that even adjusted figures of 8 per cent becoming full-time and 4 per cent Home Church members may be inflated in view of her inability to contact *all* participants in the crucial 21 day workshops. Nevertheless, assuming that these figures represent conservative maxima, it is clear that very many people fail to remain in association with the UC for long enough to become full-fledged members. It remains to be seen from Barker's research what proportion of members withdraw within, say, six months or a year after joining.

First estimates of the drop-out rate from the UC in the USA were made by Solomon (1977). Reporting on Judah's (1977) research, she claimed that 'it is well known that the movement has a 55 per cent turnover rate in recruits during their first year. This means that nearly half of the new recruits will not even fulfil one year of their commitment to the movement' (Solomon 1977: 62–3). In a more comprehensive report on the findings of her survey by mailed questionnaire of ex-members of the UC she calculated that the mean length of membership was 'just over one year' (Solomon 1981: 280), thereby suggesting that the drop-out rate in the first year is probably higher than was earlier estimated.

On the basis of their study of the UC in the USA Bromley and Shupe (1979) infer that defections are 'frequent' and that about 15 per cent of students fail to complete their courses at the Barry-town Seminary. Moreover, Galanter's (1980; 1985) study of the induction techniques employed by the UC on the East Coast of the USA in its sequence of workshops extending over twenty-one days, showed that 74 per cent of his sample of 104 people did not stay beyond the second day. After twenty-one days nine people joined the movement but four months later only six remained in membership. It is important to recognize, however, that six of the thirty people who stayed beyond the first weekend were *asked* to leave the workshop because the leaders perceived them to be psychologically unsuitable. A few were also physically prevented by their close relatives from continuing to participate in the workshop.

Disillusionment

Contrary to what most models of religious defection imply, the grounds advanced by ex-Moonies in Britain for their decision to leave the UC have very little to do with belief or other cognitive matters. This point will be explored in greater depth in the next section, but it needs to be introduced at the very outset as a way of emphasizing the importance, by contrast, of a wide range of other considerations. The only significant exception is the complaint voiced by a few people that they had been disappointed by the UC's failure to tackle metaphysical questions. They charged the movement's leaders with constantly avoiding questions calling for more than a recital of Scripture by way of an answer. All the other grounds for deciding to disengage, however, relate to material, social, and psychological considerations.

Anti-cultists have sometimes been ridiculed for complaining about the allegedly harsh living conditions for rank-and-file Moonies, but nearly all my informants supported this complaint. They found the long hours of work demoralizing. It was not so much the fact that they were required to sell things or to solicit donations in public that adversely affected them, as the apparent indifference of their leaders to the boredom and exhaustion which overcame many of them.

In fact, the challenge of selling pot-plants in pubs and clubs late at night, for example, generally seemed to elicit a positive response. An element of danger also appealed to those who had led sheltered lives. And there was undoubtedly a thrill to be had from outwitting security staff and supervisors in order to hawk goods around offices and factories. A thin line separated initiative and daring from subterfuge and downright deception on these sorties. Some people clearly revelled in the excitement as well as in the anticipated congratulations from their 'brothers and sisters' if the mission were successful. But very few were able to summon up enthusiasm for the dreary task of trying to sell magazines day-in-day-out, in all weathers in suburban shopping precincts. They felt that this form of contact with the public was the least challenging, rewarding, and occasionally, the most abusive.

As we shall see below, members often turned feelings of disappointment back on themselves. They felt that they had personally failed to do their best for the UC, even though they could also articulate specific grievances about the movement's way of organizing their work. Certainly, many people complained about the exhausting schedules, the uncomfortable living conditions, the bore-dom, and the diet. In fact, ex-Moonies' accounts are punctuated by anecdotes about particularly 'low' moments and illicit purchases of comforts such as chocolate, Coca Cola, or a seat in a warm cinema. Yet, the theme of personal failure is invariably in the background, colouring the account in a distinctive way, and detracting from the idea that the blame for failure lay entirely with the UC. This can be illustrated by the reports of some informants that they had been cross with themselves for feeling scared when they were travelling in the movement's vehicles which were being driven by people who were plainly too exhausted to drive safely.

Dissatisfaction with other rank-and-file members was mentioned as nothing more than an occasional irritant. But a common cause for complaint was the behaviour of leaders at local and national levels. Some felt that leaders were too harsh in their criticisms of members who failed to display sufficient enthusiasm, courage, or even intelli-gence. Many informants also told anecdotes about being severely criticized for failing to 'chastise' members who broke community rules or who acted 'negatively'.[2] It offended their sense of fair play that they were expected to inform on their friends and colleagues.

In some cases, leaders were accused of emotional cruelty towards members who were found to be inadequate. For example, Paula, a drop-out from music school, was told that she was evil by one of the movement's national leaders because she had somehow conveyed her disapproval of his practice of bouncing one of his children on his knee to the chant of 'Subjugate, subjugate, subjugate Satan'. And Timothy was told 'Inside, you're shit', when he refused to take cold baths. Moreover, a female Moonie was fetched from another part of the building so that she could witness and aggravate his embarrass-ment. On another occasion a female leader was said to have 'made a girl get on her knees and cry and cry and cry' because she had worn lipstick. There were also reports of alleged scorn and indifference to the physical or mental handicaps under which some would-be Moonies were suffering at the time of applying to join the movement.

Fear of certain leaders was expressed by many informants. They were afraid of being considered inadequate or inauthentic. Sudden outbursts of anger terrified most of them, but some had special reason for being afraid. Roddy, for example, had been expelled from the British 'family' for disobedience but he quickly joined the movement's One World Crusade (OWC) in Germany. He lived in fear of being discovered, however, and was eventually spotted by the man who had originally expelled him. He then moved to a centre in France but, again, he was thrown out. Yet, he said that his only wish was to rejoin the movement if that particular leader was no longer in charge. Roddy's experience is unusual, although it is not uncommon for ex-members to return briefly to the UC after an initial disengagement. More commonly, leaders were feared for the verbal abuse that they inflicted on hapless members or for the power that they had to determine members' working conditions. A good example concerns Timothy who had often been chastised for laziness and was therefore afraid of being sent to work in Japan. His strategy, like that of several others, was to make himself as inconspicuous as possible. Indeed, some passages of ex-Moonies' accounts are very reminiscent of the autobiographies of conscripts in the British armed forces. Finally, some female ex-Moonies recalled that they had been frightened of being matched by the Reverend Moon with an unknown and possibly unsuitable fiancé. Their views on the success of such matches were not favourable because they had witnessed the kind of problems experienced by the 'blessed' couples living in UC centres. Their misgivings about the system of arranged marriages were aggravated by what they had seen of the children born to blessed couples.

Resentment was more often expressed than fear. The perceived discrepancy between living conditions for leaders and rank-and-file members created particularly bad feelings and was significant enough to be the subject of numerous anecdotes. Typical of them is the recollection that the leader and his wife in one Centre were offered fresh salad for lunch while the others had to put up with a greasy stew. It was also common for the female ex-members to scoff at the Unificationist belief that the children of 'blessed' couples were 'perfect'. Some had worked as nannies or baby-sitters for these children and the common verdict was that they were basically no better than other children. In fact, someone who had spent a lot of time with them claimed that the 'perfect' children were unusually disruptive because contact with their parents was so irregular and because they were in the care of constantly changing personnel.

Several ex-members admitted that the UC's bad image in the mass media had worried them, especially when respected outsiders had joined in the criticism. They were particularly disturbed by reports of the Reverend Moon's alleged involvement in arms manufacturing and in alliances with extreme right-wing politicians in Asia. But as there was no way to check the truth of these allegations, my informants said that they had simply put the matter at the back of their mind. Again, they considered that these suspicions were the product of their own personal weaknesses.

There was also resentment at the suddenness with which managerial decisions were taken and implemented. For example, a Moonie who had cheerfully solicited donations 'for charity' was offended when he was instructed not to use this phrase any longer. No justification for the change in policy was given to him.

Several summary points can be made about ex-members' accounts of their grounds for wanting to disengage from the UC. In the first place, little or no importance is attached to theological considerations. Second, a concern with personal failure to meet the UC's challenges runs through what superficially appear to be complaints about its organization. Third, resentment and fear of leaders are widespread, whereas affection for other fellow-members is generally strong. None of these grounds amounted to a sufficient reason for abandoning commitments to the UC. They were more akin to irritations which simply made it hard for members to devote themselves wholeheartedly to Unificationist programmes. The validity of the programmes was rarely in question. The outward sign of dissatisfaction was not therefore rebellion but declining effectiveness in everyday tasks and a growing distance from some fellow-Moonies.

There is some confirmation of my belief that dissatisfaction with life in the UC was commonly interpreted as personal failure in the fact that a number of the people who were sent for 'rest and recuperation' to a special centre in Germany returned with even stronger criticisms of the movement. Before being sent to Germany they had tended to think that the reason for criticism was personal inadequacy, but they quickly discovered in the course of relaxed conversation with other 'convalescents' that they were not alone in feeling critical. In fact, the social support of like-minded members gave them a fresh light on the UC and persuaded them that their personal failings were not the sole cause of dissatisfaction. Every one of my informants who had been sent to rest in Germany disengaged either immediately or within a few weeks of returning to the UK. Excerpts from one account are worth quoting at length

'I really had a lovely time [at the rest and recuperation centre]; I didn't have to do anything; get up anytime I wanted; go and help myself to breakfast; go out for a walk and then come back and read or whatever. That was nice. It was terribly wrong treatment, I think, because leaving you to yourself you just thought about what you'd like to be doing, you know how, places you'd like to be seeing, freedom you'd like to have. I think that's the wrong treatment especially when there were three of us there and we had quite a good time because . . . it was lovely, and then having to go back to what it had been and get up early again, sleeping on the floor, whereas we'd had beautiful beds and everything. It was too difficult to take, that.'

Other ex-members also recounted incidents in which a small group of dissatisfied members reinforced each other's doubts and misgivings to the point where the idea of disaffection was seriously entertained for the first time. In each case there was a feeling of surprise when it was discovered that other apparently committed members were actually harbouring serious reservations about their place in the UC. At least, this confirmed the wisdom of the rule that members should chastise each other for 'negativity'. In a movement that does not provide for open discussion of criticisms, secret 'confessions' and 'soul baring' are likely to give rise to disaffection.

A few informants reported that they had discussed their doubts and fears with their 'spiritual parent', i.e. the Moonie who had recruited them, or with much older and respected members. 'Special relationships' were occasionally formed around these informal 'confessions', but two considerations undermined their long-term usefulness. On the one hand, the fear of chastisement even from an intimate friend could not be entirely discounted and, on the other hand, there was always the possibility that close friends would be separated and sent to different centres.

Those who did bring themselves to make their misgivings about the UC known to members who were not close friends described the response as one of shock and distaste. They were effectively ignored when it became clear that the decision to leave had been made. Similarly, descriptions of days when someone left a UC Centre emphasized the solemnity of the occasion and the unwritten rule that the defector should not be mentioned in conversation. The other members usually arranged to be absent when the defector was removing his or her belongings. Consequently, many ex-Moonies reported that their departure had gone officially unnoticed. It was as if they no longer existed.

Separation

The decision to disengage from the UC was usually taken on the spur of the moment and in response to a particular incident or realization.

It may have been as the result of a chance conversation with a fellow Moonie; experiencing the unaccustomed freedom to decide for oneself how to spend the day at a rest and recuperation centre; feeling pangs of homesickness or remorse about abandoning close relatives; and so on. Each informant had a variant on these themes. But what most of them had in common was the dawning recognition that they were in the wrong place.

Not all of the informants could express precisely why they had felt out of place, and a number admitted that they had been reluctant to accept the consequences of their feelings. But they seemed resigned to the fact that they could see little prospect of any improvement in their position unless drastic steps were taken. The act of leaving was felt to be drastic because the UC's ideology is exclusivist and totalizing. It provides for no chance of spiritual growth outside its ranks. The situation of an ex-Moonie is therefore very different from that of a 'graduate' of, for example, many Human Potential or New Age religious groups. There is no Unificationist justification for continual 'seekership'; and no acceptance of religious pluralism as an ideal state of affairs. On the contrary, members are taught that desertion amounts to self-exclusion from the movement's allegedly unique spiritual and physical benefits. It was rare, however, for the idea of total and irrevocable disengagement initially to guide the actions of prospective deserters. Rather, they sensed that it would be better for them and for the UC if they withdrew at least temporarily.[3]

It was only when they contacted outsiders that fresh defectors achieved a clearer idea of their motives and intentions. Confusion reigned supreme in their thinking at the time of disengagement, but a kind of order gradually emerged in discussions with other people. In some cases, contact with other ex-Moonies proved to be helpful in crystallizing reasons for leaving permanently, and the support of parents helped a few others to accept that they did not have to return to the UC. As we shall see in the next section, however, relations with parents were too strained in many cases to offer much support and clarification of the situation.

As a corrective to the sensationalist reports of apostasy popularized by the mass media and by some apostates' autobiographies, special attention should be given to two particular contexts for disengagement from the UC. On the one hand, several informants reached amicable agreement with the UC's leaders in Britain that it would be in everyone's interest for them to leave the movement. This happened, for example, in the case of a married couple with a young baby. The rigours of life in the movement were creating severe difficulties for the wife in particular, and she in turn was having an adverse effect on her husband's ability to meet the movement's demanding expectations. As a result, it was suggested that they should leave, and they were given £50 towards the cost of returning home. More will be said below about other aspects of this case. Its immediate importance is as an illustration of the possibility of mutually agreed withdrawal from the UC.

On the other hand, however, some other informants were forced against their will to leave the UC with no prospect of being read-mitted. They were accused of being too lazy, insubordinate, or disruptive. Expulsion proved to be traumatic for one man in particu-lar who subsequently made two desperate attempts to rejoin but was detected and ejected on both occasions. The mother of another ex-Moonie gave a harrowing account of her son's mental illness allegedly resulting from his inability to get back into the UC after being sent home in exhaustion from work overseas.

The 'mechanics' of leaving the UC are no less varied than any other aspects of the disengagement process. Running through the accounts of all those informants who were not actually expelled, however, is a common theme: nobody made plans for leaving. As we have already seen, the decision to leave was usually taken on the spur of the moment and was not followed by any careful planning for the move. Nor was there any discussion with other members about how the withdrawal would be accomplished or where the defector would go. One of the important implications, as we shall see in the next chapter, is that parents were given no warning that the ex-member was leaving the UC and intending to return home.

The problems facing defectors were complicated by the fact that the movement lacked any form of half-way house. Nor was there an acceptable status for ex-members on its periphery. One was either a member in good standing or a defector. Of the latter, the vast majority sank immediately into oblivion from the movement's point of view; only a few were privileged to avoid disgrace by virtue of special circumstances such as overriding family commitments. Would-be defectors knew perfectly well therefore that it was most unlikely that they could withdraw with dignity and integrity.[4] By contrast, the pseudonymous The Process cult is said to have had 'elastic' rules on desertion which encouraged the prospective defec-tor to reconsider. 'He would be demoted progressively down the steps of membership as the days passed after his departure'

(Bainbridge 1978: 161). Returnees were allowed to work their way back up to positions of influence and trust in the movement. I know of no case where this has happened in the UC.

The exploits of defectors were narrated in styles borrowing variously from accounts of public school 'japes' and concentration camp escapes. Glimpses of the absurd were rarely far from the surface, but tragedy was also present. One young man, for example, was so intimidated by the chastising that he had received from a leader in London that he volunteered to go and pray at a sacred site in Hyde Park. But he actually sprinted on to the first bus that passed by and made his way home by a circuitous route for fear of being followed. Another absconded with some of the movement's money in order to purchase a train ticket for the journey home. Strong feelings of guilt were still with him at the time of interview three years later. Ruses to allow escape from Unificationist centres in the early morning hours had been devised by a number of defectors. Some left a Centre under cover of official business but never returned, while others left in such a hurry that they abandoned their clothes and other belongings. In the latter case friends or relatives were sent back to the Centre to collect the abandoned property. This sometimes turned into a farce because, with high rates of mobility between Centres and with sharing of many things including clothes, it was often difficult to find everything that belonged to the defector. This distressed some parents, but to some ex-members the frustration seemed to be a small price to pay for their freedom from the UC.

Some accounts told of angry confrontations with leaders who forbade final farewells to fellow Moonies and who dismissed defectors with nonchalance or spite. One hapless individual, for example, described in great detail a scene that took place in the laundry of the London headquarters where a leader interrupted his search for his clothes and threw some underwear at him in disgust at his defection. The situation was especially difficult for members working abroad with the OWC, for they had to borrow money to travel home, and in some cases they also had to demand the return of their passport from local leaders.

Very few of my informants appear to have left the UC on good terms with its leaders, but it is important not to overlook these exceptions. One young woman was thanked for the care with which she had looked after the children of members. Another was given enough cash to buy a train ticket for the journey home. And attempts were made to entice some ex-members back into membership.

Greater publicity has been given to incidents, also reported by some of my informants, concerning intimidating threats allegedly made to members who had signified their intention to leave the UC. Some were told, for example, that they would forfeit all chances of salvation; that they would be unable to survive outside the movement; and that their close relatives would be punished.[5] Indeed, I heard many accounts of the rumours that circulated among members about the dire disasters that had reportedly occurred to defectors. But only one informant claimed to have been threatened with a punishment as dire as permanent infertility if she left the movement. No doubt some reports of threatened retribution have been exaggerated, but it is only to be expected that a religious movement which considers itself to be part of a divine scheme for the restoration of the human and material worlds to perfection should attempt to preserve its purity by methods of social containment as well as exclusion. Threats, blandishments, warnings, retrospective degradation of defectors, and official disdain for defectors' fortunes are all part of the mechanisms of group closure and self-defence. Even the knowledge that property given to, or invested in, the movement is unlikely to be returned to defectors is believed to deter potential defectors, according to Kanter (1972: 80–2).

Most ex-Moonies seemed to be more concerned, however, about the loss of their friends in the UC. *Camaraderie* was obviously strong and was especially powerful in small cliques of those who had weathered various storms together.[6] Feelings of guilt about 'deserting' them were therefore uppermost in many informants' minds, but very few ex-members kept in touch with their former friends who remained in the movement. By contrast, communication among ex-members seemed to be quite good, although I detected some signs of reluctance to prolong relationships which reminded them of things that they would have preferred to forget. At the time of the interviews, Britain had no self-help organizations catering for the needs of ex-Moonies, so there was no formal framework for such communication. The formation of Ex-Members of Extremist Religious Groups (EMERGE) in the early 1980s may have changed this situation.

Coping

Nearly all my informants returned to their parents' home after moving out of a UC Centre, and we shall investigate the consequences of this below. The exceptions are interesting, however, for what they reveal about the social situation of ex-Moonies. One young man moved into cheap lodgings near a town where he had spent summer holidays in childhood. It was the only place with which he was familiar apart from his home town. Although he was penniless and had no change of clothing (having fled from a UC Centre in too much of a hurry to take any belongings with him) he was able to find a job and a sympathetic landlady. But he made no attempt to contact his family for a period of six weeks. Interestingly, his recruitment to the UC had been equally abrupt and unannounced eighteen months earlier. His reasoning was that, as he had 'deserted' his family, his parents would have no interest in hearing from him. At the time of interview, six months after leaving the UC, he had still given his parents no reason for leaving the movement. The topic was taboo on both sides. As his mother put it, 'I think he'll keep it to himself and he respects us because we don't mention it. And I'm sure one day when he's a bit older he'll tell us why he left.' Two other informants preferred to stay with friends for a few days after moving out of a UC Centre. They wanted time to reconsider their position in peace and did not want to face interrogation from relatives. Both of them eventually moved back into the parental home with little reported difficulty.

The reason given most frequently for returning to the parental home was that ex-Moonies believed they could thereby avoid having to make decisions about their life-course in the immediate future. Their day-to-day existence would be managed by other people, and they would be free to reflect on the meaning of the UC. That is, they saw home as a temporary refuge and as a place where decisions about the future could eventually be taken in relative peace. But their first intention seemed to be to avoid decision-making of any kind. This may be similar to what Downton (1979: 219) called 'taking the line of least resistance' among defectors from the Divine Light Mission.

Many ex-Moonies reported that they had been in a state of mental and physical exhaustion at the time of the leaving the UC, and this was confirmed by some of their close relatives. As Marilyn put it,

'I was really drained. I think it would be described as nervous exhaustion. I was, well, like a zombie. I felt very dazed and very tired, and really weak and just sort of that I couldn't cope with anything. I cried an awful lot.'

It was also not uncommon for them to sleep for more than twelve hours for several consecutive nights. Some also took to overeating, but only one admitted to heavy drinking at home. The majority described themselves at that stage as lifeless and lacking interest in anything. Leaving the UC was considered to be very much the least of available evils: not an eagerly sought alternative. Parents often mentioned their fear that ex-Moonies had been physically and mentally damaged in the UC. They could find no other explanation for the listlessness of young people who had previously been extremely energetic in Unificationist activities. The ex-members' accounts make it plain, however, that their inactivity stemmed partly from feelings of shame and confusion. Faced with concerted definitions of what they had been doing as either unworthy or unwise they tended to withdraw into themselves and to make themselves as small a target as possible. In this way they could at least preserve their own sense of what the UC had meant to them regardless of parental pressure to adopt a different view.

With very few exceptions, informants described themselves as confused about the UC and their place in it. Caroline's description of her state of mind at the time of her tearful departure from the UC in Germany speaks for many ex-Moonies:

'Then I was really upset and I would have given anything then to say I'd stay, because I then, I really felt I was saying goodbye to Heavenly Father, and you know, it was so confusing, really mixed up . . . I completely felt I was doing the wrong thing, but then again it was the draw of my parents that kept me on the train to go back.'

Caroline and many fellow-defectors had been unable to answer the questions that seemed to be all-important: Was the Reverend Moon the Messiah? Was the UC God's organization? and, What would happen to them for deserting it?

Fairly typical of their uncertainty was the following conjecture on the part of a young man who had merely flirted with the idea of joining the UC but had been deterred by allegations about its business practices:

'If things did start changing in the next four years [i.e. if the English branch became less suspect], I would think about it again. I still can't eradicate, that's why I think there must be something to do with brainwashing, I still can't eradicate that there could be some truth there in it. No matter how hard I try I still can't eradicate that feeling.'

At the same time, of course, they were also under pressure to re-evaluate the 'outside' world. 'Was Satan really in control of the world?' 'Could anyone be trusted?' 'Would they be punished for joining a "cult"?' As a result, many ex-members spent a lot of their time reading Unificationist literature or simply pondering over their experiences as a Moonie. In very few cases did this include voluntarily talking to family members about their beliefs, doubts, and fears. It usually took the form of secluding themselves in a bedroom and of avoiding the normal round of family meals and recreations.

Ex-Moonies in my sample were evenly divided between those who described themselves as too ashamed to go out of the parental home and be seen in the neighbourhood and those who spent as much time as possible away from home in public places like cinemas, libraries, and coffee bars. Yet, both patterns seemed to be based on the desire to avoid having to give an account of their past action. Some managed to achieve this by seclusion and others by losing themselves in a crowd. All experienced difficulty in adjusting to the loss of a community of constant companions with common interests and, above all, shared ideals. This had given them a *lingua franca* with distinctive codes and conventions which allowed them to converse easily about things other than the mundane topics of family chatter. On their own among strangers who did not return their smiles or among relatives who did not wish to hear about their spiritual aspirations, however, many ex-Moonies felt quite isolated and detached from their social surroundings. The mass-media seemed to emphasize the depravity of the outside world, and nobody seemed concerned to remedy the situation. They therefore experienced a form of culture shock which was aggravated by the lack of a supportive community of people who shared their views.

Regardless of their strategy for evading interrogation, nearly all informants were troubled after leaving the UC by recurrent nightmares and psychic phenomena. They interpreted their own dreams as symptoms of guilt about abandoning a would-be Messiah who required their help. But their accounts implied that they had grown accustomed to such dreams during their membership of the UC and that the dreams' persistence was one of the factors which had made them doubt whether the movement had been authentically religious. This was even clearer in the case of psychic phenomena such as visions, hallucinations, strange coincidences, *déjà vu* and out-of-body experiences. Some ex-members nevertheless felt that they were being 'pursued' by these phenomena and that it might be sensible to return to the UC as a way of becoming free from them. As with their dreams, I was given to understand that comparable, psychic phenomena had been experienced during membership but that they had been easier to handle in the context of a UC Centre.

One ex-Moonie reported seeing her friend being chased up a staircase by Satan and sensing Satan's presence in the bedroom of her parents' house. Another had had a vision of a person dressed in white approaching her during an early morning ceremony at a Holy Tree in a London park. Timothy, a young man who had been told by a leader of the UC that he was 'spiritually open', felt that he had the power to exorcize a building. He was also convinced that something psychically special was going to occur to him long after he had disengaged from the movement. A similar pattern of psychic experiences before and after disengagement was reported by Roddy who had lived in fear and dread of one of the movement's leaders. He believed that the leader had power over the spirit world and that he had used this power when chastising members. At the time of interview, Roddy was still having nightmares about spirits and was still panicking whenever he heard a voice raised in anger.

The following account of phenomena experienced by an ex-Moonie who had returned to a Centre for a few days in order to re-think his disengagement conveys the general character of these experiences:

> 'I saw some strange things. I remember one night I was lying in bed at Cleeve House and suddenly I was aware that there was someone near ... I just felt there was someone there. I woke up and I looked, and there was a figure kneeling on the floor, praying, leaning on my bed. So I sat up and I said, "Who are you? What do you want?" I was wide awake, I'm sure I was. And they just continued their praying, and then all of a sudden he finished and crossed himself. It was a monk and he just disappeared. ... [The Centre leader] said lots of people that join the Unification Church have monks as spirit guides.

> Another night ... I was lying in bed and I just felt something horrible behind me, really evil. I just had to look at it. I was so terrified, really cold, and it was boiling, it was in the middle of June, that really hot summer, and I was pulling the blankets over me I was so cold. And I just knew there was something behind me. My shoulder was just like numb, it was so cold. And I went to turn over and look, as I just couldn't stand it any more. And something

on this side pulled me back, so I went and looked. And after that lots of things actually have happened. I even exorcized a building once.'

An intriguing feature of the psychic experiences reported by ex-Moonies *after* disengagement is that so many of them related to frightening or threatening themes. Yet, some of the experiences that had occurred during membership were described as pleasant and inspiring. Informants sometimes wept when they recounted the feelings of exaltation and ecstasy that had accompanied, for example, ceremonies at the movement's holy sites, watching a film of a Unificationist rally in the USA, or observing the Reverend Moon in person. Even paranormal experiences at these times produced a 'high' or a 'buzz'. But after they had left the movement, their experiences were described as uniformly unpleasant. All that remained were fear, guilt, and scattered recollections of better times spent with lost (or, worse still, abandoned) friends.

The persistence of unpleasant and frightening experiences associated with the spirit world may have been an important deterrent from participation in other religious activities after leaving the UC. Ex-Moonies reported no inclination to join another religious group and they resented the suggestion, usually made by well-meaning parents, that they should seek advice and help from the clergy. Those who were still undecided about the meaning of the UC were naturally cautious about involvement in other forms of religion; and those who had definitely rejected its claims to unique spiritual status seemed to be 'burned out' as far as religion was concerned. Or, to change the metaphor slightly, an ex-Moonie said that she had already had her fingers burned and that, in future, she would be far more discriminating about religious commitments. Religion was something that many ex-Moonies wanted to avoid: not to experiment with again. In this respect, they depart sharply from the 'seekership' syndrome which involves frequent moves from one religious group to another in a continual quest for satisfaction of spiritual needs or interests.[7] The ex-Moonies whom I interviewed showed no inclination to regard their experiences as merely a stage towards a higher spiritual goal.

One of the reasons for the reluctance of ex-Moonies to become involved in religious groups again arises from their feeling that in the UC they had been encouraged to be entirely open to their fellow-members about their innermost spiritual concerns. Their most personal hopes, aspirations, and fears had been made semi-public, often in organized group settings. Being spiritually 'open' was strongly rewarded. Many of my informants had responded enthusiastically to the encouragement to shift the boundary conventionally erected among adults between matters that are suitable for private and public discussion. In doing so, they may have been trying to establish what Henry Stack Sullivan called 'pre-adolescent chumship'. In the words of Ernest Becker, 'the exterior or public aspect of the adult world, its jobs and rewards, no longer seem meaningful or vital to college youth; the youth try to prolong the adolescent art of communicating on the basis of internal feelings' (Becker 1980: 41). Consequently, ex-Moonies experienced feelings of betrayal when, after disengagement, it seemed that they had been unwise to bare their inner feelings to others. Many of them found it difficult to overcome this sense of betrayal and were therefore very reluctant to enter into relationships which might lead to a comparable exposure of their vulnerable, inner self to the scrutiny of others. They preferred, instead, to close themselves off from potentially 'self-revealing' relationships, and this included participation in religious groups. As we shall see below, it also entailed establishing emotional distance from formerly close relatives.

Incidentally, only one set of parents said that the experience of coping with a son who had reluctantly left the UC had given them a renewed interest in religion. Their local Methodist minister had given them valued support and had taken considerable trouble to give their son assistance in his efforts to come to grips with the theological questions that remained unanswered by the UC. The vast majority of parents, however, reported finding little consolation or inspiration in organized religion.

Floating

The most material advantage for ex-Moonies of living in the parental home was that they were at least spared the problem of providing for their own food and shelter. The question of exactly how they were treated at home will be raised below. For the moment, however, it should just be noted that my informants spent an average of five weeks doing nothing more than resting, improving their appetite, and coming to terms with the difficulty of discovering for themselves a satisfactory meaning for the UC and for their disengagement from it. During this period, a number of them seriously considered re-joining the movement. The main considerations were that, as they had been unable to resolve their doubts about the spiritual status of the Reverend Moon and as they were missing the close contact with fellow-members, it seemed on balance better to go back than to remain miserable at home. It was like a sociological version of Pascal's wager.

Although comparisons are often made between the processes of leaving religious orders and disengaging from the UC, the experiences of ex-nuns, as reported by SanGiovanni (1978), and of ex-Moonies appear to be radically different. Ex-nuns are said to find the first six weeks outside the convent full of 'heady pleasures and emotional exhilaration'. They allegedly enjoy trying to compensate for an 'arrested role-passage' in their teenage years. Ex-Moonies, by contrast, reported finding the first few weeks outside the UC a difficult period, not because they were trying to catch up on lost time, but because they experienced only a sense of having failed to persevere with a demanding set of ideals. Moreover, they lacked the friendship networks that supported ex-nuns and the opportunities to play a different role in the same church.

Similar points can be made about the weakness of comparisons between the processes of leaving the Catholic priesthood and the UC. Dellacava's (1975) research emphasized the importance to would-be defectors from the priesthood of contacts that were invariably established with supportive primary groups outside the priesthood in advance of resignation. These contacts helped to facilitate the transition to the status of ex-priest. But ex-Moonies find it virtually impossible to establish such contacts and are therefore in a much more difficult position immediately after disengagement and during the longer-term search for a new identity. The fact that ex-nuns, ex-priests, and ex-Moonies all share the experience of abandoning 'high commitment roles' should not be allowed to conceal the sharp differences between their respective experiences in other, possibly more important, respects.[8]

The psychological costs of going back to their parents were, for example, high in terms of guilt, frustration, and boredom. There are also grounds for believing that the short-term convenience of the arrangement may have been outweighed in the longer term by social disadvantages. In particular, staying in the parental home had the paradoxical effect of preventing some ex-Moonies from re-establishing contact with former friends and other social networks associated with work or recreation. It was as if the walls of the house isolated them from the outside world. Consequently, the task of establishing the basis for an independent existence took longer than it did for the few who did not go home or who quickly left again.

Three of my informants actually went back to live in a UC Centre. Caroline spent only one week at home before deciding to try again to meet the movement's challenge, but the attempt was short-lived. She finally left after another few weeks partly because she could not live with the thought of hurting her family. But she seemed to remain intellectually convinced of the movement's sacred mission – so much so, in fact, that she refused to answer some of my questions about beliefs for fear of jeopardizing her chances of salvation. She also shrank from voicing all her doubts about the *Divine Principle* (DP) because she wanted to avoid giving the readers of this book any good reason for not taking Unificationist theology seriously. Her continuing uncertainty about the UC came clearly through her reluctance to join again in case she was just wasting its time. Finally, she admitted that she would probably become a Moonie again if her parents died in the near future: she would then have no serious grounds for hesitation.

Roddy's problem as we saw above, was rather different. After serving as a Moonie for four months he had been expelled and had rejoined briefly on two occasions in Germany and France. At the time of interview he had succeeded in studying for A-level qualifications at a technical college for a year but had not fully abandoned hope of one day returning to the UC. He still read DP regularly and was deeply disturbed by persisting dreams about the Reverend Moon and about the leader who had expelled him.

Timothy's case was a mixture of elements from Caroline's and Roddy's. After six months with the OWC in Britain, Germany, and France he eventually withdrew because of serious misgivings about the harshness of the regime and the alleged insensitivity of leaders. He had been quickly demoralized by the difficulties of selling goods in public but had really enjoyed the intimate company of fellow Moonies. Indeed, his decision to rejoin after an interval of one month was partly attributed to his feelings of shame and guilt about 'deserting' his friends in the movement. But life with his parents also proved to be boring and petty by comparison, so he spent a further month trying to overcome his resistance to Unificationist forms of organization. Again, he could not reconcile himself to taking cold baths and to being chastised for laziness, especially in front of other members. He said that he had really not wanted to leave the movement permanently but that he had been made to feel useless as a member. He finally left secretly after an argument with the Centre's leader, but he retained considerable respect for the practical virtues of DP. He was less enthusiastic about the Reverend Moon's claim to messianic status.

The stories of four other returnees were recounted by their close relatives. The first concerns Geoffrey who had to be compulsorily placed in a mental hospital on his return from missionary work with the UC in Japan. After one month's treatment he was released into his parents' care. Within five weeks, however, he had left a summer job at Butlin's Holiday Camp and returned to the Moonies. They quickly sent him back to the hospital, and he agreed to a course of medication. On discharge, he found a clerical job and took an interest in amateur dramatics. Within a few weeks, however, he had drifted back to the local UC Centre, alienated his employer, and demanded money for an airline ticket back to Japan. He unsuccessfully attempted to rejoin the UC in London but persisted in demanding money from his parents. Finally, he spent a further month in the hospital and, at the time of interview, was beginning to revisit the UC Centre yet again.

The second returnee is Melody who had joined the UC at the age of eighteen on leaving school and had spent several years as a fundraiser in the USA. She was sent back to her parents' home at her own request when she began to fall seriously ill. Extensive surgery was required over a period of fourteen months to restore some of her strength. At that point she was visited by a young man who had known her in the USA. Telling her parents that he was no longer a Moonie, he stayed with the family for ten days and helped with Melody's convalescence. He returned after several weeks and spent a further two weeks with Melody and her family. During this time they began to read DP together and to sing Unificationist hymns. Finally, they left without warning and hitch-hiked several hundred miles to visit the young man's parents. They joined the UC together the following week in London. At the time of interview Melody was receiving preferential treatment in the movement as well as a regular medical check-up.

The third case which concerns Terry, the draughtsman who twice left his wife and infant daughter in order to join the UC, was outlined in Chapter 3. All that needs to be added here is that, according to his former wife, he felt torn between the pull of the movement and the pull of his family. He reportedly wept with rage and frustration because he was unable to convince any of his close relatives to see the point of becoming a Moonie. At the time of interview with his ex-wife he was working as a school teacher but continuing to live in a UC Centre.

It is debatable whether Annabel really qualifies as a fourth returnee, for she spent only three weeks with the UC before being asked to leave. The reason seemed to be that a family friend had written a critical article in a Sunday newspaper about her recruitment. She was probably considered an embarrassment to the movement. Yet, within a few weeks she had telephoned the leaders and persuaded them to readmit her. At the time of the interview with her mother, Annabel had been a member for more than a year and had apparently become completely integrated into the movement.

The other ex-Moonies whom I interviewed all expressed lingering support for various aspects of the UC as an organization, for the Reverend Moon or for the DP. In the face of stiff opposition from their parents, some clung to the movement's literature and to their notebooks dating from their period of membership. A few even brought them to interviews and allowed me to read sections of their personal diaries. It was clear that these materials represented something precious but ambiguous. Ex-members were hanging on to them 'just in case', but it was difficult for them to specify the kind of circumstances in which they envisaged finding the materials useful. For some, they amounted to a form of 'insurance policy' against the possibility that the Reverend Moon might in fact prove to be the Messiah. But for others their value appeared to be largely sentimental. Only one person had kept them as a reminder of her 'stupidity'. In their parents' eyes, the ex-Moonies' refusal to throw the UC books away was dangerous and worrying.

Only three informants mentioned the possibility that they might make use of their Unificationist books in attempts to dissuade prospective members from joining. Compared with their 'deprogrammed' counterparts in the USA, British ex-Moonies were very cautious about becoming involved in anti-cult activities. In fact, few of them had even agreed to talk to journalists about their experiences. Only one felt very strongly committed to preventing others from joining the UC, but even she expressed no hostility to the movement: merely a desire to save people unnecessary anguish and frustration.

Parents of ex-Moonies and anti-cult organizations have tended to emphasize the practical difficulties facing young people who give up jobs and education in order to live and work full-time in a NRM. By contrast, my informants did not consider that these difficulties had been overly damaging to their life chances. Of course, they found it hard to find satisfying jobs after leaving the UC but, against this, they argued that they had not been satisfied with what they had been doing before joining the UC. In fact, the number who had abandoned good career prospects was quite small. Greater difficulty faced those who had abandoned courses of higher education, although in some cases it did prove possible for them eventually to get the desired qualification and to move into satisfying employment. Others, however, were simply drifting from one temporary job to another at the time of interview and had clearly failed to 'settle down' even years after leaving the UC.[9]

Ex-members tended to regard their incomplete record of employment, education, or National Insurance contributions as relatively minor irritations. They received a lower level of unemployment benefits and were under pressure to pay higher rates of contribution when they did find employment. Some had also experienced embarrassment about their association with the UC when explaining to prospective employers why their records were incomplete. Pet subterfuges included saying that they had been working abroad as a volunteer with a Christian missionary organization; travelling with a group of musicians; or crewing on a luxury yacht on a round-the-world voyage.

The mass media and popular books on cults consistently give the impression that the effects of membership of the UC are devastating on those who manage to disengage, or who are forcibly removed, from it. The findings of my research suggest that this is both a grossly exaggerated and a crudely simplified impression. Ex-members' accounts of the process of separating from the UC actually mention few indications of serious or lasting damage; but they do make it clear that the process was more confusing and indecisive than is usually acknowledged in popular treatments of the subject. If divorce and attempted suicide can be described as 'unscheduled role passage', becoming an ex-Moonie is a considerably more bewildering experience because it has so few cultural models or scenarios. Yet, the specificity of the experience of withdrawal from a 'cult' seems to have been sacrificed by many writers for the sake of making it appear to be totally unlike any other experience of leaving a social role or movement. Of course, the UC's particular mode of insertion in society and its highly distinctive pattern of social relationships create a very special 'trajectory' for defectors, but the similarities with the ways in which young adults enter or leave other commitments should not be overlooked. Comparative research on their patterns of withdrawal from ideological, occupational, recreational, and residential groups is urgently required. Comparison between the experiences of ex-Moonies and, for example, former participants in the armed forces, the Peace Corps, or Voluntary Service Overseas would be particularly appropriate.

Family strategies

It is ironic that those models of religious disengagement which have highlighted its processual aspects have, at the same time, imposed what amounts to an arbitrary end-point on the process. They typically imply that the process comes to an end when the former member of a religious group no longer feels any attraction to its teachings, rituals, and social networks. Yet, this apparently commonsensical limitation of the process conceals, at least in the case of defectors from groups which had previously made heavy demands on their time and energies, the fact that a further phase of the process begins when the status of ex-member in assumed or imposed. Of course, this is by no means a necessary or automatic component of their changing status in the eyes of others or of their evolving self-identity. For some ex-Moonies, however, it can assume an importance no less momentous than that of joining the movement in the first place. To put it simply, they spend much more of their lives as ex-Moonies than as Moonies. Much depends on the way in which their close relatives, friends, and associates act towards them.

It is unlikely that any member of a 'totalizing' religious movement could conceal his or her involvement from people close to them for very long. Even if the precise identity of the movement were never disclosed, the fact that the member's life was effectively dedicated to it would not easily escape attention. It follows that termination of membership is also likely to be noticed and to call for an explanation. The ex-member can therefore hardly avoid being identified, willingly or otherwise, as an ex-member: this identity looms large in the eyes of intimates. In practice, this often means that the defector is put under pressure to give a coherent account of the reasons both for joining *and* for leaving the movement. In the experience of my informants this proves to be more difficult and sometimes more painful than the situation in which they had found themselves as recruits. It is therefore worthwhile taking time to reflect on the different social situations in which converts and defectors typically give accounts of their experiences to others.

The kind of accounts that *practising* members give of their reasons for joining a totalizing religious movement can be relatively easily made to sound coherent and internally consistent by reference to factors outside themselves. They can, for example, claim that the movement's teachings, activities, or personnel are invested with a self-evidently sacred quality which makes them inherently superior to, and more powerful than, any alternatives or competitors. This claim frequently casts the convert in the role of a fortunate beneficiary of supra-human forces which need no justification in themselves. The convert's testimony to the personal benefits flowing from conversion or illumination and to the wider benefits being produced by the movement serves as a practical demonstration of the movement's legitimacy. There is in fact a powerful logic of congruence between the various claims advanced in the course of conversion accounts (Beckford, 1978b; Billette, 1975; Taylor, 1976). The overall effect is to strengthen the convert's own religious convictions and commitments.

At the same time, of course, the status passage is marked, sustained, and celebrated by the group to which the convert is recruited. 'Conversion' and 'recruitment' are not synonyms; nor are they fixed stages of a continuous process. In fact, recruitment often precedes conversion. But the passage from the status of non-member to member is a culturally familiar and sanctioned event with predictable consequences for the people concerned. Passage in the opposite direction is much more problematic. The term 'deconversion' is therefore totally inappropriate because, far from representing an 'undoing' of conversion, the process of disengaging from a NRM actually involves further complication of already problematic conversions.[10]

Leaving aside defection from monastic orders, there is little in the way of a cultural 'script' for the passage of a person from being a member of an intense religious group to being a non-member. It is not a status passage that has figured, for example, in popular literature or drama. Nor is it even the subject of well-known jokes or cartoons. In technical terms it involves 'transition to a non-scheduled status'. Moreover, to continue with technical terms, it represents a 'solo status passage' in this context because it concerns the defection of only one person at a time. Mass defections from certain religions and religious groups amount to a quite different sociological phenomenon. The combination, then, of these two features of status transition in the process of becoming an ex-Moonie implies that it will be a difficult experience.[11] We have already seen how difficult it was for most people to separate themselves from the UC. We shall now examine some factors in their social situation after disengagement which added to the difficulty.

Converts are usually eager to testify to their religious convictions and commitments, whereas defectors tend to be reluctant to talk about either their conversion or their disengagement. Apostasy is essentially dissimilar from conversion in that it presupposes not simply change but also failure or error. As such, it is rarely publicized with consent, although it can be stage-managed with appropriate social support. But the only kind of social support for public recanting by ex-Moonies in Britain comes from families and organizations committed to an anti-cult position. As we shall see, most defectors had little sympathy for anti-cultism and were therefore unwilling in many cases to accept this particular form of support. Their hazy and ambiguous feelings about NRMs did not endear them to any particular group or audience. Interestingly, some of the ex-members who have been persuaded to take part in carefully arranged public testimonies to their apostasy confided in me that their participation had been largely an inauthentic attempt to conform with parental wishes. In private they maintained a quite separate version of their experiences but they knew that this would be unacceptable and painful to their intimates. Not surprisingly, therefore, most ex-members preferred to avoid making references to their religious experiences, however valid they might still be considered. Let us now consider the position in which most ex-members found themselves.

Very few informants stayed away from the parental home after leaving the UC. The vast majority returned there either immediately or within a few days. In some cases, no warning was given and no preparations were made. In no case was the homecoming celebrated, for it seemed to be an awkward embarrassment even for those who had campaigned for and looked forward to it for a long time. The imagery of the Prodigal Son seemed entirely out of place, for there was no certainty that the returnee had indeed 'repented' of his or her former way of life. Many people reported feeling that 'the clock could not be put back' because too many things had changed since the ex-member had first joined the UC.

A common response on the part of both ex-members and parents was to define the situation as if it were a case of sickness requiring nursing care and rest. Perhaps because of the prominence accorded to medical models of 'cultism' in anti-cult propaganda and in the mass media (Robbins and Anthony 1982), some parents adopted the nursing role very readily. Incidentally, my interviews with the close relatives of practising Moonies taught me that many people *anticipated* having to nurse them back to health if they ever left the movement.

Although it may be more difficult to understand why the ex-members co-operated, I believe that they did so partly in order to reduce the grounds for friction and to avoid interrogation about their actions – past, present, and future. From their point of view, it was a convenient way of temporizing without appearing deliberately to evade responsibility for themselves. By their own accounts, many were actually suffering from fatigue and anxiety occasioned by unresolved uncertainties about the wisdom of leaving the UC.

The first problem for ex-members who could not eventually avoid giving an account of their experiences was that, regardless of their audience's views about the religious group to which they had belonged, it was virtually impossible for them to talk about their former convictions and commitments without jeopardizing their integrity or their intelligence. On the one hand, they could claim that they had been the victims of external circumstances or agents; on the other, they could claim that it had been their own inner weaknesses which had let them down. But in both cases the account took on the character of an admission of guilt and failure. The fact that their formerly prized and perhaps vaunted convictions had been disowned and thereby discredited meant that their own integrity or intelligence was called in question.

Even those who refused to talk about their experiences could not escape from the logic of the situation: their silence was usually interpreted as a tacit admission of failure and/or guilt. They were caught in a bind from which it was practically impossible to escape without compromising either their competence or their attachment to intimate feelings about experiences which would not be understood by others.

The second problem for ex-Moonies was that their audiences usually wanted to hear a confession of guilt or weakness. This was not necessarily out of sadistic motives but because it was only in this way that the audience's commonly hostile attitudes towards NRMs could be confirmed. They interpreted the ex-member's account as a positive vindication, *inter alia*, of the suspicions and fears that they had previously had about the kind of movement which would remove its followers suddenly and in some cases totally from their 'normal' conditions of life (Beckford 1979). Ex-members sensed that they were under pressure from their audiences to render the kind of account which would confirm their 'spoiled identity' and the correctness of anti-cult opinions. In this context, 'rendering an account' implies not simply telling a tale: it also implies restoring a balance which has been artificially destroyed. The book-keeping metaphor faithfully reproduces the frame of mind of many intimates of ex-Moonies, for it draws attention to their feelings that, before normal social relations could be restored, they had to pay for their waywardness. Deviations from 'normal' life had to be itemized and explained before the earlier basis for mutual trust and respect could be re-established.

Rendering an account in this sense was not at all easy for many ex-members of the UC, mainly because they did not feel the need to explain away their previous commitment to a religious movement in the kind of terms expected by many of their associates. They may have had their own understanding of what had happened, but it was unlikely that it could be expressed in terms which would have satisfied the audience's expectations. To pursue the book-keeping metaphor even further, ex-Moonies and their hearers rarely employed the same unit of account. That is, there were usually differences of opinion between them concerning the choice of the most appropriate ways of talking about past experience. In brief, the hearers expected to hear experiences reduced to behavioural-psychological and/or organizational-manipulative categories, whereas the speaker was usually searching for categories which did justice to authentic aspirations, convictions, doubts, and confusion. In many cases the hearers refused to accept the speakers' units of account and therefore persisted in demanding a more satisfactory rendering of the account. There was no automatic or inevitable solution to this problem. Nor was the problem merely a matter of terminology: the preferred terms reflected deep-rooted differences in values and political (in the widest sense of the term) convictions.

The clash between these different interpretations of the 'cult experience' came to a head in some families over the question of whether the ex-member 'needed to get the UC out of his/her system'. Many parents of ex-members and of members alike took the view that the best 'treatment' was to talk endlessly about the movement and its effects on the individual in order 'once and for all' to 'clear the air' so that the whole family could 'make a fresh start'. This put the ex-member under pressure to say more than he or she wanted to for the sake of the family. In other words, this strategy actually aggravated the very tensions between the UC and the family which had caused many ex-members to re-think their religious commitments. They resented what they perceived as 'moral blackmail'.

Some parents shared the view of Robert's parents that they could only talk about the UC when the ex-member was not depressed or bitter. Nevertheless, there was a strong feeling of anxiety.

> 'that there was a certain amount [of interest in the UC] still left there that could be rekindled if he got in touch with [the Moonies] again. And we know at first, well we presume, that we did some good by drawing it out of him and getting him to talk about it. And we wondered whether it would do him good to get that last little bit drawn out of him or not.'

The result tended to be a cat-and-mouse game of tentative moves, sudden changes of direction, and slow progress – even over apparently trivial matters such as where to store Unificationist literature and mementoes: in the bedroom or in the loft?

Most of the ex-Moonies whom I interviewed returned to the parental home after leaving a UC Centre, and it is here that a third and particularly painful problem occurred. For in the family home the most disarming and probing questions were often asked. Yet, this was also the place where ex-members had hoped to find privacy, considerateness, and discretion. The tension with their close relatives was distressing and gave rise to various strategies for avoidance, containment, and direct confrontation.

From the point of view of many ex-Moonies, the chief difficulty was in trying to convey to intimates that, although they had effectively severed direct connections with the UC, they nevertheless did not wish to disown the movement entirely. One informant summed this up neatly by explaining that, although she had returned willingly to a welcoming home, she could never discuss the UC with her family 'because I can only defend it, whereas they can only criticize it'. In fact, some informants definitely wanted to preserve their own memories of the more pleasant and rewarding experiences.

Several aspects of life in the UC remained attractive to some ex-members, and even those who could find little to say in its favour felt that the experience of membership had done them at least some good. This was also a major finding of Wright's (1984) research in the USA among ex-members of three NRMs. Ex-Moonies frequently suggested that, for all their disaffection from the movement, they still wished to preserve a sense of something which had been precious to them. Most of them had invested a great deal of energy, enthusiasm, hope, and time in the movement. Some had also invested themselves heavily in intense personal relationships, and the recollection of former ties and loyalties was dear to them. The effort to persuade relatives that disengagement did not include the willing abandonment of precious experiences sometimes approached the intensity of classical drama.

The struggle to preserve precious recollections and a more subtle and balanced perspective on the UC than their intimates were usually willing to allow served as a basis for many ex-Moonies' sense of their own integrity. So long as they could maintain these struggles they could feel that they were being honest and authentic. A subtle and rarely explicit assertion of their disagreement with the family's often explicit condemnation of everything to do with the UC served as a partial guarantee of the ex-member's sanity. This tactic often took the form of a refusal to be drawn into discussions and arguments about the movement. Silence was interpreted by the family as a confirmation of its worst suspicions about the effects of the UC on its recruits' minds, but in the opinion of many ex-members it was better to ignore such provocation than to challenge it. The knowledge that close relatives considered their silence to indicate incompetence was less painful to some ex-Moonies than the alternative of making inauthentic condemnations of all that the UC stood for.

The strategies that were employed in some families to extract acknowledgements of incompetence, confessions of guilt, and disavowals of the UC were backed by a variety of tactics designed to 'aid the recovery' and to 'prevent a relapse'. At one extreme was the tactic of incarcerating the ex-member in the home, but this has occurred to my knowledge very infrequently in Britain. In the case of Marilyn, a student in the final year of teacher training, the tactic produced a disavowal after several days of anguish, but it also provoked her to say, 'I was furious, I was distressed. I felt tied in . . . I felt threatened by my parents, and I felt they wanted me back for possessive reasons.'

Nevertheless, her parents were satisfied that the 'bitter medicine' had worked and that the risks that they had taken had been worthwhile. By comparison, the unsuccessful deprogramming of

Martin, a graduate student, seemed to generate only higher levels of anger in his close relatives and a more desperate determination to remove him from the UC at all costs.

A more common tactic was to isolate ex-members, without their permission or knowledge, from 'undesirable' contact with outsiders. The main aim was obviously to prevent the UC from luring them back into membership, for some parents claimed to have evidence that concerted efforts had indeed been made to do just that. In addition, steps were taken to filter out communication with other people deemed 'undesirable' at that time. Journalists, certain former friends, and other ex-members were usually included in this category. The filtering was done by disconnecting the telephone, not passing on messages, and intercepting correspondence. In the words of Anthony's father, 'There are priorities. I mean, if one has to practise a degree of deceit against a child, if it's totally in his interest, one's got to do it.' Similarly, the parents of Robert, who had been deported from San Francisco when his visa expired, felt justified in disconnecting the telephone at home, moving temporarily to a relative's house, having incoming mail delivered to a business address, and putting secure fastenings on all windows in the house in terms of protecting their son's best interests. They treated these measures as a necessary evil. Another facet of this tactic was to arrange for the ex-member to come into contact with people deemed 'constructive'. They included close relatives, carefully selected friends, clergymen, and anti-cult activists.

Finally, virtually all the relatives of Moonies and ex-Moonies whom I interviewed considered it vitally important to collect information about the UC as a means of acquiring insights into the phenomena that they were combating. 'Better the devil you know' was often quoted in justification. In some cases the information-gathering had become a major enterprise taking up all spare time and even spare rooms in the home. Some people formed an informal communications network akin to a victims' self-help network. They exchanged information and took on assignments on behalf of others, for example, to locate Moonies whose whereabouts were unknown to their anxious relatives. But the father of one ex-Moonie kept all his 'intelligence' in a locked room and refused to discuss it with other members of the family partly for fear of 'corrupting' the other children and partly out of a strong desire to minimize the embarrassment to his son who had left the UC.

The energy and ingenuity displayed by some parents were extremely impressive. Most of them had collected press-clippings and Unificationist ephemera. Some had organized letter-writing campaigns in the hope of enlisting the support of all manner of notables and public figures. They had also acquired specialized knowledge about particular aspects of the UC or about ways of combating it. Thus, one parent had become very knowledgeable about the rights of ex-Moonies to state benefits. He had corresponded extensively with various Civil Service departments for many years and was a fount of 'insider' information and advice about ways of circumventing bureaucratic obstacles. Another had specialized in studying the movement's business enterprises. Their information-gathering was systematic and thorough, but it was motivated by a deep sense of moral indignation at the injustice allegedly committed by the UC against their families. They saw themselves as crusaders but they were not blind to the risk of being considered fanatical and righteous.

Many of the parents whom I interviewed bore no resemblance to the caricatures of them purveyed by some NRMs and by some so-called liberal opponents of all anti-cultism. I found widespread sensitivity to the moral dilemmas posed by opposition to any religious movement and a wide range of practical, considered responses to them. In short, there is a grave danger that the desperate and occasionally underhand measures taken by some people to 'rescue' a close relative from the UC may give a distorted image of the majority position.

The moral career of the ex-Moonie

The situation of the ex-Moonie who returns to the parental home has often been described to me in terms reminiscent of those used by Goffman in his delineation of the 'moral career of the mental patient' (Goffman 1968). Of course, the absence from the home of the full panoply of coercive, sedative, and punitive devices available to the staff of mental hospitals renders the parallel less than perfect. But the effect of 'moral' pressure on the person signified as irresponsible or incompetent is nevertheless strikingly similar in the two settings in some respects. For example, it is made clear in both explicit and more subtle ways that behaviour and expressed attitudes in conformity with the 'incompetent' label are the major conditions for increases in the respect and consideration to be shown by the 'competent' members of the family. Continued reluctance on the ex-member's part to accept the role of 'incompetent' is met with concerted resistance and sometimes with punitive sanctions.

In one crucial respect the experience of voluntary disengagement from the UC is possibly more distressing than that of even voluntary patients in a mental hospital, for ex-Moonies' treatment follows directly from their decision to leave the movement. They typically saw their decision to withdraw from it as a freely chosen, if not always decisive, action which had called for a searching and painful analysis of their most sensitive feelings, beliefs, values, commitments, and prospects. It had taken most of my informants a long time to reach the point of being able to withdraw from the UC, and for them withdrawal represented an attempt to establish a fresh and more authentic self-identity. In particular, going home was symbolic of new hopes, if not of new confidence. Yet, what happened in certain cases was that the inquisitorial stance of probably well-meaning relatives and the concerned 'remedial' programme mounted by them contradicted the ex-members' own definition of their situation.

The solution (going home) was interpreted by others as a problem still to be tackled ('getting it out of the system'). Even parental expressions of love and concern were felt by some to be double-edged, for they marked the ex-member as someone in need of such things. The widely reported emotional emptiness or coldness of ex-members may be a reaction against the equally widely reported emotional intensity of communal living in some NRMs; but it may also be a defensive response to the perceived threat of being swamped and manipulated by relatives who are determined to treat them as 'incompetents'. This is an especially likely response to the feeling that there is what Goffman has called an 'alienative coalition' working against the ex-member's own definition of the situation as a 'solution' rather than a 'problem'.

An interesting variation on the perception of an 'alienative coalition' was reported by a few ex-Moonies who had managed to persuade their families that their disengagement from the UC was complete. Ironically, there was still tension because the families regarded disengagement as a victory for common sense and justice, whereas the ex-members still considered it as a failure on their part to live up to the UC's high ideals. The tension sometimes gave way to open conflict when it seemed that the family members were gloating over their 'success' at the expense of the ex-members' feelings of personal failure.

From the ex-members' point of view (and perhaps unreasonably) the very people whom they had thought they could trust to be sympathetic and tactful sometimes proved to be just the opposite. They were made to feel that they were no longer moral equals with their close kin. A sense of betrayal therefore compounded their distress and their unwillingness to co-operate with the problem-defining and problem-solving scenario. It is not at all surprising, therefore, that they demonstrated some symptoms of mental disturbance in their interaction with would-be therapists.

One of the major implications of my analysis of ex-Moonies' accounts is that the prevailing wisdom about them in psychological and psychiatric circles should be questioned. The prevalent view is that such things as 'slippage into dissociated states, severe incapacity to make decisions and related extreme suggestibility' derive from the effects of 'behaviour-conditioning practices on some especially susceptible persons' (Singer 1979: 75). It is further claimed that it takes ex-members many months to recover their former equilibrium because they typically suffer from such difficulties and problems as depression, loneliness, indecisiveness, altered states of consciousness, blurring of mental activity, uncritical passivity, the 'fishbowl effect', guilt, and perplexities about altruism. These problems are attributed to the effects of 'sophisticated, high-pressure recruitment tactics, and intense influence procedures' (Singer 1979: 82) in NRMs. Not all clinicians, however, are agreed on the connection between the practices of such movements and the state of their ex-members' mental health (see Levine and Salter 1976; Galanter 1978, 1980; Galanter *et al.* 1979; and Ungerleider and Wellisch 1979).

Furthermore, when the clinical and social contexts of the kind of psychiatric investigations typically conducted with ex-members from NRMs are taken into consideration, the findings begin to take on a different meaning. The fact that, for example, 75 per cent of participants in Singer's therapeutic discussion groups had been removed 'not entirely of their own volition' from movements to which most of them had been devoutly committed cannot be irrelevant to their mental and spiritual state of mind at the time of the therapy. Some of them had also been subject, probably for the first time in their life, to an awesome and bewildering series of legal and extra-legal actions in connection with parental attempts to separate them from supposedly harmful influences. At the same time, they had been obliged to listen to attempts to explain the nature of what

various well-meaning people had felt to be the manipulative processes to which members of NRMs were allegedly exposed. In short,
the psychiatric 'evidence' is at least partially generated in a social
setting calculated to undermine and to dislodge many of the fundamental convictions, aspirations, and loyalties on which the subjects
had until very shortly beforehand based their self-identity and their
world-view (see Hardin and Kehrer 1978).

I must make it clear that I am not accusing psychiatrists and
therapists of inventing or manufacturing the evidence of mental
disturbance in members and ex-members of NRMs. Nor am I
suggesting that the subjects have faked their 'symptoms' simply to
satisfy the therapists. In some respects the problems would be more
tractable if either or both of these possibilities were true. Unfortunately, however, the situation is more complex and more problematic. For it is in the nature of the social setting in which therapists and
psychiatrists typically meet the ex-members of NRMs that the
symptoms of (sometimes severe) mental disturbance may be aggravated and registered. This reproduces in a clearer fashion a pattern of
events basically similar to the one which occurs in the confrontation
between the same 'subjects' and their aggrieved relatives at home.
The worst suspicions of both sides are thereby confirmed and
reinforced.

Very few of my own informants reported interviews or discussions
with mental health professionals in Britain,[12] but it is clear from the
accounts of those who were confronted with would-be therapists or
inquisitors drawn from the wider family that the occasions induced
at least as much disturbance as they settled. The initial labelling and
treatment of the ex-members as a 'problem' was a damaging experience to people who, as a consequence of leaving a movement in
which they had made heavy personal investments, were expecting or
hoping that their difficulties had been eased. Even those who were
less sanguine about their prospects for a 'normal' life outside the UC
were nevertheless shocked by attempts to force them into 'therapeutic' encounters. Their view was that if they still had problems,
then they were spiritual in nature and not amenable to psychiatric-
cum-psychological repair alone. Most informants in this category
had withdrawn from the UC simply to gain the opportunity to think
about themselves in more relaxed circumstances. Confrontation
with unwanted therapists or analysts only complicated the matter by
calling in question the wisdom of leaving the movement in the first
place.

Given the basic disagreement between 'subject' and 'therapist' over the meaning of their meeting, it is hardly surprising that the former should respond in ways which only confirm the latter's definition of the situation. The ex-member, as was made clear to me on many occasions, was intent on preserving a sense of personal integrity in the face of what usually appeared to be hostile and/or incomprehending questions. Their reasons for joining and leaving the UC were complex and difficult to articulate but in many cases meaningful and cogent to them. Yet, they were usually faced with questions which assumed that there could be no defensible reasons for their action and which therefore sought to investigate other considerations. The questions were felt to be at best irrelevant and at worst insulting. The effect was often to drive the ex-member further and further into a withdrawn state or, worse still, to induce a dissociated state of mind in which the gap between the surface appearance of reality and an obscurely sensed, but more persuasive, reality grew progressively wider. It was common for informants to feel that they no longer knew where they were or what they were doing during the phase of interrogation by would-be therapists.

Analogous difficulties have also been reported (Shupe and Bromley 1981) in the interaction between novitiate members of the UC and their parents. Fresh recruits are usually less well-versed in the movement's teachings than their parents expect them to be. Consequently, when parents press for answers to theological questions, the answers are frequently unsatisfactory and unconvincing to both parties. Since the parents find it hard to believe that a genuine religious conversion can have taken place in the apparent absence of doctrinal learning they naturally resort to interpretations in terms of 'inauthentic' or forced conversion.

The recruits, on the other hand, perceive no problem in their lack of doctrinal *knowledge* for they have had the benefit of *experiences* in UC Centres which have convinced them of the movement's uniquely divine mission and of their personal commitment to its goals. Parental incomprehension is perceived as a threat to these convictions, and it is quickly realized that no amount of argument is likely to change their parents' minds. The best solution is therefore seen to lie in silence or in a different topic of conversation. This is interpreted by the parents, of course, as evidence of cognitive confusion or emotional disturbance. They, in turn, feel equally threatened by a situation in which they can foresee no prospect of persuading the recruits to disown the UC completely. The result is an unsatisfactory stalemate in which neither party can appreciate the other's point of view and in which all attempts to remedy the situation are met with frustration, anger, or despair.

Conclusion

The argument of this chapter has been that major problems arise for defectors from the UC when they return to live in the parental home. They come under considerable pressure to make a disavowal of Unificationism, to confess the error of their ways and to give assurances of their freedom from the movement's influence. None of this is calculated to allow the ex-Moonies the opportunity to reflect in tranquillity on experiences and feelings related to the UC which they allegedly found to be ambiguous and disturbing. Caught between family strategies to secure unambiguous signs of irrevocable disengagement from the Moonies on the one hand and, on the other, their persisting suspicions that the Reverend Moon might still be the promised Messiah many of my informants retreated into a state of uncommunicative confusion. This, in turn, only aggravated parental anxieties and elicited further demands for proof of 'decontamination'. A stalemate was reached in some cases; in others, only the passage of time provided the desired confidence that the Moonie 'phase' or 'episode' was definitely terminated.

This discussion would be very one-sided, however, if it did not acknowledge that, for all the distinctiveness and intensity of the situation in which ex-Moonies return to the parental home, analogous problems arise in other families for quite different reasons. For example, there are strong similarities between the positions of the ex-Moonie and of the young person who returns home after unexpectedly running away. Weaker parallels might also be found with the moral status of the convicted delinquent who is released from custody into the care of parents. And there may be even more remote similarities with the place in the parental home of an unmarried mother. The social processes by which disavowals, confessions of guilt, and professions of contrition are extracted by means of 'alienative coalitions' and image-management are broadly similar. The 'panic' about cults and ex-cultists is definitely not without precedent.

It should also be pointed out that, partly as a result of the nuclear family's loss of direct responsibility for many aspects of its members' social lives, there are now few counterweights to the intense emotions that are cultivated among people living in close proximity to each other. Many cases of parental anger and frustration with a Moonie illustrate the vulnerability of social bonds in the nuclear family when very few points of common interest or ambition exist among the family members. Elsewhere (Beckford 1981a) I have tried to show that the quality of parent–child relations prior to recruitment to the UC is an important determinant of family response to the Moonie and the ex-Moonie alike. Some parents and ex-Moonies were surprised by the strength of their emotional response to what, in other people's opinion, amounted to nothing more than the necessary process whereby adult children leave their family of origin. It seems that the increasingly specialized focus of the nuclear family does not make this process any smoother. Cult controversies may therefore present in microcosm the kind of wider problems that writers such as Sennett (1970, 1977) and Gordon (1972) have diagnosed in the modern nuclear family in general. Contrary to the belief that 'modern man has suffered from a deepening condition of "homelessness"' (Berger, Berger, and Kellner 1974: 77), it could be argued that today's NRMs are evidence of a reaction against home-centredness and that anti-cultism is an assertion of the primacy of family relations over all others.

Finally, a point which is usually overlooked in discussions of the relationship between NRMs and families is that most parents who are confronted with the problems arising from a child's membership of, or disengagement from, a 'cult' are themselves at a point in their own life-cycle and in the development of their personal relations with spouses, other sexual partners, and ageing relatives where peculiarly sensitive decisions may have to be made. It is often a time when 'life investments' (Rappoport, Rappoport, and Fogarty 1971: 271) are re-evaluated with varying degrees of ease and success. The eruption of serious difficulties with young adult children may be experienced as a further aggravation of already severe mid-life problems.

Many parents whom I interviewed also hinted that it was especially frustrating to watch their Moonie children apparently wasting their prospects for successful careers and marriages at a time when their own careers and marriages were entering a phase of relative decline. In short, the peculiar volatility of Moonies' and ex-Moonies' relations with parents may be partly due to the latter's life-cycle problems. Factors internal to the dynamics of the nuclear family have certainly helped to make the process of disengagement from the UC problematic. The next chapter examines the contribution made by these problems to the public controversy about 'cults'.

Notes

1 The parallel with Synanon's course of development is striking: 'as Synanon amassed riches, its early explosive population growth had subsided, then reversed. Membership declined as rapidly as assets increased' (Gerstel 1982: 137).

2 Compare the practice of 'contract breaking' in Synanon. This alsc involves informing on colleagues and thereby breaking the bonds of friendship for the supposedly greater good of the whole community. See Gerstel 1982.

3 See McManus (1980: 50–5) for an account of temporary disengagement from the COG for the purpose of rest and prayer. She subsequently left the movement completely.

4 Research into defection from NRMs in America confirmed this point:
> 'In totalistic groups, leaving is not simply a matter of packing up and walking out the door. The individual, though estranged, remains physically and emotionally involved with what is essentially a total institution. Therefore, a public leavetaking is extremely difficult, if not impossible, for most. Because discussion is forbidden for the sake of maintaining religious solidarity, public announcement of defection would be shocking to the group and would result in tremendous social pressure being placed on the individual to repent and remain within the group.'
>
> (Skonovd 1983: 101)

5 Patricia's account was quite typical. While being interviewed she could not recall any occasion when UC members had explicitly warned her of the dangers of disengagement, but her fears were nonetheless real:
> 'Well, I believed in spirits, but it used to frighten me. I was really scared; and then, of course, coming out I used to think that, they put it in a way "Oh, something will happen". And I always thought that if I went out I'd get knocked down or, and sort of in fear all the time that something was going to happen because we'd come out of the Family ... I always felt that, you know, God would do something if people came out, that I had a chance of doing something and I let it pass.'

6 Solomon (1981: 289–90) distinguishes between ex-Moonies' nega-

tive views on the UC's organization and their more positive views on their experiences as part of its intense community.

7   On the other hand, ex-Moonies are not unlike drop-outs from the Mormon Church in Utah who were found to be more likely to abandon all religious commitment than to switch to a different religious group. The social circumstances of the two kinds of ex-member are, of course, very different, but they share a common antipathy towards further religious involvement. See Albrecht and Bahr, 1983.

8   See Greeley 1981 for comments on what it means for lay Catholics to withdraw from their church without experiencing major difficulties.

9   This contrasts with the situation of 'splitees' from Synanon who were able to capitalize on the skills learned in the movement in finding good jobs when they defected. See Gerstel 1982: 158.

10   This is the only respect in which I disagree with Kilbourne's (1982) analysis.

11   If it is true that 'the only long-term, institutionally sanctioned solution to the problem of being divorced is reassimilation into the status of "married"' (Goode 1956: 207, quoted in Hart 1976: 218), how much more difficult is the transition to the unscheduled status of ex-Moonie.

12   By contrast, Kaslow and Schwartz (forthcoming) report that four of the nine ex-cultists whom they studied in the USA had participated in psychotherapy either before or after being in a cult. For further evidence of the much higher frequency of recourse to mental health professionals in the USA than in the UK, see Galanter *et al.* 1979 and Ungerleider and Wellisch 1979.

—————— SIX ——————
Disengagement and controversy

The logic of entry and exit

One of the reasons for devoting so much of Chapter 3 to an explanation of cult controversies in terms of the mode of recruitment was to underline the point that NRMs recruit people in widely different ways. And as we saw in Chapter 4, models of disengagement imply that there is no less variety in the mode of exit than in the mode of entry. The previous chapter illustrated the extent of variation.

It will be argued in this chapter that a connection exists between entry to, and exit from, the UC. The 'way in' provides for the 'way out', as it were. This applies not only on the level of individual recruits but also on the level of NRMs as collectivities. They display distinctive profiles of disengagement. The case of the UC will then be examined in detail in order to establish its distinctiveness. The final section of the chapter will discuss the relationship between the disengagement profiles of selected NRMs and their respective contributions to cult controversies.

The accounts that ex-Moonies have given of their recruitment, participation, and disengagement demonstrate that a logic was perceived to be at work within the movement disposing them to pass through it in a certain, characteristic fashion. Three themes are prominent in their accounts of disengagement (for a more detailed analysis, see Beckford 1985a).

Challenge and failure

First, the ex-Moonies whom I interviewed repeatedly emphasized that a large part of the UC's initial attraction for them lay in the *challenge* that it put before them. They felt challenged to display the courage, determination, and energy required to work for the values which figured prominently in the movement's recruitment propaganda.[1] For example, the former wife of a Moonie reported that just before leaving his family he had said 'Pretend that it's the Crusades, and I'm going off to fight and you will stay behind until I come back'. He told his four-year-old daughter that he was 'going off to work for God' and that he would return when he had finished his work. In the words of Roddy, a much younger recruit, 'In the Unification Church, although you're you, you can belong to something; you can give everything to something. This is what appealed to me. And it was good to find so many people exactly in the same position.' What is more, the theme of challenge was kept firmly in front of Moonies during their period of membership. They were constantly reminded that their determination and stamina would be sapped by insidious temptations from satanic forces and that they carried the personal responsibility to overcome the hardships for the sake of the Reverend Moon and the movement's ideals.

About three-quarters of the ex-Moonies in my sample reported that their ostensibly positive response to the UC's challenge had actually been experimental. They were testing themselves to see whether they were capable of persevering with a commitment to ideals even though they were less than fully convinced of the intellectual grounds on which the ideals were defended by the movement. A rhetoric of heroism, sacrifice, and suffering pervaded their thoughts and conversation, as indeed it pervades the Unificationist movement as a whole.

Thus, although the UC is organized communally and can be characterized by a strong *esprit de corps*, the elementary bond between recruits and the movement appears to be a highly personal sense of commitment to the idea of subjecting self to the discipline of higher ideals. It is not the movement which is on trial: it is the members' own determination to make their commitment succeed.

I infer from this that, as we shall see below, the grounds on which many people were recruited to the UC in the 1970s provided for the possibility of their personal failure to meet the challenge. Disengagement as a result of perceived failure to live up to self-imposed, but communally orchestrated, expectations was 'written into' the form that recruitment normally took. Accounts of disengagement are therefore permeated with expressions of personal failure.

Of course, the UC's shortcomings are also emphasized in some accounts, but it is rare for ex-Moonies to put blame on the movement as such and not on themselves at the same time. This often takes the form of statements about disappointment. Ex-members recall that they had joined the UC in expectation of reaping spiritual benefits from working hard towards the realization of ideals for themselves and the movement. They had accepted 'on trust' that it would work for a symbiosis between personal and collective ideals. But when members felt that their spiritual condition had not changed drastically and, in particular, that they did not have a better understanding of metaphysical questions than when they had joined, their disappointment began to grow.

The ex-Moonies' feelings of disappointment were a mixture of resentment against the UC for failing to honour the trust invested in it and of impatience with their own inability to continue striving to meet the challenge that the movement had initially presented. This frame of mind seemed to have made many members sensitive to minor grievances about their day-to-day life and the organization of the movement. Thus, an accumulation of complaints began to build up in their minds, but there was rarely an opportunity to discuss them openly.

Dissatisfaction with such things as managerial ineptitude, organizational inefficiency, and apparent indifference to members' problems eventually drove some members to disengage from the UC temporarily in order to re-evaluate their view of it. But even these people found it hard to separate their complaints about the movement from their sense of personal failure.

One of the most interesting aspects of the personal challenge/ failure theme is the virtually total absence of references to theological considerations. It is as if ex-Moonies lacked any awareness of how their personal case might fit into a Unificationist frame of thought other than in terms of capitulation to satanic forces and abandonment of the would-be Messiah. Certainly, none of my informants could derive any hope or consolation from Unificationist theology in the wake of their disengagement. They felt 'stranded' in the months following physical separation from the movement, for the theology offered them no grounds for optimism about their spiritual condition or prospects. Many of them retained respect for Unificationist principles but they were unable to specify how the principles related to their new-found situation. Confusion of the following kind was commonly reported:

'Well, I don't know. . . . It still seems to have made sense, and I don't know *how* it made sense. It did make sense, what I was told.

But taking all the theology apart and seeing what Moon, trying to parallel Moon with Jesus Christ and seeing that he does defend himself like Jesus Christ didn't, he does have bodyguards and does live in palatial splendour, that would logically disprove that he was the Messiah.'

This particular young man had been recruited by an elder brother but had disengaged when he realized that, amongst other things, he would not be able to indulge his love of piano playing in the UC.

The apostate malgré lui

A second theme in accounts of disengagement concerns the gradual and almost accidental nature of the process of leaving the UC. Ex-Moonies often reminded me that, had it not been for their personal failure to live up to the movement's high ideals, they would have had relatively few reasons for leaving. On an intellectual level they had come to remarkably few conclusions about the validity of *Divine Principle* but many of them were adamant that the system of Unificationist thought still worked for them on a practical level. This was a further reason why the sense of personal failure was so dominant in ex-members' accounts.

This finding accords strongly with one particular feature of the mode of recruitment to the UC, namely, the often reported shallowness of recruits' understanding of the movement's basic theology. They knew so little about its teachings and philosophy that they never managed to formulate adequate criticisms of them – even when they had formally disengaged. Their recruitment and induction had been based on their response to an existential challenge: not an intellectual proposition. And their subsequent experience of mobilization in the movement's diverse missions and enterprises also failed to bring them to a firm understanding of Unificationist principles.

One of the most perplexing features of relations between UC recruits and their close kin stems from the contrast between the members' poor grasp of Unificationist doctrine and their relatives' conviction that the recruits had become totally absorbed by an all-embracing thought system. Comparisons between ex-Moonies' accounts and those of their parents, for example, reveal a stunning degree of mutual misunderstanding. Parents usually mistook fervent devotionalism and intense enthusiasm in their children for unshakeable intellectual agreement with the movement's teachings. And members usually mistook parents' opposition to their participation in the UC for rejection of its teachings. It was only much later that both sides began to recognize the misunderstanding, but in some cases it was too late for them to change their respective opinions with dignity and without loss of 'face'.

It was rare, in the circumstances, for Moonies to report anything resembling a 'crisis of belief' for the simple reason that belief rarely played a major part in their life in the UC. As a result, the process of disengaging was usually lengthy and indecisive. The same story emerges from many of the autobiographies written by ex-Moonies.[2] All manner of social and personal commitments kept them loyal to the movement, but intellectual considerations were far from prominent. Indeed, a number of informants said that they had _wanted_ to believe in the UC's teachings but that various doubts and uncertainties had prevented them from ever developing firm beliefs. Occasionally intense or mystical experiences made many members elated but rarely led to any clearer understanding of Unificationist doctrines.

This can be partly explained in terms of the priority assigned in the UC to playing the role of Moonie at the earliest opportunity. Instead of waiting for intellectual conviction to occur, leaders encourage would-be recruits and 'trainees' to act _as if_ they were fully committed members. This 'anticipatory socialization' has been observed in other settings, for example, in the Watchtower movement (Beckford 1975c); in a UFO cult (Balch 1980); and in Scientology (Straus 1976). In each case role-playing was analytically separated from intellectual commitment and conviction. It marked the recruits' entry into members' social networks.[3] In the argot of another religious movement, Synanon, it involved 'walking the walk' rather than 'talking the talk'.

In some cases ex-Moonies reported feelings of frustration because they had been unable to identify clearly enough the intellectual reasons for their dissatisfaction with the UC. They felt strongly that it was wrong for them to remain in membership, largely because their personal dedication to Unificationist goals had waned, but they could muster very few grounds for disagreement with Unificationist doctrine.

I believe that it is significant in this connection that the practice of disfellowshipping or expelling members on doctrinal grounds seems to be rare in the UC. Some people have certainly been asked to leave for breaking the moral rules or for failing to show sufficient enthusiasm. But my informants knew of no examples of 'doctrinal' expulsion. This is really not surprising for a movement which devotes so little time to critical discussion of doctrine outside the ranks of its seminary students. Rank-and-file members in Britain reported virtually no opportunity to debate or even question any basic teachings, although they were exposed to many hours of formal lectures during the induction process. Reading the DP was also a regular practice but, again, it was rarely reported as a group activity in which criticism was encouraged. In sum, the lack of formal disfellowshipping in a supposedly totalizing movement is unusual but understandable in the light of the low priority accorded to strictly doctrinal matters among fully fledged members.

A related consideration is that the UC in the west appears to have suffered from no schisms. This may also strike an observer as strange in view of the exclusiveness of its teachings. Again, I believe that the answer can be found in the combination of exclusiveness with relatively little emphasis on doctrine. Of course, this does not apply to the seminarians, the seminary graduates, or those who have pursued graduate studies in secular universities during their participation in the UC. It applies only to the rank-and-file, for they have shown no signs of schismatic sympathies.

Observers seem to be agreed, however, that the *possibility* of schism is not out of the question among the best educated Moonies who have had the opportunity to discuss doctrine critically, especially with outside experts. Lindner (1981), for example, reports a high rate of disengagement among Moonie graduate students. Rumours have also abounded among members and ex-members about the imminence of a schism between the Koreans and the non-Koreans, or between the East and West coast 'branches' of the movement in the USA (see Mickler 1980). But unlike the schisms that have occurred in some other exclusivist, totalizing religious movements, rank-and-file Moonies appear to have little grasp of the potentially divisive intellectual issues at stake.

In the absence of a crisis of belief or of serious intellectual disagreements, many ex-Moonies simply allowed minor grievances of various kinds to accumulate until it seemed best to withdraw from the UC on a temporary basis. Some believed that they were only taking a deserved rest. But others wanted the freedom to reconsider at leisure their commitment to accepting the UC's challenge.

Regardless of the reasons for seeking a temporary withdrawal from the movement, it often served as the beginning of eventual disengagement. In some cases it provided anxious relatives, friends, and other ex-Moonies with the opportunity to talk the member out of returning to the UC. In others, the experience of freedom from pressing obligations, routines, and physical hardships proved too seductive. Some never returned to the movement, but it was more common for temporary withdrawal to precede a brief resumption of participation before disengagement finally took place.

Thus, the process of leaving the UC was slow, gradual, and halting for many of my informants. In my view this is associated with the relatively small role played by doctrinal beliefs in stimulating or sustaining membership. The opportunity to formulate intellectual arguments for or against continuing participation was simply not available and this worked against the likelihood that firm decisions could be taken. Ironically, some ex-Moonies said that they had read DP more carefully *after* disengagement than at any stage of their membership. They seemed to feel that this was the best opportunity that they had had to come to grips with the UC's basic teachings. I am definitely *not* supporting the kind of 'easy-come-easy-go' or 'revolving door' theory of involvement in the UC that is held by some anti-cultists. The bond of membership is very strong in many cases, but it happens not to be based primarily on intellectual grounds. I suspect that this may also be true for the less sensationalized phenomenon of withdrawal from more conventional, and less controversial, religious groups.[4] As a result, the process of leaving has little to do with crises of Unificationist beliefs.

Spoiled identity

A third feature of the recruitment process which colours the process of disengagement from the UC is the fact that recruits effectively cut themselves off from former friends and relatives. This means that ex-Moonies cannot count on being well received in circles where they formerly felt at home. The reasons for the suspicion that is sometimes shown towards them were sketched in the previous chapter. In essence, they have to do with the widespread construction of a notion of 'brainwashing' which diminishes the members' presumed moral capacity. They are stigmatized as people who, probably through no fault of their own, have become unstable and untrustworthy. This interpretation will be discussed later.

At the time of disengagement, the brainwashing scenario may be either rejected or repaired. My findings indicate that very few close associates of UC recruits were prepared to abandon the idea that brainwashing had been employed. It remains the most widely supported 'folk' explanation of recruitment even long after ex-Moonies have left the movement. It is my view that this scenario is retained because it would be too demeaning and painful for close relatives and friends to admit that they had been wrong about it. They also cling to it because it gives them a kind of moral power over the ex-members.[5]

In the families of ex-members, the notion of 'brainwashing' has been employed for the purpose of reminding them that their moral capacity is suspect and that they are not to be fully trusted 'until they come to their senses'. Of course, family members claim to know what the relevant criteria of 'coming to their senses' are, and the ex-Moonies' own judgements are not taken seriously. This has, in some cases, set in motion a vicious spiral of degradation followed by diminished self-respect, followed by further degradation, and so on.

For my purposes, then, the dynamics of ex-Moonies' personal relationships at home and among former friends illustrate another aspect of the intimate link between entry and exit, with the difference that in this case I have been referring to people's *perceptions* of the two processes. Thus, the perceived conditions of joining the UC help to elicit corresponding perceptions of the conditions in which people leave it. Moreover, the effects of these mutually reinforcing perceptions are felt by ex-members for a long time after disengagement.

The application of a brainwashing scenario is only one feature of the ex-members' social world. Its painful effects are aggravated by the fact that, as mainly single, young, and 'unsettled' people they have few alternative social networks at their disposal. They are not, however, in the same position as defectors from some longer-established religious movements with a constituency of families and neighbourhood networks. Such people may find themselves totally isolated from kin; excluded from their places of work; and forced to leave their neighbourhood. By contrast, ex-Moonies are more likely to be able to return to their family of origin. Ironically, of course, this only heightens the pathos of their position, since it is precisely in the confines of the family that close relatives feel qualified to ask the most probing questions and to exert the most insidious influence.

To summarize, three themes are prominent in the accounts given by ex-Moonies of their disengagement from the UC in Britain. First, the highly personal nature of the challenge accepted at the beginning of participation and the equally personal sense of failure and disappointment at the time of disengagement. Second, the weak role played by intellectual considerations in the processes of joining and leaving. And, third, the intrusive role of a brainwashing scenario in driving a moral wedge between the close relatives of members and ex-members of the UC.

It should not be forgotten, however, that the trajectory of the Moonie 'career' is also affected by factors in addition to the logic of the modes of recruitment and mobilization. The fact that in the 1970s the modal age of Moonies was in the low twenties and that they were mainly people lacking large investments in careers or domestic relationships suggests that only a small proportion would *not* have dropped out after a year or so. In other words, the progression through the movement can be interpreted as a complement to the statistically normal process of identity-seeking that takes place at this point in the life-cycle (see Levinson *et al.* 1978). In addition, Greeley (1981) makes the cogent point that, for a variety of political, economic and moral reasons, young people in the 1960s and 1970s tended to defer the act of finalizing commitments and identities to a later point in the life-cycle in comparison with earlier generations in the modern era. He even speculated that the counter-cultural generation may *never* make firm commitments and may be obliged to be constant 'switchers'. Certainly, Newport (1979) discovered that the highest rate of denominational switching in America in the mid 1970s occurred among young people. It is clearly important not to lose sight of the effect of social processes which are to some extent independent of the UC's particular influence.

Each theme illustrates the logic which connects accounts of joining the UC with accounts of leaving it; the way in and the way out. This is no accident, nor is it probably unique to the UC. But the topic has not previously been studied, so comparison with other cases is not possible at present. More research into the process of accounting for disengagement from religious groups is urgently needed. In particular, we lack information about the variety of 'routes through' each group, for it is unlikely that all members experience the same disengagement career. Research into 'conversion careers' has begun to investigate this general topic (see Beckford 1975c; J. T. Richardson 1978), but this book is the first to suggest extending the notion of 'career' to include disengagement.

A longer-term aim is to integrate findings about the patterned accounts of disengagement into models or frameworks representing NRMs' patterned modes of insertion in society (see Chapter 2). That is, the recruitment and disengagement processes would be related to what is known about the movements' collective relations with other groups, institutions, and social processes. The individual members' typical modes of participation in each movement would also be taken into account. In this way, a more complete sociological picture of the operations of NRMs could be composed than has so far been attempted.

Brainwashing and deprogramming

Running in parallel with the socio-logic which disposed people to join, participate in, and eventually disengage from the UC in a distinctive fashion, there is a corresponding interpretation of events from the point of view of anxious relatives. It basically revolves around the idea of 'brainwashing' and its putative effects on members' minds. As we shall see, the aetiology of brainwashing is methodically constructed by relatives and, in a few cases, employed to justify attempts to deprogramme Moonies. This section will analyse in detail the processes whereby the close relatives of two British Moonies constructed a brainwashing-type explanation of recruitment and then mounted a 'rescue operation'. These two cases are not at all typical of family responses in terms of their relatives' decisiveness but they are being examined at some length because they clearly illustrate the main lineaments of the *reasoning* encountered in many families. This reasoning is an important contribution to cult controversies. It goes without saying, of course, that some relatives abhor both the brainwashing scenario and the practice of deprogramming.

Failure

The first case concerns a university graduate, Martin, who joined the UC at the age of twenty-five while he was travelling in California in 1975. During a visit to his dying father in Britain he was held by his family and by two American deprogrammers and forcibly subjected to strenuous attempts to break his faith. He managed to escape, however, and returned to the UC in London. He had been a Moonie for two years at the time of the interview I conducted with his elder brother and sister-in-law.

The first point to make about this case is that the recruitment took place abroad. His close relatives knew nothing about the UC and they found it very difficult to communicate with Martin about his commitment to the movement. Their frustration and puzzlement developed into alarm when it seemed to them that he was showing entirely uncharacteristic indifference to his father's illness.

Nevertheless, they eventually pieced together sufficient 'clues' from their correspondence and telephone conversations with Martin to be able to explain what had happened to him.

In the light of subsequent events, Martin's sister-in-law found it helpful to delve into his past and to interpret certain conduct as indicative of a disposition to do something drastic. It was thought significant, for example, that a long-standing relationship with a girl friend had deteriorated and that Martin had possibly been implicated in some drugs-related illegality immediately before reaching California.

The reconstruction of events after Martin's affiliation with the UC drew on such things as the perceived difficulty of communicating with him:

'it wasn't Martin. There was somebody with him, and you knew there was somebody with him. . . . We did notice his letters were getting a bit obscure, you know. . . . He sounded sort of delirious, way-out voice.

'So [Martin's father] thought he had nothing else to do but write a letter to him saying "Come home". Of course, when it didn't have any effect, his father got worried. . . . Nobody knew how to handle the situation. . . . Do you know, he couldn't tell us which flight he was coming on, what airplane he was on, he didn't know anything.'

The assumption that 'something must have happened to Martin' had been implanted soon after his affiliation to the UC, but his conduct during the visit to his father provided clinching evidence:

'We took him to a pub deliberately, you know. . . . He said it was a den of iniquity . . . But you couldn't get him away from drink once. I said "Oh, come on, you used to love it." But he thought it was dreadful.'

'[Martin] gets the salt, the holy salt, and puts salt round his meal and all these kinds of things. I mean, Martin – the old Martin – he'd have laughed at all this, wouldn't he? . . . He would have said "You're crazy" . . . yes, "Crackers". He would have had a great laugh.'

The conviction that Martin had been brainwashed grew stronger as it became clear to his close relatives that his mind was not functioning normally. Thus: 'We could see him filling the visa

application form in, and he couldn't think; he could hardly write . . .
He filled quite a few things in wrong. I said "God, look at that.". . . .
He absolutely couldn't think for himself.' These kinds of perception
made it relatively easy for the relatives to decide that deprogramming
was necessary. They had learned about it from contacts in FAIR, the
British anti-cult organization. Moreover, their faith in deprogramming increased while the process was actually taking place:

'Although we realized he was brainwashed we didn't realize the
full implications of this. At least we thought he was brainwashed.
We didn't realize how much he was brainwashed, and actually the
more we went through [the deprogramming], the more we realized
that it should be done.'

Perhaps even more significant was Martin's brother's conviction
that, although the deprogramming had failed, it ought to be repeated. Martin's powers of resistance were interpreted as yet more
proof that his mind had been controlled.

There has been a tendency in academic circles to consider belief in
brainwashing and deprogramming as irrational or ideological. Leaving aside the question of whether it is morally and legally defensible,
it is clear that Martin's close relatives had constructed a consistent
'vocabulary of motives' to account for his actions. They were
consistent in relating the 'evidence' to the 'explanation'. The choice
of deprogramming as a remedy for their problems was also rationally
related to their understanding of brainwashing. In short, reasons
were implicitly and explicitly given for their beliefs and actions.
Indeed, the problem of Martin's affiliation had preoccupied his
relatives for so long and so intensely that they had been obliged to
think the matter through repeatedly. There is consequently no lack of
method, consistency, and means–end rationality in their account.

Success

There are many differences between Martin's case and that of
Marilyn, who joined the UC in Britain during the first few weeks of a
teacher-training course at a college less than a hundred miles from
her parents' home. She quickly went into residence with the Moonies
and resigned from her course. But her parents tricked her into their
car and drove her home for the purpose of informally deprogramming her. After three days of argument she renounced the UC and, at
the time of interview with both her and her parents, was coming to
the end of a fresh course of teacher training.

Marilyn's parents' initial opinion of the Moonies with whom she was living was quite favourable. It was only when she insisted on donating the proceeds of a considerable legacy to the UC that suspicions were roused. In response to her father's protests to the group leaders,

'They were extremely impudent over the phone, and from that time onwards Marilyn completely broke with us, didn't know us any more. We rushed up to Angleton several times. She looked through us like a piece of glass, rigid. Nothing. She wanted to have nothing to do with us. . . . She was obviously not herself.'

Marilyn's father doggedly tracked down every scrap of information that he could trace about the UC. He contacted the police, a lawyer, a Member of Parliament, a University chaplain, and an ex-Moonie. But it was Marilyn's college tutor's advice which finally convinced him of the need for drastic action: 'It was obvious to me there was something very wrong, and the Tutor said "Well, I tell you in confidence she's out of her mind; she is disturbed, mentally disturbed. And if I were you I would take her away."' On the pretence of taking her to a restaurant, Marilyn's parents drove her home despite her protests. She was kept under constant surveillance for three days and isolated from all contact with the outside world. As in Martin's case, the distressing experience of forcible deprogramming nevertheless strengthened her relatives' conviction that it was absolutely necessary:

'She cried for three hours and she was most distressed. She looked like a ghost, an absolute ghost. She had a rash all over her face; she had a running ear. She was unrecognizable, physically and mentally unrecognizable.'

According to both Marilyn and her parents, it was the allegations of the Reverend Moon's implication in questionable political-cum-commercial activities which eventually led her to blurt out in distress, 'All you say is right. It all fits. How did you find out? How did you discover? It's true what you say.' After about three weeks Marilyn had gained sufficient emotional stability to face the world again and to begin thinking of taking another course of teacher training. Despite the speed of her 'deconversion' Marilyn insisted that she would not voluntarily have left the UC. In fact, she was certain that she would still have been a Moonie, three years after the event, if she had not been deprogrammed.

The very idea of professional deprogramming had reportedly filled Marilyn's parents with horror, but they were nevertheless convinced of the correctness of their own actions. In justifying it they reasoned rationally from 'evidence' to 'inference'. They were certain that her mind had been controlled and misappropriated. Her poor physical condition only strengthened their resolve to remove her from the UC at all costs. The 'information' that they had energetically sought about the movement was all consistently interpreted as supportive of the need for action which would, in different circumstances, be indefensible.

Brainwashing discourse

Three general features of the logic connecting allegations of brainwashing with justifications of deprogramming call for discussion.

In the first place, allegations of brainwashing conveyed an image of the UC member as the kind of person who might either fall voluntarily for this type of NRM or fall victim to its techniques of recruitment. Martin's brother was insistent, for example, that he had been 'searching for something' in his late teens and that 'he got worse when he went to university'. His sister-in-law even confessed to feeling some guilt for failing to take Martin's existential questioning seriously and therefore 'letting him down'. The recruit is thereby represented as a victim of various circumstances. Similarly, Marilyn's parents implicitly described her as 'convertible' in terms of some childhood traumas, religious confusion, and a strong need for companionship. In her father's words,

'She was a little – not a misfit – no certainly not. I shouldn't say a misfit, but she didn't know herself. She didn't know what she was all about. She was searching. . . . She was very isolated. She was not one of those popular girls because, again, she was a very tense youngster, always tense . . . She would have been a complete pushover, let me put it that way, for the Unification Church.'

Second, strong contrasts between the before-and-after states of recruits serve to justify the inference that recruiting methods must have been exceptionally forceful. The cumulative effect of scattered references to radical personality changes, incongruous emotions, and cognitive problems is to deny that recruits could be held responsible for themselves and to justify action which might otherwise be considered unjustifiable. As Martin's sister-in-law put it,

'You know, he is brainwashed, no matter what you think and how he is at the moment. Sometimes I think I could hit him right in the face. Then I think "No, he's brainwashed and it's not Martin".' Marilyn's father made a similar point: 'I realized very quickly that she was brainwashed. . . . She had this sort of glazed look. . . . I realized that she was not with us. . . . She was no more my Marilyn, she was quite a different person.'

Third, accounts of brainwashing imply that the UC is the kind of movement that would try, or wish, to brainwash people into joining. As much effort is therefore put into explaining its goals and practices as into understanding its recruits' position. In fact, the victim-like status of recruits in accounts of brainwashing and deprogramming seems to have the curious effect of relegating them to a position of secondary importance. Consequently, attention is focused on the claim that exceptional measures need to be taken against the UC for being the kind of organization which brainwashes its recruits.

A number of commentators have remarked on the way in which the image or metaphor of brainwashing can be employed as an ideological weapon (Robbins, Anthony, and McCarthy 1980), and its centrality to sensationalist accounts of NRMs in the mass-media cannot be ignored (Robbins and Anthony 1978). My purpose has been, however, to show that it also figures as the lynchpin for some personal accounts of recruitment to the UC and for justifications of deprogramming. It may serve rationally to explain, excuse, justify, and accuse. Whatever the mythical or demonological status of 'brainwashing', we should not overlook the fact and manner of its effective operation in personal accounts of experience.

Exit and controversy

The aim of this section is to examine the contributions made by the mode of disengagement from the UC to cult controversies. We saw in Chapter 5 that this movement's way of recruiting members fuelled various controversies: we shall now show that the fate of ex-Moonies also feeds into disquiet about NRMs in general and the UC in particular.

One could be excused for thinking that the close relatives of people who had disengaged from the UC would have lost or abandoned most of their reasons for criticizing it. After all, they had 'got their loved one back'. But the nature of the disengagement process, combined with some other social conditions, is such that some relatives of ex-Moonies actually intensified their anti-cult activities. One reason for this is that they felt freed from the fear of 'emotional blackmail': they no longer had to worry that relations with the member would be severed in retaliation for their outspoken criticism of the movement. Some also reasoned that they were demonstrating how much they cared for the ex-member by attacking an organization which had allegedly harmed him or her. In fact, several ex-Moonies confided that they were appalled by their parents' persistent grudge against the UC because it made them feel more protective towards their former friends in the movement than was their personal inclination.

Another reason for the continued involvement in anti-cultism of the parents of ex-Moonies is that they believed they had an obligation to help others to 'get their children back'. Some felt that they had to discharge a debt of gratitude towards the anti-cult organization which had supported them. They also knew that their success could raise morale in anti-cult circles and that their special expertise was sought after. In some cases, this outlook was also shared by the ex-member in the same family. On the whole, however, ex-Moonies gave very few indications of interest in attacking the UC or even of dissuading people from joining.

As a result, formal anti-cult organizations in Britain have enjoyed the support of people who had already achieved their goal of 'liberating' a member from the UC. Similarly, I found that such people were, in their own terms, no less antagonistic towards the movement at the time of interview than they had reportedly been while their child was still a Moonie. They therefore contributed strongly towards the controversy surrounding NRMs. As we shall see, this was partly because they had personally witnessed the process of disengagement and were consequently able to expose further controversial features of the UC.

From the point of view of anti-cultists, the parents or other close relatives of ex-members of NRMs are vitally important evidence in support of the main theories of 'cult control' and 'coercive conversion'. The fact that some people leave the UC, return to the parental home, and eventually become 'normal' again is sometimes used as proof that they must previously have been deliberately manipulated. The reasoning is that, if an authentic religious conversion had taken place, recruitment would have been a slower process and disengagement would not have taken place at all. In other words, the combined effect of swift induction and equally peremptory withdrawal is believed to be an indictment of the UC's authenticity. The logic of the reasoning is not at issue here. What matters is that the testimony of people who had witnessed the whole process from start to finish has great moral and tactical value for the anti-cult movement.

Of prime importance to parents was the observation that ex-Moonies had taken an apparently long time (if ever) to break entirely free from the UC. The reluctance to talk about their experiences, to denounce the movement out of hand, and to rid themselves of Unificationist literature were all interpreted as signs that the manipulative power was still working against the ex-members' presumed good sense.[6] Parents often described the first few months after disengagement in terms of a dramatic struggle between the forces of reason and unreason. These painful experiences confirmed their belief that the UC was harmful to its members and that the effects could not be easily shaken off. It is worth emphasizing at this point that the ex-members' own accounts were given in very different terms.

Parents also tended to interpret continuing friction between the ex-Moonie and themselves or siblings as further proof of the UC's allegedly pernicious influence. Many had been shocked to discover that personal relations in the family did not immediately revert to their former state, and they could only explain it in terms of the movement's lingering influence. Some parents virtually isolated the ex-member from siblings for fear that the influence would be infectious. Some households had strict rules about even discussing the member or ex-member in front of siblings. As the father of John, a former Welsh factory worker, commented:

> 'Well, see, the only problem that I would find with [John's membership of the UC] in the family is sometimes the wife would talk about John. . . . She would go on and on, and I would say "Well, it's all right to talk about John for so long but don't keep on. . . . Let's talk about him while the other kids are in bed or some other time. You needn't talk when everybody's listening because they say to themselves 'Well, what is this sort of thing that John is in?'."'

By contrast, very young siblings of members were in some cases considered helpful in preventing an ex-member from withdrawing completely from family interaction.

A 'silent bargain' was struck to the effect that the UC would not be discussed in order to avoid antagonizing the ex-member or exciting the curiosity of siblings. In a few cases the parents had also been concerned not to make siblings jealous of all the attention being lavished on the Moonie or ex-Moonie in the family.

Leaving aside folk theories of lingering Unificationist influence, other considerations reportedly weighed heavily with a few parents. They had been ashamed of their child's involvement with the UC, and various ruses had been used to conceal the facts: he or she had found work elsewhere or had gone travelling abroad. But the ex-member's return home in less than ideal circumstances had proved more difficult to conceal or to accept. It seemed to them that the problem had not become easier: it had simply changed. The Prodigal Son scenario had not come true.

The overwhelming majority of people whom I interviewed, however, did not share these views. They had obviously been delighted to have the ex-Moonie back at home and had been prepared to do whatever was necessary to cope with the problems that arose. Interpersonal friction eventually died down in most cases; talk of the UC was no longer taboo; and fears of a 'relapse' subsided. But this is not to say that the animus against the UC slackened. A wide range of anxieties and complaints about practical and material aspects of the ex-Moonie's life continued to keep many relatives active in anti-cult activities.

Accusations that the UC was irresponsible ran like a *leitmotiv* through accounts of problems that occurred to ex-Moonies. It may seem paradoxical to an onlooker that people who had campaigned for years in some cases to retrieve their child from the UC should then complain about its alleged lack of responsibility towards ex-members. But this is actually a continuation of grievances voiced about the movement at all stages of their child's involvement. They are variations on the same basic themes that were sketched in Chapter 5 but with the added twist that the UC is said to be irresponsible towards ex-members.

There is, for example, resentment at what was widely regarded as the indecent haste with which ailing members were removed from Unificationist Centres and taken home with little or no warning – in some cases, it seems, against their will. The father of Melody who had been flown back to England from missionary work overseas suffering from an undiagnosed brain tumour requiring extensive surgery and convalescence was indignant because,

'At no time had the Church attempted to get in touch with her. Not a note "How are you getting on?" Not a letter – nothing. . . . I had written a letter to [a leader] explaining how, what I thought of his dumping Melody when she was in this critical stage, when she was nearly dead, on our doorstep more or less. . . . I want to warn other people of the dangers of being a member of the Church. The dangers, in my opinion, being this attitude toward the lower members of disinterest in them if something happens to them. If the member becomes ill and is no more use to them, they get rid of them.'

He did, however, admit that the UC provided adequate supervision of Melody's health when she rejoined it after fourteen months at home.

The case of Geoffrey, a former sales assistant in his early twenties at the time of interview with his mother, illustrates a similar theme but with a different ending. He had been travelling the world with the UC for two years in the mid 1970s when his mother was informed that he would be coming home from Japan:

'[The Moonies] never mentioned anything about him being ill or anything – just said they were bringing him home. . . . When he came in he didn't recognize anybody. He was absolutely drained, physically and mentally. We had to undress him; we even had to put him into bed, he was so incapable of doing anything. Of course I rang the doctor first thing the next morning, and they got him into hospital that night. And he was in there about a month, I think. Maybe a little longer.'

In the following two years Geoffrey was hospitalized three times and made repeated attempts to rejoin the UC. His employer was dissatisfied with his work, and the Moonies, according to his mother, simply refused to accept him as a member. They sent him home from the London Headquarters:

'[The Moonies] said they'd had a talk to him, and he was coming back home. "We've put him in a taxi to go back to the station." . . . When my husband went out early on the [next day] he was stood on the doorstep. He said "Hello, I'm back" and went and shook hands with his father, a thing he's never done in his life. And he came to me and said "Hello, what's your name?" That's how far he was gone mentally.'

But Geoffrey had never been critical of the UC. He was discharged from a mental hospital on the day of my interview with his mother, and at that time she saw no solution to the bind that he was in. She put the blame squarely on the UC for adversely affecting his health and then rejecting him.

Another 'casualty' of work in Japan was Jennifer who had spent a total of three years in the UC before begging her grandfather to pay for a ticket home from Tokyo. She arrived at her parents' house unexpectedly and in a poor physical condition one month later. She has never explained why she wanted to leave Japan nor why she left the UC within three weeks of returning to Britain.

A closely related concern of many parents was that ex-Moonies who had incomplete records of contributions to National Insurance and pension funds suffered a consequent reduction in various benefits. The UC's legal status in Britain is such that it does not make employer's contributions to those funds, and members can voluntarily contract out of the benefit schemes. This is the reason given by some parents for preventing members from giving all their property to the UC. The property was either kept at home as an inducement to return or sold for cash and invested in savings accounts on the Moonie's behalf. These real or imaginary fears that their children would suffer materially only confirmed many parents in the belief that the movement exploited its rank-and-file members by extracting copious labour in return for board, lodging, and pocket money. The father of Philip, a university drop-out, felt that his son was 'being cheated of something big, and he's being cheated by a guy miles and miles away who doesn't care enough about truth. *He* seems to be feathering his nest very successfully.' In addition to the anger, there were widespread fears that ex-Moonies would be destitute if they received no assistance from their family.

Some parents also accused the UC of irresponsibility towards its members' and ex-members' material possessions. Clothes were usually pooled, with the consequence that they could rarely be returned to their owners when required. Similarly, goods such as record players, records, and musical instruments could not always be retrieved at the time of disengagement. In two cases known to me, parents forced their way into UC Centres in the search for property belonging to their children who had left the movement and could not face the prospect of collecting the property themselves. In one angry confrontation parents had to shuttle back and forth between two buildings in one city for three hours before they managed to collect most of the electronic equipment and records that belonged to their son.

Matters were made worse in some cases by the fact that

ex-Moonies had difficulty finding suitable employment after leaving the UC. It took an average of six months for my informants to settle into a job which offered satisfaction and reasonably good prospects. Given the sharp deterioration of labour market conditions since the mid 1970s, it is likely that today's defectors face a much more difficult task in this respect. Some were still unsettled at the time of interview, however, and others were taking educational and training courses. But they showed little resentment towards the movement for interrupting their employment or education. Their parents, by contrast, were mostly horrified by what they saw as the abandonment of good opportunities and prospects.[7] Consequently, the parents of ex-Moonies tended to blame the UC for their children's material problems.

Although none of the ex-Moonies whom I interviewed had been married by the Reverend Moon, their parents, no less than the parents of practising members in my sample, had strong feelings about the matter. The idea of 'arranged marriages' was in itself repulsive to many, but their worst fears were reserved for the fate envisaged for the children of Moonies who disengaged from the movement. There was a widely anticipated fear that ex-Moonie parents, deprived of the support of the movement, would be incapable of looking after young children and that marriages might also be vulnerable. Another worry was that children would become victims of legal and emotional struggles if one parent remained in the UC while the other defected.

I interviewed only one set of parents who had disengaged from the UC, but they had been married before affiliation. Their child had also been born shortly before they joined the movement. They do not therefore fit strictly into the category which worried so many people. Nevertheless, this case did illustrate some of the anticipated difficulties facing ex-Moonies who had children. On a material level, for example, they had been obliged to live for a few months with the wife's parents in a small house until they qualified for local authority housing. The husband was too disturbed by the process of leaving the Moonies to be able to contemplate full-time work, so their income came solely from state benefits and gifts. It was only after one year that he obtained a grant to resume architectural studies at a local college. A year later, at the time of interview, he was still very unsure of his career prospects. He gave the impression that, were it not for his wife and child, he would never have left the UC and that he was still feeling strongly attracted to its ethos and community.

In separate interviews, both husband and wife admitted that they were each uncertain about the other's attitudes towards the UC. In fact, each one asked me for my opinion about the other's 'real' attitude. The topic was still too sensitive to be discussed openly two years after they had formally ceased being Moonies. But their close relatives were clearly aware of the problem and had brought it to the attention of an anti-cult organization and a clergyman.

Exit and mode of insertion

In the final section of this chapter I want to draw together several strands of argument in order to weave a more unified pattern of the relations between the UC's mode of insertion in society, its distinctive profile of disengagement and its contributions to cult controversies.

In the early and mid 1970s the UC operated in Britain very largely through small teams of fund-raisers who toured the country raising income for the movement and stimulating recruitment. Other sources of income were relatively unimportant at that time. Many British Moonies were also 'drafted' by the One World Crusade (OWC), an international force of Moonies who travelled extensively in Japan for fund-raising, promotion, and proselytism. To be a member amounted to being constantly mobilizable. Increasingly large numbers of young people voluntarily accepted what was termed 'devotee status' in Chapter 2.

At the same time, however, the rate of disengagement was high by the standards of most religious groups. The reasons for this were examined in Chapter 5, but they can be summarized as follows: people were recruited in response to the challenge to work selflessly for the revitalization and transformation of the world. Idealism was vigorously promoted, but the rigours of continuous mobilization and the inevitable disappointments of communal life eventually conspired to force many members out of the movement. Although the conviction that the Reverend Moon's teachings were both sacred and sensible persisted among many ex-Moonies, the movement could not accommodate them because they did not fit into the programme of revitalization by total mobilization.

As Chapter 3 showed, the UC's mode of social insertion as an agent of revitalization elicited hostile responses from many people and gave rise to a number of controversies centred on accusations of brainwashing, exploitation, and alienation from the family. In this chapter I have argued that the same mode of insertion occasioned a distinctive process and profile of disengagement which, in turn, added new themes to controversies about NRMs in general and the UC in particular. They concerned accusations of irresponsibility towards ailing members, adverse long-term effects on ex-Moonies' life-chances, personal relationships, and capacity for home-making.

In short, the UC's mode of insertion in British society in the mid 1970s called for a rapid, sudden, and all-absorbing form of commitment. Controversies tended to be focused on allegations of psychological manipulation, economic exploitation, and disruption of familial relationships. These accusations were challenged by the movement and by a weak alliance of NRMs which found themselves either directly or indirectly involved in similar controversies. As we shall see in later chapters, the controversy has also been coloured by sensationalism in the mass media and by the influence of parallel conflicts between NRMs and anti-cultists in other countries. They represent important 'external' conditions affecting the cult controversy in Britain and they complement the factors internal to the UC which have been analysed in this and earlier chapters.

There are several reasons for the UC's prominence in the cult controversy. Although it was never significantly larger than some other NRMs and although it was only one of several movements including the Children of God, The Divine Light Mission, and ISKCON which were indiscriminately bracketed together in public opinion as typical cults, I believe that features of the UC's particular mode of insertion in society rendered it relatively more controversial than the others in the late 1970s and the 1980s.

The intense emphasis on keeping recruits permanently engaged in fund-raising and proselytism, for example, gave rise to accusations of ruthlessness which were more difficult to level against movements which devoted less of their time to confronting the public. Moonies simply spent more time in public and were most identifiable only when they were selling things or soliciting donations. They were therefore a constant target for critics, whereas other movements came under public scrutiny more sporadically or in different contexts. Thus, the Hare Krishna followers were probably even more visible in public than the Moonies, but their dancing, their chanting, their robes, and their top-knots all helped to situate their solicitation and sales procedures in a more 'religious' framework. It is significant, therefore, that the Krishnas came in for more intense criticism from anti-cultists when they adopted the practice of wearing no distin-guishing garb in fund-raising activities.

The social standing of Moonies also added to their movement's controversial nature. They were mainly white, middle-class, well-educated, and 'clean living' young people. They did not therefore conform with the public stereotype of 'cultists'. Moreover, they tended to have friends and close relatives who were in a position to influence some opinion-makers. Journalists also responded readily to the suggestion that there might be a scandal attached to the recruitment of relatively well-placed young people.

In addition, adverse publicity about the Moonies in the USA was given exposure in the British mass media at the very time when their presence was first being commented on. Sensationalist reports of the UC's allegedly dangerous character coloured the public response to the movement even before Moonies had become publicly visible in Britain.[8] The 'cult syndrome' therefore preceded their activity and prejudiced the public response. To some extent this was a function of the movement's multinational form of organization, for its critics capitalized on the charge that the UC was a co-ordinated conspiracy to abduct the youth of many countries. In time, of course, other controversial charges were levelled at it for attempting to buy political influence in Washington and for complicity in the Reverend Moon's conviction for tax evasion in the USA. Again, these charges were given extensive exposure in the British press and were fully exploited by anti-cult propagandists.

Finally, as Chapter 7 explains, the UC's aggressive reaction against what it saw as concerted attacks on its integrity helped to increase its already controversial character. Threats of libel suits were made against numerous individuals and newspapers, and at least three cases were actively prosecuted. The Moonies acquired a reputation for being litigious and thereby emulated the position of Scientology in the 1960s.

In terms of the framework outlined in Chapter 2, the internal and external factors making the UC controversial are associated with its primary mode of insertion as an agent of revitalization in the 1970s. That is, its socio-logic disposed it to generate a fast 'through-put' of young, energetic, talented recruits – with all the consequent prob-lems analysed in the last two chapters. The combination of forceful fund-raising/proselytism with a form of organization based on com-munities of devotees created a very distinctive controversy.

In the 1980s, however, the character of the controversy changed somewhat in response to the UC's modified mode of insertion. The revitalizing ideology is unchanged but it is now associated with a more varied set of strategies. The emphasis appears to have shifted away from the mobilization of young fund-raisers towards the creation of Unificationist businesses, staffed mainly by long-serving Moonies, which not only provide the movement's main source of revenue but also assist in the penetration of Unificationist principles into many areas of public life. Moonies are beginning to work openly in fields as diverse as academia, banking, commerce, manufacturing industry, fishing, publishing, and service industries.

The movement's social composition is also changing. The modal age of Moonies has risen; the length of service now tends to exceed several years; and the numbers of married couples with children have increased sharply. Since it no longer recruits large numbers of young, unattached, totally mobilizable individuals, the rate of defection has slowed down. It would be reasonable to assume, then, that the social situation of those who disengaged from the UC nowadays is different from that of most of my informants.

The movement's new strategy could be described as collective infiltration of selected institutional spheres. At the same time, however, the development of the Home Church Movement indicates a move towards a more individualist form of association with the UC and, correspondingly, a less collectivist mode of social insertion. That is, associate members may retain their jobs and home outside the movement whilst continuing to participate in Unificationist activities. Their personal influence on families, friends, and colleagues may help to improve understanding of the UC's teachings and practices.

I believe that the new strategies, taken together, represent a broadening of the UC's mode of social insertion. Not surprisingly, fresh grounds for controversy have also arisen. Accusations of political intrigue, legal chicanery, and questionable business practices, for example, began in the late 1970s to complement the older charges of brainwashing, exploitation, and irresponsibility.

By contrast, NRMs with different modes of insertion in society have generated different grounds for controversy. Movements which primarily offer a refuge from evil or illusion, for example, are accused of facilitating charismatic despotisms. The history of the Children of God and Synanon illustrates this most clearly. The former evolved from an evangelical rescue mission to teenagers into an exclusivist millenarian refuge dominated by the apparently arbitrary and unchecked power of a single leader, David 'Moses'

Berg. Each lurch towards a new direction of development for the movement has elicited a corresponding outcry among its critics. Thus, nomadism, begging, anti-Americanism, anti-semitism, and the use of sex for evangelistic purposes have all fuelled the controversies surrounding the Children of God and, by unfair implication, other NRMs as well.

Synanon's evolution from a drug and alcohol rehabilitation facility, through an idealistic community of alternative life-styles, to a full-fledged religious movement requiring absolute commitment and obedience (Ofshe 1980; Gerstel 1982) illustrates not just a distinctive pattern of change but, more interestingly, a unique pattern of combinations. For, even in its intensely religious phase as a refuge beginning in the late 1970s, Synanon remained partly dependent on operations dating from its previous forms of activity. It therefore combined the continuing solicitation of free goods from organizations in the private and public sectors with the collection of state benefits for its resident population of former addicts and delinquents; with the production and sale of advertising notions; with investment in real estate; and with the collection of fees and donations from voluntary participants in the Synanon 'Game'. Indeed, this diversity of operations lent the movement considerable resilience when it came under severe attack in the late 1970s in courts of law and in the mass media for allegedly brutalizing its members and physically attacking or intimidating outsiders. Controversy is centred on the position of devotees in the residential communities. It could be hypothesized that the level of controversy surrounding Synanon was reduced by skilful management of public relations which countered criticism of specific activities with evidence of 'redeeming' activities in other parts of the movement. In this way, one aspect was played off against another, and a general picture of the movement's direction of overall development was obscured.

NRMs whose primary mode of social insertion entails the provision of services to a clientele have, ironically, tended to be controversial first and foremost in respect of their communities of devotees. Both Scientology and the Rajneesh Foundation, for example, have been accused of allowing the residential staff in certain centres to ride roughshod over the feelings and interests of neighbouring communities. East Grinstead in Britain and Antelope, Oregon have been the sites of considerable controversy over real estate purchases; planning or zoning regulations; proselytizing among local people; aggressive defence of property boundaries; exercising concerted political influence in the neighbourhood; and the problem of 'runaways'.

In addition, controversies directly related to the movements' training and therapeutic services have occasionally attracted public attention. Some former clients have sued Scientology for deception, and in some countries attempts have been made (unsuccessfully in most cases) to enact legislation designed either to prohibit the sale of such services by unlicensed therapists or to impose disproportionately harsh penalties on religious movements found guilty of fraudulent healing claims (see Chapter 9).

In summary, then, NRMs' differential modes of insertion in society provide for different bases of public controversy. As we shall see below, however, public sentiment and organized anti-cultism do not tend to make fine enough distinctions between movements and between the grounds for complaint.

Notes

1   See also Barker 1981.

2   See the list on p. 147.

3   Compare Kotre's question and answer about a sample of one hundred Catholic graduate students,

> 'What makes one person view an ambiguous fluid set of beliefs, values and information about the Church and see one structure emerging, while someone else viewed the same set of beliefs, values and information and saw a different structure emerging? The answer seemed to lie in the web of interpersonal relationships in which these people were situated, in the past as well as in the present.'
>
> (Kotre 1971: 53)

4   Newport's (1979) analysis of a large sample of American adults shows that the factors disposing most people to 'switch' from one religious group to another were associated with a desire to practise religion either alongside people of similar socio-economic status or alongside a spouse from a different religious group.

5   See Beckford 1983d for further details.

6   I suspect that parents were hoping to hear something analogous to the first confession of Alcoholics Anonymous: 'I am powerless over alcohol and . . . my life has become unmanageable.'

7   This is a particularly sore point with the German parents of Moonies according to Hardin and Kehrer 1982.

8   See Wilson 1981b for perceptive remarks on the 'anticipatory' aspects of cult controversies.

SEVEN

The public response to
new religious movements in Britain

Many new religious movements in the west can be compared with multi- or transnational corporations in so far as they operate in different countries without apparent detriment to either their unity or their standardization. They are all controlled to varying degrees by a single leader or a centralized leadership. And there is evidence to suggest that, although the boundaries of nation states are normally adopted as bases for the movements' administrative divisions, resources are often transferred between countries in accordance with international strategies for development.

One of the concomitants of the multinational character of NRMs such as Scientology, the Unification Church, the International Krishna Consciousness Society, and the Divine Light Mission is that it is more difficult than in the case of movements confined to a single country to identify the factors accounting for their relative success or failure. The rate of their membership growth, the value of their property holdings, their economic viability, and their public prestige all vary with factors transcending the boundaries of any particular country. It is important never to lose sight of the fact that these movements appear to be deliberately managed by leaders seeking maximal effectiveness in the largest possible market.

Nevertheless, it is clear that the deliberate 'marketing' of the multinational NRMs is refracted differently in different countries and that part of the task of understanding these movements sociologically is to examine carefully the ways in which the public in each country responds to them. Such a response is complex and subtle.

This chapter will consider the public response to selected NRMs in Britain under four headings.[1] It will begin with the legal and constitutional framework within which religious groups operate; the second section will consider the strength of organized opposition to NRMs; the third topic will be the self-defence measures adopted by NRMs; and finally, the treatment of NRMs in the mass media will be analysed.

The fact that most of the illustrative evidence cited below concerns the Unification Church (UC) indicates that this particular movement has recently elicited by far the strongest public response in Britain. Scientology is the only other NRM to have been at the centre of major controversy in Britain, first in the late 1960s and again in 1984.[2]

The establishment

In considering the public response to NRMs in Britain, it is essential to begin by emphasizing that there is no requirement in English or Scottish law for religious groups to be registered or officially approved as such. Nor is there any official or even semi-official list of groups defined as NRMs. On the other hand there are complex procedures whereby any group of people wishing to constitute themselves as a legal entity for the purpose of holding property or engaging in commercial activities must apply for legal recognition. Most religious groups conform with this requirement, but they are not treated differently in this respect from the way in which non-religious groups are treated. On the other hand, the category 're-ligious' does have special significance in the legislation relating to groups which apply to the Charity Commissioners, a government department, for registration of their aims as charitable in law.[3] Such organizations benefit from various legal provisions exempting them, for example, from the burden of certain forms of taxation.

The struggle between cults and anti-cults has been carried into the murky waters of the English law on charities. Matters came to a head in March 1981 when the UC failed to win an action for libel against the *Daily Mail* newspaper in the High Court.[4] At the end of the longest ever libel case in British legal history the jury recommended, in extremely unusual and forceful terms, that 'the tax-free status of the UC should be investigated by the Inland Revenue Department on the grounds that it is a political organization'. The public outcry against the movement following this verdict was so vociferous and widespread that the Charity Commissioners came under pressure in 1983 to revoke the charitable status of the Holy Spirit Association for the Unification of World Christianity and of the Sun Myung Moon Foundation (registered respectively, in 1968 and 1974) on the grounds that both organizations are 'fronts' for the Unification Church's commercial and/or political undertakings.

The Commissioners were eventually persuaded, partly in response to a motion signed by more than 180 Members of Parliament, to reverse an earlier decision and to undertake a review of the UC's registration as a charity. Other government departments were also said to be considering appropriate action in the light of the jury's verdict and recommendation. At the time of writing, however, the Charity Commissioners' view was that they had found no reason to remove the UC's two charitable organizations from the Register of Charities. As reported in *The Guardian* on 18 March 1983, the Commissioners' opinion was that,

> 'as a matter of law, the teaching and practice of [the UC's] divine principle, which are referred to in the objects of the two institutions, do not go beyond the very wide bounds which have been applied by the court for the purpose of ascertaining whether or not the propagation and practice of any particular religious creed is charitable in law.'

This opinion has met with widespread opposition and with plans to introduce legislation which would tighten the criteria of charitable status to the point where the Moonies' organizations would necessarily be excluded. The Attorney-General's determination to press ahead with fresh legislation was said to have the Prime Minister's full support in 1984, but it is expected to be a long time before the plans materialize.

Successive British governments have responded to demands for a variety of legislative or executive actions against NRMs by requesting evidence of either illegality or social harmfulness before agreeing to investigate such demands. In 1977, for example, the Under Secretary of State for the Home Office told the House of Commons that if new religious movements,

> 'keep within the law, it is a very serious matter indeed to suggest that the Government should take action against them none the less. My right Hon. Friend and I may as individuals take the view that the doctrines advanced by [the Reverend Moon] are lunatic. We may be particularly suspicious of the motives of people who, while claiming to benefit humanity, have substantially enriched themselves. But these are matters of opinion, and surely it is one of

the principles of a free society that people may propagate ideas which the majority of us do not share and do not like.'

(*Hansard*, 23 February 1977)[5]

The only major exception to this strategy was the combined effort by the Minister of Health and the Home Secretary in 1968 to ban foreign nationals from entering the country for the purpose of studying Scientology (Wallis 1976). The Home Office stated in mid 1980 that 'The ban on foreign Scientologists in general remains. A review is going on' (*The Times* 19 June 1980). But partly in response to a petition signed by ninety-two Members of Parliament to have the ban lifted, the Home Secretary announced on 16 July 1980 that the restrictions on Scientologists were being immediately removed. He based the change of policy on the view of the Secretary of State for Health and Social Services that there was insufficient evidence on medical grounds to continue to discriminate against Scientology.

A much less public, and thus less publicized, instance of official interference in the affairs of a minority religious movement began in the mid 1970s when the Attorney-General authorized a quasi-judicial inquiry into the Exclusive Brethren (see Wilson 1983). He was responding to ex-members' complaints to the Charity Commissioners about the Brethren's practice of withdrawing from social relations with people 'convicted' of compromising the movement's spiritual purity. The Charity Commissioners showed ambivalence towards the opinion of Mr Hugh Francis, QC, who had been commissioned to conduct the inquiry, that the Brethren's practices were 'contrary to public policy'. Nevertheless, it was decided that no further applications for the registration of charitable status would be accepted from the Brethren. This was overturned in 1981 in the High Court when some Brethren successfully brought an action challenging the Commissioners' ruling. The failure of the Solicitor-General, on behalf of the Attorney-General, to present the court with any of the evidence collected in the course of the Commissioners' inquiry probably implies a high degree of uncertainty among the state's lawyers about the precise criteria by which a religion can be considered to be charitable in law. A courtroom struggle was probably considered too likely to embarrass the government with proof of the law's outdated assumptions or inconsistencies. English law makes no provision for the freedom of religion, but the law on charities does grant special privileges to those organizations which, by largely implicit and conventional criteria, are deemed to be religious. The situation is so confused and confusing that indecisiveness and arbitrariness on the government's part are bound to be repeated in the future.

The 'official' position might be summed up by saying that, with the exception of Sir John Foster's inquiry into Scientology (1971), no NRM has been the object of a published investigation by the British government or Parliament. On the other hand, however, spokesmen for various ministries and statutory organizations have made it clear from time to time that internal reviews of the activities and effects of NRMs are in continuous operation. Inter-departmental files on this topic are known to be in circulation within the Civil Service, and the police are thought to be keeping the topic under review.[6]

Unlike the situation in some other parts of Europe, responsibility for young people in Britain is not concentrated in any particular ministry but is, rather, shared by a variety of agencies concerned with, for example, health, education, and employment. The picture is made even more vague and confusing by the absence of any single agency of government with responsibility for religious affairs. The leaders of various churches have, of course, issued cautious statements warning of the so-called dangers presented by some NRMs, but no concerted policy has been devised, let alone implemented.

In comparison with the intensity of anti-cult campaigns observed in, for example, France, the Federal Republic of Germany, and the USA there has been little in the way of a formal response to NRMs on the part of organizations that might have been considered relevant. The leaders of youth organizations, trades unions, political parties, and student associations have been largely silent on the matter, although in some cases there has been a purely local response to some new religious groups. Thus, some local students' associations have refused to recognize the legitimacy of the UC's Collegiate Association for the Research of Principles (CARP) as a bona fide or beneficial student group, but the topic has not yet entered into wider debates about 'youth problems' (see Barker 1983).

The official response of the 'mainstream' churches to NRMs has also been reserved and cautious. The former Archbishop of Canterbury, Dr Coggan, epitomized this response by his denial on television that the UC, for example, is a Christian organization and by his recommendation that its prospective members or supporters should investigate very carefully its claims to religious status. Similarly, the British Council of Churches Youth Unit, in its leaflet entitled 'The Unification Church. A Paper for those who Wish to Know More' (n.d.) suggested that members of the 'Christian Churches' should be made 'aware of the differences between the Unification Church and the mainstream churches in Britain'. Numerous booklets and brochures have been produced in the same vein by evangelical churches, but the topic has failed to reach the agenda of any important gathering of churchmen. Many clergymen individually take the view that NRMs are dangerous and destructive, but their collective voice was relatively muted until 1983.

A more coherent response to NRMs from a broad range of clergy and church officials began to crystallize around opposition to plans that were framed in the European Parliament for quasi-judicial control over such movements. The plans originated with Richard Cottrell, Conservative Member of the European Parliament (MEP) for Bristol, who was successful in persuading the Committee on Youth, Culture, Education, Information, and Sport to consider the dangers possibly arising from the allegedly growing influence of NRMs within the European Community. Other MEPs had earlier raised parliamentary questions about the UC in particular, but it was Mr Cottrell who was appointed by the committee to oversee the preparation of a report on the situation. The draft report was presented in August 1983 after roughly one year's deliberation. Many submissions were made to the committee in the light of the draft report before a final report in the form of a Motion for a Resolution was overwhelmingly approved and tabled on 22 March 1984 (PE 82. 322/fin.). It called on relevant ministers of member states to 'hold an exchange of information as soon as possible on the problems arising from the activity of certain new religious movements'; it recommended the implementation of numerous rules to prevent the movements from abusing the interests of members and of their families; and it proposed the establishment of a data bank on various aspects of the movements' activities.

The report is considered in more detail in Chapter 8. The point of immediate import is that the Executive Committee of the British Council of Churches (BCC), on which most major churches and denominations are represented, took exception to many aspects of the Cottrell report and tried to dissuade MEPs from supporting its proposals when it was debated in the Assembly in May 1984. This, in turn, elicited a mixed response from clergy, and a rather heated debate took place in some newspaper correspondence columns. As a result, Mr Cottrell was invited to clarify his views to the BCC Executive Committee, but no changes in their respective positions were recorded.

Although the BCC's misgivings about the proposed curbs on NRMs do not imply support for the movements in general they have been construed in some quarters as being significantly less negative than earlier statements on the topic by leading churchmen. To add further complications, the Executive Committee's stance has received enthusiastic endorsement from other religious sources including the UC and the Church of Scientology. The fact that the issue has been carefully limited to the dangers for *all* religious groups if even *one* of them is deprived of the freedom to operate in its chosen way has often been overlooked. Indeed, the BCC's letter to MEPs acknowledged that serious issues sometimes arose 'in the way certain [religious] groups conduct their affairs' but it argued that common law remedies were already available. Nevertheless, the letter and the subsequent press coverage have finally found support in parts of the religious establishment of Britain. A large clerical body has, for the first time, made a public stand on the issue of NRMs.

It is not at all easy to summarize the official response to NRMs in the UK. This is partly because the government has mainly refused to take a visibly active role in either protecting or criticizing them and partly because specifically anti-cult associations have developed largely independently from existing religious, political, or trades union organizations. The result is a complex picture of unofficial and *ad hoc* responses to a phenomenon which has never been officially categorized (and certainly not acknowledged) as a social problem.[7] Discussion of NRMs in the British press gives no indication of an 'official' etiology for them. Rather, the 'problem' is implicitly located, in the opinion of most British critics, in the allegedly dishonest and unscrupulous practices of 'the cults'. A wider social or spiritual dimension to the phenomenon is absent from most discussions. This will be made clearer in the next sub-section.

Anti-cult campaigns

The campaign against NRMs has been mounted and effectively pursued by only two organizations in Britain: Family Action Information and Rescue (FAIR) and the Deo Gloria Trust.

FAIR

FAIR is the only 'parents association' in Britain, although it also counts among its several hundred members many people who are not parents of cult members. It also includes, for example, ex-members of cults, ministers of religion, journalists, and teachers.

The founding chairman in 1975, Mr Paul Rose, was a Member of Parliament who fought an unsuccessful defence of an action for libel against the UC and did not stand for re-election to Parliament in 1979. He was succeeded by joint chairmen who were the Anglican chaplain to the Polytechnic of Central London and the twin brother of a UC member. Subsequently, the post was held by another Anglican clergyman. Under their guidance and freed from the pre-occupation with supporting Mr Rose's libel action, FAIR has expanded and changed in several ways.

First, it has deliberately encouraged the formation of regional branches in many parts of Britain and has thereby assumed a kind of federal structure. The branches enjoy considerable freedom of manoeuvre and can therefore make the most of local resources. This has also increased the effectiveness of intervention in 'personal cases' in some regions of the country. Second, FAIR has been brought into closer contact with evangelical Christian groups partly through the mediation of its chairmen and partly through the coincidental rise in prominence of the Deo Gloria Trust. Third, FAIR has improved the efficiency of its communications with anti-cult organizations in other parts of the world. Its newsletters now contain almost as much foreign as home-based news, and the awareness of participating in a world-wide struggle against 'unscrupulous cults' has grown in accordance. And fourth, the scope of FAIR's 'remit' has been extended to all 'destructive cults'. In the early years it concentrated almost exclusively on combating the Unification Church, but the field of activity now includes virtually all non-conventional religious groups. The following quotation from FAIR's newsletter of spring 1982 highlights the problem that the organization faces in trying to decide how to define the boundary between acceptable and unacceptable religious groups even within the Christian tradition:

'*Small Christian Groups:*
While it is comparatively easy to detect and recognize a cult with a strong doctrine of its own, it may be very difficult to decide whether a small bible-based charismatic group is still acceptable and beneficial for its members, or whether it has gone "off the rails". Where this happens it is in most cases the influence of a dynamic leader who introduces cult-like practices and drags the group members into a state of exclusive narrow-mindedness and dependence on him. Some of these groups are simply called

"Christian Fellowship", even "Born again Christians" and may have in their ranks genuine Christians who have fallen under the spell of the leader.

If in doubt consult local clergy, or write to us and enclose where possible, handbills, programmes or literature of the group for easier identification.'

This 'inclusive' approach to the problem of identifying 'cults' is not, however, to the liking of all FAIR supporters. It has given rise to polemics within the organization and has aggravated the related difficulty of being labelled 'anti-cult'. The position was stated as follows:

'The word "anti-cult" is a catch-phrase, coined by academics, which conjurs [sic] up the image of medieval witch hunters or – in modern times – those who consider everything connected with cults as evil and want to see every cult member proscribed by law. We are anti-deception, anti-exploitation and against the splitting of families. But we have no religious axe to grind, and cult members are not enemies but somebody's children, people in great need of caring concern.'

(*Fair News* April 1984: 2)

Maintaining an appropriate public image is clearly of importance to any campaigning association but it is exceptionally important to FAIR because of the wide diversity of its supporters' backgrounds and interests.

FAIR's operations are entirely dependent on voluntary donations and on about eight hundred annual subscriptions. It has never received financial assistance from the government or from any local authorities. Nor has it ever made a charge to the people who have used its services. Its status has remained that of a voluntary association with individual members who offer their services to any person requiring assistance in coping with a cult-related problem.

Its main services are threefold, but there are regional variations in their relative salience and effectiveness. (a) It collects, analyses, and distributes information about NRMs by means of regular newsletters, meetings, and personal contacts. (b) It intervenes on request in cases where it is felt that a prospective or actual member or ex-member of a NRM would benefit from informed counselling; and the relatives or close acquaintances of such people may also be counselled. And (c) it participates in public debates, public relations activities, and political lobbying. There is no salaried staff, and the

administrative headquarters amounts only to rented accommodation. The regional branches are run by individuals operating (often
at their own expense) in their spare time from home.

Deo Gloria Trust

After sponsoring a conference at the Belgian Bible College on 'The
Challenge of the Cults' in May 1977 the Deo Gloria Trust emerged as
the only major complement in Britain to FAIR. Its origins were,
however, very different. The founder of the Trust is a wealthy
businessman with strong Christian convictions whose two adult sons
both spent some time in the Children of God movement. It is
impossible to disentangle the religious from the purely personal and
familial aspects of the Trust, although in the late 1970s the scale of its
operations expanded to such an extent that it began to take on more
of the appearance of a formal organization devoted to combating
what it saw as religious error and abuse with evangelical Christian
teachings. There is a small permanent secretariat in a London suburb
and at least two associate bodies, the Deo Gloria Outreach and Deo
Gloria Promotions. The latter arranged the UK première of an
American film *Cult Explosion* in 1980. The accompanying publicity
sheet described it as 'a searing exposé of these insidious groups.
Former leaders of many cults explain the secret inner core including:
People's Temple; Worldwide Church of God, Moonies; Jehovah's
Witnesses; Transcendental Meditation; Hare Krishna; Scientology;
Mormons and many others, and presents a clear Christian message
on conclusion.' The Trust maintains close contact with other Chris-
tian organizations such as the Evangelical Alliance and with various
evangelical ministries in Britain and abroad. In fact, it was formerly
represented on the Evangelical Alliance's Challenge to the Cults
Committee (as was FAIR, incidentally).

It may be a measure of Deo Gloria's influence in 1980 that its
administrator was the victim of a deliberate smear campaign. Police
investigated the possibility that the campaign had been orchestrated
by one of the NRMs being monitored by the Trust. Since then,
however, the scale of operations has shrunk considerably. Deo
Gloria still supplies anti-cult publicity but it no longer adopts a high
profile in public. And, instead of providing a counselling service it
now refers enquirers to outside counsellors.

The relationship between FAIR and the Deo Gloria Trust has been
very close and mutually beneficial – so much so that it is difficult to
distinguish between their respective contributions to some projects –

but there is still a major difference in their aims and practices. FAIR remains largely a 'parents' organization with no formal commitment to specifically Christian views, whereas the Deo Gloria Trust operates within a distinctively Christian framework. The latter was probably stronger in material and organizational resources at the beginning of the 1980s, but by 1984 FAIR had added many Deo Gloria Trust members to its own membership list and had definitely resumed its former position as Britain's leading opponent of 'destructive cultism'.

Two other anti-cult organizations have operated in Britain, but their influence has been considerably weaker than that of FAIR and the Deo Gloria Trust.

EMERGE

EMERGE (Ex-Members of Extremist Religious Groups) was founded in the spring of 1980 by a group of young defectors from NRMs. Its administrative structure has never been very formal, and its style of operation has tended to be personal. The main activities include monthly social gatherings where parents and ex-members can discuss their cult-related problems; the supply of information about NRMs to schools, youth groups, and churches; counselling individuals; public demonstrations at, for example, UC rallies; and lobbying among politicians and public officials.

The fact that most activists in EMERGE are students means that continuity of operations has not been strong. Yet, with FAIR's assistance the group has survived several crises. The result is that it has come to appear more and more like FAIR's 'youth wing' – despite its protestations to the contrary. Certainly, it adopts a less harshly critical tone, and is better equipped to adopt a sympathetic stance towards ex-cultists, than FAIR.

POWER

A curious coda to this section is provided by a now-defunct organization called People's Organized Workshop on Ersatz Religions (POWER) whose brief existence between 1976 and 1977 caused some embarrassment and annoyance to the fledgeling FAIR. It was founded, apparently single-handed, by a young man whose motivation and intentions were never clearly revealed. But his stated opposition to 'cults' was crystal clear:

'The cults must be totally destroyed; the government will not act, so people must take the law into their own hands. We must have hundreds, if not thousands of deprogrammers up and down the countryside. . . . Cult members should not be allowed to own property, drive cars, or vote. Cult members should be placed in a higher tax bracket for their non-productivity . . . Police should harass the cults into leaving the soils [sic] of Britain. Contingency plans should be drawn up by the armed forces to move into centres controlled by cults in cases where public disturbance is likely . . . The Vatican should lend a hand by training Jesuits as deprogrammers.'

(POWER *The Anticultist Newsletter* 10 August 1976: 2)

Indeed, consistently vitriolic attacks on several NRMs appeared in POWER's occasional newsletters.

It was suggested that 'deprogramming could be flanked with DHSS programmes such as internment camps for the cults'. Other proposals included 'compulsory courses in schools on the evils of these cancers [i.e. cults]'; 'a national advertising campaign similar to the anti-smoking campaign'; and 'universities should be urged to award Ph.D's in deprogramming' (POWER *The Anticultist Newsletter* 10 August 1976: 1–2).

Plans were drawn up for the establishment of a 'residential centre for former cult members' where 'they can live together as a means of strengthening their resolve to stay away from other cult members and not drift back' (POWER Press Release, 19 August 1976). And efforts were made to persuade the Home Secretary to ban the entry of foreign Moonies into the UK. 'If these Moonies are allowed to come into Britain people should take the matter into their own hands – they should be seized and deprogrammed.' Perhaps the most telling statement was that 'Religious rights and civil liberties are violated by deprogramming but the ideologies of these groups are such that it doesn't matter' (POWER Press Release, 21 September 1976). Another justification was that 'these cults represent one of the gravest dangers that the nation faces today' (POWER *Newsletter* December 1976).

POWER's most notorious publication was the brochure 'Deprogramming: the Constructive Destruction of Belief. A Manual of Technique' (1976). It achieved wide circulation in anti-cult circles in Britain and elsewhere but was discredited because it advocated brutal and degrading treatment of cultists. In fact, it resembled nothing so much as a caricature of the early publications of anti-cultist organizations. As a result it was publicly criticized, for example by FAIR, and privately ridiculed.

Nevertheless, the deprogramming manual did have one serious effect. It contained the names and addresses of individuals, including my own, and of organizations supposedly associated with the POWER project. This put them in an embarrassing position and called their integrity in question. This was one reason for the suspicion that POWER was a front organization for one of the cults which had tried to discredit the emerging anti-cultist movement by associating it with repulsive tactics for forcible deprogramming. In response to protests from some of those falsely associated with POWER's infamous *Manual*, their names and addresses were crudely obliterated in copies distributed towards the end of 1976.

POWER's founder, and probably sole member, disappeared without trace just as suddenly in 1977 as he had materialized – but not before attracting considerable publicity and, by implication at least, tarnishing FAIR's image. Some people believe that documents released by the FBI in accordance with the American Freedom of Information Act prove that POWER had been operated by one of the largest NRMs, but the evidence remains inconclusive. The POWER episode therefore remains an exotic enigma in the history of British responses to NRMs. The anger and mistrust that it generated are evidence of the emotional agitation that characterizes much of the cult controversy.

NRMs' self-defence

The activities of FAIR and the Deo Gloria Trust have been opposed in Britain by the Society for Religious Peace and Family Unity, an interfaith group with the aim of promoting 'inter-religious tolerance in the community'. It has reportedly 'had occasion to take measures in the past with regard to a few rather extremist groups opposed to the "cults"' (SRPFU n.d.). Since its foundation in 1977 this group, on which a variety of Christian, Islamic, Hindu, and Buddhist interests are represented, alongside those of Scientology, the Unification Church, and the Mormon Church, has formally aimed at working towards 'harmonious family relationships and inter-religious tolerance through dialogue and understanding'. It has organized meetings at which issues confronting minority religious groups have been discussed; and it has published a brochure on 'Family Reconciliation' designed to help restore harmonious relationships within families divided by differences of religious commitment. Its contents are closely modelled on, and in part copied verbatim from, a similar brochure published in the USA by an organization called the Alliance for the Preservation of Religious Liberty,[8] which also has strong representation from the Church of Scientology and the Unification Church among others. In addition to offering guidance on ways of restoring harmony in family relationships, the Society for Religious Peace and Family Unity offers to supply the services of ministers of religion as 'mediators or advisers in disputes'. Mention is also made of a 'rehabilitation counselling service'.

Leaving aside the support offered by the SRPFU, very few voices have been heard in public support of NRMs. A conspicuous silence has been maintained by, for example, the major civil rights pressure groups; and few opportunities have been given for dissenting opinions to be represented in the mass media's treatment of NRMs. The only significant exceptions have been the attempts by a distinguished ecologist, Sir Kenneth Melanby, and by one of Britain's foremost scientists, Professor R.V. Jones, to defend the integrity of the participants in the UC's International Conferences on the Unity of the Sciences.

The lack of any significant polemic in public between pro- and anti-cult forces lends further support to my view that the question of NRMs in Britain has not yet been associated with any other areas of public concern or dispute. In other words, no serious attempts have been made to link questions about NRMs to the kind of debates that have taken place in some other countries about their moral, political, social, economic, religious, or medical implications. Compared with the Federal Republic of Germany, in particular, the whole topic is untheorized and treated in an entirely pragmatic-empiricist manner.

Mass media and NRMs

Research into family responses to the UC in Britain has shown that the mass media are frequently the single most important influence on people's attitudes towards the movement (Beckford 1981a). Many parents who had known nothing about the UC when their child joined it acquired their first pieces of information from daily newspapers or (more rarely) the television. In some instances this happens by accident, as in the case of one of my informants who reported, for example, that he had first learned about the UC from his Church of England vicar who, in turn, had read about it in the *Reader's Digest*. Another had been no more than mildly suspicious of the Moonies until he read the same article. Only then did he launch an energetic and vigorous campaign to remove his son from the movement. He had read the article by accident only the morning after hearing by transatlantic telephone that his son, Robert, had joined a religious movement for young people in the USA. According to his wife, he said, 'My God, this is exactly what's happened to Robert'. She went on 'It fitted in exactly with what had happened to Robert . . . and that was when we realized it was. . . . The UC was the Moonies'. She continued,

> 'After reading this article we realized [the Moonies] worked in a peculiar way to keep them in, and it was a type of brainwashing. We knew that, we realized after we'd read this article in the *Reader's Digest* that they had already brainwashed Robert because he was so entirely different in the [previous day's] telephone conversation.'

Many parents who had been reasonably satisfied with the accounts given of this movement by their children were suddenly disturbed by the competing accounts supplied by the mass media. In fact, most of them subsequently made contact with other 'affected' families only as a direct result of corresponding with journalists and with the people who had been featured in their stories. Indeed, journalists have played a major part in helping to fuel anti-cult campaigns and to keep them 'in the news', if not in the headlines. In many cases journalists have functioned as an unofficial channel of communication among ex-members or anguished parents who would not otherwise have known of each other's plight. And the extensive preparations for some television programmes have brought together many far-flung components of the anti-cult movement.

The mass-media in Britain rarely discriminate between possible candidates for the designation of 'cult'. Rather, the term serves as an evocative label for any group (religious or otherwise) whose activities have aroused curiosity and puzzlement. The commonest qualifiers include 'weird', 'bizarre', and 'frightening'. Yet the British press has rarely regarded 'the cults', in a generic sense, as an important topic for exposure. With only a few exceptions, press coverage has been confined to NRMs taken singly, and this amounts to a significant difference from the pattern of press coverage in some other countries of the west, as we shall see in the next chapter.

The Unification Church has attracted more publicity than any other new religious movement since the mid 1970s, with Scientology, the Children of God, and the devotees of Krishna coming next in the order of press interest. Most of the references to these groups have been sensationalized, but aside from the major 'scare' concerning Scientology in the late 1960s, this particular movement enjoyed a better public image until it was severely criticized by a High Court judge in 1984. Until then, Scientology's campaigns for legislation on the freedom of access to official information and for reforms of the institutionalized care of the mentally ill had occasionally received favourable exposure. The 'softer' attitude towards Scientology probably owed something to the movement's well publicized adoption of a less combative outlook. The changed outlook was also associated with the excommunication of twelve members of the headquarters staff in Britain in 1983. They appear to have been punished for allegedly misusing funds for attacks on Scientology's critics. In fact, the formerly powerful Office of Guardians was closed, and the remaining staff members were transferred to other duties. Finally, the movement's international headquarters was moved from East Grinstead to Los Angeles. It might be speculated that the apparent search for better relations with the mass media and government departments also owed something to the confidence and encouragement that Scientology's leaders undoubtedly derived from the verdict of the High Court of Australia in October 1983 that, for the purposes of exemption from payroll tax, Scientology qualifies as a religion.[9]

The 'Scientology scare' in Britain preceded controversy about NRMs in general, but in some respects it set the stage for what was to follow. There were allegations, for example, about the adverse effects of Scientology's practices on the mental health of some members; the 'dangerous' influence wielded by a Scientologist who taught in a school for young children; the problems that could arise for clients who got into debt in order to purchase courses in Scientology; and the difficulties experienced by some ex-members in leaving the movement. At the time of these allegations, however, there were no suggestions that Scientology might have been a forerunner of a much larger outcry against 'cults' in general.

The harsh words used by Mr Justice Latey in describing Scientology as 'corrupt, sinister, dangerous and immoral' suggested that by 1984 it had been brought within the bounds of the public image of a 'dangerous cult'. The judge found in favour of a mother who had left Scientology and had been trying for six months to gain custody of her two young children from their father who remained in the movement. This case not only revived old fears about Scientology but it also gave journalists the opportunity to re-open the 'cults file' and to rehearse the full anti-cult repertoire. The belief that Scientology had been 'rehabilitated' in the early 1980s and that it was no longer linked with the most controversial cults was swiftly disconfirmed.

Media reports on 'cults' frequently contain objective material but they are usually published only when the topic is controversial. NRMs are constituted first and foremost as a family problem whose news value is considerable because it lends itself to a variety of emotively laden treatments. One of the results is that even supposedly in-depth analyses of NRMs tend to confine themselves to certain recurrent themes which relate only to limited aspects of the topic (see, for example, the series of three articles that appeared in *The Times*, 12–14 December 1977).

It may be an exaggeration to imply, as do Shupe and Bromley (1981), that mass media accounts of NRMs take the form of 'atrocity tales', unless 'atrocity' is defined weakly as an action that is 'extremely bad'. It more commonly has the much stronger sense, however, of action that is 'extremely evil or cruel'. Massacres of large numbers of innocent people, as at Jonestown and My Lai, for example, usually qualify as atrocities. NRMs have not been accused of this kind of action.[10] Moreover, the term implies a finality and a lack of doubt about the atrocious nature of the action which could hardly be controversial. But media accounts of NRMs emphasize the continuing or equivocal character of the cult saga.

A good example from the USA concerns Synanon's implementation of various violent tactics to discipline members and to intimidate opponents. The striking thing about this case, in which three people eventually entered 'no defence' pleas to charges of conspiring to commit murder, is not that an American local weekly newspaper's owners were awarded a Pulitzer Prize for publicizing the movement's abuses of human rights (Mitchell, Mitchell, and Ofshe 1980) but, rather, that a steady stream of exposés in various mass media failed for so long to persuade law-enforcement agencies to take action. I do not believe that the public response to 'real' atrocities is so equivocal. Although Mitchell (1980: 290) is probably correct to claim that the Attorney-General of California was eventually compelled by pressure created in the mass media to issue criminal charges against some

Synanon personnel, the state acted very cautiously and allowed the defendants to plea-bargain for inconsequential sentences.

A more appropriate, though admittedly less evocative, term for these accounts is 'negative summary events' (Rosengren, Arvidsson, and Sturesson 1978). This refers to the journalistic description of a situation or event in such a way as to capture and express its negative essence as part of an intermittent and slow-moving story. An apparently isolated happening is thereby used as an occasion for keeping the broader, controversial phenomenon in the public mind.[11] Ostensibly trivial or isolated incidents can be used to revive controversy about such 'long-range' problems as the hazards of nuclear installations; germ warfare; subversive infiltration of 'sensitive' bureaucracies; and unscrupulous pyramid sales organizations.

Thus, my opinion is that no 'atrocity tales' have been published about NRMs in the British mass media; but numerous 'negative summary events' *have* appeared in print. Their contribution towards the continuation of cult controversies cannot be exaggerated but requires careful analysis.[12] They have tended to draw on one or more of five main themes which, in turn, occur in relation to certain detailed scenarios involving NRMs. I shall give just a sample of each theme and its associated scenarios.

Strangeness

This is probably the least offensive of the main themes, since it merely draws attention to what are perceived as the peculiar features of NRMs without passing explicit moral judgment on them. It can occur in the following scenarios:

(a) The personalities, physical appearance, habits, and background of leading members are often caricatured as weird and sometimes as frightening.

(b) The main teachings of NRMs are rarely given more than a crude description, and this is usually a list of points of departure from conventional Christian doctrine. Doctrines are taken out of context and juxtaposed to create the effect of inconsistency, confusion, and intellectual shabbiness.

(c) Religious practices such as prayer, worship, or pilgrimage are also described in terms of their departure from Christian norms. The impression is often given that members of NRMs devote excessive time to devotional practices.

(d) Public curiosity about the living arrangements in religious communities must be insatiable, since this is invariably a central point of journalists' accounts of NRMs. But again the description is selective: they only choose the features which depart most clearly from patterns of nuclear family life.

Trickery

The tone of moral censure is much more evident in accounts which centre on the claim that the cults are unfairly profiting at the expense of recruits.

(a)   The most common accusation is that NRMs deceive people by persuading them to believe things and to do things which they would not do if they had normal control over their minds. The members are therefore represented as victims of a deliberate plan to deceive.

(b)   A closely allied scenario is that NRMs' leaders benefit materially from the movements at the expense of members. The contrast between the living standards of leaders and followers is a recurrent image in 'cult' stories.

(c)   The above scenarios depend implicitly on a third image. The implication of many mass media accounts is that some leaders of NRMs must be insincere in their beliefs and teachings. They are usually depicted as calculating manipulators of their 'victims'.

Misery

The consequences of cult activities are frequently framed as unacceptably harmful and painful to their 'victims'.

(a)   The counterpart to the trickery of leaders is the alleged gullibility of followers. They are presented as people who are too weak to resist the offer of instant happiness, wealth, or spiritual perfection.

(b)   Their living conditions attract a lot of journalistic attention if they depart from the norm of material comfort for middle-class homes. Again, this emphasizes manipulation by the leaders and gullibility among the followers.

(c)   Stories of the serious, long-lasting psychological damage allegedly done to people who have left NRMs are common. The 'victim' image is extended beyond the period of membership into the life of defectors. This is why ex-members' problems are so newsworthy.

(d)   The reported misery of members and ex-members actually receives less journalistic attention than that of close relatives.

This is partly because, as was shown in Chapters 5 and 6, ex-members of the UC are reluctant to criticize the movement in public. The perspective taken by journalists on NRMs is therefore dictated mainly by the protests conducted against them by angry relatives. This gives each story a major 'human interest'.

Anger

The public response to cults is not overlooked but it is usually restricted to its least positive aspects. To introduce balance or perspective would weaken the powerful theme of deeply indignant people battling against an elusive and apparently ruthless opponent.

(a) The scenario of the frustrated and angry relatives who desperately try to rescue someone from an NRM is of great interest to journalists especially if it develops into a 'tug of love' or 'Interpol manhunt' drama. And the promise that personal vendettas will be carried out against the leaders of NRMs is always exciting.

(b) Sometimes the anger of relatives gives rise to a public campaign against the NRM. In fact, the ideal scenario from the point of view of journalists occurs when the anger of relatives is supported by members of a political party or a major church. Demands for an official inquiry into an NRM or demands for action by the government are also newsworthy. Both sets of demands allow journalists to keep a slow-moving story in the public eye. Any snippet of information about NRMs, however trivial, is then used as an occasion for reviewing the whole saga. This is the essence of the 'negative summary event'.

Threat

If the story is to appeal to an audience wider than the tiny number of people adversely affected by cults, it has to contain a link with the everyday experience of 'the person on the Clapham omnibus'. This is most economically achieved by implying that cults represent various kinds of threat.[13]

(a) A favourite strategy is to suggest that NRMs represent a threat to various aspects of 'normal' society. The most dramatic scenario in this context is one in which children are 'taken away' from their families and are allegedly turned into robots. It is no accident that the *Daily Mail* chose to introduce all instalments of its long-running polemic against the UC with the catchphrase: 'The church that breaks up families'.

(b)   A second type of threat concerns material possessions. A
      frightening vision of the future is described in which the NRMs
      grow more and more wealthy at the expense of individual mem-
      bers. Associated with the theme of trickery is this additional
      element of drama which turns NRMs into an immediate
      threat to every family. The perceived threat to property brings
      everything down to a level that everybody can understand.
(c)   In some mass media accounts of NRMs the theme of strange-
      ness is supplemented with an implied threat of alien invasion
      into the British way of life. Most of these movements have
      foreign origins and foreign leaders; they also have doctrines
      which introduce alien ideas and practices. Journalists often try
      to suggest that these foreign elements are an unhealthy threat to
      the integrity of British youth and may even be part of a wider
      attack on British values. The image of the 'state within the state'
      is often evoked, with all its implications of lawlessness and
      manufactured disorder.

The fact that the mass media have been unsympathetic to NRMs
has not been ignored by their leaders. Leaders of the Process, for
example, are said to have moved from London to Nassau in the
Bahamas in order to avoid hostile journalists (Bainbridge 1978: 58).
David 'Moses' Berg has reportedly decided to reduce the COG's
visibility in Britain and some other countries because the attentions
of the mass media were felt to be too threatening. And following the
UC's loss of its case for libel against a daily newspaper, the decision
was taken to reduce the level of the movement's operations in
Britain.

The 'flight' response has not prevailed in all cases, however. In
fact, the 'fight' response was, by contrast, very evident in the strategy
of the Scientologists who used to have powerful public relations
agencies to deal with journalists. Part of their work involved warning
journalists and others about the dangers of publishing defamatory
material about the movement. In some cases, writs for libel were
issued, if not always pursued very actively.[14] The most famous case
resulted in a judgement against the Scientologists in favour of a
Member of Parliament, Geoffrey Johnson-Smith, in 1970.

In the later 1970s, however, the UC seemed to take on the mantle
of the most litigious NRM. A number of writs for libel were issued,
and the first case to reach the High Court ended in the defeat of Paul
Rose, a Labour Member of Parliament who was obliged to apologize
for defaming the UC and to pay an undisclosed amount of damages.

By far the most important case, however, was the six-month-long hearing of the UC's complaint that it had been libelled by the *Daily Mail*. Not only did the jury exonerate the newspaper but it also cast serious doubt on the UC's claims to be a purely religious organization.[15] The result was hailed in most newspapers as a victory for courage and commonsense. According to the *Daily Mail* of 1 April 1981, the former Archbishop of Canterbury, Lord Coggan, welcomed the verdict; and a spokesman for the Methodist Church was quoted as saying, 'An organization which sets itself up as a religious body . . . should not leap to litigation when it is criticized. I am very pleased about the result'. This was the cue for an outburst of anti-cult sentiment in many sections of the press, as was the subsequent news that the movement's appeal against the verdict had failed in March 1983. The three Appeal Court judges agreed that

> 'In our judgement there was evidence which was capable of being regarded as the brainwashing of prospective converts. . . . There was also evidence from which the jury could infer that, both in the United Kingdom and elsewhere, this church broke up families and carried on its activities under a cloak of deceit and in a manner which gave cause for concern about its money-collecting activities.'

The number of mass media reports favourable to NRMs in Britain has been extremely small. Newspapers, in particular, have given almost free rein to moral entrepreneurs and moral crusaders wishing to stir up distrust of NRMs. A sense of balance and objectivity has been conspicuously lacking in all but a very few articles or programmes. Even a series of three articles in *The Times* in December 1977 took an undisguised anti-cult stance.

Does this mean, then, that journalists have been conjuring up or exaggerating the actual extent of unfavourable public opinion about NRMs and, more especially, the involvement of young people in them? The answer, based on my experience of talking about 'cults' to people in all walks of life for a decade or more, is that the British are intensely suspicious of any and all would-be Messiahs, evangelists, and gurus. They are accustomed to relegating spiritual enthusiasm to a category of, at best, eccentricity, and at worst, exploitation. This disposition is reinforced by the mass media's readiness to consider religious or spiritual innovation solely in terms of its actually or potentially corrupt aspects, for this is what makes for newsworthiness. The result is that the interests of the anti-cultists are continually represented in the mass media; non-committal or differentiated opinions are ignored; and NRMs are allowed only to react to their opponents' publicized attacks. In short, journalists have not conjured up or distorted the deep-seated suspicion felt by very many people in Britain towards NRMs, but they have framed their accounts in such a *selective* way that dissenting opinions are virtually excluded. What is more, as is made clear in Barker (1983), the image created by the mass media of young people who join NRMs does not satisfactorily reflect the facts generated by empirical enquiries.

From the point of view of today's controversial NRMs it is unfortunate that they display a number of the criteria widely employed by journalists for selecting 'newsworthy' stories. In particular, the focus on youth, the suspicion of exploitation, and the hint of unconventional lifestyles all make it virtually inevitable that stories about NRMs will occasionally be given prominence and be sensationalized. Above all, it is the fact that these themes occur *in combination* in connection with NRMs that encourages journalists to treat them in this way. This is why I believe that Christopher Lasch was only half correct to describe the mass media as 'biassed, as always, not in favor of any particular program or point of view but simply in favor of novelty' (1977: 135). NRMs are newsworthy less for their novelty than for the way in which they offer an opportunity for the expression of long-standing obsessions of contemporary journalists. Stories about 'cults' are not particularly frequent; but they are remarkably standardized. The effect is therefore enhanced by sheer repetition of the same images and arguments.

The corollary of the narrowness of journalistic vision is that very rarely are NRMs presented in the mass media in any other light. Inquiries into the problems of British youth, for example, have never paid any attention to NRMs. Nor has any serious attention been paid to the movements' values, teachings, or practices. It is as if the cult problem were rigidly frozen into the sensationalist mould; no connections can be made with other problems. But, as we shall see in the next chapter, NRMs have been found interesting and problematic for very different reasons in other countries.

Policy implications

Bearing in mind the distinctiveness of the 'cult problem' as it exists in Britain, questions arise about the kind of policies which might be implemented to minimize the difficulties that have been experienced by both the detractors and the defenders of NRMs. There have already been calls for a more strenuous application of existing laws to control such things as public solicitation of financial donations, the sale of goods in public places, and the uses to which residential property may be put. Pressure has been put on the government to make it more difficult for exploitative religious movements to secure the benefits of charitable status. And various public authorities have sought to prevent certain NRMs from hiring public meeting halls for recruitment purposes. All of these initiatives have been designed to limit the opportunities for NRMs to increase in size or power. The other side of the coin should not, however, be overlooked. It concerns the kind of policies which would minimize the chances of public disorder, violence against 'cultists', and the restriction of the rights to which members of NRMs are entitled in some other countries. In other words, the question of policies should not be confined to the matter of how best to control NRMs; it should also concern itself with finding ways to permit the widest enjoyment of personal and collective freedoms consonant with public order. What are the policy options?

Legislation

There has been very little demand in Britain for *new legislation* to deal with cult-related problems. Britain's society is multi-ethnic and multi-religious to such an extent that the problem of framing suitable legislation would appear to be insuperable. Moreover, the weight of public opinion seems to be in favour of keeping religious matters largely in the sphere of the private and consequently outside the framework of law.

The enforcement of existing laws, however, figures prominently among the demands of the anti-cult campaigns. In particular, the laws relating to business practice, soliciting donations and selling in public places, public health and hygiene, charitable status, immigration, and consumer protection could, it has been argued, be profitably enforced with greater vigour than has usually been the case against some NRMs without detriment to the ideals of religious freedom or personal liberty.

Of the NRMs, only Scientology has actively campaigned for a change in the law which might facilitate its activities and shield it from prejudice and arbitrariness. It has repeatedly called for a Freedom of Information Act, not simply as a defensive measure but also as a way of promoting its own aims in the field of mental health.

This is one of the very few areas of public life in which an NRM is presently willing to play an active role alongside other organizations in the pursuit of a common goal.

Public policy

In keeping with the relatively decentralized and pluralistic character of many British institutions there is little pressure for the establishment of, for example, a Ministry for Youth, a Ministry for the Family, or a Ministry for Religious Affairs. Nor is it seriously suggested that the school syllabus should take special account of NRMs. And, while the main anti-cult organizations have put pressure on the Home Office and the Department of Health and Social Security for action to curb the influence of NRMs, governmental resources have not been sought or offered as part of their campaigns. Their strategy has largely been to exercise influence through personal contacts with clergy, youth workers, police officers, and educationalists on an *ad hoc* basis.

The relatively low level of 'official' action in the area of cult-related difficulties is also a consequence of the fact that the medical profession has shown little interest in the phenomenon. In a society where medical criteria are widely used in attempts to decide whether phenomena are problematic or not, the interest of the medical profession is crucial to the success of many social reform movements. Yet, doctors and psychiatrists have in the main refrained from involvement in the polemics surrounding NRMs in Britain, and their professional literature is virtually devoid of references to the topic. As long as they remain apparently uninterested, it is unlikely that 'official' policy will be discussed or produced (for a contrast with the USA, see Robbins 1979).

While the lack of public policy regarding all forms of religion in Britain may appear to be preferable to the situation which obtains in, for example, West Germany and France where paternalism and centralism, respectively, provide for more obtrusive intervention in the affairs of controversial religious movements, it also has its costs. There seem to be much higher degrees of administrative arbitrariness and secrecy in the official response to problems generated by NRMs in Britain. The established churches and denominations are relatively well protected by custom and convention, but newer religious bodies can fall victim to administrative prejudices and fears. In the absence of a framework of constitutional law, fewer judicial remedies are available to aggrieved interests than in the USA. On balance, minority interests enjoy greater freedom in Britain than in many other countries from judicial and administrative inconveniences when they are not deemed problematic; but as soon as problems arise, the danger of arbitrary power in the hands of officials of the state at local and national levels becomes all too clear. Again, the solution does not necessarily lie in fresh legislation tailored specifically for NRMs, but there are good reasons to believe that a Freedom of Information Act would provide a partial remedy to the potential for arbitrariness which is built into the current situation in Britain.

Aftercare

The material problems facing some ex-members of NRMs have given rise to anxiety among concerned relatives and others. Difficulties may be experienced in finding employment, training, courses of education, or accommodation. Unless contributions to National Insurance have been paid regularly during membership of an NRM (or made up afterwards), the ex-member may suffer reductions in the level of various kinds of welfare benefits or pensions.

Critics of NRMs have argued that the failure to make adequate medical and material provisions for their members is evidence of irresponsibility and exploitativeness. It is unlikely, however, that special arrangements could be made in social welfare to meet the needs of ex-members of NRMs as a distinct category of beneficiary in themselves. More practicable would seem to be self-help programmes organized by concerned parents or ex-members. This is certainly one of the aims of FAIR, but it has received a lower priority than the generalized attack on NRMs. A new organization called EMERGE (Ex-Members of Extremist Religious Groups) has recently begun to take up this kind of helping task on a modest scale.

The aggressiveness of FAIR and of the Deo Gloria Trust towards NRMs in the 1970s may have been counterproductive in so far as it undermined their credibility in the eyes of ex-members who were repulsed by the anti-cultists' total denigration and dismissal of all NRMs. These two organizations undoubtedly played an important role in informing anxious relatives about the implications of membership of NRMs, and on occasion they have been instrumental in persuading members to withdraw. But they are also shunned by some ex-members for being insensitive to their special spiritual problems. The increasing involvement of clergy and of evangelical Christians generally in FAIR has further discouraged some ex-members of NRMs from taking advantage of their services, as was explained in Chapter 6.

Some ex-members of NRMs have called for the establishment of a voluntary agency, independent from all religious interests and from anti-cult associations, which could offer counselling, rehabilitation, and practical help in the form of guided negotiation between parents and adult children. The element of independence is usually considered crucial to the success of such a venture and this is the reason why the schemes on offer from FAIR on the one hand and from the Society for Religious Peace and Family Unity on the other have often been rejected by ex-cultists. Yet, it is unreasonable to expect that special agencies and programmes could be established solely to help the minute percentage of young people whose cult-related problems are, in any case, mild in comparison with those of the much larger number of young people adversely affected by, for example, drug addiction, ethnic prejudice, or criminal environments.

A more practicable approach would be to educate the counsellors working in existing agencies about the special problems facing cult members and ex-members and their relatives. Family therapists, marriage guidance counsellors, pastoral counsellors in schools, and social workers could no doubt benefit from a heightened awareness of the difficulties that can, but do not always, arise in families when a member joins or leaves a NRM. Likewise they should be acquainted with the problems facing NRMs in a society lacking constitutional guarantees of legal protection for basic rights and freedoms but possessing a powerful establishment of social and cultural institutions resistant to new ideas and lifestyles.

Social perception

There are three main reasons for the relatively low level of public discussion about policies in relation to the activities and effects of NRMs in Britain. The first is that the total number of people committed to them at any point in the past decade or so has never exceeded about 15,000 and is therefore too small to have aroused widespread concern. Moreover, most movements have given little cause for complaint. The second is that the cult problem has not been medicalized and has consequently failed to achieve the status of a fully-fledged social problem. The third is that, apart from allegations about the UC's anti-communism and extreme right-wing connections, there has been very little resonance between anxieties about NRMs and the kinds of political problem that have occupied the

British public's attention in recent years. Even the politicized problems of youth (such as violence, drug-dependency, alcoholism, unemployment, criminality, and emergent fascism) have been kept separate from the discussion of NRMs.

As was indicated above in the section on the response of journalists to NRMs, the 'problem' is mainly constituted in Britain in terms of discrete threats and dangers to individual people or families. The perception of NRMs as a threat to the social *category* of youth is rare and probably confined to certain intellectual milieux. But even there it is unusual for the various problems listed in the previous paragraph to be perceived as part of a general 'youth problem' such as alienation or 'the flight from reality'. Consequently, the topic does not readily lend itself to policy-making in Britain. Official responses to the sensationalized stories of some NRMs in the mass media are therefore fragmented, *ad hoc*, and pragmatic.

These arguments apply equally to the British *perception* of NRMs. There is very little awareness of them as a category. Each one is probably known (if at all) for a distinctive trait, but it is unlikely that the person-in-the-street has a sense of them as a distinct type of group. There may be a confused awareness of one or two of them as vaguely menacing, exotic or powerful, but the category of 'NRM' belongs firmly to the social scientist rather than to the lay person. To talk of policy in this context would be seen by many people as a premature and inappropriate response to a problem demanding merely piecemeal treatment.

Politicization

Very few attempts have been made in Britain to remove young people against their will from NRMs, and as a result the conflict between cults and anti-cultists has failed to attract the attention of civil rights activists.[16] The conflict has been fragmented into occasional court room tussles over allegations of libel or intra-family disputes about practical matters. In the circumstances the so-called problem of cults has escaped politicization. Party political differences are certainly not apparent. It seems to have been largely accidental that FAIR's founding chairman was a member of the Labour Party. On balance, Conservative Party politicians have probably been more prominent anti-cultists in the 1980s, and the Thatcher government has gone further than any other in giving encouragement to certain demands for more stringent controls over NRMs' activities.

The conclusion is that a general policy on NRMs is not

appropriate in Britain at present and that voluntary associations of people distressed by them are probably the best agencies for handling individual cases of cult-related difficulty. On the other hand, the arguments for the introduction of a Freedom of Information Act and even a Bill of Rights are strengthened by the complaints that have been voiced by some NRMs about their vulnerability to arbitrary administrative actions. The opportunity for minority religious groups to protect their interests in American courts of law is envied by some of their British counterparts, but, as we shall see in Chapter 9, many of the gains are offset by corresponding increases in the general level of purely defensive legal action.

Conclusion

We have seen that the supposedly standardized practices of certain 'multinational' NRMs have been refracted in a distinctive fashion in Britain. An important aspect of this has been the creation of a particular version of 'the cult problem'. The following considerations must be taken into account in any understanding of the public response to NRMs in Britain.

First, the lack of a state constitution guaranteeing rights to its citizens renders minority religions potentially vulnerable to administrative sanctions which can be imposed without parliamentary discussion, let alone approval. It also means that, compared with the USA, for example, the struggle between NRMs and their opponents in Britain has taken place mainly outside courts of law. The major exceptions have been cases involving allegations of libel.

Second, the fact that no department of the civil service has overall responsibility for either youth or religion has helped to prevent disputes about NRMs from acquiring an 'official' status. The disputes have been conducted, instead, almost exclusively through unofficial, i.e. non-governmental, channels. It is no exaggeration to say that the British government has no public policy with regard to NRMs and the problems associated with them. Indeed, it is difficult to see how such a policy could even be generated in circumstances in which the 'official' concerns with, for example, the family, youth, religion, or civil rights are either non-existent or dispersed over several ministries.

The 'unofficial' character of most disputes about NRMs in Britain is closely connected with a third distinctive feature, namely, the relatively low level of involvement by medical practitioners. Informal gatherings of psychiatrists and other mental health professionals have certainly discussed the 'cult problem', but the anti-cult groups do not seem to have been able to enlist their help (with the highly significant exception of some American specialists). Moreover, the Department of Health and Social Security has not financed any research on the topic. Even the 'experts' who testified for the defence in the *Daily Mail* libel trial were American, and it is largely American evidence on which investigative journalism in Britain has been based.

The distinctiveness of the British response to NRMs can be characterized in brief as piecemeal, administrative, and occasionally arbitrary. There is very little theoretical discussion of the issue in terms of, for example, the philosophy of natural rights or the philosophy of the therapeutic state. Nor have any legal doctrines about the limits of defensible freedom in the field of religion developed out of cult controversies in Britain. Instead, the proposed remedies for both pro- and anti-cultists are strictly pragmatic. The next chapter will try to show how sharply Britain contrasts in these respects with France and West Germany.

Notes

1   Since the British public does not consistently discriminate between different types of NRMs, the distinctions introduced in Chapter 2 between modes of insertion in society would be out of place in this chapter.

2   The Rajneesh movement also caught the headlines on a few occasions in the mid 1980s, mainly in connection with the effects of its headquarters staff on the balance of political power in a small Suffolk village.

3   It seems to be assumed in English law that a religious body is charitable if it disseminates its teachings publicly and is therefore deemed to be in the public interest.

4   See commentary in *The Times* and *The Guardian*, 1 April 1981; and Hampshire and Beckford 1983.

5   A very similar statement was made in the House of Commons by the Parliamentary Under-Secretary of State for the Home Department on 14 May 1984 in replying to a debate about the Exegesis Programme, an intensive character-training organization.

6   Police officers have accepted invitations to attend regional meetings of an anti-cult organization. Special Branch officers were reported to

have investigated the activities of the probably bogus anti-cult group POWER in 1977.

7 Chapter 8 shows, by contrast, how official diagnoses and categorizations of NRMs have been generated in other countries.

8 This organization was renamed Americans Preserving Religious Liberty.

9 *The Church of the New Faith v. The Commissioner for Payroll Tax* (unreported), High Court of Australia, October 1983.

10 In any case, Richardson 1980 and others have denied that the People's Temple can be justifiably considered as a NRM or a cult.

11 In fact, the term originally referred to events *deliberately staged* by journalists to draw attention to a slow-moving story. I have adapted its meaning to suit my purposes.

12 This is why it is unfortunately necessary here to repeat statements about NRMs which could be considered defamatory, but I wish to dissociate myself from them.

13 See Shupe and Bromley 1981 for a comparison with the common themes of journalistic accounts of NRMs in the USA.

14 According to Foster 1971: 1 the Scientologists issued twenty-nine writs for libel in the UK between 1966 and 1970. The movement's litigiousness was officially and publicly regretted and abandoned in 1983.

15 The jury foreman's statement was, 'The jury is unanimous that the tax-free status of the Unification Church should be investigated by the Inland Revenue Department on the grounds that it is a political organization'.

16 In an exception to this generalization, the UC unsuccessfully applied for a High Court writ of *habeas corpus* against the parents of a Moonie who was believed to have been removed from the movement and held against her will in an effort to deprogramme her.

EIGHT

Cult problems in France and West Germany

Just as scholarly interpretations of today's 'cults' are becoming more diverse (Barker 1982; Robbins, Anthony, and Richardson 1978; Robertson 1979; Wallis, 1984; Wilson, 1976), so it is becoming clear that these movements raise different *practical* problems in different countries. The situation in the USA has been analysed in several places (Shupe and Bromley 1980; Bromley, Busching, and Shupe 1982; Delgado 1977; Melton and Moore 1982), but an attempt will be made here to draw together material from other countries. This chapter is focused mainly on the practical responses to the major NRMs in the Federal Republic of Germany (FRG) and France. Church–state relations form part of the background to these practical responses, although it will be shown that this is not a salient aspect of what is popularly called 'the cult problem' in Europe. The USA is the only western country where cult-related problems have resonated with a wider debate about church–state relations (Robbins 1984).

It goes without saying that an analysis comparing many different movements in two countries can only result in rather tentative generalizations in the compass of this chapter. Finer distinctions and closer attention to detail, in particular to the pattern of legal responses to new religious movements, are an urgent priority for future research.

Ideally, it should also be possible to discriminate between the *modus operandi* of each of the supposedly monolithic 'Religious Multinationals' in different countries. The present state of reliable knowledge about them is not sufficient, however, to permit such discrimination. There are even wide discrepancies, for example, between different estimates of the numerical strength of the main movements in question. Thus, Müller-Küppers and Specht (1979) estimated that the Unification Church had 6,000 members in the FRG and ISKCON about 200. The combined membership of the Family of Love, TM, and the Divine Light Mission was put at 65,800. By contrast, Kehrer (1980) put the total at no more than 2,000 and credited the Unification Church with 500 fully committed members and ISKCON with 100 monks and nuns. The authors of the most extensive report on NRMs in Germany (Berger and Hexel 1981) estimated the strength of the UC's full-time membership as 700 in 1980. Ananda Marga was said to have 150 members and DLM about 200.

There is less discrepancy between estimates of the number of members of the 'new sects' in France. A reliable estimate (Woodrow 1977) is that the Unification Church has 1,000 members and ISKCON 'several hundreds'. The total following of the Family of Love, and the Divine Light Mission is put at 2,300. Vernette (1976) is entirely in agreement with these figures. All that can be safely claimed here is that some NRMs adapt their operations to suit prevailing conditions and that the image of them conveyed in some American commentaries (e.g. Stoner and Parke 1977; Horowitz 1978) is excessively influenced by local conditions and is inappropriate to other locations. Even the best informed American students of NRMs seem to be only dimly aware of how these movements function in Europe and elsewhere.

It is worth pointing out, in passing, that the sociological study of NRMs in Europe is beset with problems which do not arise in work on the same movements in the USA. First, the number of movements and of their participants is so much smaller that comparatively few resources have been devoted to their systematic study. Even the most basic facts about the movements' social composition, distribution, and resources are either unknown or unconfirmed. Second, there is a marked tendency to regard NRMs as American creations which are strictly marginal to European social conditions. Consequently, it is not thought necessary or instructive in some quarters to study the movements closely.

In the present circumstances, then, it is necessary to forgo a detailed description of NRMs in Europe and to focus attention, instead, on the evidence which is available about the public responses to them.[1] The fact that the public response is more evident and better documented than the movements themselves is a revealing comment on their status. Very few people have taken the trouble to study them closely, but many more people are prepared to organize defences against them. Fear of the unknown is no doubt largely responsible for this imbalance between knowledge and action. This chapter analyses in turn the responses to NRMs in the FRG and France. The material is organized under the headings of religious history, salient problems, and modes of social control.

The Federal Republic of Germany

Religious History

The ratio of Protestants to Roman Catholics in the FRG is roughly 55:45 but, in spite of tensions in some areas, there have been very few signs of serious friction between them since 1945. Indeed, they have been jointly credited with partial responsibility for underpinning the post-war stability and emergent confidence of the increasingly powerful and prosperous German nation (Fürstenberg 1974; Kehrer 1972; Schmidtchen 1979).

A number of reasons have been given for the basically harmonious division between Protestants and Catholics. First, the character of the dominant Lutheran Church is far from being exclusivist or intolerant. Second, the two groups of religionists are largely concentrated in different regions: Protestants in the north and east, Catholics in the south and west. Third, there is an underlying consensus on moral values which outweighs doctrinal differences between them (Schmidtchen 1972). Fourth, the moral consensus has been relatively undisturbed by exposure to non-Christian cultures. Finally, the more 'enthusiastic' currents within the two major faiths which in other countries have sometimes led to sectarian divisiveness have been successfully contained inside the mainstream churches (Drummond 1951). The Pietist current within Protestantism is the clearest expression of successfully 'contained' enthusiasm.

With the amalgamation of the Lutheran and Calvinist churches under the umbrella of the German Evangelical Church from 1945 onwards and with the gradual erosion of Catholic separatism symbolized by practices such as 'confessional' voting preference for the Christian Democratic Union, the overall picture has been summarized as a 'static equilibrium between the two major churches, which together encompass 95 per cent of the German population. The other religious groups hardly count. . . . [Moreover] the differentiations in the Protestant camp are of little import for the situation nowadays' (Kehrer 1972: 191).

With the exception of the Neue Apostolische Kirche and the Jehovah's Witnesses, sectarian groups have enjoyed little success in the FRG.[2] This can be explained by reference to the political history of the inter-war years when the extremes of both democracy and totalitarianism, represented in various religious sects, were widely discredited. Not only has the post-war generation of German adults been highly suspicious of extremism, it has also gone to considerable trouble to protect youth from what are considered to be the destructive attractions of all extremist ideologies. Pastor Niemöller, for example, advised that the Evangelical Church's role during Reconstruction was 'to enter the schools, rebuild youth organizations, influence the universities . . . and accept broad responsibilities in political and economic life' in order to prevent a recrudescence of all extremism (quoted in Drummond 1951: 275).

The picture that emerges from this rapid survey of the recent religious history of the FRG is that, low rates of participation in church activities notwithstanding (Fürstenberg 1974; Kehrer 1972), Christian values permeate all the major spheres of life and that relations between Protestants and Catholics do not present a serious threat to the prevailing political, social, and economic order. The scope of irreligion, non-Christian religions, and enthusiastic minorities is extremely restricted. It must be added, however, that German observers of minority religious groups have nevertheless been vigilant in monitoring their activities. Painstaking research has led to quite exhaustive surveys by Hutten (1950, 1957), Gründler (1961), Haack (1976, 1979), and Mildenberger (1979).

Salient problems

The predominantly stable and conservative ethos of the FRG has been threatened by student rebellions, political terrorism, and 'youth religions' (*Jugendreligionen*). In each case the source of the threat is identified as the disaffection of youth from the prevailing values, and this circumstance has given a distinctive character to the 'cult problem'.[3]

As Hardin and Kehrer (1982) have clearly demonstrated, there were few religious grounds in German culture and society for the rejection of new religious movements in the early 1970s. Indeed, it has been suggested that this period witnessed 'the advent of a new *secular* morality in Germany' (König 1971: 284. Emphasis added). Objections to 'youth religions' or 'youth sects' have, accordingly, been based on non-religious grounds and are directed against their practices rather than their teachings (Kehrer 1980). For the USA, by contrast, this argument has been rejected by Robbins and Anthony (1978).

One of the twin foci of anti-cult sentiment in the FRG is the allegedly harmful effect produced by 'youth religions' on the capacity of young Germans to complete satisfactorily their courses of education and to embark on conventional careers (Hardin 1983). This is not, of course, peculiar to the FRG, but what gives it special significance in that country is that it has a powerful resonance in many different agencies in various social spheres. There is a high degree of consensus in the ruling circles of the state, the civil service, provincial governments, political parties, trades unions, educational institutions, and churches concerning the prime value of personal hard work and determination in preparing for, and developing, a career or profession (see Fürstenberg 1974: Dahrendorf 1965). In other words the FRG has a complex set of interwoven, non-religious, and powerful sources of opposition to anything which interferes with the orderly and methodical progression from education to career. 'Youth religions' are one such interference. In this respect the German response to NRMs differs markedly from the American and the British: the latter is characterized by the predominance of *ad hoc* groupings of 'concerned citizens' which have had only marginal success in co-opting more powerful, pre-existing organizations into the anti-cult campaign.

The other major focus of anti-cult sentiment in the FRG is the allegedly common root of political terrorism and the 'youth religions', namely, the 'flight from reality'. This is the officially approved etiology and is widely reproduced in the deliberations of various official, semi-official, and independent bodies. The Federal Council for Youth (das *Bundesjugendkuratorium*), for example, reasoned that,

'Terrorism may legitimately be considered as the extreme behaviour of a tiny, isolated group of young people, but there are many indications – which have so far largely failed to attract attention in public discussion – that terrorism is only one form of the numerous variants on youth withdrawal from our society. Other symptoms of the sickness of social, political and cultural life are apathy, the flight into drugs or alcohol, the turning to youth sects and suicide.'
(Fetscher 1979: 115–16. Emphasis original. Trans. J.A.B.)

A similar point was made by the Minister for Employment, Health, and Social Affairs in the Province of Nordrhein-Westfalen when he argued that all groups of young extremists, including youth religions, arose from the same causes. They were listed as: the inability of young people to cope with the tensions within a liberal-democratic order of society and state and, as a result, the psychic need to form opposition groups in society (Nordrhein-Westfalen 1979: 8).[4]

One of the interesting sociological effects of the promulgation of more or less official etiologies is that they are taken up enthusiastically by widely different anti-cult groups for their own purposes. Thus, the link with terrorism is explored in the publications of various religious and secular organizations as a supplement to their more specialized analyses of 'youth religions' (Haack 1979; Müller-Küppers and Specht 1979). The result is that there appears to be an impressive degree of uniformity in the anti-cult sentiment expressed by apparently unrelated groups in the FRG.

Many common themes emerge from reports originating in organizations as diverse as the Office for Youth Work in the Evangelical Church of Hesse and Nassau;[5] the Campaign for Youth protection in Nordrhein-Westfalen;[6] the Association for the Cultivation of Political Education;[7] and the Young Democrats of Germany.[8] Above all, there is agreement on the general conceptualization of 'the cult problem' in the FRG which is defined largely in terms of the baneful influence that 'youth religions' are said to have on the motivation, the morale, and the morals of young people.[9]

Probably the best known exponent of this general conceptualization is Pastor Friedrich-Wilhelm Haack. As a specialist in matters related to religious sects and cults he has published numerous case studies of particular groups as well as large works of a more synthetic kind. His characterization of 'new youth religions' emphasizes (a) their leaders' claims to supply absolute truth and (b) the all-embracing nature of the social communities that are founded for members. Other characteristics include the movements' essential similarity of teachings; exclusive orientation towards young people; and international scale of operations. Haack's explanation of the movements' success is complex and, in places, subtle but it can be summarized as follows: young people with spiritual problems or confusions are channelled towards youth religions first by contact with a supposedly perfected family which, second, delivers a prescription for salvation and thereby, third, draws members into dependence on a Holy Master or Guru. Personality changes occur during membership as a result of practices designed to make membership synonymous with obedience to the Master's authority. The long-term consequences are said to include abandonment of education and work; rupture of personal relations with friends and family; loss of material security; criminal behaviour in some cases; and serious mental difficulties.

The phenomenon of new youth religions is interpreted as a consequence of the hegemony of a 'technical civilization' which is orientated towards the present rather than to the future, especially in the field of egalitarian social policies. People are treated as objects to be manipulated for the sake of achieving egalitarian goals. Consequently, natural social relations and groups have been broken, giving rise to a search for a sense of belonging, meaning, the future, and a place to feel at home. It is in these conditions of impersonal social manipulation that vulnerable youth can allegedly be recruited by opportunistic religious movements which profit from the general crisis of modern society.

The cult problem in Germany is grafted on to anxieties lying at the root of interest groups and agencies existing before the arrival of NRMs in the 1970s and has therefore acquired the status of a social problem which, in the opinion of some (Hardin 1983; Kehrer 1980), is out of all proportion to the numerical and material strength of the movements. Those groups which have come into existence since the mid 1970s as specifically anti-cult organizations have been strongly influenced by the politico-moral environment in which they operate.

Modes of social control

At the centre of the network of diverse agencies having an interest in controlling the operations of NRMs in the FRG is the Federal Ministry for Youth, Family, and Health. It has served as an important medium for communication between them and has initiated its own programme of research. Information and practical assistance emanating from the Ministry has been so influential that its contribution warrants extensive analysis here. Its complex role raises as many questions as it solves about the relation between church and state in Germany.

In this connection the ministry is probably best known for its 23-page brochure entitled 'Youth Religions in the German Federal Republic' (*Die Jugendreligionen in der Bundesrepublik Deutschland*) which is actually a 1980 report to a parliamentary committee investigating complaints about new religious movements. Twenty-five thousand copies of the report were printed for distribution either through the ministry's normal outlets or, by request, through anti-cult groups, churches, or youth organizations.

The minister's foreword constitutes the 'cult problem' in terms which are immediately understandable to critics of NRMs and which bear out my analysis in the previous section of this chapter. Her duty was to warn people about 'dangers' which 'threaten' young people, for she had a constitutional obligation to 'protect' young people and their families. She was most worried about the psychic 'damage' caused by the 'dubious' practices of 'youth religions', and her hope was that parents would band together for mutual assistance and support.

The main body of the report reproduces the argument that 'youth religions' form part of the more general 'flight from reality' (*die Realitätsflucht*) which, in various guises, is afflicting young people. It is aggravated, according to the report, by the fact that some movements offer to young people would-be absolute answers to life's problems which suit their needs 'like a key fits a lock' (p. 12). The problem is said to be experienced as a personal one, but the ministry's view is that it stems from social causes which can only be effectively handled through appropriate moral education. The ministry's practical response is therefore dominated by the policy of making as much information as possible available to all agencies responsible in some way for youth affairs. It aims to alert people to the 'dangers' allegedly presented by 'youth religions', to commission research into their long-term effects on members and to support the initiatives of parents who are critical of them. At the same time it encourages law-enforcement agencies to make full use of existing legislation regarding such things as the use of public places for recruiting purposes, the solicitation of donations in public, the issue of fraudulent promises, and the use of force against a person's will.

In anticipation of complaints that it may be infringing basic rights to free association and the freedoms of belief, conscience and creed, the ministry justifies its action on two grounds. First, it argues that some so-called religious groups have forfeited certain constitutional privileges by reason of their commercial activities. This means that they are disqualified from the benefits normally accorded to bona fide religious organizations. Consequently, the ministry denies that its support for anti-cultism infringes constitutional protection of religious freedom. The second argument is that special privileges are allowed to religious and ideological groups only so long as they keep within the bounds of contemporary codes or morality ('Soweit sie sich im Rahmen gewisser übereinstimmender sittlicher Grundanschauungen der heutigen Kulturvölker halten', in the words of the Federal Supreme Court). The implication is that some NRMs have failed to earn the constitutional privileges normally granted to religion and are therefore necessarily exposed to the full force of the law as it applies to non-religious groups. The conclusion is that the ministry supports anti-cultism, not in order to infringe religious freedom, but in order to discharge its constitutional responsibility to protect citizens from potential or actual harm.

The ministry's involvement in religious and cult-related matters is not, however, limited to the dissemination of information and warnings about NRMs. It has also sponsored research and conferences on the topic. As long ago as the 1950s,[10] for example, it financed a survey of the religious practices of a representative sample of young people (Wölber 1959). More significantly it financed an extensive research project conducted between 1979 and 1980 by staff at the European Centre for Social Welfare and Research in Vienna on 'Causes and effects of social dissension among young people with special reference to "youth religions"'.

The project, which merits close examination, entailed 108 in-depth interviews with members and ex-members of four NRMs in the FRG (the UC, Ananda Marga, the DLM, and Scientology) and with the parents and friends of members. In addition, short interviews were conducted with fifty-four members, and about fourteen hours of video film were made about the movements' activities. In a second part of the project, specialists from the USA, the UK, the Netherlands, and the FRG were commissioned to prepare reports on the situation of NRMs in their own countries.[11]

The 381-page report of the Vienna project (Berger and Hexel 1981) reviews much of the social scientific theorizing about NRMs before presenting its main findings. Major sections are devoted to life in the movements, withdrawal from them, and the consequences of the group experience. There are extensive recommendations about the best ways for churches, public authorities, trades unions, youth organizations, schools, and families to deal with members of NRMs. The most important conclusions are summarized as follows.

(a) The process of identity-formation in early adulthood is experienced by many as difficult, especially in a society characterized by high degrees of complexity, competitiveness, and pressure to conform. As a result, young people may retreat into themselves in the hope that, if they can only change themselves, then society and the whole world might also be transformed into something better. Political parties are rejected in this process of 'internal migration', but NRMs are found to offer a feeling of belonging, people with whom they can identify, and unambiguous meanings.

(b) It is mistaken to regard NRMs as a unitary phenomenon. There are major differences between them in respect of teachings, practices, and forms of organization. The evidence of shared characteristics, such as structures of authoritarian relationships, is undeniable but ambiguous because many other, quite different types of social collectivities share the same characteristics. Scientology's emphasis on correct knowledge rather than religious faith sets this particular movement clearly apart from the others.

(c) The numerical strength of NRMs has commonly been exaggerated. In fact, the number of members is very small. It would therefore be sensible to keep the scale of the cult problem in perspective: it is less important than, for example, youth unemployment, drug addiction, and the lack of any clear picture of work opportunities in the future. The dangers that extremist political movements present to young people are also considered more worthy of close examination than are today's NRMs.

(d) Conflicts between NRMs and the rest of society must be understood as the result of clashes between different sets of values.

(e) The conditions which make NRMs attractive to young people are summarized as:

  (i) The contradiction between the idealistic values articulated mainly in families and the experience of life's realities gives rise to a sense of directionlessness in adolescence.

 (ii) This leads to a process of searching for answers which are not found in families, schools, or churches.

(iii) Matters are aggravated by problems of communication and personal relationships which partly stem from disrupted relationships in childhood and puberty caused by excessive residential mobility and changes of significant others.

But not all informants claimed that these problems had reached a crisis point at the time of joining a NRM.

(f) Members of NRMs refused to describe their action as a flight from social reality but saw it, rather, as an attempt to construct a new social and religious alternative which might call for harder work than is involved in simply conforming with the prevailing system.

(g) There was no conclusive evidence from the in-depth interviews or the psychological tests that NRMs generated mental pathology. Mentally unstable people mainly experience greater stability on joining a movement, and this enabled many to conquer a drug problem. But definitely more serious mental strain occurs among those who leave a NRM; and those who had been mentally disturbed before joining could lapse into serious crises.

(h) Members of NRMs are positive about the significant changes which occur in their personality and behaviour patterns. They consider that they have made gains in direction, self-confidence, effectiveness, balance, etc. Even former members repeatedly mentioned these aspects and eventually came to consider their period of membership as a mainly constructive phase of their life which they had then outgrown. Other changes included a narrowing of interests, forms of language-use, and personal freedom of decision.

(i) In no case were there any indications of so-called psychomutation. Even parents maintained repeatedly that their child's basic character had not been altered.

I think that it would be fair to sum up this project's findings by saying that they confirm and strengthen many features of the federal ministry's etiology of NRMs but that they also play down the alleged dangers attributed to the movements. The report constantly seeks to situate 'youth religions' in a wider context of social problems. In this context they slip almost into insignificance alongside much more serious, pressing, and widespread problems affecting young people generically.

The highly intrusive role of the Federal Ministry for Youth, Family, and Health has been seen as an encouragement to groups and agencies concerned primarily with combating the influence of 'youth religions'. The major churches, for example, have responded by either setting up special posts of responsibility in this area or by strengthening the work of existing units which could be adapted to the new situation. The best known examples are the Evangelical Lutheran Church's Office for Sects and Ideologies in Bavaria to which Pastor Haack is attached, and the Evangelical Centre for Ideologies in Stuttgart to which Drs Reimer and Mildenberger are attached. The Roman Catholic Church maintained a residential centre for ex-cultists near Cologne. This may be partial confirmation of the view that, 'in the area of social welfare the churches carry out a considerable part in the integration of West German society; it must still be kept in mind that state and church institutions differ very little either in their structure or in their estimation of what cultural role they play.'

(Kehrer 1972: 208)

The contrast to the church–state relations which prevail in the USA could hardly be sharper, as we shall see in the next chapter.

Associations of anti-cultists have received moral and material support from the ministry. The most powerful is the Aktion für geistige und psychische Freiheit, Arbeitsgemeinschaft der Elterninitiativen e.V. (AGPF) which was founded in 1977 as an umbrella body to co-ordinate a number of existing organizations and individuals working against 'cults'. It receives regular subsidies from the ministry and has had a Member of the Bundestag as President. It appears to benefit from both formal and personal contacts with many branches of the federal civil service.

The targets of AGPF's work are invariably described as 'destructive cults'. They are said to be destructive for (a) destroying family and personal relationships, even the personality of members, and (b) inciting members to revere a Master or Guru as if he were God or godlike. Special importance is attached to the capacity of parents to maintain contacts with, and compassion for, their adult children even when they have cut themselves off from friends, spouses, and colleagues in order to join a NRM. The exchange of information and experiences among parents is also regarded as valuable in itself as well as often leading to the release of members.

Less prominent anti-cult groups in Germany include the Aktion Psychokultgefahren of Düsseldorf and the Arbeitskreis of Herford. The latter has close connections with the Christian Democrat political party. Special mention must also be made of an organization which is not specifically anti-cult but which has energetically countered the public recruitment campaigns of the Church of Scientology. This is the Stuttgart-based body for consumer protection in the field of education, Aktion Bildungsinformation (ABI). By the early 1980s it had won all fifteen of the legal cases that it had brought against Scientology for alleged infringements of laws prohibiting recruitment in public places. Yet, even this privately funded organization has close links with other anti-cult groups and, after the publication in 1979 of its 130-page book 'The Sect of Scientology and its Front

Organizations',[12] it has been treated as a part of the broader alliance of forces mobilized by the churches and the federal government. In addition to exposing the allegedly exploitative and fraudulent character of Scientology's organizations, ABI's book argues that the movement is anti-democratic and bent on imposing its own values on society. Scientology's founder, L. Ron Hubbard, is accused of scorning the achievements of democracy as nothing more than inflation and income tax. Moreover, the movement is said to abuse the basic laws protecting the freedom of religion and freedom of opinion by insisting on the right to approach people in public with the aim of changing their opinions and by frequently threatening legal action against critics. Since the book was written, its author, Ingo Heinemann, has become the Executive Secretary of the anti-cult group AGPF. This is yet another instance of the overlapping constituencies of German anti-cult circles.

Finally, federal officials from various ministries have discussed concerted action against 'youth religions' in accordance with the general policy adopted towards them by the Ministry for Youth, Family, and Health and the Interior Ministry. For example, at a conference of federal and provincial ministers of youth and senators in May 1979 it was agreed that the cult problem had to be primarily tackled by improved understanding and intensive spiritual discussion. At the same time, though, officials from the provincial Ministries of Finance began to consider ways of preventing abuse of the laws granting fiscal privileges to charitable organizations. And Interior Ministry officials at the federal and provincial levels discussed the need for customs and border police to be extra vigilant in scrutinizing the applications from foreign members of NRMs to enter Germany. Finally, provincial Ministers of Public Worship and Education agreed in a meeting in 1979 that school teachers, especially teachers of religion, social studies and philosophy, had a special duty to inculcate the kind of self-responsibility, independence of thought and political responsibility required for effective citizenship. Officials in provincial governments have been encouraged to devise ways of disseminating anti-cult literature as widely as possible among young people (see Nordrhein-Westfalen 1979).

Moreover, funds have been made available to organizers of conferences dealing with cult-related problems. For example, the federal Ministry for Youth, Family, and Health subsidized a two-day conference in February 1978 on 'New Youth Religions' organized jointly by the German Society for Child and Youth Psychiatry and the

Federal Conference for Educational Counselling. The proceedings were published in Müller-Küppers and Specht (1979). The editors' foreword precludes any possible uncertainty about the participants' negative stance towards NRMs: 'The dangers facing young people who join [NRMs] have become more significant' (p. 6). And the selection of published papers reflects the range of anti-cult thinking at that time. The federal ministry's financial support was later given to the parents' association, AGPF, for organizing an international conference on 'The effects of new totalitarian religions and pseudo-religious movements upon society and health' in Bonn in 1981. The list of organizations participating in the conference included the federal government, the Federal Medical Association, the Federal Association for Health Education and the German Society for Child and Youth Psychiatry. The ministry also subsidized a meeting of the Federal Conference for Educational Counselling on the theme of 'Counselling in the area of youth religions' in November 1983. It is significant for my interpretation of the dense network of official and voluntary organizations in German anti-cult circles that the conference report was subsequently circulated by yet another organization, German Family Service.

Another example of co-operation between official and voluntary organizations is the plan announced in *Die Welt* on 12 April 1983 for West Berlin's municipal Youth Department to set up, in conjunction with the Protestant Church, a telephone 'lifeline' for young people seeking urgent help with cult-related problems. The announcement also mentioned that the Youth Department had already set up a special unit for full-time monitoring of the activities and recruitment methods of youth religions in Berlin.

In conclusion, the distinctiveness of the response to NRMs in the FRG can be characterized in terms of (a) the very high levels of agreement about the nature of the 'cult problem' which prevail in a wide variety of social spheres, (b) the connection made between 'youth religions' and the roots of terrorism, (c) the dense network of agencies in federal and provincial government, churches, political and social service organizations which co-operate in combating cultic influence, and (d) the strongly intrusive role played by the Federal Ministry for Youth, Family, and Health in giving encouragement to diverse expressions of anti-cultism.

France

Religious history

The very hegemony of the French Catholic Church has been the occasion of a strong undercurrent of opposition to it from various quarters (see Dansette 1953–56; Isambert 1972). Thus, in a country where between 89 and 94 per cent of the inhabitants have been estimated to be at least nominal Catholics (Boulard 1954), Catholicism has also led to 'large political and social fissures, organic oppositions and secularist dogmas of various kinds' (Martin 1978: 119). Protestantism has often given rise to this kind of opposition, and although relations between the two major religious communities in France are nowadays improving, there is still a wide social and cultural gulf between them (Fouilloux 1975; Mehl 1965). Matters have been aggravated in the twentieth century by the growth of enthusiastic movements outside the 'official' Protestant camp such as Jehovah's Witnesses, Pentecostals and Mormons (Chéry 1954; Dagon 1958; Séguy 1956; Vernette 1976). Such movements have always been an object of intense suspicion for the French Catholic Church, and the response to the growth of various NRMs in the 1970s has been to regard them as the natural successors of intransigent Protestantism. The problem of the 'new sects' has therefore been grafted on to an ancient root-stock, namely, suspicion of Protestantism's potential for 'subversion' of the natural, organic order of French society. In Martin's view 'The intégrisme of the Catholics defined [Protestants], along with freemasons and Jews, as amongst the alien elements in France and they accepted this role *vis-à-vis* the Catholics' (1978: 123).

Salient problems

The 'cult problem' in France is distinctive by reason of the dominant Church's ambivalence towards what it patronizingly terms '*dissidences*'. It recognizes that NRMs can be a response to genuine spiritual difficulties; but it insists at the same time that the proliferation of such movements can only aggravate the difficulties. This was clearly illustrated in the Bulletin of the French Bishops Office:

'The scouring effect of secularization and the tidal race of unbelief go together with a renewal of interest in spiritual things. The "death of God" is giving way to His return to reality: the one being

no doubt as ambiguous as the other. This is the context in which
the phenomenon of sects today must be located.'

(*Documents. Episcopat.* 1975: 5. Trans. J.A.B.)

The significance of NRMs is thereby reduced to the function of
'warning lights': they indicate that something has gone wrong in the
machinery. This theme has been taken up and reproduced in the mass
media and in popular books on NRMs (see Woodrow 1977; Leduc
and de Plaige 1978; Facon and Parent 1980; Le Cabellec 1983;
D'Eaubonne 1982) as well as in Catholic publications (see Vernette
1976, 1979).

The 'new sects' are disparaged in France, as were the so-called
'classical sects' before them, for being closed off from the would-be
universal Church. Self-imposed isolation is seen as proof of an
organization's merely human weakness, whereas the inclusiveness of
the Church is considered the guarantee of its divine favour. Spiritual
enthusiasm and vitality are not regarded as healthy unless they are
cultivated and controlled within the overarching framework of the
historic Church (Séguy 1977). This point was symbolized in the
caption to a photograph of roped-together mountaineers printed in a
special issue of a popular Catholic magazine devoted to the theme
'What to make of the Sects?': 'Roping yourselves together is fine. But
where can you go without an experienced guide? The members of a
sect are tied together by real brotherly friendship. But without the
Church to guide them they cannot reach the summit' (*Fêtes et Saisons*
1963. Trans. J.A.B.).

From this point of view there is no significant difference between
the 'new' and the 'classical' sects. Thus, Alain Woodrow, religious
affairs correspondent for *Le Monde* and author of the influential *Les
Nouvelles Sectes*, is content to propose a unitary explanation for the
development of movements as diverse as the Unification Church,
Jehovah's Witnesses, the Family of Love, Seventh Day Adventism,
Nichiren Shoshu, and Christian Science. For him they are all 'politi-
co-religious sects . . . captivating a young generation, which has gone
adrift, with the lure of the craziest utopias' (1977: 12). They are all
said to meet a need for friendship and community among marginal
people who are vulnerable to the high-pressure sales techniques of
sectarian recruiting organizations. The only distinction that he
permits is between those groups which confine themselves to meditation or charity work and those whose leaders have fallen prey to
the temptations of personal, economic, and political power.

In view of the formerly hegemonic position of the Catholic Church in France it is not surprising that the problem of the 'new sects' is intimately tied in many analyses to the perceived threat of a conspiracy against 'normal' social structures and cultural assumptions. Thus, whereas in the USA the dominant anxiety about 'cults' concerns their effects on the minds of individual recruits, anti-cult sentiment in France is dominated by a basically political anxiety about the power that is allegedly being sought and accumulated by their leaders. Of course, this necessarily involves reference to the pyschology of manipulation, as, for example, in the argument that 'Systems of human liberation are more often than not agencies of tyranny. . . . The Multinationals of Consciousness are set up by informed men who have often had a career in business or in scientific and academic circles' (Leduc and de Plaige 1978: 41. Trans. J.A.B.)

A more psychologically biased version of this general explanation can be found in D'Eaubonne's (1982) survey of numerous sectarian movements in France. In the light of the findings of Stanley Milgram's experiments on the willingness of volunteers to apply electric shocks to disguised victims in conformity with instructions from the experimenters, she interprets the readiness of young people to follow modern gurus and prophets as just one instance of a societal problem with authority. Widespread despair in the midst of various social crises is cited as the factor which disposes people to be nostalgic about authority and, therefore, to adopt a conformist stance towards leaders who issue firm orders. Lack of strong social ties and of a sense of belonging is also said to explain the allegedly irrational and dangerous desire of young people to throw themselves into high-demand groups.

It is also common in France for discussion of psychological manipulation in 'new sects' to be set in a wider context of conspiracy. The treatment in French publications of the People's Temple tragedy in Guyana, for example, was dominated by the idea of conspiracy, and most notably by the suspicion that there had been various conspiracies of silence. A popular book on the topic (Facon and Parent 1980) concluded that the following questions remained unanswered: why did the California State Prosecutor not investigate allegations of criminal activity in the movement until Jim Jones had fled to Guyana in 1977? Why was his eventual report on the movement never published? Why did the State Department deny that people were being held against their will and in pitiable conditions at Jonestown? Why has none of the survivors, known to have been members of Jones' armed bodyguard, ever been prosecuted? And so on. Such questions have been asked in other countries, but in France they form the main framework for a great deal of the thinking about cultism in general.

A closely allied aspect of the 'cult problem' in France is the accusation that there is a totalitarian intent behind the conspiracies. Nowhere is this more clearly demonstrated than in a document published by France's leading anti-cult organization in 1977. *A Comparative Study of Two Ideologies* consists of juxtaposed quotations from Hitler's *Mein Kampf* and Sun Myung Moon's aphorisms, and its conclusion is that 'the Unification Church has appropriated all the guiding principles of Nazism.' Moreover,

> 'It is time to understand how our children are, in good faith, being manipulated, blinded and subjected to a sect as if they were slaves. They cannot see the secret aims of their organization and, anyway, they are not allowed the time for reflection nor the material opportunities to understand what kind of a plot is being hatched around them. They fail to realize what an evil role they are being surreptitiously made to play against the national interest.'

The theme of subversion is finally reinforced by a note of xenophobia:

> 'The problem is serious enough for the government and our elected representatives to take the necessary steps to prevent the nation from suffering a dictatorship which would be all the more terrible for being the work of foreigners with an outlook different from ours.'

> (ADFI 1977: 17–18. Trans. J.A.B.)

These are extremely serious charges and they go far beyond the accusation, which is widely heard in North America, that the leaders of 'cults' are spiritual confidence tricksters. The strength, if not the volume, of organized anti-cult sentiment in France is of a different order altogether. The difference probably reflects the deep-rooted feeling in some sections of French public opinion that the country's formerly unitary and dominant value-system is under concerted attack. The whole tone of the opposition to 'new sects' in France is different from that which pervades the North American claims that the 'destructive cults' merely abuse the privileges properly accorded to bona fide religions in a pluralistic culture. The value of pluralism is not yet conceded in some anti-cult circles in France.

The special prominence accorded in French anti-cult sentiment to the themes of conspiracy, subversion, and totalitarianism has to be understood in the light of the scandal which surrounded a Franco-Belgian sect in the early 1970s. This event has indelibly coloured public opinion in France in a way which is unknown in other countries. It concerns the sect of The Three Holy Hearts, a small familial community founded by a graduate of the University of Louvain whose doctoral thesis on 'Terror as a system of domination' seems to have served as its blueprint (Lecerf 1975). Allegations of adultery, fraud, and sexual abuse of an under-age girl led to police investigations, criminal charges, an Interpol man-hunt, and the eventual conviction of the leader, Roger Melchior, for abducting a young person and for abandoning his family. In French anti-cult circles these events represent the most clear-cut instance of cultic infamy because of the apparently systematic use of terror. Moreover, there are suspicions that both the Catholic and Protestant hierarchies in France and Belgium connived at the sect's excesses and have not had the courage to admit their mistake. The case is said to illustrate 'the fragility of the defences of major institutions confronting schemes for infiltration which are cleverly conducted by mini-churches in search of legitimacy' (Baffoy 1978: 55), and it is frequently cited as justification of the need for vigilance in France against would-be subversive and totalitarian cults.

A further complication of the conspiracy theory is the suspicion that government officials have tried to turn a blind eye or feign ignorance of cult-related problems. This was the view taken most forcefully and expressed most volubly by a socialist Député, Alain Vivien, who has been conducting a campaign against 'new sects' since the mid 1970s. We shall consider some aspects of his campaign below, but for the moment it is important simply to note his complaints about the silence of officialdom:

'We know about the Moonies' brainwashing, the attacks on the family rights of Melchior's followers [the Three Holy Hearts sect], the psychological and economic pressures of the Church of Scientology, but no official steps have been taken, especially in France, to carry out a serious investigation and, if necessary, to impose sanctions. The written and oral questions raised by Members of [the French] Parliament have so far received, at best, derisory replies and most of the time no response at all. This is a violation of the statutes.'

(*Le Monde* 26 June 1977)

The fact that Monsieur Vivien was subsequently appointed to conduct a parliamentary fact-finding inquiry into NRMs in France does not seem to have shaken his belief that a conspiracy of official silence had previously hampered attempts to expose the 'cult problem'.

Modes of social control

The thorough integration of conspiracy-theory into the main anti-cult organization in France is illustrated in the following quotation from its vice-president, a sociologist with personal knowledge of some aspects of The Three Holy Hearts scandal:

> 'There is cause for concern that a sect can become dangerous with a theory which defies the most elementary good sense. It is surprising that it can recruit followers on a massive scale. But the most disturbing thing is that a sect can be certain that the highest-ranking civil and ecclesiastical authorities will keep quiet about it and even actively collude with it.'
>
> (Baffoy 1978: 54. Trans. J.A.B.)

Indeed, the theory is also said to explain why various Pentecostal and charismatic movements have been favoured by regimes in Latin America: their non-involvement in politics, in contrast to the Roman Catholic Church, supposedly makes them *ipso facto* attractive to hard-pressed, repressive regimes.

The organization to which Baffoy belongs, L'Association pour la Défense de la Famille et de l'Individu (ADFI), enjoys an ambivalent relationship with the state. On the one hand, it is critical of the state for turning a blind eye to the 'dangers' presented by the 'new sects'. In fact, it accuses the government of profiting from the sects' capacity to recruit and rehabilitate various kinds of marginal people for whom the state is thereby relieved of the burden of providing social welfare. The 'pay-off' for the government was not lost on the Député who argued that 'It is better for a youth to join Moon than to join the barricades', and it is this reasoning which, according to ADFI, lies behind the government's refusal to act against the new religions unless evidence of their criminality is provided. Thus, when the Interior Minister was questioned about the possible dangers to French nationals in the wake of the Jonestown tragedy in Guyana he gave an assurance that the police were satisfied that no organization comparable with the People's Temple existed in France. More importantly, he added:

'Nevertheless, the activities of sects are under constant surveillance by the relevant services of my department so that warnings can be made of any attack on basic liberties and, if proven, crimes committed by their members or leaders can be recorded. . . . I remind the Chamber . . . that no serious crime has hitherto been attributed to sects and that, as enquiries stand at present, it does not seem possible to proceed against them with the powers of dissolution available to judicial and administrative authorities under the law of July 1901 concerning their charters and the law of January 10 1936 concerning military groups and private militias.'
(*Journal de Débats. Assemblée Nationale.* Item 9389.
November 30 1978. Trans. J.A.B.)

On the other hand, ADFI receives an annual grant from the Ministry of Health to help cover its administrative costs and it has considerable support in the Chamber of Deputies. In fact, as a direct result of pressure from two Députés who are closely associated with the ADFI, the French Parliament agreed in 1979 that its Legislative Commission should conduct an enquiry into NRMs in France. ADFI has been energetically amassing information for presentation to the commission and is receiving widespread public support for its work. It could hardly be said to enjoy official status but it is certainly looked on with favour in many official circles.

In its origins ADFI represented an independent organization of parents seeking to oppose the NRMs which their children had joined. It developed spontaneously in half a dozen provincial centres in the early 1970s and was eventually given a federal structure in 1975. In Paris it has a permanent headquarters provided by a city-centre Catholic parish, and from this base it maintains close relations with the mass media and with those agencies of the Church which specialize in the study of sectarian movements. It publishes vast amounts of information and can provide an effective 'personal cases' service for people disturbed in any way by a 'new sect'. At the same time, and in imitation of the Catholic Church's practice, it maintains files on the so-called classical sects and generally accepts the Church's official explanations of their growing strength in France.

The parliamentary inquiry into new sects was authorized by Pierre Mauroy, Interior Minister in the socialist government which came to power in 1981.[13] The objective was not simply to investigate the practices of sects but also, and no less importantly, to consider their legal and material position in France. For the government's intention was no less to protect the basic freedoms of association than to expose the putative abuses of their individual members by religious sects. In other words, the aim was to find a way of balancing the rights of religious collectivities to conduct their affairs in their chosen manner against the rights of individuals to be protected against exploitation and deception.

A brief account of the legal mechanisms whereby religious groups can achieve recognized status in France is necessary at this point. The legal status of religious sects in France can take one of two forms. Under a law of 1901 they may have the status of non-profit associations but only if they submit themselves to, and successfully pass, a formal process of evaluation to determine their social usefulness. Alternatively, they may apply for recognition as religious 'congregations' but only on condition that they be approved by the Interior Minister and that their finances be open to public inspection. Neither of these procedures appears to recommend itself to minority religious groups, but there has been growing pressure on them to achieve legal recognition of one kind or the other in the recent past.

Although the full report of the parliamentary inquiry has not been published at the time of writing, enough has already been leaked to the press to permit a general picture of its main proposals to be sketched. The most important concerns the establishment of an interministerial agency in the civil service with responsibility for co-ordinating the various departments having an interest in the activities of NRMs. A number of other proposals have a bearing on ways of monitoring, disseminating, and using information about religious movements for the benefit of the public at large. Finally, there are proposals for improving the material position of defectors and would-be defectors.

The inquiry, which was led by Monsieur Vivien, Député for the Hauts de Seine constituency, reached its conclusions early in 1983. But the final report was confined to the Interior Minister's office. Public speculation about the reasons for the delay in publishing it has added further fuel to the widespread suspicion of an official conspiracy of silence.

The dominant responses to NRMs in France can be summarized in terms of (a) the pervasiveness of 'organicist' or *intégriste* assumptions about the natural order of French society derived from the Catholic Church's teaching, (b) the widespread currency given to themes of authoritarianism and conspiracy, and (c) the semi-official status enjoyed by the country's main anti-cult organization.

Discussion

Three generalizations can be made about anti-cult sentiment in the FRG and France.

First, the nature of 'the cult problem' clearly varies with the social, political, and cultural conditions prevailing in each country. In order to understand the distinctive animus against certain NRMs it is essential to examine not only their individual structures and teachings but also each country's religious communities in the case of European societies. Thus, in the absence of an all-encompassing constitutional separation of Church and state the nexus of inter-religious relationships is more important in the FRG and France than, for example, in the USA.

On this point I take issue with Kehrer (1980) who believes that there are no special features in West German society to account for its generally uniform and hostile response to NRMs. His argument is that recent events are simply the latest episode in the continuing historical dynamic affecting *all* societies and which intermittently opposes new salvation religions against the prevailing social values. (For an alternative formulation of a similar view, see Ellwood 1979b). This may well be true at one level, but what it ignores is that the ways in which this dynamic of challenge and counter-challenge is expressed are, at another level, heavily conditioned by their historical context. Indeed, given the speed and efficiency with which information is communicated between anti-cult groups in various countries today, it is hardly surprising that they employ a 'standard repertoire of attacks' (Kehrer 1980: 10). What this chapter has tried to show, however, is that the repertoire is arranged differently in the FRG and France because its 'standard' components have differential resonance with each country's social, political, and cultural structures. In other words, the charges against NRMs are layered in a different order in each country, and the order is far from arbitrary. The quick recourse to arguments about the level of 'deep structures' at which all religions are one is guaranteed to remove all human meaning from human affairs and is therefore of little help in explaining any particular historical juncture. It precludes the possibility of comparative study and would have been anathema to Max Weber whom Kehrer paradoxically cites in support of his argument.

Second, the trajectory of anti-cult sentiment in the FRG and France confirms the usefulness of focusing sociological attention on social networks and 'multi-organizational fields' (Beckford 1977; Gerlach and Hine 1970; Curtis and Zurcher 1973). The evidence indicates that pre-existing movements and movement-organizations have played a crucial role in canalizing nascent anti-cultism along particular channels. Thus, even the relatively autonomous and spontaneous initiatives of 'concerned citizens' and 'aggrieved parents' have been heavily influenced, if not guided, by older and stronger organizations.

The intrusive role played by the federal and provincial governments in the FRG is the clearest example of how popular sentiment can be effectively moulded by the forces which take it up for their own purposes. But this is no less true of the distinctive direction imparted to anti-cult sentiment in France by Roman Catholic agencies for studying sectarian movements. In view of the evidence concerning the importance of pre-existing social networks and multi-organizational fields it is advisable to think of anti-cultism as an emergent product of the interrelationships among many diverse interest-groups.

Third, it will be readily apparent to the reader familiar with the recent dynamics of cult/anti-cult relations in the USA that the issue of civil rights has played only a relatively minor role in my account of events in the FRG and France. This is partly because the practice of deprogramming is rare in Europe, and the use of legal conservatorships in connection with NRM members is virtually unknown. But it is also because the German and French legal systems do not encourage or facilitate the individual's defence of personal rights through courts of law. In fact, the levels of litigation in this area are much lower in Europe than in the USA.

In addition, the relevant legislation in both the FRG and France places limits on what properly constituted religious organizations are allowed to do. Their aims must be officially approved and registered before they can enjoy the status of a legitimate organization for legal purposes, and any deviation from their registered aims could be used as grounds for revoking their legal status and rights. Until 1980 the Church of Scientology, for example, could not obtain official recognition in France as a religious body. More importantly, the Interior Minister of the Province of Nordrhein-Westfalen in the FRG reported in 1979 that his border officials would scrutinize very carefully any foreign members of the Unification Church who wanted to enter the country and, if necessary, refuse them entry (Nordrhein-Westfalen 1979). This is a good example of the use of purely *administrative* discretion within a constitutional framework which actually 'imposes' freedom of religion. An equally glaring example of this practice was the British government's administrative ban on the entry to the country of foreigners intending to study Scientology between 1968 and 1980 (see Foster 1971).

One of the most intriguing aspects of this phenomenon is that, unlike some of the outlawed medieval and Reformation movements, of which the present-day NRMs are sometimes said to be the successors, none of today's groups is avowedly (or covertly) hostile to the state. In this respect they are not even comparable with, for example, the Jehovah's Witnesses or the Mormons who have on occasion defied various states over issues of principle. Rather, most of the new movements take the state's authority as given and seek to operate within its constitutional provisions. Occasional infringements of minor statutes concerning fund-raising should hardly be counted as challenges to the state's authority. So closely do some movements adhere to the norms of present-day business and therapeutic practices that they are in fact criticized for merely 'masquerading' as religions. The situation begins to resemble a double-bind when a movement comes under suspicion for being simultaneously too religious and not religious enough.

NRMs do not present a threat to the state but in some respects they *are* felt to threaten certain cultural and social norms (see Beckford 1979). At this point the state's resources can be mobilized against NRMs by well-placed groups and individuals acting out of concern for their own interests. The interest groups might be quite separate in their origins – aggrieved parents, religious competitors, political opponents, family organizations, youth groups, etc. – but to varying degrees in different countries they have coalesced. The influence of the state in the FRG has greatly assisted the process of coalescence; but in France this process is still at an early stage partly because the state apparatus has not yet been fully mobilized in the interests of anti-cultism.

By contrast, the more rigid separation of Church and state in the USA has helped to reduce the scope for state intervention against NRMs (see Kelley 1977; Robbins 1979; Annals 1979). But at the same time and perhaps for the very reason that the American state has not been easily mobilized on this issue the strength of independent anti-cult organizations is so much greater than in any European country. Similarly, the volume of cult-related litigation is much greater and cannot be explained simply in terms of the larger numbers of people involved in the USA.

In short, the level of *overt* conflict associated with NRMs is higher in the USA than in Europe, but thanks to the American legal system the movements in the USA are in a position to struggle on equal terms with their adversaries. In Europe, however, the conflict is far less visible and is obscured by the administrative measures taken by some states to control the activities of NRMs. It is therefore more difficult for the movements to see clearly where their adversaries lie and correspondingly more difficult for them to bring the struggle for the freedom to operate as they see fit into public view. As a result, energies are diverted into apparently symbolic, but none the less vicious, conflicts in courts of law over alleged libels and petty offences.

Just as David Martin (1978) was able to account for the differential trajectory of the process of secularization in various countries by means of a notion of a 'frame', so I have argued that the tensions between NRMs and their critics in the FRG and France have been conditioned by a metaphorical 'contour of dykes and canals'. Sentiments and events have been canalized in distinctive ways in accordance with a range of identifiable social, cultural, and political factors.

Notes

1   But see *Social Compass* 30 (1) 1983 for several articles describing NRMs in Europe. See also Beckford and Levasseur (forthcoming).

2   But King 1982 demonstrates the lengths to which the Nazi state was prepared to go to stifle even relatively weak religious sects.

3   'Research into systems of personal and social values [in the FRG] shows that the major themes are those of peace and orderly existence, meaning in life and control over existence as well as freedom and independence .... Above all, it is young people who are clearly seeking systems of orientation and meaning.'
      (Lukatis and Krebber 1980: 95–6. Trans. J.A.B.)

4   This is why the children of 'guest workers' in the FRG are also considered to be a potentially difficult problem at a time of high rates of unemployment for young adults.

5   Amt für Jugendarbeit der Evangelischen Kirche in Hesse und Nassau, *Jugendreligionen*. Darmstadt, 1978.

6   Aktion Jugendschutz Landesarbeitsstelle Nordrhein-Westfalen, *Auswertung eines Fragesbogens zur Ermittlung von Daten über die Jugendsektenszene*. Köln, 1978.

7   Verein zur Pflege Politischer Bildung e.V., *Dokumentation 'Neue Jugendreligionen'*. München, n.d.

8   Deutsche Jungdemokraten, Kreisverband Neuss, *Jugendreligionen – Dokumentation*. Neuss, 1978.

9   This emerged very clearly in the material assembled for a conference of the Bundeskonferenz für Erziehungsberatung e.V. in 1983 on the topic of 'Counselling in the area of youth religions'.

10   At this time, it was a division of the Interior Ministry.

11   *Social Compass* 30 (1) 1983.

12   *Die Scientology-Sekte und ihre Tarnorganisationen*. Stuttgart, 1979. See also Heinemann 1981.

13   A summary of the findings and recommendations can be found in Beckford and Levasseur (forthcoming).

NINE

Significance and state control of new religious movements

Instead of recapitulating the arguments of previous chapters I shall try to draw the discussion to a conclusion by raising general questions about the significance of today's NRMs and the controversies which surround them. This means that I shall situate them in the context of major social changes. The objective is therefore to assess the social and cultural meaning of the phenomena which have given rise to so much controversy in the past two decades. Prominence will finally be accorded to the role of the modern state in guiding the path of 'cult related' controversies.

It cannot be repeated too often that the NRMs which have been at the centre of controversy have affected the lives of a minutely small fraction of the population in any country. Even among the population of young adults, who are supposedly most 'at risk', it is unlikely that more than 1 per cent have taken a serious interest in NRMs. The percentage who have been adversely enough affected by them to fuel the controversies is even smaller still. The personal cases on which antipathy towards NRMs is mainly based are few and far between, but this has not prevented the antipathy from becoming widespread and intense on occasion. The general point must be made, then, that NRMs are of little significance in terms of the sheer numbers of their members or followers. Yet, controversy has raged over their activities.[1]

The same conclusion is reached when the material and organizational strengths of NRMs are considered. With the possible exceptions of the UC, Scientology, and the Rajneesh movement, their material resources can be considered no more than modest, especially when it is borne in mind that some movements have been striving for growth for more than twenty years and that they have had the benefit of a considerable amount of voluntary and highly committed labour, various fiscal privileges, donations, bequests, etc. For the most part, however, NRMs have remained outside the main centres of political and cultural influence. Their links with political, business, educational, religious, or welfare organizations have remained, at best, tenuous. Synanon represents an important exception, of course. And other movements have certainly *tried* to establish close links with centres of power in the 'outside' world. Yet, the results have generally been meagre, if not actually counter-productive. There are few indications that this situation is likely to change in the foreseeable future.

In terms of the framework developed in Chapter 2, the NRMs which have tried to achieve insertion in society as 'refuges' have managed to secure a supply of members. But their collective impact on events in the outside world has been negligible. Their virtuous example has been ignored, and they have contributed little to the culture of their host societies. Those NRMs which have sought to 'revitalize' the social world in accordance with their own precepts have certainly attracted greater publicity and, in some cases, notoriety. Yet, it is doubtful whether they have positively influenced any spheres of life for people other than their own members. Many of these movements have made good use of the latest organizational, technical, and cultural resources for promoting their message, but evidence of their positive impact on the everyday life of the majority of people in the West is hard to find. Only in the case of NRMs offering 'release' or 'liberation' services to their clients can one discover evidence of influences on everyday life. Yet, even here the evidence is scanty, impressionistic, and not entirely unambiguous. For it is difficult to separate the influence of specific NRMs in the 'release' mode from that of more diffuse milieux such as the Counterculture, Gestalt psychology, Encounter groups, and holistic health. The specific contributions of, for example, Scientology, Transcendental Meditation, and Synanon are easily lost against the general background of humanistic psychology, Eastern mysticism, and psychotherapy. It is therefore more practicable to think in terms of the reciprocal relationships and parallel developments between these movements and certain currents of ideas and therapeutic practices in the wider society. They reinforce each other in many indistinct ways, but it is impossible to be more precise than this about the independent contributions made by NRMs.

It is even more difficult to assess the impact of NRMs on culture.

Given the vast circulation of books and leaflets produced by some movements, it is conceivable that their ideas have influenced the thoughts and feelings of untold numbers of people. Moreover, the fact that there is a buoyant market for books and films dealing with some of the phenomena which figure prominently in the world views of some NRMs may also suggest that their cultural influence has been greater than their limited size would imply. Concerns with, for example, the occult, magic, astrology, holistic healing, and humanistic psychology are certainly shared at present between some NRMs and sections of the adult population in many western societies. But it is impossible to separate causes and effects here. All that can be safely said is that the interests of some NRMs chime with some elements of popular culture. There is no reliable evidence to suggest that NRMs have contributed in any significant ways to the themes of popular culture.

More to the point of this discussion is the fact that none of today's NRMs has appreciably influenced the terms in which major political, social, and economic issues are discussed or presented. Some movements have published their own distinctive diagnoses of such problems as drug addiction, crime, terrorism, and poverty, but I have found no resonance of their diagnoses in public discussion of the same problems. Indeed, with the exception of Scientology and Synanon, it is rare for NRMs to give prominence to their distinctive interpretations of moral and social problems. They are usually treated as relatively minor or incidental aspects of the more central spiritual and/or theological teachings. For this reason, one should be circumspect about arguments which credit NRMs with either the capacity to generate new systems of moral meaning or the power to influence prevailing moral sentiments.

A good case in point is Tipton's *Getting Saved from the Sixties* which interprets the success of three NRMs in the San Francisco Bay Area as responses to the disruption of meaning-systems occasioned by the 1960s Counterculture. The title of the book captures the sense of this particular reading of the growth of a fundamentalist Christian group, the San Francisco Zen Center and the *est* organization (now re-named the Centers Network). Tipton shows how each group has aided its members to piece together a distinctive moral meaning system which, in turn, copes with the cognitive, existential, and moral problems generated by the Counterculture and its associated lifestyles by means of a process of 'ethical recombination':

'Neo-Christian groups recombine the expressive ethic of hip culture with the authoritative ethic of revealed biblical religion, with particular plausibility for the lower middle class. Neo-Oriental groups recombine the expressive ethic with the regular ethic of rationalized religion and humanism, with particular plausibility for the upper middle class. The human potential movement recombines the expressive ethic with the consequential ethic of utilitarian individualism, with particular plausibility for the middle middle class.'

(Tipton 1982: 232)

Tipton's assessment of what he prefers to call 'alternative religions' stresses that they are 'better adapted to survival within utilitarian society than was the counterculture' (p. 233) and that they have therefore 'saved sixties youth caught between the devils of self-interest, law and order authority, and heartless rules on one side and the deep blue sea of boundless self-expression on the other' (p. 234).

It seems doubtful, however, that Tipton's interpretations can be translated into a convincing account of the impact of NRMs on more than a small number of people and in areas other than the San Francisco Bay Area. The effects of the expressive counterculture were felt most extensively in California. *Est* is the only one of Tipton's sample of NRMs to have enjoyed a large following in Europe. And the movements which have flourished there deploy moral meaning systems which cannot easily be interpreted within the terms of Tipton's theory of 'ethical recombination'. His analysis may be perfectly appropriate to his rather isolated groups in California, but its relevance to the rest of North America and Europe must be questionable. There is an urgent need for further research on the implications of NRMs for moral meaning systems in general.

European researchers have tended to concentrate on the capacity of NRMs to confer identity on members. Feelings of alienation and anomie have therefore been highlighted among the factors leading to affiliation (Hardin and Kehrer 1978; Berger and Hexel 1981). The Counterculture's specific contribution to these feelings is far less important than it was in the San Francisco Bay area. But the *indirect* contribution may have been highly significant. In particular, the mainstream churches' responses to the Counterculture's call for self-expression and self-realization acted as a catalyst for interest in NRMs. The churches' growing preoccupation with personal relationships and social responsibility removed much of the mystery and experiential richness from their religious activities. The appeal of some NRMs is precisely to young people searching for mystical experiences. Consequently, European NRMs benefited from the mainstream churches' attempt to come to terms with one aspect of the Counterculture (see Pace 1983).

Another indirect contribution of the Counterculture to the growth of NRMs in Europe was mediated by the churches and many other social institutions. In response to demands for greater freedom of self-expression in the 1960s, a tolerant, liberal, and pluralist ethos began to find expression in the spheres of religion, education, and social welfare. The relativization of values and the abandonment of previously absolute standards were widely welcomed. But many people found the fluidity and insubstantial nature of values, teachings, and practices to be psychologically and spiritually unnerving or, at least, unsatisfactory. Some NRMs have recruited young people who share these misgivings about the liberal ethos prevailing in social institutions which directly affect them (see Martin 1982).

Finally, the Counterculture has indirectly contributed to the growth of NRMs in Europe by articulating themes which were already rooted in American culture but were, until the 1960s, confined to strictly peripheral groups. Notions of personal growth and self-actualization, all of which received great impetus from the Counterculture, have played a major role in the long and continuing history of 'positive thought' in the USA (Meyer 1980). This is a tradition of thought which emphasizes, in a multitude of different ways, people's capacity to harness their mental and bodily powers for the attainment of chosen ends. It is part of an optimistic, expressionistic ethos which has occurred in such diverse currents as Transcendentalism, New Thought, Christian Science, and humanistic psychology.

NRMs such as Scientology, *est*, TM, and the Rajneesh Foundation have systematized aspects of positive thought and have given it novel forms of expression. In doing so, they have drawn on philosophical resources which clearly ante-date the Counterculture but which nevertheless came to represent many of its major preoccupations. The very pervasiveness of the Counterculture therefore helped to popularize positive ways of thinking. But this is not to deny that they were also incompatible with some other countercultural tendencies.[2] What matters here is that some NRMs benefited indirectly from the currency given to certain key, positive notions by the Counterculture.

In short, the Counterculture outside California gave a considerable boost to ideas of a mystical, relativist, and positive nature. In so far as NRMs have variously conveyed similar or reactive ideas they have benefited from the Counterculture's *indirect* influence. But the evidence of a more direct influence of the Californian kind analysed by Tipton is not available for other parts of the western world.

In fact, there is little evidence in support of the argument that NRMs have had any kind of significant positive impact on western societies. But this is not to say that they lack sociological interest. On the contrary, the limited success enjoyed by NRMs is indicative of a number of important aspects of social structure and process. They show, for example, that at a time when most churches find it difficult to recruit or to retain young adult members it is still possible to mobilize such people in certain NRMs. They are mainly movements which offer direct personal experience of the transcendental or numinous; methodical ways to gain self-confidence and to strengthen self-identity; intensely practical ways of putting religious faith into action for idealistic purposes; and an urgent sense of the critical character of the present era. The denominational form of religious organization does not seem to offer the same kind of opportunities. Nor is it clear that many people would take up these opportunities even if they were available in conventional churches. The NRMs have therefore demonstrated that it is possible to mobilize religious enthusiasm and idealism by means of high-commitment, strictly disciplined, and age-specific groups. But the cost of these gains in commitment and energy may be a reduced impact on society at large.[3]

There is evidence to suggest that, at least among the mystical and occult NRMs, commitments are frequently transferred from movement to movement in a 'cultic career'. Serial involvements of this kind are, of course, very different from the conventional modes of belonging to mainstream religious organizations. The 'seekership syndrome' which is evident in some members of NRMs (but rarely in the more controversial ones) may help to weaken the impact that the movements could possibly have on their host societies. The long-term effect of periodically re-directing spiritual enthusiasm may be to prevent the accumulation of the knowledge and skills required to exert a significant long-term influence on public thinking or action. The lack of parish-based or neighbourhood organizations only aggravates the fragmentation effect of serial commitments in NRMs.

NRMs are illustrative of the general tendency towards the fragmentation of social and cultural structures. They tend to be exclusive
of other interests and divisive in the sense of cultivating distinctive
outlooks and ways of life which are only accidentally part of wider
meaning systems and social networks. As 'havens in a heartless
world' they may be effective in counteracting feelings of alienation,
but this is achieved at the cost of reducing their members' involvement in public life (Lasch 1977, 1980).

Many NRMs also illustrate the tendency to translate public
problems into private troubles. That is, they encourage members to
develop a way of looking at the world which offers the possibility of
overcoming most difficulties by means of personal accomplishments.
Positive attitudes, methodical practices, and a willingness to monitor
inner states of mind and body are cultivated as ways of handling all
problems, including those which inhere in social structures. In this
way the problems are reduced to a matter of 'how can I cope with
them?' Their reality is 'defined away' in the process of screening out
all considerations other than one's personal response. *Est*'s 'Hunger
Project' is a classic example of this process at work in relation to an
eminently 'public' problem.

In short, today's NRMs are significant mainly for being indicative
of several tendencies emerging in contemporary western societies.
The movements may be relatively unimportant in themselves, but
their limited success and modes of operation can throw light on the
social conditions which facilitated them. At the same time, however,
it is essential to keep in mind that, as was emphasized in Chapters 3
and 6, the *opposition* to NRMs is in itself no less indicative of
prevailing social and cultural conditions. 'Cult controversies' are
very revealing about taken-for-granted notions of normality. And
anti-cult campaigns in particular have brought to light some interesting cross-national differences in ideas about the nature of perceived
threats to the social, moral, and religious fabric of western societies.
Some of them were examined in Chapters 7 and 8, but it remains in
this final section to ask questions about the role of agencies of the
state in lending a distinctive character to cult controversies in the late
twentieth century. The aim will be to show how state involvement in
these controversies is indicative of certain structural tendencies in
contemporary societies.

A few notes of caution must be sounded at this point. First, we
should not overlook the fact that control by the state over religious
groups has been no less forceful in the past than in the present.

Indeed, the intensity of control has on occasion been far greater than it is at present in western countries. We should also not lose sight of the fact that current attempts to control NRMs are less violent, less arbitrary, and probably less effective than many earlier attempts.

Second, state control over specifically *political* organizations and movements is considerably more strenuous and effective. And, in comparison with attempts to curb terrorism, drug trafficking, smuggling, and espionage, the state's interest in controlling NRMs pales into insignificance.

Third, the visibility of controversies surrounding NRMs has more to do with the effectiveness of modern means of communication than with the allegedly more intrusive role of the state in matters of religion. The overwhelming importance of mass communications has boosted the 'sound and the fury', but this is not to be mistaken for evidence of increasing state control.

Finally, it should be noted that, in spite of extensive litigation and numerous projects for new legislation, no western[4] state has yet enacted legislation designed to control NRMs. Attempts have certainly been made, as we shall see below, to apply existing laws for this purpose; but it is not at all clear that this represents action by the state as such.

Characteristics of state control

The first observation is that the movements which are most heavily controlled by the state are those which provide the most comprehensive services for members. Commune-type movements, for example, have invariably been subject to stringent scrutiny. Robbins (1981) has taken this argument one stage further:

'The underlying source of tension contributing to controversies over "cults" involves the diversification or multifunctional nature of these movements, which proselytize aggressively and ultimately solicit from devotees an intense and diffuse loyalty which appears to undermine participants' obligations to other groups and institutions. . . . The emergence of diversified and omnicompetent spiritual movements plus the increasing governmental regulation of non-religious organizations highlights the "regulatory gap" between "churches", other organizations, and the ambiguity of the "boundary" of governmental authority in the area of religion.'
(Robbins 1981: 221)

This may be true for some NRMs, particularly in the USA, but I would like to emphasize that fully communal or 'omnicompetent' movements are no longer the most numerous. Indeed, it is doubtful whether this was ever the case. Social and economic circumstances now allow NRMs to sustain themselves by various types of activity which, as we saw in Chapter 2, combine communal living for some members with other modes of affiliation. Consequently, the 'regulatory gap' to which Robbins refers has less to do with the distinction between religious and non-religious organizations and more to do with the elusive distinction between the purely religious and the political or productive aspects of *all* religious organizations. The move from 'refuge' to 'revitalization' and 'release' entails increasing surveillance by statutory agencies of the stage.

In fact, the case of NRMs simply illustrates the increasing statutory surveillance by agencies of the modern western state over *all* social (and therefore religious) activities. It follows that, the more comprehensively a group tries to provide services for its members, the more subject will it be to state control. Thus, the plethora of rules and regulations governing virtually all aspects of commerce, manufacturing, hygiene, and safety in places of work, health hazards in therapeutic practice, and the use of land and buildings makes a strong impact on those NRMs which cater comprehensively for their members and which attempt to revitalize their host societies.

For the most part, state control over NRMs is achieved by indirect and bureaucratic means which employ such procedures as certification, licensing, and scrutinizing. The fact that some opponents of NRMs seek to exploit these procedures as a way of containing the movements does not affect my contention that the procedures are part of the state's apparatus of societal control but are not aimed *specifically* at NRMs. What has happened is that NRMs have expanded into new fields of activity which are increasingly controlled by statutes of all kinds. The simultaneous growth of NRMs *and* of state surveillance may have given the mistaken impression that the latter was designed to control the former.

How can my interpretation of events handle the undeniable fact that numerous attempts have been made in many countries to frame legislation specifically designed to control NRMs alone? My response is in three parts. First, no such legislation has yet been enacted in the west. Second, the initiative has usually come from private or their elected representatives: not from state officials. The record shows that, with the exception of prosecutions of

Scientology in West Germany, NRMs have been highly successful in defending themselves against attempts to use existing laws against them in novel fashion.[5] The facts simply do not confirm the view that the state is manipulating the law in order to control NRMs.

In sum, state control over NRMs is indirect, bureaucratic, and not markedly different from the way in which it applies to other, comparable organizations.

A second observation is that there is a discrepancy between official disclaimers of anti-cult bias or policy and administrative actions taken against some NRMs. Statements by government ministers or civil servants have tended to be circumspect and strangely uniform. Official concern is said to be confined to matters of crime or practices harmful to citizens' physical or mental health.[6] On the other hand, however, agents of the state have occasionally imposed administrative sanctions against NRMs. In the USA, for example, the Food and Drug Administration made strenuous efforts to obstruct the Scientologists' use of the E-Meter in the 1960s. And the Attorney-General's office in the State of California intervened in the affairs of Synanon as well as in those of the Worldwide Church of God (Worthing 1979). In Britain, the Minister of Health in 1968 banned the entry of foreign nationals into the country for the purpose of studying Scientology. More recently, the charitable status of two sections of the UC in Britain has been under sustained attack from the government's chief law officer. In West Germany, border officials have been instructed to prevent the Reverend Moon from entering the country.[7] And staff of the General District Attorney in Munich forcibly confiscated documents from two offices of the Church of Scientology in May 1984. Police launched surprise raids on a number of UC offices in France in June 1982, removed church documents, and interrogated many people found on church premises.

It is also characteristic of this kind of piecemeal, administrative action that it places law enforcement agents under suspicion of colluding with anti-cult groups and with the would-be kidnappers of NRM members.[8] There is some evidence to suggest that they have supplied damaging material about NRMs to the mass media; given wide circulation to unconfirmed reports of NRMs' alleged harmfulness or criminality; and threatened to curtail NRMs' access to important benefits and resources in punishment for non-cooperation.

In short, the lack of official policy with regard to NRMs and of laws aimed specifically at them creates the conditions in which piecemeal, administrative sanctions can be applied behind a curtain of official detachment.[9] These conditions also encourage the growth of public distrust and paranoia. The clearest example is provided by the European Parliament's approval of a 'Motion for a Resolution on the activity of certain new religious movements within the European Community' in May 1984.[10] The preamble stressed that 'freedom of religion and opinion [was] a principle in the Member States and that the institutions of the European Community have no right to judge the value of either religious beliefs in general or individual religious practices' but it added that it was 'convinced that in this instance the validity of religious beliefs is not in question, but rather the lawfulness of the practices used to recruit new members and the treatment they receive'. This is a classic attempt to avoid the danger of involvement in religious matters by claiming to be concerned solely with matters of recruitment and conditions of membership. The 'problem' is thereby reduced to a form in which purely 'legal-rational' criteria can be applied to its assessment and solution. Wider issues of ethics and policy can be ignored.

The motion, which had been prepared by Mr Richard Cottrell, MEP for Bristol, on behalf of the Committee on Youth, Culture, Education, Information, and Sport contained two sets of recommendations. The first was for 'an exchange of information' among the Ministers of Justice, the Interior and Social Affairs of member states on the problems arising from NRMs with particular reference to procedures for conferring charitable status; compliance with the law; attempts to find missing persons; infringements of personal freedoms; creation of centres to assist defectors; and legal loopholes permitting NRMs to transfer activities proscribed in one country to another.

The second set of recommendations was for guidelines to be followed by NRMs. They included: minors and temporary residents of a country should not be induced to make long-term commitments to NRMs; fresh recruits should have time to reconsider their commitments and to have access to friends and relatives; courses of education should not be interrupted; members' freedom of movement and communication should be respected at all times; inducements to break the law must be forbidden; potential recruits must be made aware of a movement's name and principles; the whereabouts of members must be supplied on request to competent authorities; members must be in a position to receive any social security benefits to which they are entitled; members sent abroad should be brought home if necessary, especially if they become ill; and the health and education of members' children must be safeguarded.

In addition, the Motion called on the European Commission to collect and collate all relevant information on NRMs and to advise the Council of Ministers on how to protect citizens against them. The longer-term aim was to encourage a common approach among member states to the problem of protecting people 'from the machinations of these movements and their physical and moral coercion'.

Although the Motion, which was accepted by a vote of 98 for, 28 against and 27 abstentions, is not strictly speaking an initiative of any single state it nevertheless illustrates the type of thinking which underlines administrative action against NRMs. Legislators shrink from the task of confronting the spiritual and moral challenges presented by NRMs. Instead, they hide behind the excuse that only piecemeal sanctions are required to prevent harm to people.

A third observation concerns the state's readiness to commission research on NRMs and/or to sponsor public hearings about them. Whilst such activities cannot be said to have had any appreciable effects on public policy, it can hardly be denied that they have worked against the general interests of NRMs by appearing to impugn their integrity.

The first wave of official investigations was concerned almost exclusively with Scientology and gave rise to reports in the State of Victoria, Australia;[11] South Africa;[12] and Britain.[13] The second wave began with the State of New York's investigation of the COG[14] and continued with other hearings in the States of Vermont,[15] California,[16] Massachusetts,[17] and in Washington, DC.[18] The Federal Republic of Germany's Ministry for Youth, Family, and Health published a brochure on 'Youth Religions' in 1980 without conducting a public hearing.[19] The third wave of official reports is marked by a greater concern for social scientific findings and theories about NRMs. This is true of a report commissioned by the Canadian province of Ontario (Hill 1980); a project conducted under the auspices of the Vienna Centre for Social Welfare Training and Research on behalf of the Federal German Government[20] (Berger and Hexel 1981); and an inquiry into new religious movements in the Netherlands conducted by a sub-committee of the Second Chamber of the Dutch Parliament.[21] It is less true of the parliamentary inquiry conducted in France between 1981 and 1983.[22]

Official reports and investigative hearings offer to the state considerable advantages. They allow it to be seen to be acting in an enlightened, liberal manner without imposing the inconvenient necessity to act on the recommendations and findings. The investigative activity itself can sometimes serve as a substitute for decision-making and can thereby create valuable leeway for *ad hoc* manoeuvres. Above all, however, such activity obviates the necessity to frame policies which might be considered socially divisive.

The western states' typical modes of controlling NRMs can be summed up as indirect, piecemeal, administrative, *ad hoc*, and liberal. There is no underlying policy, and separate agencies of the state seem to act independently of each other except in the Federal Republic of Germany where federal and provincial ministries have at least exchanged information about the problems posed for them by NRMs. Nevertheless, there is a rationale behind the state's apparently confused modes of control. The next section will examine the affinities between this rationale and the dominant characteristics of the state in western societies.

Capitalism, the state, liberal ideology, and religion

The governments of western states with predominantly capitalist economies are under pressure to support and maintain capitalist accumulation. This requires fiscal measures which, in turn, call for statutory regulation and surveillance of increasingly wide swathes of life. Control by the state is therefore rational in so far as it is related to the logic of increasingly collectivist strategies of accumulation 'in the national interest'. But it is also *ad hoc* to the extent that it lacks any clear reference to policy affecting specific phenomena such as religion. Indeed, the generally liberal ethos of most western regimes in the 1980s could be considered to be antithetical to the very idea of such policies. This makes the actual practice of controlling NRMs by purely administrative expedients all the more contradictory.

It helps to create a paradoxical situation in which one of the greatest threats to the independence of religious institutions arises from the state's concern for the welfare of its citizens in a world economic order dominated by advanced capitalism. Progressive intervention in all spheres of life is determined by the need to protect national capitals and all the relations of production and distribution that they sustain. The ideology underlying this strategy holds that the freedom of opportunity and the basic equality of each individual are thereby preserved (Sullivan 1982). They amount to some of the fundamental values of most western societies and are deeply entrenched in all major social institutions. The state's controlling role is therefore legitimated in terms of the allegedly impartial arbitration that it provides in the event of conflicts between free and equal individuals seeking to maximize their benefits in the market-like conditions of modern life (see Habermas 1974).

There is a strong affinity between this ideology and the increasing prominence of religious pluralism and diversity in western societies. Ideas of a 'spiritual supermarket' and of an ecumenical 'circulation' of Christians among different churches all committed to the view that religion is a matter of personal choice or preference reinforce the dominant 'market' ideology. The corresponding tendency in the sociology of religion has been to theorize religious commitments as a matter of the personal construction of peace of mind, self-realization, and identity in 'conversation' with others (see Beckford 1983e for criticisms of this tendency).

Another implication of the liberal, utilitarian individualism which currently prevails in the West is the tendency to separate the sphere of religion from other spheres of life in accordance with the dominant model of man as an individual, rational, cost-benefit accountant. Religion is thereby compartmentalized as a basically personal realm of self-actualization with only incidental connections to other social roles and institutions. In current jargon religion is something with which one should ideally 'feel comfortable'.

It follows that, faced with the teachings and practices of NRMs which are not all compatible with liberal, utilitarian individualism, agents of the state tend to become suspicious. They are affronted by what is perceived as authoritarian, sectional, and irrational collectivism in some movements. And this general perception is reinforced by more specific observations of the ways in which the operations of some NRMs conflict with statutory regulations governing a wide range of activities.

Conflicts with the state are not confined, however, to the relatively simple question of whether NRMs have broken statutory regulations. They tend also to widen out into more general conflicts centring on the definition of 'authentic' religion. This is because the ideology of liberal utilitarianism has been used in many states to justify a variety of arrangements for giving bona fide religious groups a number of official privileges. Indeed, the privileges used to make very good sense from the state's point of view at a time when religious groups served as the foremost defenders of the dominant culture and as agents of moral socialization. Exemption from some fiscal obligations and from some statutory regulations has traditionally been the privilege of religious organizations in many countries.

Since access to these privileges or constitutional freedoms is conditional upon demonstration of religious authenticity, conflict with some NRMs has tended to centre on the question of definition. Courts of law, administrative tribunals, and individual law enforcement agents therefore find themselves obliged to decide what is to count as 'religion' for legal purposes. Their decisions have serious consequences for the extent to which NRMs are allowed to put their teachings into practice and thereby to assure their stability or growth as organizations. This is just another facet of my earlier argument that the modern state's mode of control over NRMs is largely administrative and *ad hoc* in the absence of agreed upon policies.

One of the many ironies of this situation is that it is precisely in a country like the USA with its constitutional guarantee of the freedom of religion from entanglement with the state that the full force of the legal-administrative control over religion is felt most keenly. This is because NRMs can legally contest the constitutionality of any regulation or action which allegedly limits their freedom. The legal doctrines which are then invoked in court invariably turn on the definition of religion. The court therefore decides what is to count as 'religion'. The result is that NRMs are drawn into realms of legal discourse to which their own ideologies may in fact be indifferent or even hostile.[23] Would-be world-rejecting movements find themselves confirming the legitimacy of legal-rational procedures so that they can disseminate their message that the very same procedures are 'satanic' or part of the 'corrupt' world. NRMs defend their action by claiming that it would be worse to be at the mercy of regimes unconstrained by constitutional protection of religious freedom. This may be true; but it overlooks the fact that by seeking legal redress for their grievances against the state they are strengthening the legal system's dominion over religion.

The irony is aggravated by the fact that, in the name of liberal ideals, a number of civil libertarians and mainstream church executives in the USA have recently begun to associate themselves with the legal causes of some decidedly non-liberal NRMs.[24] Their argument is that any and every encroachment on the so-called separation of Church and state represents a potential threat to the freedom enjoyed by *all* religious groups, regardless of their doctrinal or ideological position.[25] The logic of this purely formal argument can hardly be faulted. But one of its consequences is that the legitimacy of deciding issues of religious authenticity in courts of law is thereby reinforced. A sceptic might interpret this as a further step towards the total subjection of religion to the rational-legal logic of the state's mode of operation in western societies.

Indeed, the specificity of religion may be threatened by such procedures in the long term.[26] For, if the defence of religious freedom is to rest on purely formal, legal grounds without reference to the substance of belief or practice, the question arises of whether a notion like 'conscience' would not be a more appropriate object of constitutional protection. What is more, the case for the protection of conscience is obviously strong in societies characterized by the growing privatization and diversification of all beliefs, including religion (see Hammond 1981). But, again, the problem arises that legal tests and criteria of conscience would only tend to draw upon, and therefore reinforce, the prevailing psychologized and philo-sophically individualist images of the person in western democracies. In this way, the presumptive independence of conscience from the social conditions of its definition is called in question.

I believe that all of these considerations support my initial conten-tion that control over NRMs (as well as other religious and non-religious organizations) in western states has been more complex and more subtle as a result of social and ideological forces rooted in the changing relationship between the state and civil society under conditions of advanced capitalism (see Urry 1981). It is not that NRMs have been singled out for repression or suppression. Rather, they have been partly co-opted by various agencies of state control whose intended functions have little to do with religion. Another way of putting this is to suggest that some NRMs have been seduced by the rhetoric of constitutional rights discourse into methods of self-defence and self-promotion which have the effect of weakening their potential independence. For it is in the interest of the state in liberal democracies that religious conflicts should be seen to take place in terms of individual rights and personal freedoms. So long as conflicts are framed in this way, the 'normal' processes of legal conflict-resolution can be employed without necessarily alienating any of the parties. Modern western states have been remarkably successful in minimizing religious conflicts in this way, although there are distinct signs of a worsening of Church/state relations in the USA, at least, in the mid 1980s.[27]

It is significant that the controversies surrounding today's NRMs are mostly about individual rights' issues having to do with disputed possession of minds or property. Alternatively, they concern the practical methods employed by some movements to recruit members and to disseminate their message. Far from being challenges to the prevailing order, they tend to be demands for further extension of its liberal, utilitarian benefits. To the extent that NRMs have chosen to become embroiled in legal struggles for their constitutional rights they may have forfeited the opportunity to promote values other than those on which the constitutional systems of the western states are founded.

It is quite another matter, of course, to know whether any of today's NRMs actually wish to promote novel values. Wilson's (1976) view is that NRMs are irrelevant to the integrative function of culture, but Wuthnow (1978) seems to sense in them the possibility of a new brand of populism. And Bellah (1975) sensed that they contained at least the possibility of a 'renewal of religious imagination'. This view was extended by Anthony and Robbins into the claim that some NRMs displayed 'belief in an implicit universal order [which] can provide a value framework that supports participation in a society in which shared values are disintegrating' (1982: 226). David Martin's assessment of their potential is more nuanced but it recognizes that 'new religious movements ... provide a language and vocabulary within which spiritual experiences and comprehensive meanings can be found' (1982: 69). Tipton (1982), on the other hand, discovered only recombinations of conventional ethical systems in the movements that he studied. And Bird (1979) could find only various ways of reducing 'moral accountability' among NRM members. 'Cults' were also dismissed by Daniel Bell as nothing more than illustrations of the cultural confusion which flourishes at a time when 'the institutional framework of religions begins to break up' (1980: 348). They are said to represent a chaos of competing notions of 'authenticity' and of a search for direct, ecstatic experience by means of esoteric knowledge.

It would be a serious mistake to forget, however, that the controversial NRMs are still adjusting their stance towards the prevailing order. It may be unreasonable, therefore, to expect them to have articulated any values clearly enough to challenge or support it. It would certainly be premature to interpret the state's attempts to control them as a response to perceived challenge or threat.

I have argued here that the controversies surrounding NRMs in the mid 1980s are both perennial and novel. They are perennial in so far as they reflect opposition to movements which are seen to threaten the integrity of the family institution, the boundary between 'real' and 'bogus' religion, and deep-seated assumptions about the autonomy of 'normal' minds. On the other hand, today's cult controversies are novel in so far as they (a) are not primarily about doctrines; (b) are concerned with more than one group at a time; and (c) reflect the interests of methodical anti-cult campaigners and the presumptions of welfare states to know what is best for their citizens.

This combination of perennial and novel sources is a formidable obstacle for NRMs. Some, especially those which operate as retreats from the world's evil or illusions, may resist by simply reducing their contact with outsiders to a minimum. But those movements which are attempting to revitalize and transform the world or to market schemes of release from its constraints are compelled to resist by using the economic, political, and legal rationality of their opponents. The result is a kind of stalemate in which the NRMs' protests of spiritual authenticity are matched by their opponents' cries of 'charlatan!' It is characteristic of secular societies that such disputes are increasingly marginalized and couched in psychological, medical, and social terms.

Notes

1   A similar point has been made about the disproportionate degree of public concern about communes in the 1960s (see Berger 1981).

2   This is close to the thesis that the expressiveness of the Counterculture was eventually superseded by a different sensibility (see Foss and Larkin 1976; Martin 1981).

3   This is superficially similar to Yinger's (1946) thesis about what might be termed the zero-sum game played in religious sects between purity and power. See also Eister 1973. But I make no value judgements about purity and compromise in NRMs. My thesis is solely about the non-ideological costs and benefits of different strategies for insertion in society.

4   Legislation to control Scientology and other 'psychological practices' was enacted in the states of Victoria, Western Australia, and South Australia in, respectively, 1965, 1968, and 1969. By the mid 1970s, however, each Act had been repealed. In 1983 the Scientologists won recognition for their movement as a religion for the purposes of exemption from payroll tax in Australia.

5　See Shepherd 1982 and Robbins 1983 for reviews of the position in the USA. The serial publication, *Religious Freedom Reporter*, is an indispensable guide to current litigation concerning religion in the USA.

6　There is a striking similarity between the statement made by the French Interior Minister (quoted on p. 269) in response to questions about repercussions of the People's Temple tragedy in France and the statements made by various representatives of successive British governments about the best way to tackle cult-related problems.

7　Immigration officials in the UK and the USA have also excluded, or tried to exclude, the Reverend Moon, the Bhagwan Shree Rajneesh, and David 'Moses' Berg from their countries.

8　See Lucksted and Martell 1982 for an insight into the dilemmas presented to American FBI agents by disputes between members of NRMs and their relatives who wish to deprogramme them.

9　'Action affecting religious movements may be taken at official, but sub-political, levels to which neither the public at large, nor the victim in particular, have much access, and in the counsels of which they can exert virtually no influence.' This is Bryan Wilson's (1983: 82) assessment of the difficulties facing religious movements in dispute with the British government.

10　PE 82.322/fin. It was agreed in debating the Motion that, in view of problems with defining 'NRM', they would be referred to as 'new organizations operating under the protection afforded to religious bodies'.

11　State of Victoria, *Report of the Board of Inquiry into Scientology*, 1965. ['The Anderson Report'].

12　G. R. C. Kotzé *et al.*, *Report of the Commission of Inquiry into Scientology for 1972*. Pretoria, South Africa: Government Printer, 1973.

13　Foster, 1971.

14　State of New York, Office of the Attorney General, *Final Report on the Activities of the Children of God*. A report submitted by the Charity Frauds Bureau. Albany, 1974.

15　State of Vermont, *Hearing of the Committee for the Investigation of Alleged Deceptive, Fraudulent and Criminal Practices of Various Organizations in the State*. Burlington: August 1976.

16　State of California, Hearing of the Senate Sub-Committee on Children and Youth, *Impact of Cults on Today's Youth*. Northridge: August 1974 ['The Dymally Hearings'].

17 State of Massachusetts General Court, Senate Committee on Commerce and Labor, *Public Hearing on Solicitation Methods Utilized by Religious and Charitable Groups*, 1979.

18 Transcripts of Proceedings. *Information Meeting on the Cult Phenomenon in the United States*. Washington, DC: February 1979 ['The Dole Hearings'].

19 Bundesministerium für Jugend, Familie, und Gesundheit, *Die Jugendreligionen in der Bundesrepublik Deutschland*. Bonn, 1980.

20 See also *Social Compass* 30 (1) 1983.

21 Tweede Kamer 1984.

22 See Beckford and Levasseur, forthcoming.

23 This is clearly not true of *all* NRMs. There is no tension between, for example, the Church of Scientology's teachings and its extensive recourse to litigation.

24 See, for example, Kelley 1977; Annals 1979. An *amicus curiae* document was submitted to the court considering the Reverend Moon's appeal against conviction for tax evasion in December 1982 by the leaders of many mainstream denominations. His jail sentence began in 1984.

25 One of the arguments advanced by the Council of the French Protestant Federation in February 1984 to try to dissuade members of the European Parliament from approving a proposal to encourage member states of the European Council to monitor and control NRMs was that, 'Religious freedom is indivisible. It is both too precious a blessing and too important a right of our society for selective limitations to be applied to it, and then for legislation concerning it to be enacted on a selective basis'.

26 Richard Fenn 1981 has spelled out the way in which this happens.

27 See Annals **446** 1979; *Sociological Analysis* **42** (3) 1981; Demerath and Williams 1983.

REFERENCES

Abrams, P. and McCulloch, A. (1976) *Communes, Sociology and Society*. Cambridge: Cambridge University Press.

Ahlstrom, S. E. (1978) From Sinai to the Golden Gate: the liberation of religion in the Occident. In J. Needleman and G. Baker (eds) *Understanding the New Religions*. New York: Seabury Press.

Albrecht, S. and Bahr, M. (1983) Patterns of religious disaffiliation: a study of lifelong Mormons, Mormon converts, and former Mormons. *Journal for the Scientific Study of Religion* 22 (4): 366–79.

Allan, J. (1980) *The Rising of the Moon*. Leicester: Inter-Varsity Press.

Annals of the American Academy of Political and Social Science (1979) Special issue on *The Uneasy Boundary: Church and State* 446 November.

Anthony, D. and Robbins, T. (1978) The effect of detente on the growth of new religions: Reverend Moon and the Unification Church. In J. Needleman and G. Baker (eds) *Understanding the New Religions*. New York: Seabury Press.

—— (1980) A demonology of cults. *Inquiry Magazine* 1 September: 9–11.

—— (1982) Spiritual innovation and the crisis of American civil religion. *Daedalus* 111 (1); 215–34.

—— and Needleman, J. (eds) (1985) *Conversion, Coercion and Commitment*.

Association pour la Défense de la Famille et de l'Individu (1977) Étude comparative de deux idéologies. Rennes, mimeo.

Baffoy, T. (1978) Les sectes totalitaires. *Esprit* January: 53–9.

Bainbridge, W. S. (1978) *Satan's Power: a Deviant Psychotherapeutic Cult*. Berkeley, California: University of California Press.

Balch, R. W. (1980) Looking behind the scenes in a religious cult: implications for the study of conversion. *Sociological Analysis* 41 (2): 137–43.

——— (1982) Bo and Peep: a cast study of the origins of messianic leadership. In R. Wallis (ed.) *Millennialism and Charisma*. Belfast: The Queen's University.

Barker, E. V. (1978) Living the Divine Principle: Inside the Reverend Sun Myung Moon's Church in Britain. *Archives de Sciences Sociales des Religions* 45 (1): 75–93.

——— (1981) Who'd be a Moonie? In B. Wilson (ed.) *The Social Impact of New Religious Movements*. New York: Rose of Sharon Press.

——— (1983) New religious movements in Britain: the context and the membership. *Social Compass* 30 (1): 33–48.

——— (ed.) (1982) *New Religious Movements: A Perspective for Understanding Society*. New York and Toronto: Edwin Mellen Press.

Becker, E. (1980) *The Birth and Death of Meaning*. Harmondsworth: Penguin Books (1st edn 1962).

Beckford, J. A. (1975a) Organization, ideology and recruitment: the structure of the Watchtower movement. *Sociological Review* 23 (4): 893–909.

——— (1975b) *Religious Organization: a Trend Report and Bibliography*. The Hague: Mouton. (Published under the auspices of the International Sociological Association and the International Committee for Social Sciences Documentation as *Current Sociology* 21 (2) 1973.)

——— (1975c) *The Trumpet of Prophecy. A Sociological Analysis of Jehovah's Witnesses*. Oxford: Blackwell.

——— (1976) New wine in new bottles: a departure from the church–sect conceptual tradition. *Social Compass* 23 (1): 71–85.

——— (1977) The explanation of religious movements. *International Social Science Journal* 29 (2): 235–49.

——— (1978a) Through the looking-glass and out the other side: withdrawal from the Rev. Moon's Unification Church. *Archives de Sciences Sociales des Religions* 45 (1): 95–116.

——— (1978b) Accounting for conversion. *British Journal of Sociology* 29 (2): 249–62.

——— (1979) Politics and the anti-cult movement. *Annual Review of the Social Sciences of Religion* 3: 169–90.

——— (1981a) A typology of family responses to a new religious movement. *Marriage and Family Review* 4 (3–4): 41–55.

——— (1981b) Cults, controversy and control: a comparative analysis of the problems posed by new religious movements in the Federal Republic of Germany and France. *Sociological Analysis* 42 (3): 249–64.

——— (1983a) The State and control of new religious movements. *Acts of the 17th International Conference for the Sociology of Religion*. London.

Beckford, J. A. (1983b) Some questions about the relationship between scholars and the new religious movements. *Sociological Analysis* **44** (3): 189–96.

—— (1983c) Talking of apostasy, or telling tales and 'telling' tales. In N. Gilbert and P. Abel (eds) *Accounts and Action*. Aldershot: Gower.

—— (1983d) 'Brainwashing' and 'deprogramming' in Britain: the social sources of anti-cult sentiment. In D. Bromley and J. Richardson (eds) *The Brainwashing/Deprogramming Controversy: Sociological, Psychological, Legal and Historical Perspectives*. New York: Edwin Mellen Press.

—— (1983e) The restoration of 'power' to the sociology of religion. *Sociological Analysis* **44** (1): 11–31.

—— (1984) Religious organisation: a survey of some recent publications. *Archives de Sciences Sociales des Religions* **57** (1): 83–102.

—— (1985a) Conversion and apostasy: antithesis or complementarity? In D. Anthony, T. Robbins, and J. Needleman (eds) *Conversion, Coercion and Commitment*.

—— (1985b) Religious organizations. In P. Hammond (ed.), *The Sacred in a Post-Secular Age*. Berkeley: University of California Press.

—— and Levasseur, M. (forthcoming) New religious movements in Western Europe. In J. Beckford (ed.) *New Religious Movements and Rapid Social Change*.

—— and Richardson, J. T. (1983) A bibliography of social scientific studies of new religious movements. *Social Compass* **30** (1): 111–35.

Bell, D. (1980) *Sociological Journeys. Essays 1960–1980*. London: Heinemann Educational.

Bellah, R. N. (1975) *The Broken Covenant. American Civil Religion in Time of Trial*. New York: Seabury Press.

Benn, S. I. and Peters, R. S. (1959) *Social Principles of the Democratic State*. London: Allen & Unwin.

Berger, B. M. (1981) *The Survival of a Counterculture: Ideological Work and Everyday Life among Rural Communards*. Berkeley: University of California Press.

Berger, H. and Hexel, P. (1981) Ursachen und Wirkungen gesellschäftlicher Verweigerung junger Menschen unter besonderer Berücksichtigung der 'Jugendreligionen'. Vienna, European Centre for Social Welfare Training and Research. Mimeo.

Berger, P., Berger, B., and Kellner, H. (1974) *The Homeless Mind*. Harmondsworth: Penguin Books (first published by Random House 1973).

Bibby, R. W. and Brinkerhoff, M. B. (1973). The circulation of the Saints: a study of people who join conservative churches. *Journal for the*

Scientific Study of Religion 12 (3): 273–84.

Billette, A. (1975) *Récits et Réalités d'une Conversion*. Montréal; Presses de l'Université de Montréal.

Bird, F. (1979) The pursuit of innocence: new religious movements and moral accountability. *Sociological Analysis* 40 (4): 335–46.

—— and Westley, F. (1983) The political economies of new religious movements. Unpublished paper.

Bjornstad, J. (1976) *The Moon is not the Son*. Minneapolis: Dimension Books.

Boulard, F. (1954) *Premières Itinéraires en Sociologie Religieuse*. Paris: Ouvrières.

Brinkerhoff, M. B. and Burke, K. L. (1980) Disaffiliation: some notes on 'Falling from the Faith'. *Sociological Analysis* 41 (1): 41–54.

British Council of Churches (n.d.) The Unification Church: A paper for those who wish to know more. Paper prepared by the Youth Unit.

Bromley, D. G., Busching, B. C., and Shupe, A. D., Jr. (1982) The Unification Church and the American family: strain, conflict and control. In E. V. Barker (ed.) *New Religious Movements: A Perspective for Understanding Society*. New York and Toronto: Edwin Mellen Press.

Bromley, D. G. and Richardson, J. T. (eds) (1983) *The Brainwashing/Deprogramming Controversy: Sociological, Psychological, Legal and Historical Perspectives*. New York: Edwin Mellen Press.

Bromley, D. G. and Shupe, A. D., Jr. (1979) *The Moonies in America*. Beverly Hills: Sage.

Bryant. D. (ed.) (1980) *Proceedings of the Virgin Islands Seminar on Unification Theology*. New York: Rose of Sharon Press.

—— and Foster, D. (eds) (1980) *Hermeneutics and Unification Theology*. New York: Rose of Sharon Press.

—— and Hodges, S. (eds) (1978) *Exploring Unification Theology*. New York: Rose of Sharon Press.

—— and Richardson, H. W. (eds) (1978) *A Time for Consideration. A Scholarly Appraisal of the Unification Church*. New York: Edwin Mellen Press.

Buckle, R. (1971) Mormons in Britain. *A Sociological Yearbook of Religion in Britain*. 4: 160–79.

Campbell, C. B. (1977) Clarifying the cult. *British Journal of Sociology* 28 (3): 375–88.

—— (1978) The secret religion of the educated classes. *Sociological Analysis* 39 (2): 146–56.

Caplowitz, D. and Sherrow, F. (1977) *The Religious Drop-Outs: Apostasy among College Graduates*. Beverly Hills: Sage.

Carey, S. (1981) A sociological study of the Ramakrishna Mission in Great Britain. Unpublished PhD thesis, University of Newcastle-upon-Tyne.

Carey, S. (1983) The Hare Krishna movement and Hindus in Britain. *New Community* 10 (3); 477–86.

Carlson, D. A. (1981) A commentary on the Pledge service focusing on the children's Pledge: one tradition observed by the Unification Church movement. Unpublished MA dissertation, Pacific School of Religion.

Carney, F. (1981) Letter to the Faculty, Perkins School of Theology. In H. Richardson (ed.) *Ten Theologians Respond to the Unification Church*. New York: Rose of Sharon Press.

Chéry, H. C. (1954) *L'Offensive des Sectes*. Paris: Cerf.

Children of God (1976) *The MO Letters*. Vol. 1. Hong Kong: Lion Press.

Chinnici, J. P. (1979) New religious movements and the structure of religious sensibility. In J. Needleman and G. Baker (eds) *Understanding the New Religions*. New York: Seabury Press.

Church of Scientology of California (1978) *What is Scientology?* Los Angeles, CA: Publication Organization United States.

—— *Freedom* (occasional magazine of the movement).

Clark, J. G. (1979) Cults. *Journal of the American Medical Association* 242 (3): 279–81.

——, Langone, M., Schechter, R., and Daly, R. (1981) *Destructive Cult Conversion: Theory, Research and Treatment*. Weston, Mass.: American Family Foundation.

Cohn, N. (1957) *The Pursuit of the Millennium*. London: Secker & Warburg.

Conway, F. and Siegelman, J. (1978) *Snapping*. New York: Lippincott.

—— (1982) Information disease: have cults created a new mental illness? *Science Digest* 90 (1): 86–92.

Cooper, P. (1971) *The Scandal of Scientology*. New York: Tower.

Curtis, R. C. and Zurcher, L. A. (1973) Stable resources of protest movements: the multi-organizational field. *Social Forces* 52: 53–61.

Dagon, G. (1958) *Les Sectes en France*. Strasbourg-Cronenbourg: chez l'auteur.

Dahrendorf, R. (1965) *Gesellschaft und Demokratie in Deutschland*. München: Piper.

Daner, F. (1976) *The American Children of Krsna. A Study of the Hare Krsna Movement*. New York: Holt, Rinehart, & Winston.

Dansette, A. (1953–56) *Histoire Religieuse de la France*. 2 vols. Paris: Flammarion.

Davis, R. and Richardson, J. T. (1976) The organization and functioning of the Children of God. *Sociological Analysis* 37 (4); 320–41.

D'Eaubonne, F. (1982) *Dossier S . . . Comme Sectes*. Paris: Alain Moreau.

Delgado, R. (1977) Religious totalism: gentle and ungentle persuasion under the First Amendment. *Southern California Law Review* 51 (1): 1–98.

Dellacava, F. A. (1975) Becoming an ex-priest: the process of leaving a high commitment status. *Sociological Inquiry* **45** (4): 41–9.

Demerath, N. J. III and Williams, R. H. (1983) The separation of church and state? Notes on a mythical past and uncertain future. Unpublished paper.

Downton, J. V. Jr. (1979) *Sacred Journeys: the Conversion of Young Americans to Divine Light Mission*. New York: Columbia University Press.

Drummond, A. L. (1951) *German Protestantism since Luther*. London: Epworth.

Durham, D. (1981) *Life Among the Moonies: Three Years in the Unification Church*. Plainfield, NJ: Logos International.

Ebaugh, H. R. F. (1977) *Out of the Cloister: a Study of Organizational Dilemmas*. Austin, Texas: University of Texas Press.

Edwards, C. (1979) *Crazy for God*. Englewood Cliffs, NJ: Prentice-Hall.

Eister, A. W. (1973) Richard Niebuhr and the paradox of religious organization. In C. Glock and P. Hammond (eds) *Beyond the Classics?* San Francisco: Harper & Row.

Elkins, C. (1980) *Heavenly deception*. Wheaton, Ill: Tyndale House.

Ellwood, R. S. Jr. (1973) *Religious and Spiritual Groups in Modern America*. Englewood Cliffs, NJ: Prentice-Hall.

—— (1979a) Emergent religion in America: an historical perspective. In J. Needleman and G. Baker (eds) *Understanding the New Religions*. New York: Seabury Press.

—— (1979b) *Alternative Altars: Unconventional and Eastern Spirituality in America*. Chicago: University of Chicago Press.

Enroth, R. (1977) *Youth, Brainwashing and the Extremist Cults*. Exeter: Paternoster Press.

——, Ericson, E., and Peters, C. B. (1972) *The Jesus People: Old-Time Religion in the Age of Aquarius*. Grand Rapids, Mich: Eerdmans Publishing.

Ernst, E. (1979) Dimensions of new religion in American history. In J. Needleman and G. Baker (eds) *Understanding the New Religions*. New York: Seabury Press.

Evangelische Zentralstelle für Weltanschauungsfragen (n.d.) *Vereinigungskirche*. Stuttgart.

Facon, R. and Parent, J. M. (1980) *Sectes et Sociétés Secrètes Aujourd'hui. Le Complot des Ombres*. Paris: Lefeuvre.

Fenn, R. K. (1981) *Liturgies and Trials*. Oxford: Basil Blackwell.

Fetscher, I. (ed.) (1979) *Jugend und Terrorismus*. München: Juventa Verlag.

Fichter, J. (1954) *Social Relations in an Urban Parish*. Chicago, Ill: University of Chicago Press.

Flasche, R. (1981) Hauptelemente der Vereinigungstheologie. In G. Kehrer (ed.) *Das Entstehen einer Neuen Religion: das Beispiel der Vereinigungskirche.* München: Kösel-Verlag.

Foss, D. and Larkin, R. (1976) From 'the Gates of Eden' to 'Day of the Locust': an analysis of the dissident youth movement of the 1960s and its heirs in the 1970s – the post-movement groups. *Theory and Society* 3: 45–64.

Foster, J. G. (1971) *Enquiry into the Practice and Effects of Scientology.* London: HMSO.

Fouilloux, E. (1975) Les églises contestées. In J. M. Mayeur (ed.) *L'Histoire Religieuse de la France. 19e et 20e Siècles. Problèmes et Méthodes.* Paris: Beauchesne.

Freed, J. (1980) *Moonwebs: Journey into the Mind of a Cult.* Toronto: Dorset Publishing.

Fürstenberg, F. (1974) *Die Sozialstruktur der Bundesrepublik Deutschland. Ein soziologischer Überblick.* Opladen: Westdeutscher Verlag (3rd edn).

Galanter, M. (1978) The 'relief effect': a sociological model for neurotic distress and large-group therapy. *American Journal of Psychiatry* 135 (12): 588–91.

——— (1980) Psychological induction into the larger group: findings from a modern religious sect. *American Journal of Psychiatry* 137 (12); 1574–579.

——— (1985) Group induction techniques in the Unification Church. In D. Anthony, T. Robbins, and J. Needleman (eds) *Conversion, Coercion and Commitment.*

———, Rabkin, R., Rabkin, J., and Deutsch, A. (1979) 'The Moonies', a psychological study. *American Journal of Psychiatry* 136 (2): 165–70.

Gallup, G. and Poling, D. (1980) *The Search for America's Faith.* Nashville: Abingdon Press.

Garrison, O. V. (1980) *Playing Dirty. The Secret War against Beliefs.* Los Angeles: Ralston-Pilot.

Geertz, C. (1968) *Islam Observed.* Chicago, Ill: University of Chicago Press.

——— (1979) From the native's point of view: on the nature of anthropological understanding. In P. Rabinow and W. Sullivan (eds) *Interpretive Social Science.* Berkeley: University of California Press (first published 1976).

Gerlach, L. P. and Hine, V. (1970) *People, Power, Change: Movements of Social Transformation,* Indianapolis: Bobbs-Merrill.

Gerstel, D. A. (1982) *Paradise Incorporated: Synanon.* Novato, CA: Presidio Press.

Glaser, B. and Strauss, A. L. (1971) *Status Passage*. Chicago, Ill: Aldine.

Glock, C. Y. and Bellah, R. N. (eds) (1976) *The New Religious Consciousness*. Berkeley: University of California Press.

Goffman, E. (1968) *Asylums*. Harmondsworth: Penguin Books (first published by Doubleday & Co. 1961).

Goode, W. J. (1956) *After Divorce*. Glencoe, Ill: The Free Press.

Gordon, M. (ed.) (1972) *The Nuclear Family in Crisis: the Search for an Alternative*. New York: Harper & Row.

Goswami, S. d. (1980) *Planting the Seed*. Los Angeles: Bhaktivedanta Book Trust.

Greeley, A. M. (1981) Religious musical chairs. In T. Robbins and D. Anthony (eds) *In Gods We Trust*. New Brunswick, NJ: Transaction Books.

Gründler, J. (1961) *Lexikon der Christlichen Kirchen und Sekten*. Vienna: Hender.

Haack, F.-W., (1976) *Die Neuen Jugendreligionen*. München: Evangelischer Presseverband.

—— (1979) *Jugendreligionen. Ursachen, Trends, Reaktionen*. München: Claudius Verlag.

Habermas, J. (1974) Legitimation problems in the modern State. Paper presented to a meeting of the Deutscher Verein für Politsche Wissenschaft, reprinted in translation in his *Communication and the Evolution of Society*. Boston: Beacon Press, 1979.

Hall, D. T. and Schneider, B. (1973) *Organizational Climates and Careers*. New York: Seminar Press.

Hammerstein, O. von (1980) *Ich war ein Munie*. München: Deutscher Taschenbuch Verlag.

Hammond, P. E. (1981) The shifting meaning of a wall of separation: some notes on church, state and conscience. *Sociological Analysis* 42 (3): 227–34.

Hampshire, A. P. and Beckford, J. A. (1983) Religious sects and the concept of deviance: the Moonies and the Mormons. *British Journal of Sociology* 34 (2): 208–29.

Hardin, B. (1983) Quelques aspects du phénomène des nouveaux mouvements religieux en République Fédérale d'Allemagne. *Social Compass* 30 (1): 13–32.

—— and Kehrer, G. (1978) Identity and commitment. In J. J. Mol (ed.) *Identity and Religion*. London: Sage.

—— (1982) Some social factors affecting the rejection of new belief systems. In E. V. Barker (ed.) *New Religious Movements: A Perspective for Understanding Society*. New York and Toronto: Edwin Mellen Press.

Harper, C. L. (1982) Cults and communities: the community interface of three marginal religious movements. *Journal for the Scientific Study of Religion* 21 (1), 26–38.

Hart, N. (1976) *When Marriage Ends: A Study in Status Passage.* London: Tavistock Publications.

Heftman, E. (1983) *The Dark Side of the Moonies.* New York: Penguin Books.

Heinemann, I. (1981) *Aus der Schule in die Sekte.* Stuttgart: ABI (Aktion Bildungsinformation).

Hervieu, B. and Léger, D. (1980) Ebyathar ou la protestation pure. *Archives de Sciences Sociales des Religions* 50 (1): 23–57.

Hill, D. G. (1980) Study of Mind Development Groups, Sects and Cults in Ontario. A report to the Ontario Government, Toronto, Ontario Legislature.

Hirschman, A. O. (1970) *Exit, Voice and Loyalty.* Cambridge, Mass: Harvard University Press.

Hoge, D. R. (1981) *Converts, Dropouts, Returnees. A Study of Religious Change among Catholics.* New York: Pilgrim Press.

Hollis, C. (1976) *Models of Man.* Cambridge: Cambridge University Press.

Horowitz, I. L. (ed.) (1978) *Science, Sin and Scholarship.* Cambridge, Mass: MIT Press.

Hubbard, L. R. (1950) *Dianetics: The Modern Science of Mental Health.* New York: Hermitage House.

—— (1968) *The Phoenix Lectures.* Los Angeles: Church of Scientology of California (delivered 1954).

—— (1969) *Scientology D-8. The Book of Basics* 3rd edn. Los Angeles: Church of Scientology of California.

—— (1974) *Introduction to Scientology Ethics.* Los Angeles: Church of Scientology of California.

—— (1982) The aims of Scientology. *Freedom*, special edn, 8 (first published 1965).

Hultquist, L. (1977) *They Followed the Piper.* Plainfield, NJ: Logos International.

Hunsberger, B. (1980) A reexamination of the antecedents of apostasy. *Review of Religious Research* 21 (2): 158–70.

Hutten, K. (1950) *Seher, Grübler, Enthusiasten. Sekten und Religiöse Sondergemeinschaften der Gegenwart.* Stuttgart: Quell Verlag.

—— (1957) Die Kirche und die Sekten. In his *Die Einheit der Kirche und die Sekten.* Zollikon: Evangelischer Verlag.

International Society for Krishna Consciousness (n.d.) A Report to the Media: Please Don't Lump Us In. Los Angeles, CA: ISKCON.

—— *Back to Godhead.* Los Angeles, CA: ISKCON (the movement's principal magazine).

Isambert, F. A. (1972) France. In J. J. Mol (ed.) *Western Religion*. The Hague: Mouton.

Johnson, G. (1976) The Hare Krishna in San Francisco. In C. Glock and R. Bellah (eds) *The New Religious Consciousness*. Berkeley: University of California Press.

Jud, G., Mills, E., and Burch, G. (1970) *Ex-Pastors*. Boston: Pilgrim Press.

Judah, J. S. (1974) *Hare Krishna and the Counterculture*. New York: Wiley.

—— (1977) Attitudinal changes among members of the Unification Church. Paper presented to the Annual Meeting of the American Association of Social Anthropologists, Denver.

Jules-Rosette, B. (1985) Disavowal and disengagement: a new look at the conversion process in religious sects. In D. Anthony, T. Robbins, and J. Needleman (eds) *Conversion, Coercion and Commitment*.

Kanter, R. M. (1972) *Commitment and Community*. Cambridge, Mass: Harvard University Press.

—— (ed.) (1973) *Communes: Creating and Managing the Collective Life*. New York: Harper & Row.

Kaslow, F. W. and Schwartz, L. D. (forthcoming) Vulnerability and invulnerability to the cults: an assessment of family dynamics, functioning and values. In D. Bagarozzi (ed.) *New Perspectives in Marriage and Family Therapy*. New York: Human Sciences Press.

Kaufman, R. (1972) *Inside Scientology*. London: Olympia.

Kehrer, G. (1972) Germany: the Federal Republic. In J. J. Mol (ed.), *Western Religion*. The Hague: Mouton.

—— (1980) Kirchen, Sekten und der Staat. Zum Problem der religiösen Toleranz. Mimeo.

—— (ed.) (1981) *Das Entstehen einer Neuen Religion: das Beispiel der Vereinigungskirche*. München: Kösel-Verlag.

Kelley, D. M. (1977) Deprogramming and religious liberty. *The Civil Liberties Review* July/August: 23–33.

—— (ed.) 1982) *Government Intervention in Religious Affairs*. New York: Pilgrim Press.

Kemperman, S. (1981) *Lord of the Second Advent*. New York: Regal Books.

Kilbourne, B. K. (1982) Deconversion: ritual and myth. Unpublished paper.

—— (1983) The Conway and Siegelman claims against religious cults: an assessment of their data. *Journal for the Scientific Study of Religion* 22 (4): 380–85.

Kim, S. K. (1981) A critical study of the Reverend Sun Myung Moon's movement. Unpublished PhD dissertation, San Francisco Theological Seminary.

Kim, Y. O. (1976) Unification Theology and Christian Thought. New York: Golden Gate.

King, C. (1982) *The Nazi State and the New Religions: Five Case Studies in Non-Conformity*. New York: Edwin Mellen Press.

Knoke, D. H. and Wood, J. R. (1981) *Organized for Action: Commitment in Voluntary Associations*. New Brunswick, NJ: Rutgers University Press.

Knox, Ronald (1950) *Enthusiasm*. Oxford: Oxford University Press.

König, R. (1971) West Germany. In M. Archer and S. Giner (eds) *Contemporary Europe: Class, Status and Power*. London: Weidenfeld & Nicolson.

Kotre, J. N. (1971) *The View from the Border*. Chicago, Ill: Aldine.

Kotzé, G. R. C. (1973) *Report of the Commission of Inquiry into Scientology for 1972*. Pretoria, South Africa: Government Printer.

Lanarès, P. (1982) Sectes et nouvelles religions. *Conscience et Liberté* 23: 33–42.

Lasch, C. (1977) *Haven in a Heartless World*. New York: Basic Books.

―――― (1980) *The Culture of Narcissism*. London: Sphere Books.

Le Cabellec, P. (1983) *Dossiers Moon*. Mulhouse: Salvator.

Lecerf, Y. (ed.), (1975) *Les Marchands de Dieu. Analyses Socio-Politiques de l'Affaire Melchior*. Brussels: Complexe.

Leduc, J.-M. and de Plaige, D. (1978) *Les Nouveaux Prophètes*. Paris: Buchet/Châstel.

Léger, D. and Hervieu, B. (1983) *Des Communautés pour les Temps Difficiles*. Paris: Le Centurion.

Levine, S. L. and Salter, N. E. (1976) Youth and contemporary religious movements: psychosocial findings. *Canadian Psychiatric Association Journal* 21: 411–20.

Levinson, D., Darrow, C., Klein, E., Levinson, M., and McKee, B. (1978) *The Seasons of a Man's Life*. New York: Knopf.

Levitt, Z. (1976) *The Spirit of Sun Myung Moon*. Irvine, CA: Harvest House.

Lindner, K. M. (1981) Kulturelle und semantische Probleme beim Studium einer neuen Religion. In G. Kehrer (ed.) *Das Entstehen einer Neuen Religion: das Beispiel der Vereinigungskirche*. München: Kösel-Verlag.

Lofland, J. (1966) *Doomsday Cult*. Englewood Cliffs, NJ: Prentice Hall.

―――― (1977) *Doomsday Cult*. New York: Irvington.

―――― and Richardson, J. T. (in press) Religious movement organizations: elemental forms and dynamics. In L. Kriesberg (ed.), *Research in Social Movements, Conflicts and Change*. Greenwich, Conn: JAI Press.

Lucksted, O. D. and Martell, D. F. (1982) Cults: a conflict between religious liberty and involuntary servitude? *FBI Law Enforcement Bulletin* April: 16–20; May: 16–23; June: 16–21.

Lukatis, I. and Krebber, H. (1980) Recherches empiriques concernant la religion en Allemagne Fédérale, en Autriche et en Suisse allémanique. *Social Compass* 27 (1): 85–100.

Lukes, S. (1973) *Individualism*. Oxford: Basil Blackwell.

McBeth, L. (1977) *Strange New Religions*. Nashville: Broadman Press.

MacCollam, J. A. (1979) *Carnival of Souls*. New York: Crossroads.

McGuire, M. (1981) *Religion: the Social Context*. Belmont, CA: Wadsworth.

McIntyre, A. (1981) *After Virtue*. London: Duckworth.

McManus, U. (with J. Cooper) (1980) *Not for a Million Dollars*. Nashville: Impact Books.

Magnouloux, B. (1977) *Pionnier du Nouvel Age: Témoignage d'un Ex-Adepte de Moon*. Andancette, chez l'auteur.

Malko, G. (1970) *Scientology: the Now Religion*. New York: Delacorte Press.

Martin, B. (1981) *A Sociology of Contemporary Cultural Change*. Oxford: Basil Blackwell.

Martin, D. A. (1978) *A General Theory of Secularization*. Oxford: Basil Blackwell.

——— (1982) Revised dogma and new cult. *Daedalus* 111 (1): 53–71.

Martin, R. (1979) *Escape*. Denver: Accent Books.

Martin, W. J. (1980) *The New Cults*. Santa Ana, CA: Vision House.

Mauss, A. L. (1969) Dimensions of religious defection. *Review of Religious Research* 10: 128–35.

Mehl, R. (1965) *Traité de Sociologie du Protestantisme*. Neuchâtel: Delachaux & Niestlé.

Melton, J. G. (1978) *Encyclopedia of American Religions*. 2 vols. Wilmington, North Carolina: McGrath.

——— and Moore, R. L. (1982) *The Cult Experience. Responding to the New Religious Pluralism*. New York: Pilgrim Press.

Meyer, D. (1980) *The Positive Thinkers*. New York: Pantheon Books (first published 1960).

Mickler, M. (1980) A history of the Unification Church in the Bay Area 1960–1974. Unpublished MA dissertation, Graduate Theological Union, Berkeley, CA.

Mildenberger, M. (1979) *Die Religiöse Revolte. Jugend zwischen Flucht und Aufbruch*. Frankfurt-am-Main: Fischer Verlag.

Mitchell, D., Mitchell, C., and Ofshe, R. (1980) *The Light on Synanon*. New York: Seaview Books.

Müller-Küppers, M. and Specht, F. (eds) (1979) *Neue Jugendreligionen*. Göttingen: Vandenhoeck & Ruprecht.

Naipaul, S. (1980) *Black and White*. Harmondsworth: Penguin Books.

National Council of Churches in Christ (1977) A critique of the theology of the Unification Church as set forth in 'Divine Principle'. *Occasional Bulletin* of the Commission on Faith and Order, July: 18–23.

Needleman, J. (1972) *The New Religions*. London: Allen Lane.

—— and Baker, G. (eds) (1979) *Understanding the New Religions*. New York: Seabury Press.

Newport, F. (1979) The religious switcher in the United States. *American Sociological Review* 44 (4): 528–52.

Nordquist, T. (1978) *Ananda Cooperative Village*. Uppsala University: Religionshistoriska Institutionen Monograph Series 16.

Nordrhein-Westfalen (1979) Sogenannte Jugendsekten in Nordrhein-Westfalen. Sachstandsbericht des Ministers für Arbeit, Gesundheit and Soziale des Landes Nordrhein-Westfalen, Köln.

Ofshe, R. (1980) The social development of the Synanon Cult: the managerial strategy of organizational transformation. *Sociological Analysis* 41 (2): 109–27.

Pace, E. (1983) *Asceti e Mistici in una Società Secolarizatta*. Venezia: Marsilio Editori.

Patrick, T. (with Dulack, T.) (1976) *Let Our Children Go!* New York: E. P. Dutton.

Peter, K., Boldt, E., Whitaker, I., and Roberts L. (1982) The dynamics of religious defection among Hutterites. *Journal for the Scientific Study of Religion* 21 (4): 327–37.

Pritchett, W. D. (1979) Charismatic leadership and the evolution of the Children of God: a deviant new religious group. Unpublished paper.

Prus, R. C. (1976) Religious recruitment and the management of dissonance: a sociological perspective. *Sociological Inquiry* 46 (2): 127–34.

Quebedeaux, R. and Sawatsky, R. (eds) (1979) *Evangelical-Unification Dialogue*. New York: Rose of Sharon Press.

Rappoport, R., Rappoport, R., and Fogarty, M. (1971) *Sex, Career and Family*. London: Allen & Unwin.

Rasmussen, M. (1976) How Sun Myung Moon lures America's children. *McCall's* September: 102–15, 175.

Rice, B. (1976) Honor thy Father Moon. *Psychology Today* 9 (8): 36–9.

Richardson, H. W. (1978) A brief outline of Unification theology. In D. Bryant and H. Richardson (eds) *A Time for Consideration. A Scholarly Appraisal of the Unification Church*. New York: Edwin Mellen Press.

—— (ed.) (1981) *Ten Theologians Respond to the Unification Church*. New York: Rose of Sharon Press.

Richardson, J. T. (ed.) (1978) *Conversion Careers*. Beverly Hills: Sage.

—— (1979) From cult to sect. Creative eclecticism in new religious movements. *Pacific Sociological Review* 22 (3): 136–66.

———— (1980) Peoples Temple and Jonestown: a corrective comparison and critique. *Journal for the Scientific Study of Religion* 19 (3): 239–55.

———— (1982) Financing the new religions: comparative and theoretical considerations. *Journal for the Scientific Study of Religion* 21 (3): 255–68.

———— and Davis, R. (1983) Experiential fundamentalism's revisions of orthodoxy in Jesus Movement groups. In W. Shaffir and L. Greenspan (eds) *Identification and the Revival of Orthodoxy*. The Hague: Mouton.

———— Stewart, M. and Simmonds, R. (1979) *Organized Miracles: a Study of a Contemporary, Youth, Communal, Fundamentalist Organization*. New Brunswick, NJ: Transaction Books.

Robbins, T. (1979) Cults and the therapeutic State, *Social Policy* May/June: 42–6.

———— (1981) Church, state and cult. *Sociological Analysis* 42 (3): 209–26.

———— (1983) Sociological studies of new religious movements: a selective review. *Religious Studies Review* 9 (3): 233–39.

———— (1984) Marginal movements. *Society* 21 (4), 47–52.

———— and Anthony, D. (1978) New religions, families and brainwashing. *Transaction/Society* June: 77–83.

———— (1979a) The sociology of contemporary religious movements, *Annual Review of Sociology* 5: 75–89.

———— (1979b) Cults, brainwashing and counter-subversion. *Annals of the American Academy of Political and Social Science* 446: 78–90.

———— (1980) Brainwashing and the persecution of the 'cults'. *Journal of Religion and Health* 19 (1), 66–9.

———— (eds) (1981) *In Gods We Trust*. New Brunswick, NJ: Transaction Books.

———— (1982) The medicalization of new religions. *Social Problems* 29 (3): 283–97.

————, and Curtis, T. (1975) Youth culture religious movements: evaluating the integrative hypothesis. *Sociological Quarterly* 16 (1): 48–64.

————, and McCarthy, J. (1980) Legitimating repression. *Society* 17, 39–42.

———— and Richardson, J. (1978) Theory and research on today's 'New Religions'. *Sociological Analysis* 39 (2): 95–122.

Robertson, R. (1979) Religious movements and modern societies: toward a progressive problemshift. *Sociological Analysis* 40 (4): 297–314.

Rochford, E. B. Jr (1982a) A study of recruitment and transformation processes in the Hare Krishna movement. Unpublished PhD dissertation, University of California, Los Angeles.

———— (1982b) Recruitment strategies, ideology and organization in the Hare Krishna movement. *Social Problems* 29 (4): 399–410.

Roozen, D. A. (1980) Church dropouts: changing patterns of disengagement and re-entry. *Review of Religious Research* 21: 427–50.

Rosengren, K. E., Arvidsson, P., and Sturesson, D. (1978) The Barsebäck 'panic': a case of media deviance. In C. Winick (ed.) *Deviance and Mass Media*. Beverly Hills: Sage.

SanGiovanni, L. F. (1978) *Ex-Nuns: a Study of Emergent Role-Passage*. New Jersey: Ablex.

Schmidtchen, G. (1972) *Zwischen Kirche und Gesellschaft*, Freiburg: Herder.

—— (1979) *Protestanten und Katholiken. Soziologische Analyse Konfessioneller Kultur*. Bern: Francke Verlag.

Séguy, J. (1956) *Les Sectes Protestantes dans la France Contemporaine*, Paris: Beauchesne.

—— (1977) Les sectes comme mode d'insertion sociale. In Université de Strasbourg, *Eglises et Groupes Religieux dans la Société Française*. Strasbourg: Cerdic Publications.

—— (1980) La socialisation utopique aux valeurs. *Archives de Sciences Sociales des Religions* 50 (1): 7–21.

Seidler, J. (1979) Priest resignations in a lazy monopoly. *American Sociological Review* 44: 763–83.

Sennett, R. (1970) *Families against the City*, Cambridge, Mass: Harvard University Press.

—— (1977) *The Fall of Public Man*. New York: Knopf.

Shapiro, R. W. (1983) Of robots, persons, and the protection of religious belief. *Southern California Law Review* 56 (6): 1277–318.

Shepherd, W. C. (1982) The prosecutor's reach: legal issues stemming from the new religious movements. *Journal of the American Academy of Religion* 50 (2): 187–214.

Shupe, A. D. Jr. and Bromley, D. G. (1980) *The New Vigilantes. Deprogrammers, Anti-Cultists and the New Religions*. Beverly Hills: Sage.

—— (1981) Apostates and atrocity stories: some parameters in the dynamics of deprogramming. In B. R. Wilson (ed.) *The Social Impact of New Religious Movements*. New York: Rose of Sharon Press.

Singer, M. T. (1979) Coming out of the cults. *Psychology Today* January: 72–82.

Skonovd, L. N. (1979) Becoming apostate: a model of religious defection. Paper presented at the Annual Meeting of the Pacific Sociological Association, Anaheim.

—— (1981) Apostasy: the process of defection from religious totalism. Unpublished PhD dissertation, University of California, Davis.

—— (1983) Leaving the 'cultic' religious milieu. In D. Bromley and J. Richardson (eds) *The Brainwashing/Deprogramming Controversy:*

Sociological, Psychological, Legal and Historical Perspectives. New York: Edwin Mellen Press.

Snow, D., Zurcher, L., and Ekland-Olson, S. (1980) Social networks and social movements: a microstructural approach to differential recruitment. *American Sociological Review* 45: 787–801.

Society for Religious Peace and Family Unity (n.d.) *Family Re-Conciliation. A Booklet on Family Conciliatory Procedure.*

Solomon, T. (1977) Programming and deprogramming the 'Moonies': brainwashing revisited. Unpublished paper.

—— (1981) Integrating the 'Moonie' experience: a survey of ex-members of the Unification Church. In T. Robbins and D. Anthony (eds) *In Gods We Trust.* New Brunswick, NJ: Transaction Books.

Sontag, F. (1977) *Sun Myung Moon and the Unification Church.* Nashville: Abingdon.

—— (1981) The God of Principle: a critical evaluation. In H. Richardson (ed.) *Ten Theologians Respond to the Unification Church.* New York: Rose of Sharon Press.

Sparks, J. (1977) *The Mind Benders. A Look at Current Cults.* Nashville: Abingdon.

Stark, R., Bainbridge, W. S., and Doyle, D. (1979) Cults of America: a reconnaissance in time and space. *Sociological Analysis* 40 (4): 347–59.

Stark, R. and Glock, C. Y. (1968) The switchers: changes in denomination. In R. Stark and C. Glock, *American Piety: the Nature of Religious Commitment.* Berkeley: University of California Press.

State of New York (1974) *Final Report on the Activities of the Children of God.* Submitted to the Attorney General by the Charity Frauds Bureau of the State of New York.

Stoner, C., and Parke, J. A. (1977) *All God's Children. The Cult Experience – Salvation or Slavery?* New York: Penguin Books.

Straus, R. (1976) Changing oneself: seekers and the creative transformation of life experience. In J. Lofland (ed.) *Doing Social Life.* New York: Wiley.

Streiker, L. D. (1978) *The Cults are Coming!* Nashville: Abingdon.

Sullivan, W. M. (1982) *Reconstructing Public Philosophy.* Berkeley: University of California Press.

Swatland, S. and Swatland, A. (1982) *Escape from the Moonies.* London: New English Library.

Tate-Wood, A. (with Vitek, J.) (1979) *Moonstruck: a Memoir of my Life in a Cult.* New York: William Morrow.

Taylor, B. (1976) Conversion and cognition: an area for empirical study in the micro-sociology of religious knowledge. *Social Compass* 23 (1): 5–22.

Taylor, D. (1982) Becoming new people: the recruitment of young Americans into the Unification Church. In R. Wallis (ed.) *Millennialism and Charisma*. Belfast: The Queen's University.

Tipton, S. M. (1982) *Getting Saved from the Sixties*. Berkeley: University of California Press.

Tobey, A. (1976) The summer solstice of the Healthy-Happy-Holy organization. In C. Glock and R. Bellah (eds) *The New Religious Consciousness*. Berkeley: University of California Press.

Tribe, L. H. (1982) Church and state in the Constitution. In D. Kelley (ed.) *Government Intervention in Religious Affairs*. New York: Pilgrim Press.

Troeltsch, E. (1931) *The Social Teachings of the Christian Churches*. Trans. O. Wyon. London: Allen & Unwin (first published in German 1911).

Tweede Kamer der Staten-Generaal (1984) Onderzoek betreffende sekten. *Overheid en nieuwe religieuze bewegingen*. The Hague (16, 635 no. 4).

Tworuschka, U. (1981) Die Vereinigungskirche im Religionsunterricht. In G. Kehrer (ed.) *Das Entstehen einer Neuen Religion: das Beispiel der Vereinigungskirche*. München: Kösel-Verlag.

Underwood, B. and Underwood, B. (1979) *Hostage to Heaven*. New Jersey: Clarkson N. Potter.

Ungerleider, J. T. and Wellisch, D. K. (1979) Coercive persuasion (brainwashing), religious cults, and deprogramming. *American Journal of Psychiatry* 136: 279–82.

——— (1983) The programming (brainwashing)/deprogramming controversy. In D. Bromley and J. Richardson (eds) *The Brainwashing/ Deprogramming Controversy: Sociological, Psychological, Legal and Historical Perspectives*. New York: Edwin Mellen Press.

Unification Church (1977) *News and Views from the Unification Church*. Vol. 1. Rowlane, Reading: Holy Spirit Association for the Unification of World Christianity (HSAUWC).

——— (1978) *New and Views from the Unification Church*. Vol. 2. Rowlane, Reading, UK: HSAUWC.

——— (1979) *Our Response to the Report of October 31, 1978 on the Investigation of Korean–American Relations Regarding Reverend Sun Myung Moon and Members of the Unification Church*. New York: HSAUWC.

——— (1980) *Introduction to the Principle. An Islamic Perspective*. New York: HSAUWC.

Unification Thought Institute (1973) *Unification Thought*. New York: Unification Thought Institute.

——— (1974) *Unification Thought. Study Guide*. New York: Unification Thought Institute.

United States House of Representatives (1978) Investigation of Korean–American Relations. Report of the Subcommittee on International Organizations of the Committee on International Relations. Chairman Donald M. Fraser, 7 vols.

Urry, J. (1981) *The Anatomy of Capitalist Societies*. London: Macmillan.

Vernette, J. (1976) *Sectes et Réveil-Religieux*. Mulhouse: Salvator.

——— (1979) *Des Chercheurs de Dieu 'Hors Frontières'*. Paris: Desclée de Brouwer.

Vosper, C. (1971) *The Mind Benders*. London: Neville Spearman.

Wallis, R. (1974) Ideology, authority and the development of cultic movements. *Social Research* 41 (2): 299–327.

——— (1976) *The Road to Total Freedom. A Sociological Analysis of Scientology*. London: Heinemann Educational.

——— (1979) *Salvation and Protest*. London: Frances Pinter.

——— (1981) Yesterday's children: cultural and structural change in a new religious movement. In B. R. Wilson (ed.) The Social Impact of New Religious Movements. New York: Rose of Sharon Press.

——— (1982) The social construction of charisma. *Social Compass* 29 (1): 25–39.

——— (ed.) (1982) *Millennialism and Charisma*. Belfast: The Queen's University.

——— (1984) *The Elementary Forms of the New Religious Life*. London: Routledge & Kegan Paul.

——— and Bruce, S. (1983) Accounting for action: defending the common sense heresy. *Sociology* 17 (1): 97–111.

West, L. J. (1982) Contemporary cults – utopian image, infernal reality. *Center Magazine* 15 (2): 10–13.

Whitehead, H. (1974) Reasonably fantastic: some perspectives on Scientology, science fiction and occultism. In I. Zaretsky and M. Leone (eds) *Religious Movements in Contemporary America*. Princeton, NJ: Princeton University Press.

Wilson, B. R. (ed.) (1967) *Patterns of Sectarianism*. London: Heinemann Educational.

——— (1976) *Contemporary Transformations of Religion*. London, Oxford University Press.

——— (ed.) (1981a) *The Social Impact of New Religious Movements*. New York: Rose of Sharon Press.

——— (1981b) Time, generation, and sectarianism. In his *Social Impact of New Religious Movements*.

——— (1983) A sect at law: the case of the Exclusive Brethren. *Encounter* 60 (1): 81–7.

Wilson, J. F. (1974) The historical study of marginal American religious movements. In I. Zaretsky and M. Leone (eds) *Religious Movements in Contemporary America*. Princeton, NJ: Princeton University Press.

Wölber, H. O. (1959) *Religion ohne Entscheidung*. Göttingen: Vandenhoeck & Ruprecht.

Woodrow, A. (1977) *Les Nouvelles Sectes*, Paris: Seuil.

Woodrum, E. (1982) Religious organizational change: an analysis based on the TM movement. *Review of Religious Research* **24** (2): 89–103.

Worthing, S. (1979) The State takes over a church. *Annals of the American Academy of Political and Social Science* **446**: 136–48.

Wright, S. A. (1983) Defection from new religious movements: a test of some theoretical propositions. In D. Bromley and J. Richardson (eds) *The Brainwashing/Deprogramming Controversy: Sociological, Psychological, Legal and Historical Perspectives*. New York: Edwin Mellen Press.

—— (1984) Families and cults: familial factors related to attrition of youth from new religions. Unpublished paper.

Wuthnow, R. (1978) *Experimentation in American Religion*. Berkeley: University of California Press.

—— (1981) Political aspects of the Quietistic Revival. In T. Robbins and D. Anthony (eds) *In Gods We Trust*. New Brunswick, NJ: Transaction Books.

—— (1982) World order and religious movements. In E. V. Barker (ed.) *New Religious Movements: A Perspective for Understanding Society*. New York and Toronto: Edwin Mellen Press.

—— and Glock, C. Y. (1973) Religious loyalty, defection and experimentation among college youth. *Journal for the Scientific Study of Religion* **12** (2): 157–80.

Yamamoto, J. I. (1977) *The Puppet Master*. Downers Grove, Ill: Inter-Varsity Press.

Yanoff, M. (1981) *Where is Joey? Lost among the Krishnas*. Chicago: Swallow Press.

Yinger, J. M. (1946) *Religion in the Struggle for Power*. Durham, North Carolina: Duke University Press.

Zaretsky, I. and Leone, M. P. (eds) (1974) *Religious Movements in Contemporary America*. Princeton, NJ: Princeton University Press.

NAME INDEX

SUBJECT INDEX

Note: The following abbreviations are used in sub-entries:
COG = Children of God
ISKCON = International Society for Krishna Consciousness
NRM = New Religious Movement
UC = Unification Church